HyperProgramming

Building interactive programs with HyperCard

HyperProgramming

Building interactive programs with HyperCard

George Coulouris

Queen Mary and Westfield College
University of London

Harold Thimbleby

Stirling University

Addison-Wesley Publishing Company

Wokingham, England • Reading, Massachusetts • Menlo Park, California
New York • Don Mills, Ontario • Amsterdam • Bonn • Sydney • Singapore
Tokyo • Madrid • San Juan • Milan • Paris • Mexico City • Seoul • Taipei

The programs in this book have been included for their instructional value. They have been tested with care but are not guaranteed for any particular purpose. The publisher does not offer any warranties or representations, nor does it accept any liabilities with respect to the programs.

Many of the designations used by manufacturers and sellers to distinguish their products are claimed as trademarks. Addison-Wesley has made every attempt to supply trademark information about manufacturers and their products mentioned in this book. A list of trademark designations and their owners appears below.

Cover design by Designers & Partners of Oxford.
Cover printed by The Riverside Printing Co. (Reading) Ltd.
Typeset using MicroSoft Word version 4.0 converted into FrameMaker 3.0 on an Apple Macintosh with camera ready copy produced on an Apple LaserWriter IIf by George Coulouris.

Printed in Great Britain by William Clowes Ltd, Beccles, Suffolk.

Printed 1992.

ISBN 0–201–56886–1

British Library Cataloguing in Publication Data
A catalogue record for this book is available from the British Library.

Library of Congress Cataloguing-in-Publication Data
Applied for.

Trademark notice
MicroSoft Word is a trademark of MicroSoft Corporation.
FrameMaker is a trademark of Frame Technology.
HyperCard, HyperTalk, Apple, Macintosh are trademarks of Apple Computer, Inc.

Preface

HyperProgramming is the book to read if you can already program in Pascal, Basic or any other language. This book describes the principles of HyperTalk programming and illustrates their use through many examples, ranging from a simple program that makes labels for diskettes to a sophisticated hypertext authoring system. Most other books on HyperCard merely tell you what HyperTalk is – and they are often no more than extended dictionaries; this book tells you what you can do with it and how to use it to the full.

HyperCard is Apple Computer's application-building tool for the Macintosh. It is a system that you can use to build new applications quickly because it already 'knows about' many of the kinds of component that modern computer applications are built from – various kinds of *graphical objects* that can be used to display information, to respond to the user's actions and so on. In HyperCard you build applications that incorporate the features of standard Macintosh applications – pull-down menus, multiple windows, pop-up dialogs, buttons and multi-font text boxes – and you can develop your own interactive techniques to produce distinctive applications with their own 'look and feel'. It is not surprising, then, that HyperTalk is one of the most popular and widely used programming languages today.

HyperCard combines an accessible programming language that's quick and easy to learn with a graphics system that provides useful graphical and text objects. The objects are dynamic – the changes that you make to their size, shape, or other properties are visible instantly. HyperCard applications are called *stacks*. Many useful stacks can be built without programming, using HyperCard's menu operations and tools for stack development. But HyperTalk, the programming language built in to HyperCard, enables much more to be done.

To build high-quality applications in HyperCard, you need two kinds of knowledge: about designing and constructing graphical user interfaces in HyperCard, and about programming in HyperTalk. *HyperProgramming* tells you how to use HyperTalk to construct easy-to-use, highly interactive user interfaces and whole applications. You can build good user interfaces and bad ones with HyperCard and HyperTalk. Good user interfaces require careful design. We hope that the many projects described in this book will serve as illustrations of good user interface design practice, but we haven't been able to devote much space to discussing their design. For more information on user interface design, you should study one of the books on the subject from the list of *Further Reading* starting on page 351.

This book isn't only for people needing to learn HyperTalk. The examples throughout the book illustrate the design and construction of interactive techniques that can be exploited in other systems for building applications with graphical interfaces. They provide a starting point and some specific techniques for constructing applications using a wide range of user interface features, not just in HyperCard, but in any graphical user interface environment. Many more 'professional' programming environments have a lot to learn from HyperTalk.

Who this book is for

This book will be of interest to several sorts of people who might want to get more out of HyperCard by programming in HyperTalk:

Novice programmers

Unlike most other application programs, HyperCard applications, stacks, are written in a readable language. That means that you can readily examine and modify other people's stacks to do what you want, or you can easily 'borrow' good ideas from them – simply by using the Macintosh's cut-and-paste tools.

HyperCard is very easy to program. If you have programmed at all you will have acquired some basic ideas that are common to all programming languages. *HyperProgramming* builds on these, describing the facilities of HyperTalk, illustrating them and showing useful programming techniques through the examples. The book is full of interesting projects: you can either copy them and get to work straight away, using the book's disk, or you can learn from the ideas and devise your own programs.

We won't claim you can become a fully fledged programmer just by reading this book but it does provide you with enough knowledge of programming to get you properly started. (There are many other books for learning the general concepts that underlie programming languages and the skills needed to exploit them; beginners are advised to study one of them in tandem with this book if they want to become accomplished programmers.)

Novice programmers should read Chapters 1 to 4 carefully, working through the examples on the Macintosh for themselves. After that, they should choose chapters that describe the techniques they want to learn about, always making sure that they understand the material by programming their own versions of the examples.

Experienced programmers

HyperCard is *very* quick to program. Even if you use other programming languages, you will be interested in using HyperCard as a powerful prototyping tool: you can use it to design and plan programs very quickly. Half an hour of prototyping with HyperCard is worth weeks in a conventional language like Pascal or C.

Compared with other programming environments, HyperCard combines some features that are found only in isolation in other languages, and adds some of its own:

- It incorporates a set of high-level *graphical objects* which are sufficiently configurable and flexible that they can be tailored to represent or simulate many of the components found in modern graphical interfaces. Compared with systems like X/Windows or the Macintosh ToolBox, building graphical user interfaces in HyperCard is heaven.

- It is *object-oriented*. Messages are sent to the objects in stacks. Objects contain pieces of program (called *handlers*) that receive the messages and act on them. Handlers can send messages to other handlers. But compared with conventional object-oriented languages, HyperCard is small and manageable – just five types of objects (*buttons, fields, cards, backgrounds* and *stacks*). You don't define new classes of object, but you can create new instances of each type of object and you can change their *properties* (so-called instance variables in other object-oriented languages) and their *handlers* (methods). HyperCard's five types of object are surprisingly versatile; in this book we'll show you how to use them for a wide range of purposes.

- It supports the re-use of program components by providing a form of *message passing* – messages are passed from object to object along a defined path until one is found that can handle each message. This enables programmers to develop general-purpose *tools* that can be used with many stacks.

- HyperCard's graphical objects are mouse-sensitive. Messages are sent to objects automatically when the user moves the mouse cursor into the object or clicks the mouse button over the object. Much of the work of interactive programming has already been done for you.

- It is event-driven at other levels too. For example, the display of a new card sends a message and this can be used to invoke a HyperTalk program that might, for example, record the identity of the card in a list of 'cards the user has seen'.

- Hypercard objects are *persistent*. That is, when an object is created, it is recorded in the current stack, with all of its properties and contents, and it remains until it or the stack is deleted. Much of the work of database programming has already been done for you.

Chapters 2, 3 and 4 provide an overview of HyperCard as a programming environment and describe HyperTalk as a language. Chapters 5 to 15 describe a wide range of techniques for programming interactive applications in HyperTalk.

Students

HyperCard is useful and fun to work with because you can develop programs quickly. If you have already done a programming course, then after reading this book you should be able to use HyperCard to do projects that involve highly interactive, graphical user interfaces far more quickly than you could in Pascal, C or whatever language you have studied. *And* you can do interesting and creative work even when your teacher thinks you are learning database techniques, graphics, object-oriented programming, recursion or other terribly difficult topics!

In most other languages, you wouldn't be able to do such exciting things without writing mammoth programs (and, all too often, learning an awful lot about the computer you use – like details of its windowing system – something that HyperCard protects you from).

Because HyperCard is an interactive programming environment, debugging your programs is more interesting too. You can quickly evaluate new programming techniques – the program debugging tools in HyperCard are comparable with ones you'll find elsewhere.

Students who have studied programming but have no experience with HyperCard should start at Chapter 1. Those who have some experience in building simple HyperCard stacks may like to go straight to Chapter 3, or perhaps go straight into one of the projects later in the book. If you know Pascal (or Modula-2), Appendix B will help you into HyperTalk's concepts.

Advanced students

If you are a student taking a degree in computer science or a related topic, you should be attracted by the advantages listed above: HyperCard provides an excellent way to get some interesting programs working quickly, to experience the benefits of an interactive graphical development environment and to learn the elements of interactive software design. But it's not a panacea – HyperCard's fixed set of object types can be restrictive and HyperTalk has limitations compared with a conventional programming language.

For example, you can't write much HyperTalk without using global variables, and everybody knows global variables are bad for you. In HyperTalk you soon find out why – which is another good reason for teaching HyperTalk as a first programming language. If, instead, you always used a 'sensible' language like Ada or Modula-2 you would need a team of students working for months before you encountered some of the programming style issues that are obvious to HyperCard programmers!

If you are already familiar with object-oriented application programming, start at Chapter 2, otherwise, start at Chapter 1. Read Chapters 3 and 4 carefully, then use Chapters 5 to 15 as a resource, providing details of useful programming techniques and approaches to application development in HyperTalk. Appendix B introduces HyperTalk assuming you are familiar with Pascal's programming concepts.

HyperCard designers and developers

HyperCard isn't perfect! We don't hold back from criticizing HyperCard and HyperTalk where necessary. So even people who already know a lot about HyperCard should benefit, as will anyone wishing to implement a new system inspired by HyperCard. We have included an epilogue on what hyperprogramming really is: this will help stimulate developers and researchers to go beyond HyperCard and HyperTalk into the next generation of interactive programming systems.

Even if you are already familiar with HyperCard and HyperTalk, you should scan Chapters 3 and 4 to make sure you haven't missed anything. Then use Chapters 5 to 15 as a source of ready-made techniques for programming your own applications. Read the epilogue that defines HyperProgramming.

The HyperProgramming disk

A disk is available with this book. To help you get started with the stacks on the disk, there is a stack called *About HyperProgramming*. This stack contains a navigator card that lists all of the stacks on the disk, and a card describing each stack. Click on the name of a stack on the navigator card to go to its description card, and then click on the **Open It** button to open and use the stack described there.

Some readers will want to use the scripts and objects from the stacks on the disk in their own projects. You are free to do so, with the usual disclaimer – we cannot take responsibility for any problems that may arise, but we will, of course, be pleased to hear from you about your experiences with them.

The copyright on all of the material in the book and on the disk is the property of Addison-Wesley Publishers and is subject to the normal copyright restrictions. You may not republish any part of it without their written permission. Addison-Wesley will be happy to hear from you if you wish to use our material in any way. They have however agreed to make a special concession to enable the stacks on the disk to be distributed for teaching purposes: copies of the stacks may be distributed to students for strictly non-commercial educational purposes without restriction.

Getting going

Compared with other HyperCard books, we introduce HyperTalk right away and cover the non-programming aspects of HyperCard only where we need to. We introduce HyperTalk with examples and exercises enabling you to become familiar with most of its facilities. The book is arranged so that we don't tell you lots of confusing details until after you've had some experience from earlier chapters. This informal, tutorial approach is complemented by two appendices. Appendix A provides a systematic overview of the features of HyperTalk and Appendix B compares HyperTalk with Pascal, acting as quick conversion route for readers who are already familiar with Pascal.

There are also two indexes: the *Index of Handlers* contains page numbers for all of the HyperTalk handler definitions (HyperTalk's equivalent to procedures) given in the book. This should be helpful, for example, when you want to follow up a reference to a handler in the text of the book or when you want to look up the description of a handler found on the book disk.

The main *Index* includes page numbers for all the main ideas and techniques discussed in the book, and for each of the HyperTalk features mentioned or used in the book. You can refer to it when you need information about HyperTalk – virtually all of the features of HyperTalk are discussed or used in scripts in the book. The main index also has a list of all the worked projects described in the book; see under *projects* in the index.

For information on the non-programming aspects of HyperCard we expect our readers to rely on the perfectly adequate *HyperCard Help* stack (or one of the many Macintosh 'point and click' books). Books that tell you how to draw pictures in HyperCard are difficult to read:

if you are going to learn how to use HyperCard as a programmer, you may as well start using it that way right away rather than read a book of tedious recipes. Our approach gives you a strong HyperTalk programming foundation so that you can exploit HyperCard for your own designs.

We assume that you have already installed HyperCard on your Mac and have at least had a quick browse. If you are new to HyperCard, you should spend an hour or so browsing through the *HyperCard Tour* and *HyperCard Help* stacks and the various ideas stacks and sample applications supplied with HyperCard. They provide a good introduction to the non-programming aspects of HyperCard, which we don't intend to spend any time on in this book.

Once you have grasped the basic principles of using stacks, you are ready to start using this book and the stacks that go with it.

Using HyperCard

A basic copy of the HyperCard 2 system is supplied free with every new Macintosh. It is suitable for running HyperCard 1 and HyperCard 2 stacks, but it doesn't include the *HyperCard Help* or any of the other information and tool stacks.

You can use this basic HyperCard 2 system to program in HyperTalk. The HyperCard user level has to be set to 5. To make sure that it is, go to the last card in your Home stack (**Last** on the **Go** menu) and click on the button labelled **Scripting** to set the user level to 5 permanently. If there isn't a button visible labelled **Scripting**, open the message window (select **Message** on the **Go** menu), type magic and hit the return key. This will reveal three extra buttons including the **Scripting** button. If none of this seems to work, try just typing:

    set userLevel to 5

in the message window and hitting the return key; this should work.

The material supplied with the 'free' distribution of HyperCard doesn't included the stacks and other documentation and development aids that Claris, Apple's software company, distribute to people who wish to develop stacks. They are supplied, along with a comprehensive reference manual for HyperTalk as a part of the *HyperCard 2 Developer's Kit*, available from your Apple/Claris dealer.

Actually, you don't need the *Developer's Kit* to start using this book and the stacks on the accompanying disk. You can use the stacks on the disk with the 'free' HyperCard system and you can start to program in HyperTalk using the information in this book. But you will probably covet the stacks in the *Developer's Kit* if you intend to do any serious development work. The *Guided Tour* stack and the *HyperCard Help* stack describe all of the features of HyperCard that are accessible to a user without programming. The *HyperTalk Reference* stack and its *Help Extras* stack provide a comprehensive reference source on the HyperTalk language in a convenient – hypertext – format, together with many useful examples and tips; it comes with a convenient search facility that you can use as you develop HyperTalk programs. There is a *Power Tools* stack, which we describe in Chapter 2. It contains a set of tools for extending

HyperTalk in several directions and some useful HyperTalk scripts. The *Developer's Kit* is a source of ideas and ready-made examples of buttons, fields, backgrounds and stacks.

What is HyperProgramming?

You don't need to know the answer to this question in order to benefit from the book! If you're curious, you'll find our answer in the epilogue, entitled *So, What is Hyperprogramming?* starting on page 345.

About this book

This book was drafted in Microsoft's Word 4, then converted to Frame Technology's FrameMaker 3 for final page layout and typography, which we did ourselves, with help and advice on the layout from Susan Keany and Leoni Vidali. The main fonts used are Garamond for the body text and Helvetica for headlines and scripts. HyperCard was of course used for the preparation of all the scripts and almost all the illustrations. We both worked on all the chapters, corresponding using email and, less often, by posting floppy disks. (We also used face-to-face meetings, lunches and telephone calls – if authors *can* write a book without seeing each other, that isn't what we did.)

We would like to acknowledge the enormous help freely provided by our many guinea pigs (mice?) who have read drafts and provided us with continual encouragement and corrections. The following helped us to make substantial improvements: Andrew Cockburn, Alan Dix, Jean Dollimore, Gary Marsden, Gabriel Mennerat, Prue Thimbleby, Will Thimbleby, Leoni Vidali and Steve Wilbur. Nicky Jaeger at Addison-Wesley provided her enthusiastic support and the anonymous referees made useful and constructive criticisms.

Internet

George Coulouris, London   *george@dcs.qmw.ac.uk*
Harold Thimbleby, Stirling   *hwt@compsci.stirling.ac.uk*

August 1992

Contents

Chapter 10 Finding Things

Chapter 11 Collecting Things

Chapter 12 Do-it-Yourself Hypertext

Chapter 13 A Hypertext Framework

Chapter 14 Hypertext Tools

Disk Contents

The table below lists the stacks on the *HyperProgramming* disk that is supplied with this book. The table gives the name of each stack, the main chapter and section in which it is discussed, and a short description of it.

Stack	Chapter	Description
About HyperProgramming		This is the *Home* stack for the *HyperProgramming* book. It provides information about the authors, the publishers, and about all of the stacks described in the book.
Music machine	1.3	Makes the keyboard of the Mac behave like a piano keyboard.
Direct manipulation	1.4	A simulated window manager.
Dice	1.5	Illustrates the use of sound in a simple way and the use of button icons for animation.
Bibliography	1.6	A bibliographic database stack with a scheme for locating books.
Disk labeller	1.6	For making disk labels, includes details on printing and rotating text.
Simple graphics	2.5	Two cards of simple drawing functions.
HyperCard objects	3.2	This tutorial stack illustrates the properties of buttons and fields and gives examples of some of their more unusual uses.
Bookmark	4.6	Keeps track of which cards in a stack you have visited, and makes it easy to go back to them, rather like a bookmark.
Turtle graphics	5	How to do turtle graphics: drawing pretty pictures. Illustrates background scripts being used between several cards.

Stack	Chapter	Description
Timing tests	**6.2**	Script timing techniques.
Graphical techniques	**7**	Charting and business graphics techniques.
Animation	**8**	Various ways of animating stacks.
Cannon game	**8.1**	A game that uses dragging for its animation.
Animating sorting	**8.3**	Provides demonstration of several sorting algorithms, using buttons to represent the numbers to be sorted.
Talk menu	**9.4**	An example menu for helping present talks using an overhead projector.
Handlers menu	**9.4**	A tool stack to add facilities to other stacks: a menu showing all of the currently accessible handlers to open them for editing.
Property tool	**9.4**	This stack creates a menu providing quick interactive access to properties of objects, such as the **lockText** and **visible**.
Finding things	**10.1**	Various ways of finding text in stacks: from improving HyperCard's standard menu **Find...** to a 'Find by example'.
Collecting things	**11.1**	Various scripts for collecting things from fields and scripts throughout a stack.
Shortcuts	**11.3**	Collect helpful handler comments from scripts.
DIY hypertext	**12**	Generate a hypertext-linked document using a grammar.
Stable matching	**12.11**	A hypertext that pairs people up, respecting their preferences.
HyperText framework	**13**	A generic hypertext system which supports authoring and reading of hypertext. The stack is generic – scripts can be copied and installed in almost any stack to add hypertext facilities to it.
HT tools	**14**	A tools menu for *HT* hypertext stacks; provides a menu of operations that are helpful when authoring new *HT* stacks and a tool for converting hypertexts into pure text.
HT browser	**14.4**	A tool stack which adds facilities to other *HT* stacks: a graphical browser – a diagrammatic representation of a stack, showing the nodes and the links, and you can click on a node to open it.

CHAPTER 1

Introducing HyperTalk

HyperTalk concepts, projects and ideas

In this chapter, we introduce HyperTalk by describing some simple interactive programs that you can write in HyperTalk, explaining the necessary features of HyperTalk as we go along. This is a good way to get started in most programming languages, and we recommend that you work through the examples yourself to make sure that you understand the details. Then in Chapters 2, 3 and 4 we go into HyperTalk in more detail, describing the main features of the programming environment, the objects that you can work with and the features of the HyperTalk programming language.

1.1   Objects

The world and everything in it is an object. Most of those objects are inanimate things like stones. You kick a stone and it moves; in fact, kick most things and they move, though some break. If we were talking the language of object-oriented programming, we wouldn't say 'kick' so much as 'send a message'. In object-oriented programming, you ask objects to do things by sending them messages. Sometimes, you send a message, and the object does not understand it. Of course, if you asked a stone something complicated, you would be wasting your breath, but if you sent an object a message it doesn't understand, it will pass the message on to someone else, who (hopefully) does know. You can imagine object-oriented programming as a bureaucracy: you can ask a clerk to do something, and generally they do; other times, when they don't know what to do, the clerk has to pass on your request to a superior. Object-oriented programming can be thought of in many ways, as these examples show. That's why it is such a useful way of programming.

HyperTalk is a simple object-oriented programming language. The objects in HyperTalk are designed to make writing interactive programs easy. The basic concepts of HyperTalk are easy to grasp: there are *messages* (instructions sent to objects); *handlers* (bits of program that understand messages; and the *objects* themselves, of which there are several kinds – buttons, fields, cards, backgrounds, stacks. A program in HyperTalk is called a *script*: since most objects have scripts, we will use the word quite a lot and it's nice to have a shorter word than program!

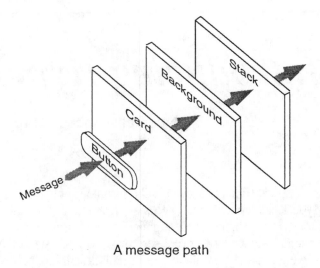

A message path

What happens if an object does not have a script? That means it cannot have any handlers, which means that it cannot understand any messages. If it can't understand messages, the messages are passed on through it to another object. The order in which messages are passed to other objects depends on the current *message path*. So a message might be sent to a button: but if the button does not handle the message it passes automatically to the card that contains the button to see whether it can handle it: if the card doesn't handle the message, it passes in turn to the background and to the stack and then ... we'll pick up the details later!

These concepts may seem difficult at first: we'll explore them quite gradually by developing some programs that, starting from simple ideas, we are able to build up to realize the full potential of these ideas.

1.2   Trying simple messages

HyperCard lets you type simple messages to see what they do. Choose **Message** from the **Go** menu to bring up the message window. You can type commands for HyperCard into this window and see what happens. Try typing **beep**, or **23+56**.

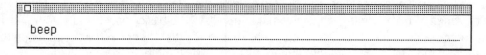

Typing **beep** takes a bit of effort. If you like beeps, HyperCard can let you program an easier way of getting them than typing into the message window! Our next example tries some real programming to do just this. Anything you can do from the message window, like beeps, can be done by mouse operations that you have preprogrammed.

1.3 A mouse that beeps

Select **Message** on the **Go** menu (or type *command–M*, *command* and *M* at the same time) to bring up the message box – a small window into which you can type HyperTalk commands to see what they do. Type **beep** and hit return. You should find that HyperCard beeps – not surprisingly!

Select **New Button** on the **Objects** menu. This will put a rectangular object on the current card, a new button: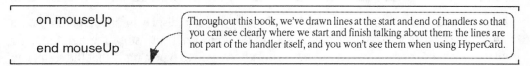

Double-click on the button and this brings up a dialog box telling you about the button. (Note: not *all* about the button! We will describe the properties of buttons and other objects in full in Chapter 3.) You should experiment with the various options provided by the dialog box: they enable you to change the appearance of the button: to a rectangle, a check box, with the button's name showing or not, and so on. Note that you have to click **OK** to see the changes take effect.

Click on the button labelled **Script**, and you can now make a script for this button. The script is already partly written by HyperCard:

```
on mouseUp

end mouseUp
```

> Throughout this book, we've drawn lines at the start and end of handlers so that you can see clearly where we start and finish talking about them: the lines are not part of the handler itself, and you won't see them when using HyperCard.

This is what a *handler* looks like (though as yet it's an empty handler).

This handler tells the button what to do when it is sent the **mouseUp** message. So, the button can handle **mouseUp** – it does nothing. If, instead, the button was sent the message **mouseDown**, say, it would not understand it, because there is no **mouseDown** handler anywhere in the button's script. MouseDown, then, would be sent to the card with the button on it, to see if the card can handle it. So the fact that a **mouseUp** message always and inevitably comes after a **mouseDown** (you must press the mouse button down before it comes up!) is something we don't need to worry about when making the button's script – unless we add a **mouseDown** handler.

If you have no handler for a message, it gets processed by HyperCard itself. HyperCard ignores many messages like **mouseDown** and **mouseUp**, but some messages – **beep** for example – get worked on.

As a first experiment, add the instruction **beep** to the handler in the button script:

```
on mouseUp
  beep
end mouseUp
```

This means that when this button handles **mouseUp** (when you click on it – or, rather, when you let the mouse button up and *stop* clicking on it), it will beep.

To test your script, you will have to first choose the Browse tool on the **Tools** menu (see illustration). The Browse tool is the one that HyperCard normally selects when you open a stack. The Button tool is the one that you use when you want to modify a button or its script. In the sequence of actions described above, the Button tool was chosen automatically when we created a new button. See Chapter 2 for more information on selecting HyperCard tools.

You can of course write far more interesting code in handlers than this example might suggest. The following are some simple suggestions – you can either edit the script of one button to each of these suggestions in turn, or you may prefer to have several buttons, each with one of these scripts:

```
on mouseUp
   answer "Did you click?"
end mouseUp
```

When you are debugging scripts, **answer** can be very useful to display information (the values of variables or whatever) so that you can see what's going on; it also stops the script running until you click **OK** (ask is similar to **answer**, but allows you to type a reply that the script can use). However, the **answer** dialog box appears in a fixed part of the screen and may obscure other things you want to look at. Instead, you can use **put**, as below. This displays information in the message box, which you can move around by dragging in the usual way for a window. Unlike using **answer** and **ask**, putting text into the message box doesn't wait for the user to do anything: the script will carry on (and of course, it may put something else into the message box that replaces what it just put there).

```
on mouseUp -- this should show 9 in the message box!
   put 4+5
end mouseUp
```

```
on mouseUp
   put the name of me -- the name of this button appears in the message box
end mouseUp
```

Note that put *something* (like put the name of me) is short for put *something* into the message box. If you want to, you can get back anything that you've put in the message box by using **the message** like a variable. Thus, **put the message+1** will add one to a number already displayed in the message box.

Here are some more example button **mouseUp** handlers for you to try.

```
on mouseUp
  put the message into lastMessage
  put the date
  answer "I've changed the message box to show the date"
  put lastMessage -- and now changed it back to what it was before
end mouseUp
```

```
on mouseUp
  set the name of me to "beeper"
  beep -- useful to do this before an answer to wake people up!
  answer "Did you click?"
  put the name of me
end mouseUp
```

```
on mouseUp
  repeat 20 times
    set cursor to busy -- spins the beachball cursor
  end repeat
end mouseUp
```

If you create another button, that button will have its *own* script and its *own* handlers. So if you create a new button now, and click on it (using the Browse tool), the code you have just written for the first button will not be executed. The new button has an 'empty' script (later on you will want to distinguish between a button with a *really* empty script, and one that has an outline mouseUp handler, as helpfully supplied by the script editor, that does nothing – other than absorb mouseUp messages).

Now you know how to write scripts into buttons: all that remains to do is to learn HyperTalk so that you can take full advantage of its features! We shall give an outline of the language in Chapter 4; if you are already familiar with a language such as Pascal, C or even BASIC, you shouldn't have much difficulty in picking it up. The structure of HyperTalk programs is similar to other languages in many respects:

- scripts have a simple nested structure (using keyword pairs such as: on and end, repeat and end repeat, if ... then and end if as brackets);

- you can use procedures (handlers can be used as procedures and there are functions too);

- repetition (repeat while and other variants of the repeat instruction enable you to make all the same sorts of loops that you can in other languages);

- HyperTalk's conditional instructions are similar to those in other languages (if ... then and if ... then ... else).

On the other hand, the ability for programs to operate on objects and the message-passing scheme is quite novel, and these are best understood at first by exploring some examples and making some simple programs for yourself. The following examples all run and can be typed into HyperCard directly as you read them; however, you'll find that we leave some details of HyperTalk till later chapters so that for now you can have useful hands-on experience. Use the HyperTalk Reference stack to clarify the meaning of any HyperTalk instructions that you don't understand.

1.4   A 'musical' diversion

Now that we have an idea of how HyperCard sends messages and how you can write HyperTalk scripts to handle them, let's put them to use in almost the simplest interesting HyperTalk script possible: a simple musical instrument.

When you press any key **x**, HyperCard sends the message **keyDown x** along the current message path. If you don't have the cursor in a field, the message goes to the current card's script (from where it will pass to the background, the stack, home script, and so on). We'll handle the **keyDown** message in the current card and use it to play a note. If we made our proposed modifications, say, in the home script, we would still be able to play notes. The problem would be that pressing keys would *always* play notes, whichever card we were on! Sometimes we might have such a brilliant idea that we do want to be able to use it everywhere, but playing notes from the keyboard isn't one of those bright ideas! So, we make the changes to the script of the current card: this keeps the innovations to just this card.

The following script can go in the card of a new stack. It will be the only thing in the card's script:

```
on keyDown aKey
    play harpsichord aKey
end keyDown
```

With this script in place, when you type a key, such as **A**, HyperCard will play note A on its harpsichord. But, if you have a QWERTY keyboard, your key layout won't have low notes on the left and high notes to the right as you might want for a real keyboard instrument! To achieve this in HyperCard, the easiest thing is to use the built-in function **offset**. Offset takes two parameters (s and t, say) and returns the position of the string s in the string t (or 0 if s is nowhere in t). Thus, offset("h", "abcdefghij") is 8, as is offset("hi", "abcdefghijkl"), but offset("hello", "abcdefghijkl") is zero.

```
              1 2 3 4 5 6 7 8 9 10
         t: a b c d e f g h i j
         s:                 h i j
offset(s,t): |←——————— 8 ———————→|
```

So if we define the sequence of keyboard keys in a variable called, say, musicKeys:

```
put "qwertyuiop" into musicKeys
```

we can use offset to index into another variable, say notes, that we have initialized with the names of the notes we want:

```
put "c4 d4 e4 f4 g4 a4 b4 c5 d5 e5" into notes
play harpsichord word offset(aKey, musicKeys) of notes
```

But play can also take a numeric parameter, the smaller the number the lower the note, with 60 being middle C. So play harpsichord offset(x, musicKeys)+60, for example, would play notes according to a keyboard layout defined in the variable keys. Here's an example layout that uses the three alphabetic rows of the QWERTY keyboard to play a chromatic scale:

```
on keyDown aKey
  play harpsichord tempo 180 offset(aKey, "qazwsxedcrfvtgbyhnujmik,ol.p;/")+60
end keyDown
```

It would be more fun to be able to change the instrument: why not use HyperCard's flute? If we add a button, we can use the name of the button to hold the name of the instrument, and change it whenever the button is pressed:

```
on mouseUp
  if short name of me = "flute" then set name of me to "harpsichord"
  else set name of me to "flute"
end mouseUp
```

Then our choice of instrument can change the instrument that keyDown is using:

```
on keyDown aKey
  put short name of card button 1 into theInstrument
  play theInstrument tempo 180 offset(aKey, "qazwsxedcrfvtgbyhnujmik,ol.p;/")+60
end keyDown
```

Finally, a computerized music machine perhaps ought to be able to play its own tunes when you get fed up with it. When nothing else is happening, HyperCard sends the message idle to the current card; we'll simply handle idle and play a little tune. (The # character used in the next handler isn't visible on some keyboards. If you can't find it on yours, type *option–3* to get it.)

```
on idle
  put short name of card button 1 into theInstrument
  play theInstrument "a es eq es f# g# a b c#5q a4s aq g#3s a b aq ew"
end idle
```

Unfortunately, this will swamp our keyboard, since HyperCard is idle most of the time, and each time it is idle this handler gives it a lot to play. Instead, we ought to set a timer, and test it each time HyperCard is idle. Here are two handlers (what Pascal programmers call procedures and functions) to manage a timer. They use a global variable to record the time when the timer should expire. (Global variables are discussed in Chapter 4.) Global variables retain their values from one execution of a handler to the next:

```
on setTimer n
  global timer
  put seconds() + n into timer
end setTimer

function timedOut
  global timer
  if seconds() > timer then return true
  else return false
end timedOut
```

We set the timer to expire after 30 seconds from now whenever a key is pressed and after playing the 'idle' tune:

```
on keyDown aKey
  put short name of card button 1 into theInstrument
  play theInstrument tempo 180 offset(aKey, "qazwsxedcrfvtgbyhnujmik,ol.p;/")+60
  setTimer 30
end keyDown

on idle
  if timedOut() then
    put short name of card button 1 into theInstrument
    play theInstrument "a es eq es f# g# a b c#5q a4s aq g#3s a b aq ew"
    setTimer 30
  end if
end idle
```

To understand why this works, you need to know that the **play** command differs from most other HyperTalk commands in that it does some of its work in parallel with the program. When a **play** command is executed, it passes a request to the sound driver in the Macintosh system and then returns control to your program. The sound driver plays the sounds requested at the requested speed, and meanwhile your program executes at its own speed. So, if it has been more than 30 seconds since the user last hit a key, the next **idle** message will find that **timedOut()** is true, so we play the fixed tune and set the timer for another 30 seconds – this will work nicely so long as the fixed tune is over before the 30 seconds is up!

The line in the **idle** handler: **play theInstrument "a es eq es f# g# a b c#5q a4s aq g#3s a b aq ew"** is probably too long to fit in your script-editing window. The solution to this is to use HyperTalk's *continuation line* facility (or make your script editing window wider!).

This is done by typing **option–return** to break the line at an appropriate point (not within a quoted string). Continuation lines are indicated by the ¬ symbol on the preceding line:

```
play theInstrument ¬
"a es eq es f# g# a b c#5q a4s aq g#3s a b aq ew"
```

1.5   Direct manipulation: a simple window system

Below is a picture of a simple scrolling window somewhat resembling a Macintosh window. In

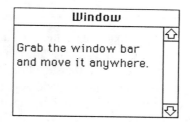

fact, it is a sham. It is a simulation of a window constructed out of a rectangular HyperCard button (called **Window**) and beneath it a scrolling field. You should have no difficulty creating a button and field like this on a blank card, using the button tool and the field tool to manipulate the size and position of the button and field and the **Button Info…** and **Field Info…** dialog boxes to set the appropriate properties.

What we plan to do is make a simulation of a 'window manager,' so that we can use the title bar (simulated by the **Window** button) like a *real* window's title bar. Clicking on the title bar and dragging should make the window move around the card.

We first need to get the button to handle mouseDown, the message that is sent when the user presses the mouse button down on the **Window** button. After the initial mouseDown message, and with the mouse button still held down, HyperCard will continuously send the mouseStillDown message: we will have to write something to handle this message to make the button move with the mouse:

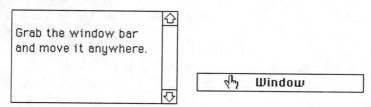

We will also want the scrolling field to follow suit, but that will be the easy part! There is a subtle complexity. The first mouse click on the button may not be right in the centre of the button:

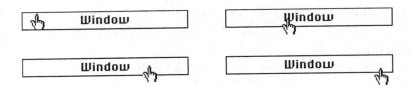

Make a new button and try the following experimental button handler to see what happens when you *don't* take account of the mouse's relative position:

```
on mouseDown
   set the location of me to the mouseLoc
end mouseDown
```

With this handler, when you click on the button, it centres itself around the mouse. If you want to get a better idea of what is happening you can add a line **put the mouseLoc**, and this will make **the mouseLoc** value be displayed in the message box. (It will be two numbers, like 231,43.) The name **me** refers to the object where this handler is, namely the button; so **set the location of me to …** moves the centre of the button to the specified coordinates, in this case wherever we happened to click on the button.

So, we need to save the position of the mouse click within the button, so that when the mouse is dragged, wherever it was initially clicked, it stays in the same relative position to the mouse. We'll use the variables **dx** and **dy** to measure the mouse's position when the button is first clicked. The following script will do to initialize them:

```
put the mouseLoc into mousePos
put the location of me into buttonPos
put item 1 of buttonPos - item 1 of mousePos into dx
put item 2 of buttonPos - item 2 of mousePos into dy
```

The **mouseLoc** gives us two items, like **127,32**, which represent the position of the mouse. Here, **item 1** of this will be **127** and **item 2** will be **32**: thus **item 1 of mousePos** will be the horizontal position of the mouse (measured in pixels from the left of the card), and **item 2 of mousePos** will be the vertical position (measured in pixels from the top of the card).

Thus, **put item 1 of buttonPos - item 1 of mousePos into dx** puts the horizontal offset of the mouse from the centre of the button into **dx**. Similarly, we work out the vertical offset and put it into **dy**. Now the problem is that we know **dx** and **dy**, but HyperTalk is inside a **mouseDown** handler, called when the button is first clicked. But we need to know these values while the mouse drags the button around. HyperCard will send **mouseStillDown** as the mouse is dragged, so a separate handler is needed. In short, **dx** and **dy** must be global variables: they must stay around even after the handler **mouseDown** has finished:

```
on mouseDown
   global dx, dy
   put the mouseLoc into mousePos
   put the location of me into buttonPos
```

```
    put item 1 of buttonPos - item 1 of mousePos into dx
    put item 2 of buttonPos - item 2 of mousePos into dy
  end mouseDown
```

Putting it together: when the button gets **mouseDown**, it works out and saves the relative offset of the mouse in the two global variables **dx** and **dy**.

We now need only add a **mouseStillDown** handler so that we can drag the button around. MouseDown is sent when the mouse's button is first pressed down, and **mouseStillDown** is repeatedly sent while the mouse button remains held down. We need, therefore, to have a handler for **mouseStillDown** to keep the button moving with the mouse. The following handler does this:

```
  on mouseStillDown
    global dx, dy
    get the mouseLoc
    add dx to item 1 of it
    add dy to item 2 of it
    set the location of me to it
  end mouseStillDown
```

These two handlers together make a button that can be dragged at will around the screen.

To complete our window manager we need a field, and we need it to follow the button around.

Create a field and make it scrolling. Call the field 'window' and position it carefully beneath its 'title bar' – the button. Adjust it to fit the width of the button. As an experiment, type

set loc of card field "window" to loc of button "window"

into the message box and see what happens. This makes the field have the same central position as the button. That's not quite what we want! (You can abbreviate **location** to **loc**, and with the set command you can miss out the 'the' as well. Notice that it does not matter if windows and buttons have the same name, in this case **window**.)

If you type **the loc of card field "window"** into the message box, you'll find out where the field is. Suppose HyperCard says its at 170,146. Try typing **set loc of card field "window" to 200,146** to see what happens. It should move a bit to the right, in fact from 170 to 200.

Maybe this suggests how to make the field end up in the right place? It needs to have its top left set to be the same as the button's bottom left. We just add the line **set topLeft of card field "window" to left of me, bottom of me** *after* we have set the location of the button correctly.

If you try this you will notice that the field is actually one pixel too low because of the way HyperCard measures the sizes of things. We need to make the field one pixel higher:

```
  on mouseStillDown
    global dx, dy
    get mouseLoc()
```

```
    add dx to item 1 of it
    add dy to item 2 of it
    set the location of me to it
    set the topLeft of card field "window" to the left of me, the bottom of me-1
  end mouseStillDown
```

When you test this, you will probably find that the field appears to lag behind the button as you move the mouse around. This is because the screen is being updated too fast! Sometimes it is updated after the instruction **set the location of me to it** but before the instruction **set the topLeft of card field "window"**. The solution is to lock the screen while these two operations are performed:

```
    lock screen
    set the location of me to it
    set the topLeft of card field "window" to the left of me, the bottom of me-1
    unlock screen
```

If you are using a Macintosh with a screen that is larger than the standard-sized HyperCard cards, try dragging the simulate 'window' outside the card on which it is displayed. HyperCard allows you to do so, but it the image of the 'window' is clipped so that you can only see the portion that is on the card. This is an example of a point that is worth bearing in mind – buttons and fields can be placed at locations that are completely off the card, making them invisible. This often occurs as a consequence of programming errors in which a new location for a button or field is incorrectly computed!

1.6 Variables, global variables and fields

HyperCard has global variables and we've seen these can be used to communicate from one handler to another. Like all HyperCard variables, they can be used to store numbers or strings. In fact, numbers *are* strings, as you can find out by typing an expression like **char 2 of (23+44)** into the message box.

All the variable names you use in a handler, unless declared as global, are 'secret' to the handler; in the jargon they are called 'local variables'. No other handler can affect them, and this is precisely why they are so useful: they are safe from unintended changes if you send messages or call other handlers.

A special variable is **it**. You can use it like any other local variable, with two provisos. First, and most usefully, you can put values into it more easily (and faster) than other variables. Instead of writing **put 5 into it**, you can simply write **get 5**. The result in both cases is **it** having the value 5. Secondly, some – but not all – HyperTalk commands put useful values into it.

The commands **answer** and **ask** both put their result into it. You should try:

```
    get "hello"
    answer it
```

This will put up the expected dialog box:

But if you try **answer it** *again* (type another return to get **answer it** run from the message box
– it will still be there from the first time) the answer dialog box will say **OK** not **hello**! When
you clicked on **OK**, answer set the value of it to OK. Had you tried:

   answer "Make a choice:" with "Apple", "Pear", "Orange"

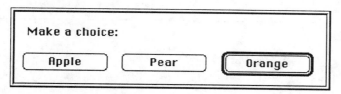

then you would have got it set to Apple, Pear or Orange according to which choice you had
clicked on.

Apart from the way **answer**, **ask** and a few other commands mess with it, it is an
ordinary local variable, and it is useful to think of each handler having its own it.

Global variables, unlike local variables, are used to share information with other
handlers (as we saw above with the **mouseDown**, **mouseStillDown** handlers); this is often a
mixed blessing. If you accidentally use a global n (say) to mean one thing for some handlers
over here, and you also use n to mean something else for a pair of handlers over there, then
things certainly won't work out as you expect! Your global variable n is shared, but you've
forgotten about some of the handlers that affect it. It is very easy to do this when you are writing
scripts, even ones of comparatively modest size. It can be pretty difficult to track down the bugs
that arise. One moral is to use long names for global variables, and to make the names as
specific as you possibly can to their purpose (so you are unlikely to use them for some other
reason).

Human nature being what it is, you are bound to use one global variable called t or i
because it is just so useful. But tomorrow you may do the same thing (a global t is so
convenient!) in another script – and it may be some time before you notice the effects of the
clash! A big problem in HyperCard is that variables are either local to a single handler or global
to *everything*: every handler, even in every stack. Someone else may have written a stack that
uses the same name for one of its globals as you have – and this may spell disaster (if you have
both stacks open at the same time)! We can only say that it's a shame that there isn't a semi-
global variable that is global only to handlers within a single object's script. One might envisage
such a global also being known in contained objects – so buttons can see their card's or
background's semi-globals, but backgrounds and other buttons would not see a button's own

semi-globals. There are all sorts of schemes, and HyperCard had to choose the simplest and most unreliable!

Fortunately HyperCard provides three ways to avoid global variables and their dangers.

First, a technique available in any decent programming language: functions. You may already know about functions from other programming languages, but even so it is very useful to think of them as a good way of making programs better, particularly by eliminating global variables. One of the most common requirements to get information from one handler to another is when they call each other explicitly. In our example of mouseDown/mouseStillDown, the handlers did not mention each other, and this technique won't work.

Here is a really simple idea. On mouseUp on some button we want to throw a die and answer the number thrown.

```
on mouseUp
  global dice
  throw
  answer dice
end mouseUp

on throw
  global dice
  put random(6) into dice
end throw
```

The idea is that throw rolls the die and sets the global variable dice, so we can look at it in the mouseUp handler. Of course, it is far better to make throw a function:

```
on mouseUp
  answer throw()
end mouseUp

function throw
  return random(6)
end throw
```

This solution, which does exactly the same thing, is not only 34 characters shorter (it will take you less time to type) but there is no global variable dice to get messed up! Bigger programs written this way will take you less time to debug.

Of course you may want to get several values out of a function, perhaps someone's name and age and sex and so forth. Since all values in HyperCard are strings of characters, you can simply make a big string out of the values you want to return. Furthermore, if you use commas, returns or blanks between the values, HyperTalk provides char, item, line and word as convenient selectors to get the various values out of the string. Here's how you might make throw deal with two dice:

```
function throw
    return random(6) & "," & random(6)
end throw
```

Calling throw will get us values like **2,3** or **6,6**. These values can be put into variables like any others. For example:

```
get throw()
if item 1 of it = item 2 of it then answer "You rolled a double"
```

If the first way to avoid globals is to use functions, the second way is to use parameters. Parameters get values *into* both handlers and functions, just as functions get values *out*. In fact, you've already seen HyperTalk using parameters: **random**, for instance, takes a single parameter (such as 6) to tell it how large a random number it can generate. A handy little function that will improve almost every stack you write is **plural**. It takes two parameters and returns a grammatically correct string.

plural(0, "card")	→ "no cards"
plural(1, "card")	→ "1 card"
plural(2, "card")	→ "2 cards"
plural(13, "card")	→ "13 cards"

It is implemented as follows:

```
function plural count, text
    if count ≠ 1 then put "s" after text
    if count = 0 then put "no" into count
    return count && text
end plural
```

When you consider how awkwardly you would have written this function using global variables (you need three), you can see that functions and parameters are a good idea. You would find scripting things like:

```
answer "I found" && plural(f, "field") && "on" && plural(c, "card")
```

pretty tedious without a **plural** function!

(In fact, the branch of programming called functional programming manages to do away with global variables *and* puts (assignments) altogether using nothing other than functions and parameters. It is a very reliable way of programming.)

The third way to avoid globals is to use fields.

Global variables in HyperCard have two glaring problems for most purposes: they are shared between stacks (when you may not want them to be shared) and they disappear when HyperCard is exited. Fields are HyperCard's way of keeping data within stacks, safely and permanently. You may only have thought of fields as places on cards that can be used for storing text: well, that's exactly how you can use them from HyperTalk, as a substitute for global variables.

Even for simple situations, fields have a big advantage over globals: you can see what they contain, and this makes debugging much easier. Once you have debugged a script you can say **hide field "data"** (or whatever you called it) in the message box, and the field will disappear from view. (You can also use HyperCard's variable watcher for this purpose, though not to change values or to display exactly what you want to watch.)

More generally, you will find uses for hidden fields for storing things that the user may not be interested in, but your program is: the date and time a stack was last used or last printed (you can then tell the user whether the stack has changed since it was last printed, perhaps even if it was printed some time ago on a different machine); secret passwords; how many times a card has been looked at by the user.

Here is a simple example. We want our stack to remember where the user left it: so that next time the stack is used, instead of going to the first card (as usual) we go straight to where the user last left it.

We need to know that HyperCard sends the messages **openStack** when a stack is first opened and **closeStack** when it is closed.

So we create a field on the first card, say it is called **card field "kickoff"**, and we hide the field by typing **hide card field "kickoff"** in the message box.

When the stack is closed, we arrange for a handler to save the current card number in this field on the first card:

```
on closeStack
    put the number of this card into card field "kickoff" of card 1
end closeStack
```

When **closeStack** is sent by HyperCard, the user might be on any card, so it is important to refer to the field of card 1 explicitly – which is done by saying **card field "kickoff" of card 1**. This refers to the right field whichever card the user is on; of course, if we knew the user was on card 1 already, we could more simply write **card field "kickoff"** (but the whole idea is that we don't know which card the user will be on!)

On opening the stack, HyperCard sends the message **openStack**, which we handle as follows and automatically go to that card whose number has previously been stored in the card field:

```
on openStack
    go to card (card field "kickoff" of card 1)
end openStack
```

This is the idea; there are several ways to improve it that we needn't go into here.

There is even a fourth way to avoid the use of global variables. Use the properties of objects to hold the information that you want to store. This one is especially useful when you need to store a small amount of information that is closely associated with a button or script. Of course you can only use properties in this way that aren't already being used and won't affect the appearance of the object. For example, if a button's **showName** property is always **false**, then you can use the button name to hold a string (of up to 31 characters). It would be nice if we could invent our own properties for objects and the **set** them and **get** them, but unfortunately HyperCard objects aren't extensible in this way. However the scripts of objects offer an almost unlimited storage space for strings. You can use the script of any object as a container for a string of any length of to 32k characters, as long as the string doesn't contain any lines that begin with **on** or **function**! To access the string use **get the script of**.... To update the string, you must replace the entire script with a new version of the string, using **set the script of**....

Our next HyperTalk example is the classic HyperCard database, but we have used a field – rather like a global variable – to keep track of a simple sequence number.

1.7 Simple databases

You can build simple databases with HyperCard quite quickly, often with very little HyperTalk programming, but it is also possible to make them a lot more useful and relevant to the real world by adding some special features programmed in HyperTalk. You might make yourself a HyperCard database of your favourite records, CDs, or a catalogue for all of your books. HyperCard would let you flip through the database with the greatest of ease, but it wouldn't help very much when it actually came to putting your fingers on your records or books.

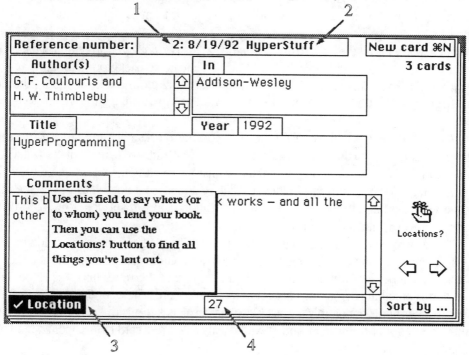

Here's a way of using global variables to solve the problem. (The only other thing you need is a pen!) The idea is that as you add new items to your database, HyperCard gives you a reference number, 1, 2, 3, 4, … . You simply write the reference number on your CD (or book or whatever), and keep your CDs in reference number order. Now HyperCard can tell you exactly where your CDs are. The great thing about this scheme is that you don't have to keep your books or papers in a 'sensible' order (like by their authors, titles and dates), just in their reference number order – HyperCard can be used to find the reference number from any of the things you have put in the database. Indeed, you can keep track of who you lend your books to (and get HyperCard to make a list of fines and who should pay them): who you lend books to would be silly information to keep in the books themselves!

The card design illustrated on the preceding page shows one way of doing it. Numbers indicate special features. 1 is the reference number itself, generated by HyperCard. We often find it helpful to keep track of the date when we get new things, so the date is also generated automatically as part of the reference number. 2 is anything you want to add to the reference number as a mnemonic. In fact 1 and 2 are two separate fields (both transparent) and the rectangle around them was drawn on the background using the paint tools. So it looks like a single field, but the automatically generated part has its lock text property set, so it cannot be changed by accident. 4 is a shared background field that is used to record the most recently allocated reference number, see below.

Sometimes we lend CDs or books to friends, and it helps to keep track of them. 3 is a button which pops up a field where we can write in details, like where something has gone. It is shown highlighted here, to help remind you to click it to make the location information disappear.

Let's worry about the **Location** button first. This is a *background button*. That is, it is repeated on every card with this background. To create a background button, use the **Background** menu item (on the **Edit** menu) to select background editing mode, then use **New Button** on the **Objects** menu and finally, use **Background** again to revert to normal editing.

As a refinement, when *we've* got the item (on our bookshelf), the **Location** button looks like this: | **Location** |, but when an item is lent out, we'll make it look like this: | ✓ **Location** |. The tick is supposed to remind us that we've written who or where we've lent the item to in the location information field (which is hidden, so it doesn't clutter up the card). Also, we want the button highlighted when the location field is displayed, to remind us that clicking on it will again hide the location information.

The way to do this is to arrange for HyperCard to peek into the location field and see if there is any information there: if there is, then the button name must be ticked; if not, then the tick, if any, must be removed. An **openCard** handler is used, because this gives HyperTalk a chance to do something before the user gets a look at the card. The **openCard** handler should be in the background (or possibly the stack), so that it catches *any* card being opened. If it was placed in the script of the current card, it would only catch *that* card being opened, and we'd have to have a copy of it in each card.

```
on openCard
   if number of words in field "location" = 0 then
      set name of background button id 38 to " Location"
   else
      set name of background button id 38 to numtochar(18) && "Location"
   end if
   hide field "Location"
end openCard
```

There are several features of this handler to note:

- First, we didn't say simply: if field "location" is empty then..., because quite often a field that looks empty in fact contains a space or a return character. Counting the number of words is a more reliable way of finding out if the field looks empty to a user.

- Since we keep changing the **Location** button's name, we have no idea what it is going to be called! We therefore use its ID number, which for our stack happens to be **38**. *It might be a different number for your stack – you'll have to bring up the button dialog box to find out what it is (use the* **Objects** *menu).*

- In the Chicago font (the one that is normally used for button names), the tick character has code 18 (you can use the Desk Accessory Key Caps to help find out – press **control**, and you'll see that is control+R, and R is the eighteenth character in the alphabet), so we set the name of the button to numToChar(18) && "Location" to get it ticked.

- Fields and buttons are either card or background – the script above uses a background field and a background button. In HyperTalk, we can refer to a background field simply by saying field, but a card field *must* be referred to by saying card field (perhaps abbreviated, like cd field or cd fld). Contrariwise, buttons when referred to simply as button are card buttons, not background buttons. Thus we refer to a card button by saying button (or card button, if we wish to be long-winded) and a background button by saying background button (bg button or bg btn).

The handler for the complete **Location** button has two different things to do, depending on whether the location information field is displayed. If the location field is displayed, then hide it, otherwise show it. It is easy to see if the field is displayed by testing its visible property. If the field location is visible, hide it, and set the hilite property of the location button to false (make it look normal). Note that we can say the hilite of me, to avoid naming the button (this trick makes it a handler that can be copied to other buttons more easily). Note that we can easily decide whether to put a tick in the button's name (the user may have deleted or added text to the field) by sending the openCard message ourselves, even though the card hasn't been 'opened' again.

```
on mouseUp -- the location button
  if visible of field "location" then
    hide field "location"
    set hilite of me to false
    openCard -- to reset name of this button if necessary
  else
    show field "location"
    set hilite of me to true
  end if
end mouseUp
```

We need to get the reference numbers organized. Each time the user makes a new card, we need a new reference number. Should we use a global variable? No, because the global variable will lose its value when the stack is closed. Instead, we need to keep the reference number in a field, as we discussed in the previous section. Fields, of course, keep their value between uses of the stack, so if we keep the reference number in a field, HyperCard will remember it in the stack indefinitely, which is exactly what we want here.

The best way is to have a shared text background field (set the **Shared Text** box in the **Field Info** dialog in the **Objects** menu); this means that the field's text is available in every card on that background. Let's call it counter, and for simplicity assume that it is visible – it is shown as 4 in the picture. Whenever the user makes a new card (to record the details of the latest CD), we must intercept the newCard message, sent by HyperCard when a new card is made, and adjust the reference number accordingly. That is easy to do by the command: **add 1 to field "counter"**. Since counter is a shared field, this single command will add one to it on every card in the background.

All that remains to do is to copy the new reference number into the reference number field on the new card. The newCard handler below shows how we can also easily add today's date as part of the reference number. The handler for newCard should be in the background (or stack) script:

```
-- make reference number correct
on newCard
  add 1 to field "counter"
  put field "counter" & ": " & the short date into field "reference number"
end newCard
```

Making your own labels

The database described in the last section generated reference numbers that you were supposed to write on the books, papers or disks that you wanted to keep track of. You might have thought that you would use HyperCard to generate the reference number which you then wrote by hand onto your treasured object – but why not get HyperCard to print the reference labels for you?

```
┌─────────────────────────────────────┐
│  Various HyperCard Stacks            │
│  ·································    │
│  ·································    │
│    Turtle Graphics                   │
│    Graphical Tools                   │
│  ·································    │
│                                      │
│  ·································    │
│                                      │
│  ·································    │
│    #3 [May 16, '91]                  │
│                                      │
│  ═══════════════════════════════    │
│       #3 [May 16, '91]               │
│  ◀ ⅃ƆƎTOꓤꓑ ƎTIꓤW    [Ɩ6, '9Ɩ ʎɐꟽ] Ɛ# │
│  ◀ Ǝ⅃ꓭA𝖭Ǝ ƎTIꓤW                     │
└─────────────────────────────────────┘
```

We shall briefly describe how to organize your stack so that you can print labels easily, then – for fun – we'll show how HyperTalk can be used to take control of HyperCard's graphics. (Can you guess how to put the upside-down text in the disk label?)

The design of a stack to be used for managing your database, and the design of your labels may or may not be the same. If you can make your video stack look like video cassette labels (or wine labels), then so much the better: the stack will have an attractive look and feel about it, and the purpose of various fields will be fairly obvious. However, if your database style and your labels are going to look different, perhaps because labels have to be tiny and would be unreadable on the Mac screen at the appropriate size, you won't be able to simply get HyperCard to print the stack as it stands.

Since we are learning HyperTalk, we may as well design a completely new stack. The cards for the basic database part of the stack will look like the one illustrated at the top of the next page.

The two places the user can type into are the disk label and the notes background fields. The other visible field on the card is the disk reference number: this is locked and cannot be changed by the user. Indeed, the easiest way to get the text 'Notes:', 'Disk label:' and so on is to use shared-text background fields; shared text means the same text is shown in the field on every card, and incidentally the text is locked.

We'll start at the easiest end of the stack.

First, the home button: its **mouseUp** handler simply says **go home**. In full,

```
on mouseUp -- home button
  go home
end mouseUp
```

The left and right arrow buttons are more complicated. They could simply have **mouseUp** handlers like the home button, with **go previous card** (or **go prev**, for short) and **go next card**. However, it's nice if the next button doesn't **go next** when you are already on the last card, for here telling HyperCard to **go next** actually takes you to the *first* card. So on the last

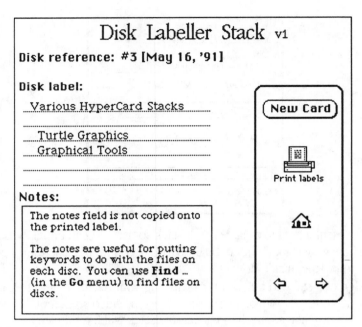

card, it's generally better to **beep** than end up on the first card! Likewise, for going to previous cards, we should check we are not on the first card, else we'd end up on the *last* card by mistake. The necessary tests are straightforward. The script for the ⇨ button is:

```
on mouseUp -- go to next card (if there is one)
   if ID of this card = ID of last card then beep
   else go next card
end mouseUp
```

and for the ⇦ button:

```
on mouseUp -- go to previous card (if there is one)
   if ID of this card = ID of first card then beep
   else go previous card
end mouseUp
```

Later we will need another background in this stack to make the actual disk labels, so we need to refine these handlers to stay within the same background: we don't want the buttons to let the user stray onto any other backgrounds that may be in the stack. Rather than talk about the first or last card (first or last in the stack), we want to talk about the first or last card in the current background:

```
on mouseUp -- go to next card of this background (if there is one)
   if ID of this card = ID of last card of this background then beep
```

```
      else go next card of this background
   end mouseUp
```

```
   on mouseUp -- go to previous card of this background (if there is one)
      if ID of this card = ID of first card of this background then beep
      else go previous card of this background
   end mouseUp
```

The new card button is also very simple. Its **mouseUp** handler uses HyperTalk to select from the HyperCard menus to make a new card:

```
   on mouseUp
      doMenu "New Card"
   end mouseUp
```

This button doesn't change the reference number, because it isn't the only way of getting a new card. The user might, for instance, select **New Card** from the menu, or even copy-and-paste an existing card. As before, then, we put a **newCard** handler in the background script. (Do not put this handler in the stack script! It would be run when any new card was made in any stack.)

Here's one suggested background handler for **newCard**:

```
   on newCard
      add 1 to field "Reference"
      get the long date
      delete item 1 of it
      delete char 1 of it
      delete char 1 to 2 of last word of it
      put " ' " before last word of it
      put "#" & field "Reference" && "[" & it & "]" into field "Refno"
   end newCard
```

Most of this script converts the current date in long format (e.g., "Friday, May 10, 1991") successively into " May 10, 1991" by deleting the first item (i.e., up to the comma); then into "May 10, 1991" by deleting the first character (a space); then to "May 10, 91" by deleting the first two characters of the last word, before finally inserting an inverted comma before the year digits to get "May 10, '91".

The field **Reference** is a hidden, shared text field that is used to record the highest reference number used so far; the field **Refno** is locked but not shared (since each label has a different reference number) and can be seen in the picture: it is visible near the top of the card. You can create a background field with shared text (they have the same contents on all of the cards in the background) by creating the field in the normal way (remember to select background editing mode first) and then selecting the **Shared text** option in the **Field Info** dialog. To hide the reference field you would type hide field "Reference" into the message box; but you may want to be able to see it while you debug the stack.

Now we've built the basic disk catalogue stack, we need to work out how to print labels. The two fields the background uses that we want to work with are: Label, the main text of the label, and Refno where our newCard handler puts the disk's reference number.

The way we shall make the labels is by copying the relevant information onto a different background, itself called label. The idea is that one background (user interface, say) is designed to look smart for interaction; the other background (label) is designed to look smart when it is printed. The label background, then, won't have buttons for going to the next and previous cards!

Use **New Background** in the **Objects** menu to make a new background, which creates a new background with one new card. Then use **Background Info** dialog to give this new background the name label.

Before copying the data from the user interface background onto the label background, we need that background to have the same number of cards:

```
on mouseUp -- for button 'print labels'
  -- first make the right number of labels
  put number of cards in background "user interface" into numbui
  repeat while numbui < number of cards in background "label"
    -- delete a few labels
    go background "label"
    doMenu "delete card"
  end repeat
  repeat while numbui > number of cards in background "label"
    -- create a few labels
    go background "label"
    doMenu "new card"
  end repeat
```

> Throughout the book we use hairlines like this to delimit portions of handlers that will be continued later in the text.

One repeat loop reduces the number of cards, the other increases it. Notice how each time we delete or create a new card, the loop re-evaluates the expression number of cards in background "label", which therefore either decreases or increases, accordingly, until it is equal to numbui, the number of cards in the user interface background.

Next we zip through the user interface buttons, copying the two fields over to the label background. In fact, we need to do more work on the label background, so, as it comes to the same thing, we zip through the label cards and copy the user interface fields to them. At the same time we will mark just those cards we want to print as labels:

```
unmark all cards
repeat with i = 1 to number of cards in background "label"
  go card i of background "label"
  put field "label" of card i of background "user interface" into field "label"
  put field "refno" of card i of background "user interface" into field "refno1"
  put field "refno" of card i of background "user interface" into field "refno2"
```

```
      mark this card
      rotate
   end repeat
```

Now we ask the user if they really want to print the labels. HyperCard is currently displaying a sample label (we are still on the label background):

```
   -- we are left looking at a label
   answer "Print all labels?" with "Cancel" or "OK"
   go background "user interface"
   if it = "OK" then print marked cards from 0,0 to 220,220
end mouseUp
```

The 'magic numbers' 0,0 to 220,220 were worked out so that we make the printed label just the right size (remember that the card size is larger so that the user interface background has enough space for its extra buttons; there may also be junk on the label background we don't want printed). You can easily find positions on a card by a **mouseUp** handler in the card script:

```
on mouseUp
   put the mouseLoc
end mouseUp
```

A detail to note is that HyperCard may not print as many cards per sheet of paper as possible. Unfortunately, you can't control the printing size of cards from within HyperTalk, the user has to do it from a dialog box. We should therefore improve the printing by reminding the user:

```
if it = "OK" then
   answer "Have you already set the card size to Half?" with "Yes" or "Set"
   if it = "Set" then
      answer "Choose card size, then Print" & return & return ¬
      & "•• Then Cancel the print dialog box! ••"
      print marked cards from 0,0 to 220,220
      close printing
   else print marked cards from 0,0 to 220,220
end if
```

Writing upside down

Let's now do the fun graphics for the disk labeller. Specifically, we want to write the reference number upside down so that it will be readable when the label is folded over the edge of a diskette. The basic idea is to use the **Text** tool to write the appropriate text onto the card image, select it, then rotate it right twice (thus turning it over).

The first problem is to know where the text is that we want to turn over! Although we could write a **mouseUp** handler to **put the mouseLoc** and hence by hand work out all the coordinates, it is far easier to use a button to define the region of the card we want to work in.

If there is a background button **X** (a transparent, rectangular button so that it is normally invisible) we can resize and move it around with the Button tool with ease. Saying **get rectangle of background button "X"** in HyperTalk then gives us four coordinates, specifying the positions of its left, top, right and bottom. The **rect** will be something like **110, 186, 206, 210**: we use **item** to pick off the various numbers. This is not an obvious use for a button – but then we sometimes use buttons in the real world in similar, and equally unexpected ways – haven't you ever used a button to draw circles?

Before doing any graphics, we need to make certain that the drawing region we have selected is free of any junk. If you were a human user, you would now choose the select tool and drag the mouse over the region covered by the **X** button, then select **Clear Picture** from the menu. We can do exactly the same in HyperTalk:

```
on rotate
    get rectangle of background button "X" -- first clear the rectangle
    choose select tool
    drag from item 1 of it, item 2 of it-1 to item 3 to 4 of it
    doMenu "Clear Picture"
```

We are dragging from the line above the rectangle of the button (that's the **item 2 of it-1** bit in the drag). A few experiments revealed that it was necessary to do so (otherwise some of the rotated text 'leaks')!

Next we pick up the text to rotate and type it (having chosen the **Text** tool and clicked where we want it to go – just as we would by hand). Then we choose the select tool again, drag across the button rectangle again, and flip it over.

```
    -- now type the text
    choose text tool
    set textFont to "New York"
    set textSize to 9 -- need a small size so lots of text fits
    click at item 1 of it, item 4 of it-1
    type field "refno1"

    -- then turn it over
    choose select tool
    drag from item 1 to 2 of it to item 3 to 4 of it
    doMenu "Rotate Right"
    doMenu "Rotate Right"

    -- and back to the browse tool
    choose browse tool
end rotate
```

You can speed up **rotate** by adding **hide tool window**, and much more by **lock screen**. In its present form, without locking the screen (and hence saving HyperCard from drawing directly on the screen) the user can see something is really happening. So if you lock the screen (the best place to do this is before the last **repeat** of the **mouseUp** handler), insert a **set cursor to busy** in the loop. Each time **set cursor to busy** is executed, the beach-ball cursor rotates a bit, and makes things look busy.

Deleting spare cards

The label stack creates lots of labels (in the label background) that can always be generated from the other cards at any time. It's not necessary to leave them lying around in the stack, wasting space. One is sufficient (to keep the button, various fields and graphics on).

When a stack is closed, HyperCard sends the message **closeStack** to it. We'll simply handle this message and use it as a cue to delete all the spare cards from the stack: the **repeat loop** in the **closeStack** handler deletes cards until there is just one left. Having deleted all these cards (and, indeed, having deleted cards earlier from the print labels button on the other background), HyperCard may have lost track of free space in the stack: it's wise to compact the stack to make it as small as possible.

```
on closeStack
  lock screen
  repeat while number of cards in background "label" > 1
    go background "label"
    doMenu "delete card"
  end repeat
  unlock screen
  doMenu "Compact stack"
  pass closeStack
end closeStack
```

This handler should be put in the stack script. Later in this book (Chapters 4 and 9) we'll explain the final **pass closeStack** line.

Printing what hasn't been printed

We've used the last two examples to illustrate the use of fields for keeping values around from one use of a stack to the next. Both examples used a shared-text (background) field to do this, so that the same values stored in the field were accessible from all cards on its background.

We used a field to help generate unique reference numbers that could be written by hand or printed on labels and stuck onto your *objets d'art*, or the other things you were cataloguing.

Another use of the same sort of idea – keeping values around in a stack – which is both simple and very useful is to have a way of getting HyperCard to print just those cards that you haven't already printed. Indeed, this idea is very appropriate for both of the database stacks we've just been describing.

Suppose you keep an address list. For safety, or for when you are away from a Macintosh, you may want to keep a paper or card index backup. Naturally, you will use

HyperCard to print the address stacks cards (perhaps using a report so you only print the relevant fields) on your printer; you then cut them up and glue them to the new cards in your card index. The thing is, you want to print only the new cards.

Life would be easier if HyperCard sent a startPrinting and stopPrinting message to each card as it was printed, just as it sends openCard and closeCard. Unfortunately it doesn't!

Suppose each card has a field printed that keeps track of whether that card has been printed, then when we print a card we update put true into field printed, and when a card is changed or newly made, we put false into field printed. In fact, since the user might like to see what's been going on, we could put "Printed" or "Not yet printed" into the field as this is much easier to understand when it is displayed.

So how do we print the cards whose printed field is (contains the text) Not yet printed? One way to do this in HyperCard is to look for these cards, mark them and then use print marked cards.

```
repeat number of cards times
  set the mark of this card to field "printed" = "Not yet printed"
  go next card
end repeat
print marked cards
repeat number of marked cards
  go next marked card
  put "Printed" into field "printed"
  unmark this card
end repeat
```

HyperCard provides other ways of marking cards. This isn't the fastest way of doing it, but it gives us more control over what is going on. Thus it would be nice for this script not to change the marking of the cards (perhaps the user has marked certain cards for other purposes?). All you need to do is use the second line of the printed field to save the original mark. You can arrange for the field, as displayed on the card, not to be big enough to expose its second line. Here's one way to do it:

```
repeat number of cards times
  put the mark of this card into line 2 of field "printed"
  set the mark of this card to line 1 of field "printed" = "Not yet printed"
  go next card
end repeat
print marked cards
repeat number of marked cards
  go next marked card
  put "Printed" into line 1 of field "printed"
  set the mark of this card to line 2 of field "printed"
end repeat
```

By the way, the faster ways of marking cards are: mark cards where field "printed" = "Not yet printed" and, even faster, mark cards by finding "Not yet printed" in field "printed". Both of these methods do not unmark other cards that might not have Not yet printed in their printed field, so they should both be preceded by unmark all cards to make sure.

Finally, how do we know which cards have been changed, and therefore haven't been printed in their current form? Obviously, we can find new cards (which cannot have been printed) easily, simply by having a **newCard** handler. But the user may update an existing card: how do we find out which these cards are? (Besides, a new card that has not been 'changed' probably isn't worth printing yet.)

There are two parts. First, a handler for **newCard** should initialize field **printed:**

```
on newCard
   put "New card" into field "printed"
end newCard
```

Note that the text **New card** has the right effect in the script for printing cards we worked out earlier! Next, we have a **closeField** handler; **closeField** is sent when the user leaves a field that has been changed – just what we need.

```
on closeField
   put "Not yet printed" into field "printed"
end closeField
```

These two handlers should go in the background script of the cards we are concerned about.

1.8 Commands versus messages

Some parts of HyperTalk look like other programming languages, like **if...then...else**. The assignment statement, **put**, is a little different. Some commands produce messages which, if received by HyperCard, actually perform the command.

Thus **put** doesn't so much do an assignment, but sends a message to HyperCard, which *then* does the assignment. You can discover this for yourself by writing a stack handler that catches **put** messages.

```
on put
   beep
   pass put
end put
```

Notice the line **pass put:** although we've handled the **put** message (by beeping imaginatively), we still want HyperCard to *do* the put. So we pass the **put** message on.

However, it would be more interesting to try and see what **put** actually does. We could do this by using the message box. There is a problem, however, for the handler:

```
on put
   put the params
   pass put
end put
```

– which has serious problems! The line **put the params**, which is intended to tell us what **put**'s parameters are, will simply cause the handler to recurse, as it tries to handle the **put the params** message itself. Instead, we should specifically send this **put** directly to HyperCard, so bypassing our own **put** handler:

```
on put
   send "put the params" to HyperCard
   pass put
end put
```

Send specifies where the message is to be handled; we could have sent the message to **this card**, **this background**, or anywhere else, but in this case, to do so would have been pointless (because we are certain we really want HyperCard to do *this* put). An alternative solution to the recursion problem would have been to use **answer**: this wouldn't cause a recursive call to **put**, and as an added benefit would have given you a chance to read the **put** message (since you have to click **OK** before **answer** returns to the script). With **put the params**, any other **put** messages in a more complex script would make the message box too busy to read! Here's how:

```
on put
   answer the params
   pass put
end put
```

Unfortunately, it turns out that some versions of HyperCard don't seem to know what the parameters of **put** are, and you'll get the misleading impression that **the params** returns nothing; in fact, it will work properly with your own handlers and can be very useful. A very worthwhile trick in such cases as this when you are debugging scripts is not to write something as bare as **answer the params**, but to write something like **answer "the params=" & the params & "."** so that you can see clearly whether **the params** (or whatever you are testing) returns nothing or a space that you wouldn't otherwise have been able to see.

Perhaps you are wondering whether you'd ever want to intercept **put** commands with your own handlers, if you can't find out the parameters of **put**? One useful idea is to simply count how many **put**s your scripts are executing, something like this:

```
on put
   global put_counter
   add 1 to put_counter
```

```
      pass put
      end put
```

By seeing how **put_counter** increases when your stack does things, you'd try and modify it to make it do fewer **put**s and so be more efficient.

Most messages are not caused directly by commands, but are caused by the result of HyperCard doing something. Thus **closeCard** is not a command, for issuing it as a command would beg the question of what to do after closing the card! Should HyperCard show the next card, delete the current card, show another stack, or what? Instead, **closeCard** is sent by HyperCard to the current card when a command such as **go** has been executed. Just before HyperCard goes from the current card to the next card, the message **closeCard** is sent to the current card. Of course, if the card we're going to is in a different background, then the current background will get **closeBackground**. If the next card is in a different stack, **closeStack** will also be sent, and so on.

You can of course send **closeCard** yourself (and all the other messages) if you need to. For example, you might have an **openCard** handler that initializes your card (making the right buttons visible, say). It may be easiest to re-initialize the card when it has changed by sending an **openCard** message. HyperCard will ignore the **openCard** message if it gets it (the card is anyway already open). But the effect is that all your card initialization script can be kept together in the **openCard** handler (which is probably on the background, so that all cards on that background can be initialized the same way).

Although you can have scripts to handle **closeCard** and other like messages, it is too late if you want to stop HyperCard closing (or opening, or whatever) the card. HyperCard has already embarked on the process of closing the card, and trying to do something else at this stage will cause problems (for example, uncontrolled recursion). Instead, you should have had a handler for **go** and any other card-closing circumstances you want to catch – though this is trickier than it sounds, for a card can be closed when HyperCard deletes cards, creates new cards, and so on, actions which are caused by commands other than **go**. It's best to keep a handler for **closeCard** just to make a note, perhaps setting a global variable **error** (you can **put ID of this card into error**) so that you can sort out the mess later, perhaps on an **openCard** or **openStack**. Better still, say **put … after …** so that your global variable **error** can accumulate a whole series of errors which you can sort out later. Otherwise there is a danger that if two or more errors occur in succession before you have a chance to handle them, you'll forget the earlier ones.

1.9 Programming safely

The next chapter provides some useful high-level suggestions to help your HyperTalk programming and stack design. Here, we'll content ourselves with some basic but important advice on writing HyperTalk safely. If you don't write safely, you'll sometimes find things you write going wrong in very obscure ways.

We wrote things like the location of card field "window" when we *could have* written the location of card field 1 because we knew card field window was the only field, and therefore field number 1. But we didn't, because it doesn't take much programming before you forget which field is which: particularly if you use the **bring closer** or **send farther** features (in the **Objects** menu) which change the numbers.

Furthermore, we wrote "window" using quotes, when in fact HyperTalk would have let us get away with the slightly briefer: the location of card field window. We did that because of the ever present danger that we may later make window a HyperTalk variable: then its value won't necessarily be window as we need it here, but something else.

It is important to realize this point of HyperTalk. If you write the string "x", its value is x, for this is a *string literal*: it means what it literally says. You should try typing "x" (i.e., quote, x, quote) into the message box (then hit return): you will see HyperCard evaluates it to simply x. Now type the variable name x. It's value is whatever value you last put into it; for instance, if you had just said, put 3 into x, then x would have the value 3. But if you have not put a value into x, then HyperTalk treats it as if it had the value "x". (Try typing fooblebrox – or some other name you haven't yet used if you've already got a global variable already called x.)

This is a nasty source of confusion. For example, it means that HyperCard gets confused if you give a card a name that is a number, because HyperTalk cannot tell the difference between going to a card *called* "3" and going to card *number* 3, which may be quite different cards. It is best to program systematically, putting quotes around all of the literal strings in your programs, so that this confusion never catches you out.

We prefer a slightly more long-winded way of writing in HyperTalk than is sometimes necessary, to reduce the risks of things going wrong in obscure ways. We've found that it's easier to program defensively than to get into a mess later. If you do the same, then when you do get into a mess, as you inevitably will do from time to time, you'll have fewer kinds of error to worry about !

CHAPTER 2

Working with HyperCard

Accessing and editing scripts, programming style and stack design,
using the debugger, other tools and resources

This chapter deals with the things it helps to know before you start programming in HyperTalk. It is best read in conjunction with a running HyperCard system that you can use to experiment with. We assume that you've become familiar with ordinary HyperCard operations like making new cards, making new fields and entering text as well as doing graphics. We tell you about the basic new ideas you need to start hyperprogramming.

We also tell you about other things (like resources and XCMDs) that you may not need for a while, but will be useful to know a bit about so you recognize their names. This book does not require any resources or XCMDs that do not come as standard with HyperCard.

After reading this chapter you will be able to access and edit the scripts in your stacks quickly and conveniently, to make new icons and to use HyperCard's debugging tools. We'll introduce HyperCard's system of coordinates for referring to positions on cards and how to use it in HyperTalk programs, and we'll discuss two topics that are important in producing high-quality stacks – programming style and stack design. Finally, we introduce some useful ways to extend HyperCard and HyperTalk – creating new icons for buttons, creating new menus and palettes and extending the HyperTalk language with XCMDs and XFCNs.

2.1 Saving and undoing changes

The treatment of stacks in HyperCard differs from the treatment of files in most Macintosh applications – any changes made to a stack are permanently recorded as soon as they are made and no user action is needed to bring the file up to date. Hence there is no **Save** operation in HyperCard's **File** menu. Note that this means that you *cannot* undo the changes that you make to a stack, apart from the most recent change – but don't rely on **Undo**, as there are a few things that cannot be undone (like deleting a card). If you think you may want to go back to a previous version of a stack, make sure that you save a copy *before* you start to modify the stack.

Conversely, when you edit scripts within a stack, the stack's scripts are *not* saved until you say so. Viewing and editing HyperTalk scripts is simple and quick; as soon as you have altered a script and **Saved** the altered version, the changes take effect. You must save a script before it is 'really' changed, which means that you can run a script *before* you have saved any changes you made to it. This feature may help you in working out what you want to put in the script (because you can still run the old version of the script), but just as easily it can become very confusing, because the script won't work the way you might think you've changed it!

Hints

Rather than save a copy of the entire stack before embarking on changes, if you are only editing one card, it is quicker and uses less disk space to copy that card and paste it back into the same stack (**Copy Card** and **Paste Card** operations are in the **Edit** menu; **Paste Card** doesn't appear until you have a card to paste). If all goes well, you delete the old card – but make sure you can remember which is which!

Compacting a stack (which you can find in the **File** menu) makes it smaller, so this is useful to do before you save a backup copy.

HyperCard saves changes you make to a stack automatically, but it doesn't bother to do saves all the time, as this would slow things down. If you are working with graphics, you'll find **Keep** in the **Paint** menu can be used to save graphics changes you want to keep as you go along. To recover from a mistake, you can try **Undo** (from the **Edit** menu) or **Revert** (from the **Paint** menu) which takes you back to the last kept picture.

2.2   Accessing and editing scripts.

You can open the script of any object that you can see. Scripts contain the source texts of HyperTalk handlers and they are attached to the individual objects of a HyperCard stack. In the next chapter we'll give a complete list of the kinds of HyperCard objects and their properties, but you have probably already discovered that there are *fields, buttons, cards, backgrounds* and *stacks*. Every object has a script although, in most stacks, many of the scripts are left empty. A stack is itself considered to be an object and it too has a script.

There are several ways to open the script of an object when you can see the object on the screen. The simplest and slowest method is to use the **Objects** menu. To open the stack script, choose **Stack Info...** on the **Objects** menu; this opens a dialog box (a window without bar across the top); then to access the stack script use the **Script** button in the dialog box. Similarly, to access the script of the current background or the current card, use **Bkgnd Info...** or **Card Info...** from the **Objects** menu and then the **Script** button in the relevant dialog box.

To access the script of a button, choose the Button tool from the **Tools** palette (the menu labelled **Tools**; note that once you have chosen a tool it will remain selected until you choose another) and select a button by clicking on it. Use the **Button Info...** operation from the **Objects** menu to open a dialog box showing the properties of the button. Use the button in

the dialog box labelled **Script** to open a window for viewing and editing the button's script. The scripts of fields are opened in the same way, but you must, instead of the Button tool, use the Field tool to select the required field and then use the **Field Info...** operation. You can open the scripts of several fields and buttons in this way. Remember to choose the Browse tool to revert to the normal browsing mode when you have finished.

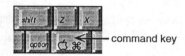

Now for the short cuts:

- You can make the **Tools** palette stay on the screen by typing *option–tab* or by choosing **Tools** on the menu bar and then dragging it to a convenient position.

- Using the Button tool or the Field tool, you can open the dialog box for a button or a field by double-clicking on it.

- You can open the script of any object with a single mouse click. Using the Browse tool, hold down the *option* and *command* keys, then click on any button to open its script. To open the script of the stack, press the *s* key while holding down the *option* and *command* keys. Similarly, press the *b* key to open the script of the current background and the *c* key to open the script of the current card. Finally, to open the script of any field, hold down the *option*, *command* and *shift* keys and click on the field.

HyperCard opens scripts in a window that is managed by the script editor. Whenever the script editor is active the menu bar contains text-editing operations similar to those found in other Macintosh text editors. The **Edit** menu provides **Cut**, **Copy** and **Paste**, so that you can move and copy portions of scripts, both within a single script and between scripts. The **Script** menu provides **Find** and **Replace** operations. You can make any changes you like to a script while it is open. The changed script is not recorded in the object until you use the **Save Script** operation on the **File** menu (short cut: type *command–s*). When you are developing a HyperTalk program, you may need to have several scripts open. That is no problem; each script is opened in a separate window, and they may remain open as long as you like, but use the **Save Script** operation in each window before testing any modifications.

The script editor tries to indent your script correctly to show the structure of your script. The lines that make up the body of each handler are indented, and the indenting within each handler shows the levels of nesting between **on**, **if** or **repeat** instructions and their corresponding **end** instructions. The script editor checks for matching **end** instructions and the indentation is adjusted whenever you use the *return* key or the *tab* key (the *tab* key has no other effect in script editing, since the indentation is automatic). Whenever there is an error in the matching of **ons**, **ifs** or **repeats** with **ends** the script editor removes the indentation to show that there is an error and gives you an idea where to start looking.

2.3 Stack design

The Apple Macintosh is famous as the computer platform that launched graphical user interfaces – windows, mouse-based interaction and the desk-top metaphor. HyperCard is a tool for developing applications that exploit those ideas, although it replaces the desk-top with a metaphor of its own – the stack of cards.

Graphical user interfaces bring new opportunities and challenges to the designers of interactive systems. There isn't a guaranteed method for designing a system that is easy to learn and effective to use; the development of systematic methods for user interface design is an area of current research. Meanwhile, experienced designers and human scientists have developed useful sets of guidelines, and it is these that have resulted in the look-and-feel that you see in today's applications on the Macintosh, HyperCard and other windows environments.

The two cards below, from a HyperCard project about the human body, illustrate the difference between designing and programming. The card on the left is starting to look terrific: it has a promising design. The one on the right looks boring: it has not yet benefited from visual design effort. The one on the left, however, doesn't even have a single working button – even what look like buttons are pictures of what the designer wants! Yet the card on the right works – the buttons already have carefully worked-out scripts. Neither project is finished. Note that

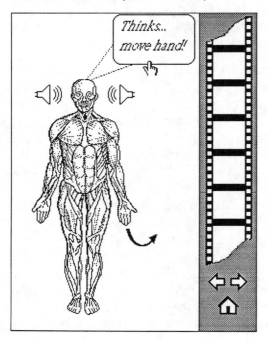 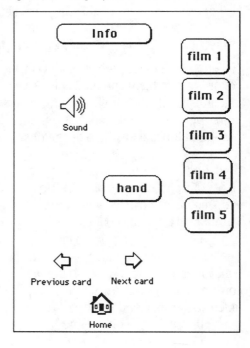

one button is not visible in the lefthand card: there is a danger that checking its script may be overlooked.

From this very simple comparison, you can see that good stacks need *both* design *and* programming. If all you want to do is enter a fantasy world, design alone is sufficient (left card); if all you want to do is get work done on your own, you may wish to do it without worrying about what it looks like (right card). Mostly, however, you will want your stacks to look good and to work! It is largely a matter of taste and circumstance whether it is better to add working scripts to a well-designed card (left) or whether it is preferable to add graphics to working scripts (right); you will probably end up doing a bit of one then a bit of the other, repeatedly making adjustments so that design and program are unified, and so that users get what they want (simplicity, help, power, information...) out of it.

To avoid confusion over our own and the reader's goals, we shall refrain from discussing issues of interface design for the HyperCard techniques stacks that we describe, although some of our own ideas on good design practice will no doubt be evident in the examples that we use. This book is not a design guide: it is a programming guide. Our aim is to give you an understanding of how to program interactive systems in HyperTalk that you can use to build all sorts of interactive programs. These may range from simple databases to sophisticated hypertext and hypermedia systems and from simple information tools to prototypes of full-scale business applications. The users' interface requirements for HyperCard applications are equally diverse. The aim of the book, then, is to provide designers with the tools and techniques they will need to construct many kinds of user interface.

2.4 Programming style

HyperCard is used for many purposes. Some HyperCard stacks are developed just to test out an idea or to do some simple once-off task; others are developed to a point where they become 'production' applications, fully documented and intended to be error-free and suitable for users who have no knowledge of HyperCard or HyperTalk. There are many points between these two extremes; the amount of attention that should be paid to the programming style issues discussed in this section (and the stack design issues discussed later in this chapter) depends on the purpose for which a stack is developed.

But let's assume that you want at least some of the stacks that you develop to be high-quality programs that can be supplied to other users and meet the requirements of 'production quality' software. If you have programmed in other programming languages, then many of the rules and guidelines that you have learned there are still applicable in HyperCard. The clarity and style of your programs can make all the difference to your success in producing high-quality HyperCard applications.

You should aim to make your finished programs:

* *easy for yourself and others to read*: even when you return to them months or years later.

  Use meaningful names, spelled out in full – almost all of the built-in names and keywords of HyperTalk follow this rule. Names made from two or more words have the initial letters of the second and subsequent words capitalized: **mouseUp**, **topLeft**, **myString**, **aDate**, **todaysDate**, **theFieldName**. However, the HyperCard system does not distinguish between upper- and lower-case letters in names and keywords, but you should do so when writing programs, to enhance their clarity.

Use comments to improve readability. Annotate each handler stating its purpose and any important preconditions; add clarifying comments on anything that isn't obvious. Here is an example:

```
function throw  -- returns two items containing random numbers in the range 1-6
   return random(6) & "," & random(6)
end throw
```

- *easy to debug and maintain*: algorithms should be as simple as possible, so that you can be reasonably confident that they are correct.

  Simplicity is of far greater value than efficiency, especially when you are developing a stack: you can leave the question of performance until you have constructed a working stack and determined where the performance problem (if any) lies.

- *general-purpose*: avoiding the proliferation of handlers that do 'almost the same thing' and ensuring that they can easily be re-used in different contexts.

  Handlers should be shared wherever possible. If several buttons have **mouseUp** handlers that perform the same action, then the **mouseUp** handler could go in the card script, with a test at the start of the handler to ensure that only **mouseUp** messages sent to the relevant buttons will invoke the action.

  Handlers should be defined at the lowest level that enables them to be accessed by all of the scripts that share them. Chapter 4 explains HyperCard's hierarchy of objects.

  Global variables should be used only to retain the values of variables across several activations of the same handlers, never as an alternative to using parameters. Global variables should always be given an initial value as soon as they are declared.

  Leave no 'dead wood' in your scripts. It is tempting to leave handlers that have ceased to be used in a stack in case they may be needed later. This is a false economy. When an old handler that has been out of use for some time is brought back into use, it is very likely to contain some assumptions that have ceased to be valid.

  It is also remarkably easy to forget about handlers – they can lurk in invisible fields or in card scripts where you don't remember putting anything. When you have finished working on a stack, therefore, print out *all* its scripts on paper using an automatic method that won't miss any (we show how to do this in Chapter 11) and then hunt down any dead wood.

- *portable*: so they work anywhere.

  Your stacks may be used on different sorts of Macintosh from the one you developed them on. If this is likely, you should check your stack particularly on smaller Macs, ones with less memory and smaller screens. It is very easy to overlook that on smaller screened Macs you cannot both see the top of a card and the menu bar at once without some difficulty: so don't put important things near the top of cards, in case they get covered up by the menu bar and not noticed on smaller screens.

  Your stack should check which version of HyperCard it is running under, and tell the user if the version is different from the versions the stack was developed on. The user may not want to risk your stack not working correctly with their system!

  Your stack may use fonts and other resources that are not universally available. Does your stack use any handlers or XCMDs in your home stack? You should distribute the relevant resources along with your stack, unless there are licensing reasons not to.

Do we practice what we preach? Not entirely: while the *HyperProgramming* stacks that accompany this book do follow many of the guidelines given above, their scripts are not fully annotated. This is because they are not intended to be used independently: this book supplies the necessary explanations. Moreover, we have often had to decide between clear and direct programming versus efficient and thoroughly error-proofed programming that would have been too complex to be worth explaining. The stacks are intended to illustrate the techniques that we describe in the book and to provide a basis for your own experimentation and developments. They are not intended as production systems.

2.5   Using the debugger

There is no substitute for thinking clearly about your programs and making sure that they are easy to test and debug. But when the inevitable 'mysterious bug' arises, it is helpful to have a tool to hand that helps you to find out what your program is *really* doing. The HyperCard debugger is a good example of such a tool. The purpose of a debugger is to tell you what your program is doing while it is running. You can arrange for your program to stop at a predetermined *checkpoint* and then you can execute it in steps (each step executing a single HyperTalk instruction). The debugger can show you which instructions are being executed and can display the changing values of global and local variables as your program progresses.

A checkpoint is an instruction with a check mark alongside it. You can set checkpoints by selecting a HyperTalk instruction using the script editor and then using the **Set Checkpoint** operation (or typing *command-d*) on the **Script** menu. A quicker way is to hold the option key down (the cursor should change to a ✓) and click on any line of the script. **Clear Checkpoint** removes the checkpoint from the current line.

A checkpoint is displayed as a check mark (✓) next to a line in the script. When a script containing a checkpoint is run, the debugger halts the program when any checkpoint is reached. A window containing the script is opened, the checkpoint instruction is outlined and a debugger menu (named: ☒) is displayed in the menu bar. The illustration below shows the debugger menu pulled down and a script halted on the instruction: **get script of card field….**

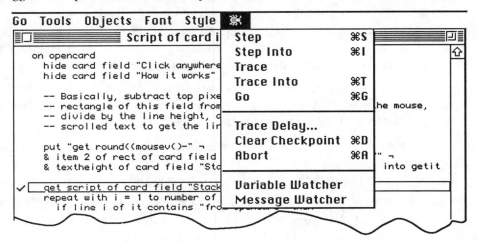

To see the values of the local variables select the **Variable Watcher** on the debugger menu. This will display a small variable watcher window containing the names and values of all of the variables in the currently active handler.

To see what messages have recently been sent to handlers in your script, select **Message Watcher** on the debugger menu. The message watcher window displays a list of the most recently sent messages (HyperTalk's message sending is described fully in Chapter 4).

Once you have made one or both of these windows visible, you can allow the script to proceed one instruction at a time using the **Step** operation on the debugger menu (or by typing **command–s**). This executes one line at a time and halts so that you can see the resulting changes to the variables in the Variable Watcher window and any messages that are sent in the Message Watcher window. If you **Step** through an instruction that calls another handler, that entire handler will be executed before halting again. Use **Step Into** if you want to halt after each instruction in the called handler.

You can alter the values of variables in the variable watcher window while the program is halted; to do so, click on the name of the variable that you want to alter. An editable copy of the variable's value appears at the bottom of the Variable Watcher window. Type the new value and press the **enter** key to replace the variable's value.

The **Trace** and **Trace Into** operations provide a sort of 'slow motion' facility; the script is executed continuously but the instructions are outlined as they are executed, and you can control the speed using the **Trace Delay...** operation. **Abort** turns the debugging mode off, so that you can return to normal browsing, or edit the script – you can't edit the script while in debugging mode.

2.6 Basic graphics

HyperTalk uses a two-dimensional coordinate system to specify positions for placing objects on cards and to report positions. The system is based on the conventional coordinate system in which every point is addressed by a pair of numbers (x,y). The first number (x) specifies the horizontal offset of a point from the left edge of the card and the second (y) specifies vertical offset downwards from the top of the card – reversing the sense of y used in most coordinate systems.

The values of x and y must be whole numbers – this is because the picture on the Macintosh screen is made up of distinct picture elements (pixels) and the points mentioned in HyperTalk programs must coincide with the positions of the pixels. If you write scripts that calculate positions, it's useful to use trunc(x) or round(x) to make x a whole number.

Here is a good way to explore the coordinate system. Put the following handler in the card script: it will give continuous feedback showing the current coordinates of the mouse cursor in the message box:

```
on idle
   put the mouseLoc into message box
end idle
```

You can write **put the mouseLoc**, if you wish to be brief: **put** without somewhere to put things puts into the message box.

And here is another way to explore the coordinate system: the illustration on the next page shows a small card with some points labelled with their coordinates. The labels were produced using the following handler, placed in the card script:

```
on mouseUp -- this handler is invoked whenever the mouse is clicked in the card
   put item 1 of clickLoc() into X       -- clickLoc() returns the coordinates of
                                         -- the last  mouse click
   put item 2 of clickLoc() into Y
   -- items 1 and 2 are now the X and Y coordinates respectively
   choose line tool                      -- use the line tool to make a dot
   click at X,Y                          -- draw a line from X,Y to X,Y to make the dot
   choose text tool                      -- use the text tool to make the label
```

```
    click at X+5, Y+5          -- the label is offset from the dot by 5 pixels
                               -- horizontally and vertically
    type X&","&Y               -- simulates the user typing "15,75" or
                               -- whatever the coordinates are
    choose browse tool         -- revert to the browse tool
end mouseUp
```

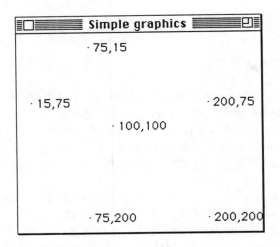

This is an example of a very simple HyperTalk graphics program. You can find far more interesting examples in Chapters 5, 7 and 8.

2.7   Card sizes

All of the cards in a stack are the same size, but the size of a stack's cards can be anything from 64 by 64 pixels to a size that is limited only by the amount of memory that is available to the HyperCard system on your computer. The 'standard' size is 512 by 342 pixels. This is the screen size of the smallest Macintoshes (Plus, SE, Classic, portables, etc.), so standard-size cards can be viewed on the screens of those Macintoshes without scrolling, which is a problem these machines have for viewing larger cards; see the comments above on programming style.

HyperCard displays each stack in a window (called the Card Window), and when necessary (for example, when the screen is smaller than the cards) the stack can be displayed in a window that is smaller than the cards. When this is the case, a scrolling tool is available (on the **Go** menu) to enable the user to scroll the cards to see the hidden portions.

To change the size of a stack's cards, use the **Resize...** button in the **Stack Info...** dialog. Stacks with much larger cards can be created. For example, on the Apple 12" monochrome and 13" colour monitors, you can display cards with up to 640 by 480 pixels. If you intend to create or use stacks with large cards, you should make sure that HyperCard is allocated at least 1500 kilobytes of memory. This will allow you to use stacks with up to about

800 by 800 pixels. To modify the amount of memory allocated to HyperCard, quit HyperCard and use the **Get Info...** operation on the Finder's **File** menu.

2.8 Choosing and making icons for buttons

HyperCard has many built-in icons that you can assign to buttons. To assign a new icon to a button, select the button with the button tool and use the **icon** button in the **Button Info** dialog. This opens a window with a scrolling sub-window showing the icons that are available. To assign an icon to the currently selected button, click on an icon and then select **OK**. The selected icon will be assigned to the button, replacing any previous icon. Note that you may have to enlarge the button to show all of the icon. To remove the icon from a button, leaving it with no icon, use the **None** button in the icon selection window:

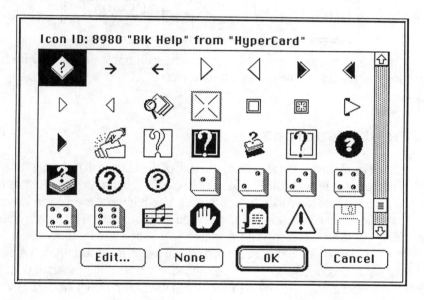

You can also create new icons using HyperCard's Icon Editor (illustrated overleaf). To create a new icon or to modify an existing icon, use the **Edit** button in the icon selection window. This opens the Icon Editor in a new window, showing an enlarged image of the current icon. You can draw on the enlarged image using the 'pencil tool' that is provided. There are two other tools – a 'selection tool' is invoked by holding down the **command** key. It can be used to select portions of the icon image in order to cut, copy or paste them. A 'dragging tool' is invoked by holding down the **option** key. It can be used to move the whole icon image in its frame. When you are in the icon editor the menu bar contains operations that pertain to icon editing. These include operations (on the **File** menu) to create a completely new icon, to duplicate the existing icon (so that you can modify it without altering the original), operations for cutting and pasting on the **Edit** menu, an operation (on the **Icon** menu) for picking up a small rectangle

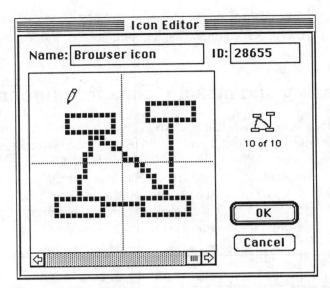

from any portion of the screen and pasting it into the icon frame and several useful image transformation operations on the on the **Special** menu.

2.9 About resources

When you edit an icon's image the icon changes in all of the buttons that share it. To make this possible, each stack contains a small 'database' of icons and other resources. Buttons that have icons contain a reference to the database of resources. This reference is called an icon identifier (icon ID). Icons are assigned a name and an ID when they is created. The ID is an integer that is different for every icon. When you attach an icon to a button, the button's icon reference is updated to contain the ID of the desired icon. You can attach icons to buttons using the icon selection window as described above, or you can make a HyperTalk program do it by using **set the icon of button ... to ...**. In HyperTalk, you can refer to an icon by its ID or by its name, but the icon reference attached to a button is always the icon ID.

The small database attached to each stack that is referred to above is a generic feature of Macintosh software called the *resource fork*. Any file may have resources attached to it, and they go in this fork; the other fork is the stack itself. There are many types of resource that are recognized and used by Macintosh software. Some of the more important types of resource that can be used in HyperCard are listed in the table opposite.

Resources can be stored in the resource fork attached to a particular stack or in the HyperCard application itself. In fact, a stack can access any resource that is in one of the stacks on the current path, the HyperCard application or the Macintosh System File.

As we shall see below, you can move resources between files in several ways, including cutting and pasting. In fact there is an application available from Apple (ResEdit, the Resource

Resource	Created using	Hypertalk examples	Storage format	Type
Icons	Icon editor	set icon of button 3 to 4124	32 x 32 black & white image	ICON
Cursors	ResEdit	set cursor to watch	16 x 16 black & white image	CURS
Palettes	Palette Maker in the Power Tools stack	palette "tools", topleft of this card	Description of a window containing an array of buttons	PLTE
Pictures	The Picture XCMD can open any PICT format file, or resource. Pictures can be created using most Mac graphics programs.	picture "Sunset", resource	Description of graphical objects in Macintosh PICT format, may include images, geometric objects and text	PICT
Sounds	Sound recording using the Audio palette.	play flute	Digital sound recording	SND
Fonts	ResEdit	set textfont of field x to Courier	Bit maps or outlines	FONT
XCMDs	C or Pascal compiler	the name of the XCMD is used as any HyperTalk command	Macintosh machine code	XCMD
XFCNs	C or Pascal compiler	the name of the XFCN is used as any HyperTalk function	Macintosh machine code	XFCN

Editor) that is designed specifically to enable you do these and other editing operations on the resource database attached to any Macintosh file. For moving resources between HyperCard stacks, however, a much easier Resource Mover tool is available in the *Power Tools* stack.

When objects that include resources are moved between stacks in HyperCard, for example a button with a home-made icon, the resources are copied as well. The scripts inside a copied object may not work properly in the new stack if you forget to copy resources they assume will be there, such as sounds and XCMDs. Also, note that sometimes resource numbers will change when an object is copied from one stack to another: thus, what used to be icon ID 231 may now be some other icon.

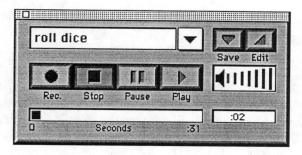

Sounds are named resources, and can be copied and renamed easily using the Audio stack. The audio palette (illustrated) also conveniently allows you to try out sounds and, if you wish, to extract snippets. You might have recorded a sound like 'mumble mumble hello folks mumble' and it is easy to extract the 'folks' from this – if that's what you want.

2.10 The Power Tools stack

The *Power Tools* stack is supplied by Apple/Claris as part of the *HyperCard Developer's Kit*. It contains a set of 16 very useful aids to building stacks and adding extra features to them. The tools are listed in the table below.

Super Grouper	Palette that moves and aligns groups of objects (fields, buttons)
Window Manager	Palette that helps you to manipulate the windows when you have several stacks open
Paint Palettes	Palettes to set the painting properties (lineSize, brushShape, polySize)
Export a Stack's Scripts	Puts all of the scripts in a stack into a text file that can be opened with a word processor
Function and Control Keys	Gives examples of how to write handlers for the Function keys on extended keyboards and the Control keys on all keyboards
Stack Menus	Adds menus to the menubar for keeping track of all of the currently open stacks and the stacks in use
ListObjects	Displays a list of the buttons and fields in the current card and background and allow you to hide or show each of them
Picture XCMD	HyperTalk command to display a picture in an external window. Can read PICT description of the picture from a file, a resource or the clipboard. If window doesn't exists, it is created
Search Container XFCN	HyperTalk function to find a given string within a text. Returns the line and item number in which the string occurs
ShowList XFCN	HyperTalk function that displays a dialog box containing scrolling list of items and allows the user to select one of them
Multiple Scrolling Fields	Example (written in HyperTalk) showing how to implement several fields that scroll together
Script Library	HyperTalk examples showing how to: handle double mouse clicks; detect whether there is anything in the card picture, remember the last thing typed in the message box, etc.
Palette Maker	A tool for making palettes (see Chapter 9). A palette is a small separate window (windoid) containing a set of buttons with icons
Menu Maker	A tool for making menus (see Chapter 9)
Resource Mover	A tool for moving any of the resources in a stack to another stack
Export to TextFile	Write the contents of all background fields in a stack to a text file, so you can import them to a wordprocessor, database, etc.

2.11 XCMDs and XFCNs

In Chapter 4 we shall introduce much of the HyperTalk language, and the *HyperTalk Reference* stack provides complete listings of the commands and functions in the language. But in one sense, it is impossible to describe all of the available commands and functions because HyperTalk is extensible – new HyperTalk commands and functions can be implemented in languages such as Pascal and C and then installed in your stacks and used in exactly the same way that you will use the built-in HyperTalk commands and functions. These are the so-called external commands, XCMDs and XFCNs.

XCMDs and XFCNs are code resources that can be installed in stacks or in HyperCard itself using the Resource Mover tool or the ResEdit application. Both end up appearing as ordinary HyperTalk: XCMDs are simply handlers written in a language other than HyperTalk;

XFCNs are functions. Some XCMDs are already built-in to HyperCard, including the Picture and Palette XCMDs already mentioned in connection with the Power Tools stack. Others are included in the Power Tools stack and can easily be added to any of your stacks.

The advantage of using another language for XCMDs, such as Pascal, is that for some things it can be much faster and you may be able to access bits of the Macintosh that aren't accessible directly from within HyperTalk. If you want HyperCard to use, say, a special TV camera, some of your programming would have to be done in external commands.

The disadvantage of XCMDs is that not only do you need to know Pascal or C, but you have to know quite a bit about the Macintosh and how it works. Although there are many books about programming the Macintosh in both Pascal and C, it's a much more risky operation than programming in HyperTalk. If an XCMD crashes, your stack and probably your Macintosh along with it will *really* crash! In short, programming with XCMDs may make your stacks faster and more flexible, but they will make developing your stack and getting it working in the first place a very much more tedious process.

Fortunately, there are many collections of generic XCMDs available from public domain, shareware and commercial sources. These include XCMDs for interfacing HyperCard to hardware devices – scanners, video cards, video cameras, modems and many more. There are XCMDs for interfacing HyperCard to networks – Ethernet, Internet and AppleTalk. And there are XCMDs that are just for adding functionality to HyperTalk.

This book does not use any of these XCMDs or require any further knowledge of them; it is entirely devoted to programming in straight HyperTalk.

2.12 Printing and reports

HyperCard offers several ways to print from stacks. The trick lies in deciding which of HyperCard's printing facilities to use. The basic distinctions are between printing scripts, cards and reports.

It is sometimes useful to make a hard copy of a script – so you can look at it when you are away from your Macintosh. The Script Editor has a **Print Script** menu operation that provides a simple way to print individual scripts. There is an Export Stack Scripts button in the Power Tools stack that will make a text file containing all of the scripts in a stack, with each script labelled to show which object it belongs to. You can then open the text file with a text editor or a word processor to examine the scripts, print them, etc. Chapter 11 will give you ideas of ways in which you could make similar buttons.

Cards can be printed with one or several to a page. You can get half- or quarter-sized card images in order to fit more on each page, but the result of this is often unsatisfying, with the text in fields unreadable. A more useful way to approach fitting the cards to the printed pages is to use the **Reduce or Enlarge** option (available for PostScript printers only). A reduction to 75% or so often produces card images that will conveniently fit two on an A4 page, even when using larger than standard-sized cards.

Cards printed on laser printers and other high-resolution printers have high-quality typeset text in the fields and buttons, combined with bit-map images for the card and background pictures. Buttons and their icons are usually redundant on the printed page and they constitute a distraction for the reader. A solution to this problem is to add a printing script that hides all of the buttons and other unwanted objects before printing the cards and shows them again when printing is finished.

If you just want to print the text in fields, report printing may offer a better solution. This is a convenient way to print text from selected fields. Report formats can be constructed that will print the contents of several cards on each page, producing a tabulated report similar to those produced by conventional database systems. The HyperCard Help stack provides further information on report printing. It is not possible to define or alter report formats by program, but once a format has been defined it can be saved in the stack and accessed by name, enabling programs to generate reports using any of the existing formats in a stack.

Cards and reports can be produced using the printing operations on the **File** menu, but printing can be much more flexibly controlled by HyperTalk scripts, using commands such as **open printing**, **open report printing**, **print card**, **close printing**, etc.

The decision chart below will assist you in deciding how to get a high-quality print-out of a stack, formatted the way you want it:

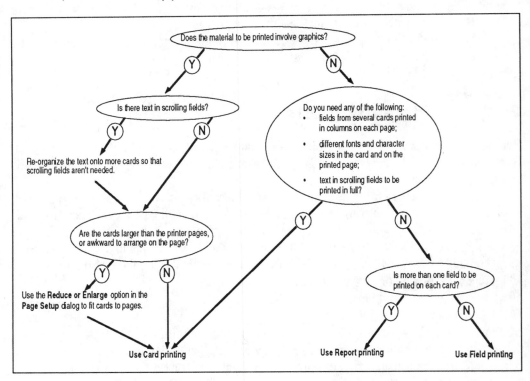

CHAPTER 3

HyperCard Objects

The programmer's view of stacks, backgrounds,
cards, buttons and fields

3.1 Why objects?

Objects are the building-blocks of HyperCard applications. HyperCard's designers set out to supply a kit of parts for building applications consisting of a small number of highly configurable types of object. They have succeeded in doing so with just five types of object – stacks, cards, backgrounds, fields and buttons.

Let's consider the analogy between HyperCard objects and actual building blocks for a moment. Buildings are made from components such as bricks, timbers, tiles and so on. Each type of building component comes in many shapes, sizes and colours and they often have other properties that can be specified to suit different uses too. Thus when bricks are bought, the buyer can specify their colour and the texture of their surface depending on the final appearance desired for the building in which they are to be used. Bricks may be specified with different sizes (half-height, half-width), and shapes (with rounded corners, etc.) and with different behaviours (waterproof, fireproof, load bearing, etc.). The characteristics of HyperCard objects, likewise, are determined by their *properties* in a similar way. For example, a button has a size (width and height), a style (one of: transparent, opaque, rectangle, shadow, roundRect, checkBox, radioButton) and some other properties that determine its appearance. Most importantly, it has a script, and this determines its behaviour, what it will do when HyperCard sends it messages.

HyperCard objects are far more flexible than bricks. They don't have to be ordered in advance with specified properties, they can be created on demand and their properties can be changed at any time at will. For example, if a building were constructed from components as flexible as HyperCard's, its walls could be rendered transparent or opaque on demand – one would not need curtains!

Buildings are constructed from fixed components – you can see them and feel them. But modern buildings wouldn't be effective without some more abstract elements too. Every building needs a postal address; office buildings need a telephone system with a scheme for allocating numbers to rooms; shared buildings need a procedure for renting portions of the

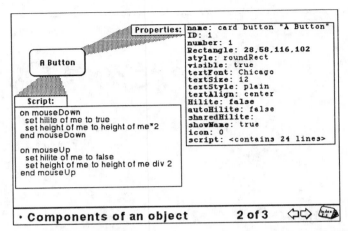

building, equipped with furniture, telephone lines, etc. You can't see or touch all of the things that go to make an effective building – the phone system, the procedure for renting and occupying portions of the building are abstract, invisible parts of the building. Likewise, HyperCard objects can be similarly subdivided into 'concrete' objects that are normally visible and can be manipulated: cards, buttons and fields; and more abstract objects – stacks and backgrounds – that are used to contain and organize the concrete ones. As with buildings, objects inside a HyperCard system have names and 'addresses' so that they can be referred to.

3.2   Properties of objects

The properties of objects are the basis for giving them the appearance and the behaviour that you want them to have. And HyperCard itself can be configured using properties. The properties of HyperCard are called global properties. They include all of the painting properties that can be changed in the user interface to HyperCard (e.g. lineSize, pattern, brush, textFont) and many others that affect the behaviour of stacks and of HyperTalk programs (userLevel, lockMessages, lockScreen).

In the following sections, we discuss the properties of HyperCard objects and some of their uses in HyperTalk programs. Appendix A at the end of this book gives tables listing the properties of each of the HyperCard object types, and a further table listing the global properties associated with the HyperCard system. The illustrations in this chapter are taken from the *HyperCard Objects* stack on the book disk, which provides an easy way of exploring HyperCard's objects and their properties.

Apart from a few exceptions, all types of HyperCard object have the following properties: name, identifier, number, script and rectangle. The name, identifier and number are ways of referring to an object; the script is what the object does; and the rectangle is where and how big the object is. We'll discuss each in turn.

Objects have *names*. Object names are text strings containing up to 253 characters. They are not necessarily unique. Object names can be set by the user or by a HyperTalk program.

When an object is created, its name is empty, except for stacks, which have the name of the file that contains them – this can only be changed by re-naming or moving the file.

Object names provide a convenient way for HyperTalk programs to refer to specific objects. They also provide a rapid method for accessing cards: it is much quicker to access a card by its name than to search for a card containing a particular string in one of its fields.

Stack names are the full name of the Macintosh file: the disk, the various folders, and the file name itself. A full name is unique, but the same file name might be used (without confusion) in different folders. If you simply ask for the name of an object, such as a stack, you get its full unique name. Alternatively, you can ask for its **short name**, which is just the last component of its full name; this need not be unique.

All objects other than stacks have *identifiers* or *IDs* for short. This is a positive integer that is assigned to each object when it is created. An object's ID cannot be changed. An object's ID is unique amongst all the objects of the same type within the containing object – that is, cards and backgrounds have IDs that are unique within the stack that contains them; card buttons and fields have IDs that are unique within the card that contains them; background buttons and fields have IDs that are unique within the background that contains them (see the discussion of background and card buttons and fields below).

Objects other than stacks also have a **number**. An object's number determines its position in a sequence of other similar objects. For cards, the number determines the position of the card in the sequence of cards in the stack that contains it. If the position of the card in the stack changes – as it would if it is moved or if another card is inserted in front of it – its number changes. A button's or field's number determines its position in the front-to-back ordering of the buttons and fields on a card. Buttons and fields with low numbers appear behind buttons and fields with higher numbers that overlap them.

Since numbers (unlike IDs) start at 1 and are always sequential within a particular type of object, they are useful for programming actions on all of the objects of a particular type. For example, the following program assigns names to all of the cards in the current stack using the letters of the alphabet as names and repeating them after each 26 cards:

```
repeat with i = 1 to number of cards of this stack
  get i mod 26
  set name of card i to char it of "ABCDEFGHIJKLMNOPQRSTUVWXYZ"
end repeat
```

All objects have **scripts**. A script is a (possibly empty) text string containing a set of HyperTalk handlers. The script can be accessed and modified by the user using the script editor, or by a HyperTalk program. For example:

```
get script of this stack
if "©" is not in it then
  put "-- © Addison-Wesley Publishing 1992" & return before it
  set script of this stack to it
end if
```

Buttons, fields and cards have a **rectangle** property. A rectangle is represented by four integers separated by commas. The integers give the coordinates of the object relative to the frame in which the current stack is displayed. The first pair of integers gives the coordinates of the top left corner of the rectangle and the second pair gives the coordinates of the bottom right corner. For cards, the first pair of coordinates is always 0,0 since cards are always the same size as the stack frame. In HyperTalk you can get at these numbers using item: item 1 of the rectangle of button "x" will give you the left coordinate; item 2 the top, and so on.

The rectangle of an object defines all of its geometric properties, but for convenience there are several other ways to refer to an object's geometry. These other geometric properties are derived directly from the rectangle of the object. They are:

height, width	the dimensions of the object in pixels
top, bottom, left, right	the individual coordinates
topLeft, bottomRight, location	pairs of coordinates, representing points; the location of an object is the mid-point of its rectangle

Whenever any of these derived geometric properties is set, the rectangle is changed to correspond, and whenever the derived properties are accessed, they are calculated from the rectangle. You should be cautious: for example, changing the top of a button is not the same as changing the second item in its rectangle! If you set the top, the button will stay the same size but move so that its top is positioned where you want it. If, instead, you set the second item of its rectangle property, the bottom of the button would be unchanged, so the bottom would stay in the same place. The button's shape would have changed.

The properties can be abbreviated to make programming more convenient: location can be written loc, rectangle can be written rect. Appendix A provides the full range of abbreviations for these and all other properties.

Properties of buttons

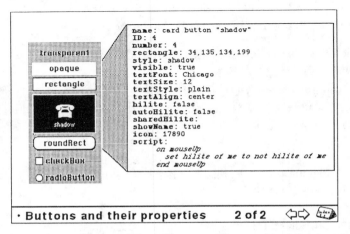

which the current stack is displayed. The first pair of integers gives the coordinates of the top

The illustration above shows the properties of buttons. The graphical representation of buttons is quite flexible. The position, size, shape, style, text font and other presentation properties can be set by the user and by HyperTalk programs.

Properties of fields

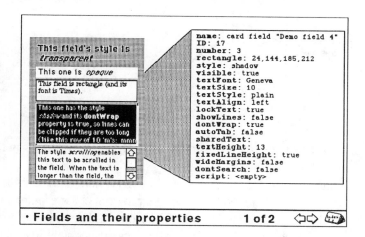

```
                                      name: card field "Demo field 4"
                                      ID: 17
                                      number: 3
This field's style is                 rectangle: 24,144,185,212
transparent                           style: shadow
                                      visible: true
This one is opaque                    textFont: Geneva
This field is rectangle (and its      textSize: 10
font is Times).                       textStyle: plain
                                      textAlign: left
This one has the style                lockText: true
shadow and its dontWrap               showLines: false
property is true, so lines can        dontWrap: true
be clipped if they are too long       autoTab: false
(like this row of 10 'm's: mmm        sharedText:
                                      textHeight: 13
The style scrolling enables           fixedLineHeight: true
this text to be scrolled in           wideMargins: false
the field. When the text is           dontSearch: false
longer than the field, the            script: <empty>
```

· **Fields and their properties**   **1 of 2**

Despite their apparent differences, fields are very similar to buttons. Their differences are limited to the facility of a field to hold text, and the facilities of a button to hold an icon and to highlight. Thus a field will serve as well as a button in some roles, and a button can be used in place of a field where there is no need to display multi-line or editable text (the name of a button can be used to display short single lines of text, though the user cannot type directly into a button's name as they can a field's text).

Properties of cards and backgrounds

As we have seen, HyperCard objects can be configured, like the objects used for constructing buildings, by specifying their properties. But unlike building construction objects, the properties of some HyperCard objects may be shared between many similar objects. We can see this in many stacks, because they contain several cards with similar fields and buttons on them and a similar background picture. This sharing is achieved through the use of *backgrounds*.

A background itself is not directly visible, but acts as a shared template that defines the properties of some fields and buttons – the background fields and buttons – on each of the cards that are on that background. The background also contributes a common picture that is merged with the individual card pictures.

What a user sees of a card is composed using information from both the card and its background, rather as if the card image and other card things are drawn on a transparent overlay through which the background can be seen. The card picture and the representations of the card fields and buttons are superimposed on the background picture and background

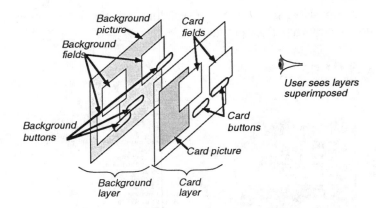

fields and buttons. Objects in the background layer are obscured by objects in the card layer unless they are transparent.

For buttons and fields in the same layer, the sequence number determines the object's position in the layer – higher-numbered buttons appear in front of lower-numbered ones, and similarly for buttons. There is no defined priority for buttons and fields in the same layer.

Graphics on the card layer of the picture can be black, white, or transparent allowing the background to show through. Thus a card picture can selectively modify the background picture. Typically, the background provides a common structure or graphical theme (such as a decorative border) for each card. The card image can be hidden or revealed under control from HyperTalk; **hide card picture** makes it invisible, and **show card picture** makes it visible.

If you have a complicated card on its own background, the card image can be used to provide helpful information about how to use the card. Normally, you'd arrange for the card picture to be hidden. When the user clicks on the help button, the card picture is shown. It can have arrows and text, and so on, to explain things:

```
on mouseUp -- a help button
   show card picture
   wait until the mouse is "down"
   hide card picture
end mouseUp
```

Properties of stacks

Stacks are the largest units of construction for HyperCard applications. Stacks are stored as Macintosh files. Several stacks may be open simultaneously. There is a separate window for each open stack. The size of each window is a property of the associated stack, and one of the cards from the associated stack is always visible in each window.

The containment structure of stacks

The objects in a stack are contained in a hierarchy based on their types:

- Stacks contain cards and backgrounds. At least one background and one card is required in any stack.

- As we have noted above, backgrounds are invisible. Their purpose is to organize and describe the background objects and the picture associated with a set of cards. Each card in a stack is associated with one of the backgrounds in the stack. The cards in a stack can be stored in any sequence: cards of different backgrounds can be interleaved.

- Cards contain buttons and fields. These are of two kinds. *Card* buttons and *card* fields are individuals – they are present only in the card where they were created.

- *Background* buttons and *background* fields are replicated on all of the cards with the same background. That is, there is an instance of the button or field in each card of the background. Many of the properties of buttons and fields are shared between all their instances, meaning that they are the same on every card they appear on. They will be the same size, same position, and have the same script on all cards.

In the case of background fields, all of the properties except the text of the field (and its fonts and styles) are shared between the instances. Even the text of background fields can be made

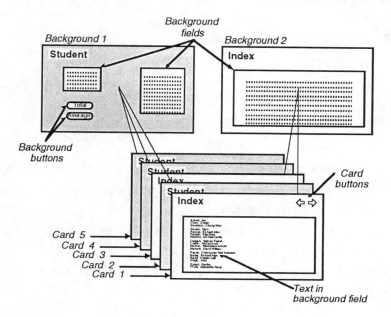

The relationship between backgrounds and cards
Cards 2, 4 and 5 are associated with background 1; cards 1 and 3 are associated
with background 2. The backgrounds act as templates for the representation of
the cards.

shared by setting the **sharedText** property to **true**; this means that the same text will be shown on all cards in that background, which is useful for things like titles. (You can also use the Text tool to paint shared text on the background, but then you won't be able to control it so readily from HyperTalk.)

In the case of background buttons, all of the properties are shared between the instances, except that the **hilite** property can be made unshared by setting the **sharedHilite** property to **false**. This means that the highlights of buttons can be set independently on different cards, even though they share everything else. The sharing of properties between objects is something that doesn't often occur in the physical world; it's as though all of the bricks in a wall of our building got their colour from a single point!

It is sometimes confusing when a stack appears to share fields or buttons, but does not. You may find what seems like the same button on several cards. Yet it may not be a background button: it could be a card button that has been copied-and-pasted onto every card. Of course this is inefficient, because it wastes space in the stack: there are many copies of the button when one would do. Much worse, it makes the stack very hard to debug. You have to fix a bug in the script of a card button on every card where it appears. You fix a bug in a background button just once, and then you've fixed the bug for every appearance of that button on all cards in the background.

To make a card button a background button, choose the Button tool, cut the button, change to background and then paste the button. Likewise, you can convert background buttons to card buttons (but this removes the button from every card, and only pastes it onto one card). Fields are changed the same way.

3.3 Uses for objects

HyperCard objects can be used:

- as components of graphical user interfaces;
- to store information as text or in graphical form;
- to store related items of information together so that they can be retrieved by searching, browsing and several other methods;
- to store programs in the form of HyperTalk scripts and to execute them in response to user actions and other events.

In this chapter we shall describe each of the five types of object, mentioning their more important properties and giving examples of their use. Appendix A contains a tabulation of the properties of each type of HyperCard object, indicating the type of data required to specify each property.

The properties of objects and the facilities to access and modify them in HyperTalk programs are what make HyperCard objects so flexible. The range of uses to which they can be put is limited only by your imagination. You can, for example, put transparent objects over graphics that look like completely different things. If you want to simulate a dialog box that HyperCard doesn't give you, you can draw it (say, in the card picture, or perhaps on another card in the same background) as if it was really displayed.

Uses for buttons

The most common use for buttons is as controls to initiate actions, as you would expect, but they can be used to display a short piece of text (in the name of the button); to represent small moving images (by the icon in a transparent button whose position is continually being changed under the control of a script) and to show a sequence of small pictures (by changing the icon).

Transparent buttons can be used to highlight any portion of a card or field (by setting the rectangle of the button to overlap the required area and then setting its hilite property to true. Transparent or invisible buttons can also be used to delimit an area on a card. For example, the rectangle of a button can be used to discover whether the mouse cursor is in a certain portion of a card, as follows:

if mouseLoc() is within the rectangle of cd button 3 then ...

Uses for fields

Fields can be used to hold and display text in different styles, sizes and fonts as you would expect, but they can also be used to store information in numbered containers (each *line* of a field can be a container, or if it isn't convenient to use lines in that way in your application, then each *item* can be a container – where items are separated by commas); they can be used to hold information that your HyperTalk program needs to store, but you don't want the user to see (by putting the information in a field that is hidden – its visible property is false – or in a field that is on a card that the user can't go to, or by putting the information in parts of a field that the user can't see – lines that are off the bottom of the visible area of the field). Like buttons, fields can respond to mouse clicks and other events to initiate some action. For example, when the user clicks on a field, the field can determine which word or phrase the user clicked on and use the word or phrase as a key to search for another card.

To respond to mouse clicks, a field must be locked (lockText must be true) or it must have its sharedText property set, which makes it behave as if it is locked, except when editing the background. It seems complicated! The reason for this is that HyperCard lets the user edit text in fields, which of course has to be done using mouse clicks and so forth. Such operations do not generate messages in themselves, though an edited field will be sent closeField if it has been changed. If the field is sharedText, its text can only be edited in background mode. Thus, in normal mode the field behaves as if it is locked, and messages like mouseDown are sent to it, and these can be processed by its script. Both locked and unlocked fields get mouseWithin and mouseLeave messages.

Since all this is getting confusing, we suggest you get a feel for the sorts of messages that are available – look in Appendix B – and then play with HyperCard with the message watcher running; to do this most easily, simply type show message watcher in the message window.

Uses for cards

Of course, cards are the main building blocks for HyperCard stacks. Using HyperCard's visual effects, you can produce convincing simulations of turning pages in a book or shuffling a stack of index cards or you can use several cards to display an animated sequence in which each card differs only slightly from the previous one (for example, see the dice in the animation stack in the *HyperProgramming* disk).

It is sometimes convenient to collect information and store it in fields on a card that is not normally accessible to the user. Programs can still access the information on such cards using constructs such as **get card field "user name" of card "customization"**. If you wanted to make sure that a card is never accessible to the user, you put a handler:

```
on openCard
  go back
end openCard
```

into the card script. The user will never know if you use **lock screen** before going to any card, since this will stop the screen changing momentarily to the card you want to lock out.

Uses for backgrounds

The main use for backgrounds is to make it easy to generate many similar cards, all having the same background fields and buttons. Once a set of cards has been created with the same background, you can process them in HyperTalk scripts. For example, here is a handler, **printCards**, to print all of the cards with a given background, hiding the card buttons (buttons are often distracting when included in printed pages):

```
on printCards
  open printing
  repeat with j = 1 to number of cards of bg "title cards"
    set cursor to busy
    go card j of bg "title cards"
    repeat with i = 1 to number of cd buttons
      hide cd button i
    end repeat
    print this card
  end repeat
  close printing
  -- see below for revealing the hidden buttons
end printCards
```

In this script, all of the buttons remain hidden until the **close printing** command has been executed, since the cards on which **print this card** was executed are not actually printed until then. You will certainly want to make the buttons visible again afterwards. You should append these instructions to the handler:

```
repeat with j = 1 to number of cards of bg "title cards"
  set cursor to busy
  go card j of bg "title cards"
  repeat with i = 1 to number of cd buttons
    show cd button i
  end repeat
end repeat
```

Uses for stacks

A single stack is usually the most appropriate container for all of the cards needed in an application, but stacks are not just containers for cards. They are objects themselves with scripts and other propertie,. and they can be used to produce some interesting effects.

Originally, HyperCard could not open more than one stack at a time, but HyperCard now extends the uses of multiple stacks in several ways. The main ones are:

- If you need cards of different sizes in an application, you can do this is by making a stack for each card size. Alternatively you can use HyperTalk to change dynamically the size of cards when necessary.

- You can open two or more stacks to display information to the user in different windows. This is useful where the user needs to compare information from different sources. The hypertext tools of Chapter 14 will exploit this feature.

- You can develop libraries of handlers and place them in the script of a stack that can be shared by any number of other stacks by the **start using** construct. This approach, called *stack using*, is discussed in detail in Chapter 4, and some examples are given in Chapter 9.

- Stacks can also 'talk' to each other across a network, sending messages from machine to machine. The reliable programming of networked HyperCard systems is difficult and beyond the scope of the present book.

HyperTalk as a Programming Language

A guide to HyperTalk programming

By now, you'll have a good idea of HyperCard and HyperTalk. We've taken a practical, hands-on approach, and before we go on to the main projects of the book, this chapter goes into the details of the language in more detail to answer any remaining questions. In this chapter we describe the basic principles of HyperTalk programming: the structure of programs and the interpretation of HyperTalk commands; as in all other chapters, there are plenty of ideas and small projects as well.

Some features of HyperTalk will be familiar to readers with a knowledge of other programming languages. The procedures and functions, and the control structures (like **repeat** and **if**) in HyperTalk are similar to those in procedural languages such as C and Pascal. HyperTalk's object-oriented model of program structure is derived from Smalltalk-80. The representation of data values in HyperTalk is based entirely on text strings. If you are familiar with Pascal, an appendix to this book tells you how to convert from Pascal to HyperTalk. We do not assume a knowledge of any of these languages, but we provide some links to them for readers who have such knowledge.

The HyperTalk language has three basic parts: control structures (like **if..then..end if**), commands (like **beep** or **go to card 1**), and expressions (like **2+3**) which can form parts of control structures and commands. Control structures put commands together, just as commands put expressions together. We'll start our description of HyperTalk with expressions, the basic building block.

4.1 Expressions

Expressions enable us to specify the *values* in HyperTalk programs. Values are needed in many places in HyperTalk programs – not only to do sums, but in control structures, **put** commands, **set** commands, and as parameters in calls to handlers.

Whenever values are required in HyperTalk programs, what is expected is a *text string* representing the value. Strings may be numbers, truth values (true, false), as well as the sort of data that is more commonly represented in strings ("the 29th of January", "Mr. David Brown"). There are a wide range of ways of manipulating text strings, and of course there are the standard arithmetic operators, +, - and so on.

Expressions are composed of constants, container references, operators and function calls. We have identified examples of each in the illustration below. We discuss these four components of expressions in the next four sub-sections. In addition, parentheses work as usual to sub-divide expressions and to ensure that operators are applied to the correct portions of the expression.

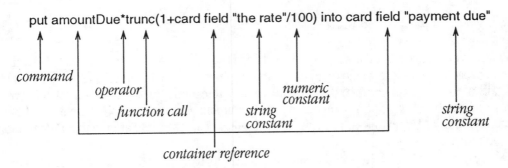

The definition of HyperTalk has been dramatically simplified by restricting the number of data types to one – namely strings of characters. 'What about integers, reals, logical values, etc.?' – you may ask. The answer is that all of these are represented as strings without loss of generality.

Whenever a HyperTalk expression is evaluated, the result is a string. Whenever a string value is used in an expression or a command, the value of the string is checked to ensure that it represents a data value of the correct type. For example, an integer or a real number is required in an arithmetic expression, a valid name is required when referring to a field or a button by name and a truth value – true or false – is required in conditional expressions, as in if control structures.

The use of strings to represent numbers does incur some penalty in the speed of evaluating numerical expressions, but HyperCard uses a high-precision floating-point representation (up to 19 decimal digits) internally to perform arithmetic and numbers as large as 10^{72} can be manipulated.

Strings of any length that do not represent numbers may be constructed and stored in HyperTalk variables provided that sufficient memory is available to HyperCard, but strings containing more than 30,000 characters cannot be stored in fields.

A more serious apparent problem is – how are data structures constructed in HyperTalk? HyperTalk is rich in facilities for manipulating text strings, but at first glance, it appears to be deficient in facilities for representing data structures such as the arrays, records and lists found in Pascal and other procedural languages.

In fact, there are two approaches that will meet most needs for the representation of structured data in HyperTalk: the first of these is the use of *chunks* to sub-divide text strings. Chunks are described in the section *Chunks* below. These enable sequences of data items to be represented, with up to three levels of nesting, and the structures represented in this way may be dynamic, since chunks may be inserted into and deleted from strings. The second approach is the use of collections of fields on cards to represent collections of data values. Cards provide natural 'data structuring', as good as Pascal's records: indeed fields on cards can be used in exactly the same way as Pascal fields within an array of records.

For problems that require more general pointer-like structures, we can use the identifiers of cards, fields, and so on in a similar manner to the use of stored pointers in languages such as Pascal and C. This technique is often used to construct the links in hypertext applications of HyperCard, as discussed in Chapter 13.

Constants

When we wish to include a specific string in a HyperTalk expression, we enclose it in double quotes, thus: "United Kingdom", "deoxyribonucleic acid", "3.14159" and "z". Numbers and truth values need not be quoted, thus: 123.25 and "123.25" are both valid and have the same meaning, as do false and "false".

HyperTalk provides various named constants to represent characters that don't have textual representations. These named characters include: return, space, empty, quote and tab. There also some constants that correspond to frequently used strings. These include pi, up and down. See Appendix A for a list of named constants.

Container references

There are three kinds of container for strings in HyperTalk – variables, fields and the properties of objects.

There is no need to declare variables before they are used; the names of variables are noted by HyperTalk on the first occasion on which they are used. A variable name is any sequence of up to 30 letters and numerals starting with a letter. The underscore character '_' counts as a letter. Upper- and lower-case letters are not differentiated when they are used in names, so the variable called theTotal can also be referred to as THETOTAL or thetotal, and both are different from the_total.

Objects (stacks, backgrounds, cards, fields, buttons) can have names that include any characters, including spaces and funny characters like •, though stacks (being files) must have names that the Macintosh Finder is happy with, so they can't contain colons.

The following examples illustrate the use of references to variables and fields to construct expressions. The names theTotal, theCredit and amountDue are variables and "the rate", "payment due" and "last name" are the names of card fields. Fields and other objects can also be referenced by name, by identifier or by number. (Since HyperTalk's syntax doesn't distinguish between the use of the name of an object and the number, it will get confused if the name happens to be a number.)

```
put theTotal - theCredit into amountDue
put amountDue *(1 + card field "the rate"/100) into card field "payment due"
set height of card field "last name" to max(height of card field "payment due", 25)
```

If you type these commands straight into the message box, you'll get the complaint that HyperCard expected numbers. Of course, you should first do something like:

```
put 10.00 into theTotal
put 9.00 into theCredit
```

otherwise the variables won't be properly initialized to numbers. That you can set the height of objects (here, a field) by calculating numbers in scripts can be used for simple graph plotting; the idea will be used powerfully in Chapter 8 for animation.

Chunks

HyperTalk lets you get at bits of strings, called *chunks*. Expressions can contain references to chunks of containers as well as whole containers. Such references are called *chunk expressions*.

A chunk is some sub-sequence of a string. The selection of sub-sequences is quite flexible, allowing reference to the *characters, words, lines* and *items* of a string, as well as to the positions of the first and last characters. All of the following expressions are valid chunk expressions:

```
first word of "John Smith"          -- which will be John
item 4 of "234,54,645,13"           -- which will be 13
word 2 of name of this stack        -- which could be "About HyperProgramming"
lines 3 to 5 of field "Description" -- which will be lines 3, 4 and 5 of that field
char 2 of 3.14                      -- which will be a dot
char 2 of 27+3                      -- which will be 10
char 2 of (27+3)                    -- which will be 0
```

Chunk expressions are of the form: *chunk* of *string*, where the *chunk* denotes a suitable sub-sequence of the string. A chunk may be a sequence of *lines* (separated by **return** characters), *items* (separated by commas, but not including them), *words* (separated by, but not including, **space** characters; if the resulting word starts with a quote it ends with a quote, if there is one – words starting with quotes can therefore contain spaces), or individual *characters* within a string.

In addition to their use in expressions, where they get values from portions of containers, chunks can be used in **put** and some other commands to insert new values into portions of strings.

For example, when the variable aRect is 234,54,645,13 then after:

```
put 20 into item 3 of aRect         -- aRect contains "234,54,20,13"
add 20 to item 3 of aRect           -- aRect contains "234,54,665,13"
```

If the variable theRoute is I'll take the high road then after:

```
put "You'll" into word 1 of theRoute   -- theRoute contains "You'll take the high road "
```

We can also use chunk expressions to insert non-existent chunks of strings, producing the extra delimiter characters where necessary. For example, if aRect is initially **empty**, then after:

    put 50 into item 4 of aRect   *-- aRect contains ",,,50"*

Put can also be used with the prepositions after and before to insert strings non-destructively. For example if aColour contains "blue", then after:

    put "dark " before aColour   *-- note space after "dark "*

aColour contains "dark blue".

Operators

HyperTalk includes a full set of operators for performing arithmetic operations, making comparisons between numbers and forming simple logical expressions. There are also operators for combining and comparing text strings and for testing the types of strings and testing for the existence of objects.

    The operators are listed and described in Appendix A. Here we describe some of the less usual operators. The arithmetic operators +, -, *, / and ^ (raised to the power) can be applied to integers or to real numbers. There is a div as an alternative to / that always produces an integer result and a mod that produces the integer remainder. Thus:

    10/3 = 3.3333....
    10 div 3 = 3
    10 mod 3 = 1

The standard functions trunc and round can be used to truncate or round a fractional number to an integer.

    There are six comparison operators that can be used to compare pairs of numbers or pairs of strings. They are used mainly in the construction of if and repeat commands. Some of the comparisons have synonyms, like = and is; ≠ and is not. Each takes two operands and produces true or false.

    Since strings can be numbers, HyperTalk has to work out whether both strings are numbers before it makes a comparison. Thus " 1"<"2" is true because what is really compared are the numbers 1 and 2, but " z"<"a" is true, because the string space & space & "z" is compared with "a", and spaces come before a in the alphabetic ordering.

    There are the usual logical operations and, or and not, for combining the results of comparisons and other truth values. The negating operator not can be used flexibly when you use is: a=b can be written as a is b; a≠b can be written either as not(a=b) or a is not b.

    There are only two operators for constructing strings:

    &   Takes two strings and produces a new string containing a copy of the first followed by a copy of the second. For example, the expression "UB" & "40" produces "UB40". Similarly, 3&6 produces 36.

    &&   Takes two strings and produces a string containing a copy of the first, followed by a space and a copy of the second. For example, the expression "friendly" && "people" produces "friendly people" (This is most useful when combining the contents of variables or the results of functions. for example date() && time() produces a string of the form: "11/9/91 9:54 am").

Note that put into, put after, put before also serve as string construction operations. Thus, if you find yourself writing put x & y into y, you could better write put x before y and save the & operation.

The contains operation and its equivalents (x contains y is the same as y is in x) are useful for locating sub-strings in larger strings: contains produces true if the second operand is a substring of the first. For example, "Mr. Jones" contains "Mr." produces true.

You may find the function offset is more useful than contains, since it also gives the position of the string it finds: offset(x, y) is 0 if x is not in y, otherwise the index of the char of y at which x starts.

The is within operation takes a string representing a point (two integers separated by a comma) and another string representing a rectangle (which will be four integers separated by commas, the top left point and the bottom right point). It produces true if the point lies within the rectangle and false otherwise. For example, "75,75" is within "50,50,100,100" produces true. The point 75,75 is inside a rectangle with top left corner at 50,50 and bottom right corner at 100,100.

Item lists are just ordinary strings; HyperTalk provides no special help in constructing them. If you want to make a two item list from the values of the variables x and y, you have to write x & "," & y. Confusingly, in some contexts such as set commands, HyperTalk will be happy with x,y. You can also use put to make item lists, and then commas *are* added automatically:

```
put empty into x
put 5 into item 3 of x
```

ends up with ,,5 in the variable x, that is with the 5 in the third item position, and the other items being left as empty.

Function calls

Function calls in HyperTalk, as in most programming languages, are represented by a function name followed by a pair of parentheses which may be empty or may contain one or several comma-separated parameter values.

In the following examples, the expressions following put contain calls to the built-in functions sqrt, offset and mouseLoc:

```
put sqrt(x)*3 into aValue
put offset("/", x) into aSlash
put mouseLoc() into newPoint
```

In the case of the functions that are built-in to HyperCard, and when you do not want them to be redefined, the parentheses can be omitted if the function name is preceded by the; if there are parameters you say of, and may omit the. So the date and date() are synonymous, as are the clickLoc and clickLoc(); for functions with parameters, such as sqrt(4) you may write the sqrt of 4 or simply, sqrt of 4.

When you use **the**, a function cannot be redefined. In the last example above, **mouseLoc**, although defined by HyperCard, can be redefined by you or some other script. If, instead, you wrote **put the mouseLoc into newPoint** then this would always use the standard HyperTalk function **mouseLoc** even if there was an alternative definition defined in a script. Using **the** would also be faster, since HyperTalk would not have to determine if there were any alternative definitions.

Whatever form is used, the parameters of functions are always *passed by value* which means that a string containing a copy of each parameter is passed to the function, and it is therefore impossible for a function to alter the contents of variables appearing in the parameter list of the function call.

There are more than sixty built-in functions (see Appendix A for a list of them – the HyperTalk Reference stack contains full details on each of them), ranging from standard mathematical functions such as **cos**, **sin**, **tan** and **sqrt**, to functions for getting information from the HyperCard system, such as **mouseLoc** (which returns the coordinates of the mouse relative to the current card) and **selectedText** (which returns the sequence of characters that is currently highlighted, if any, in a field on the current card). You can define any further functions that you need. We'll describe how to define functions later.

We'll introduce most of the built-in functions in the context of the examples throughout the book, but we'll describe one function, **value**, here because its behaviour affects the interpretation of programs.

The value function

The value function evaluates strings as expressions. For example:

> value("3+4")   = 7

If **x** contains **16,22** then

> value("item 2 of"&&"x")   = 22

If the parameter doesn't contain an expression, then it is assumed to be a string, and any surrounding quotes are removed (because the 'value' of a string constant is the string that it represents). You have to think very carefully when using **value** (and the related command **do**); for example, **value("item 2 of"&&x)** (that is, without the quotes around **x**) is **empty**, since its parameter (**item 2 of 16,22**) is a syntax error for an expression.

You can write scripts that construct HyperTalk expressions, and then use **value** to evaluate the expression. This is very useful when you want to generalize a script in one of several ways. For example we might want to write a function that will compute the area of *any* button or field.

The following function takes two parameters; the first indicates the type of an object ("**card field**", "**card button**", "**background button**", etc.) and the second identifies the particular object (by giving its number, ID or name):

```
function area objectType, anObject
     -- put the string that we're going to evaluate into 'it' first,
     -- so that we can examine it for debugging if necessary
     get "width of" && objectType && anObject && ¬
     "*"&& "height of" && objectType && anObject
     return value(it)
end area
```

Area can be used like this:

    put area("card field", 3) into msg

In this example, the **get** command will assemble a string **width of card field 3 * height of card field 3**, which it puts into the variable **it**. **Area** then returns the value of **it**, which will be the product of the height and width, in this case, of card field 3.

More usefully we might use **area** when we have no idea what the object in question is. Here we see it being used with **the target**, which gives us the object that first received a message:

    put area(word 1 to 2 of the target, number of the target) into a

4.2 Commands

Commands in HyperTalk enable us to give instructions to the HyperTalk interpreter. HyperTalk commands can be included in handlers for execution whenever the handler is invoked, or they can be typed into the message window for immediate execution. Each HyperTalk command occupies a line in a script and can be extended on continuation lines if necessary (continuations are created by typing **option–return** and are indicated by a ¬ mark appearing at the end of the preceding line).

It's helpful to divide commands into those that you define and those already provided by HyperCard – HyperCard's commands have a much more readable syntax than anything you can define! Thus HyperCard's **answer** is used as in **answer "Hello!" with "OK"**, but you can only define a command to be called in the form **answer "Hello!", "OK"**, without any helpful words like **with**. This inequality between you and HyperCard is also a problem with functions: HyperCard's functions can cope with variants like **the short date** or **the long date**, but you can't do that unless you pass **"short"** or **"long"** as a parameter: **date("short")** or **date("long")**.

There are more than 68 built-in command names and many of them have several variants (such as **put...into, put...after, put...before**). See Appendix A for a list of the built-in commands – the HyperTalk Reference stack contains full details on each of them. In this book we aim to introduce them and illustrate their use by example – you will have already learned about many of them when reading Chapter 1. Later in this section we'll deal with the **go** command and with **push** and **pop** because an understanding of their operation is needed to comprehend fully the way in which other commands are interpreted. In the next section we deal with the control structures and with control-related commands such as **do, pass** and **send**.

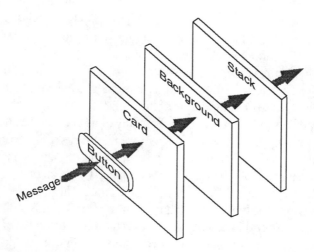

Command execution

Commands consist of a line containing a command name followed by zero, one or several parameter values. If there is more than one parameter value, they are separated by commas, but unlike the parameters of function calls, the parameters of commands are not surrounded by parentheses. Commands in HyperTalk resemble procedure calls in other programming languages. Their purpose is either to invoke one of the procedures built-in to the HyperCard interpreter or to invoke one of the handlers defined by the user in the current execution environment. The current execution environment is also known as the current message path, and is described in detail below.

Each command in a HyperTalk script begins with the name of a built-in or user-defined handler that it invokes. There are many useful commands built-in to HyperCard. See Appendix A for a list of them; the *HyperTalk Reference* stack also gives full details on each of them. You can also define handlers for commands. They may have different names or the same names as built-in commands. If the name of a user-defined handler is the same as a built-in command, the user's version overrides the built-in one. Handler definitions may include parameters and use local and global variables. We shall discuss these and other aspects of defining handlers in greater detail below.

The execution of a command has two stages: first any expressions embedded in the command are evaluated and the values are substituted for the expressions, and then the resulting line of text is executed as a command.

Commands are executed by the invoking a handler in the current execution environment that has a name matching the first word of the command. HyperCard seeks a matching handler by scanning the scripts of the objects in a list of objects called the *current message path* (CMP). In most cases the CMP contains all of the objects on an imaginary path traced from the object whose script is currently being executed to HyperCard via the current card, the current background, and the stack, as illustrated in the above diagram which we first introduced in Chapter 1.

If a command is executed in the script of a button or a field, the search for a matching handler starts in the script of that button or field and passes through: the current card, the current background, the current stack, any stacks that are in use, the *Home* stack and finally, HyperCard itself. The first matching handler that is encountered in the CMP is executed and, unless anything stops HyperCard, control returns to the next command in the original handler in due course. It follows from this description of the CMP that a handler in the background does not normally use handlers in the current card, or in any of its fields and buttons.

The current message path is so-named because the process of executing a command is analogous to sending a message; the message is the string of characters that make up the command and the destination of the message is determined by a scan of the CMP. The message is intercepted by the first handler in the path with same name. This message-passing metaphor is a useful way to describe the binding (matching names) of commands to their handlers, but it should not be taken to imply that commands are executed concurrently (as you might expect if the messages were real ones passing between computers in a network); when a handler receives a message, it takes control and retains it until it has completed its execution, when control returns to the original point of execution.

The message-passing metaphor emphasizes that the choice of the handler to interpret each command is determined dynamically and that the path along which the message is sent can be modified as a result of the actions of scripts. For example, if there is a handler called **put** in the CMP, it will be invoked to handle any **put** commands, pre-empting the usual interpretation of **put** that is built-in to the HyperCard system. If a command name does not match any handler in the current message path it passes through to the HyperCard system, and if there is a built-in handler for it, it is executed, otherwise an error is indicated.

This so-called late binding of commands to handlers and the concept of the current message path are important features of HyperTalk. They enable system events (**mouseUp**, **openCard**, ...) to be treated in the same way as program commands and they ensure that handlers can be shared between many objects by placing them in an appropriate position in the message path. They also support a notion of *specialization* similar to that found in other object-oriented languages, since the implementation of a command or the handling of a message resulting from a system event can be specified in a generalized way by a handler in the background or stack script, while special cases can be dealt with by separate handlers in card, field or button scripts where required. These concepts will inevitably seem a little strange at this stage; however you will grow used to them and learn to appreciate their potential applications as you read the book!

The go command

After **put**, HyperTalk's assignment, the command used most frequently is probably **go**. **Go** changes the card HyperCard is using, and it does for a script much what changing cards does for the user. Thus the command **go card 1** changes the current card to the first card, card number 1. This has two important effects: the user sees the card change to the first card; HyperTalk sees the fields and other objects on the card change.

Suppose we are on a background that has a field called **Address**, and we are currently on card 2 of this background. Then the HyperTalk expression **field "Address"** is, as you'd expect, the text in this field in card 2. But after **go card 1**, the *same* expression **field "Address"** is now the text of the field in card 1. Likewise, all the other objects change: so expressions like **the number of buttons** really mean **the number of buttons on this card**, and so as you go to another card, the value of the expression changes to the number of buttons on that card.

Since changing card is such a fundamental concept, it can be done in several ways: you can go to a specific card (giving its name, number or ID), you can go to the next card in a specific background (giving the background's name, number or ID), or you can go to a card or background in a specific stack. When you go to a background, if the current card happens to be on that background already, **go** does nothing. When you go to another stack, you go to its first card unless you specify otherwise; if the stack you go to is not the current one (it doesn't matter if you go to the stack you're already in) then you can either close the old stack, or open the new stack in a new window: this is provided by the optional **in a new window** part of the **go** command. Finally, if you go to another stack and HyperCard can't find it, HyperCard will ask the user to find it with a dialog box – unless you use the **without dialog** form of the **go** command.

We will use a simple notation to describe the form of commands, in which literals are in our usual typeface (**Helvetica**) for HyperTalk code and italicized text indicates names of components of control structures. Square brackets [ ] surround optional parts – and are not themselves part of what you would write. Here is a summary of the syntax for the forms of the **go** command described above using that notation:

go [to] *card*
go [to] *background*
go [to] *card* of *background*
go [to] [stack] *stackname* [in a new window] [without dialog]
go [to] *background* of [stack] *stackname* [in a new window] [without dialog]
go [to] *card* of *background* of [stack] *stackname* [in a new window] [without dialog]

Go is a powerful command because you can specify the card, background or stack that is the destination using an expression or a variable: if **x** is a variable whose value is the name, number or identifier of a card, background or stack, **go x** will do the appropriate **go**. The variable, however, cannot include the optional dialog parts of the **go** command: **in a new window** or **without dialog**. (If you want to do that, you may use the **do** command, which is described later in this chapter.) A typical example of using a variable is the following script:

put the long ID of this card into here
-- *do lots of complicated things*
go here -- *and this brings us back to where we started*

The commonest uses of **go** are to go to the first, last, next and previous cards. Although you have to write expressions like **field "name" of next card** in full, you can write **go** commands more concisely, omitting the word **card**:

```
go next
go first
go last
go prev -- short for go to previous card
go mid -- goes to the middle card of the stack
go any -- goes to a random card somewhere in the stack
```

You can also go to the first, next, last, middle, or any marked card, but you have to say **card** explicitly (marking cards is discussed in Chapter 10):

```
go next marked card -- to next marked card
go prev marked card -- to previous marked card
```

HyperCard keeps track of where users go to in stacks: the **Back** and **Recent** menu items in the **Go** menu are how the user can go back to cards that have been visited. Just as **back** is a card descriptor (you can say **field "Address" of card back**), you can use it in **go** commands – where it makes more sense! The command **go back** takes you back to the card you've just come from.

Sometimes you may try to go to a card that isn't there; maybe you asked the user for a card name and then attempted to go to it. There are two ways to handle this possibility. The **go** command itself sets the value of the function **the result**, which would be **empty** if the **go** succeeded or **No such card** or **No such stack** otherwise. It's generally better to use the **there is** operator (as in, **if there is a card x then go to card x**), since **the result** can get changed unpredictably by the results of other commands (for example, if you are debugging your stack, you might insert an **answer** command immediately after the **go**).

Go changes the current card by specifying that card by its name, number, or ID. You can also change card by specifying what a card contains in its fields. The **find** command finds cards with fields that contain text: we'll describe it fully in Chapter 10.

Both **go** and **find** commands can be typed into the message window so that you can get a good idea of what they do.

Push and pop

HyperCard keeps a small push-down stack of cards that you can push and pop with the **push card** and **pop card** commands. When you pop a card, you can either pop its long ID into a variable – **pop card into** *variable* (or **pop card before** *variable*, or **pop card after** *variable*) – in which case the current card doesn't change, or if you simply say **pop card**, HyperCard goes to that card. You may wish to use these commands to help with an interesting way of exploring a stack recursively, but we do not recommend their use. There are two problems: first, the push-down stack is of limited size and is too small to be reliable, and secondly, if the user does a **Back** from the **Go** menu that does a **pop** – which means that scripts cannot be certain that when they do a **pop** they are popping the card they thought they pushed.

The main use for these commands is to implement a return button, usually a bent arrow, with the script:

```
on mouseUp
  pop card                          ⏎
end mouseUp
```

Of course, this assumes that you have *already* done a push (and you haven't done one-too-many pops since!), typically in an **openStack** handler.

4.3   Control structures

The purpose of control structures is (in the case of **if**, **else**, **repeat**, **exit**, **return**) to modify the sequence of execution of the script; or (in the case of **global**, **function**, **on**) to inform HyperCard about a new global variable or handler; or (in the case of **do**, **pass**, **send**) to pass a message. Unlike commands, control structures do not themselves send any messages – their purpose is to control commands that send messages.

Although each control structure is intended to be self-contained, in some cases they depend upon the presence of related 'commands' to specify a complete structure. For example, the most general form of the **if** ... **then** command depends on the presence of an **end if** on a subsequent line, and all of the forms of the **repeat** control structure depend upon the presence of an **end repeat** on a subsequent line. Whenever a control structure is not matched by an appropriate terminating command, or the structure of a handler is inconsistent in some way, the HyperTalk editor indicates this by refusing to indent the script correctly.

Conditional structures

The **if** structure takes two forms each of which includes an optional **else** part. The most flexible form is very similar to that found in most procedural languages:

```
if expression then
  command sequence
else
  command sequence
end if
```

The **else** part of the **if** structure is optional and can be omitted. We write this as follows:

```
if expression then
  command sequence
[else
  command sequence]
end if
```

There is another form of the **if** structure for use when only a single line of commands is controlled by the condition:

```
if expression then command
[else command]
```

The use of this one or two line form produces shorter programs, but it is never essential, since the command sequence component in the first form may also be a single command.

Which of the following equivalent examples do you prefer?

```
if mouseLoc() is within the rect of bg btn "WasteBasket" then
   set hilite of bg btn "WasteBasket" to true
else
   set hilite of bg btn "WasteBasket" to false
end if
```

or:

```
if mouseLoc() is within the rect of bg btn "WasteBasket" then
   set hilite of bg btn "WasteBasket" to true
else set hilite of bg btn "WasteBasket" to false
```

or:

```
set hilite of bg btn "WasteBasket" to the mouseLoc ¬
is within rect of bg btn "WasteBasket"
```

Our answer would be that the first form is the easiest to modify – you can easily add extra commands before and after each set; though the last form is faster, it is much harder to modify.

The brief form of the if structure can produce confusing programs when ifs are nested (this is the well-known dangling else problem), and caution is needed to ensure that elses are matched with the appropriate ifs. Here is an example where the longer form should have been used for both ifs. The script has been written as if the programmer thought the else attached to the first if.

```
-- this script is incorrect (see text above)
if a < 1 then
   if hilite of button 1 then set hilite of button 1 to false
else answer "a is" && a
```

We have not mentioned that you may always put a newline before then. If we represent this optional newline by [*newline*], the *nearly* complete syntax for if is as follows:

```
if expression [newline] then command
```

```
if expression [newline] then
   commands
end if
```

```
if expression [newline] then command
else elsebit
```

```
if expression [newline] then
   commands
else elsebit
```

where *elsebit* can either of the following two forms:

```
else command
else
    commands
end if
```

We said that this is nearly the complete **if** syntax – because *command* or *commands* following **then** cannot end with an **if** command itself without **else** or **end if**. And we haven't mentioned that an empty line containing a comment is as good as a command. And maybe we *still* haven't covered all the possibilities. In short, HyperTalk's **if** syntax is bizarre, and from time to time you'll get caught out by it! Fortunately, the script editor's automatic indentation will help you see what commands are thought to be controlled by which **if** commands.

Repetitive structures

The **repeat** control structure has six forms, replicating the variety of looping constructs provided and found useful in other programming languages. The word **forever** is optional.

```
repeat [forever]
    commands
end repeat
```

This form produces an 'infinite loop', more correctly called an unbounded loop (it can't run *infinitely* many times). An unbounded loop can be stopped by the user typing **command–period** (the usual way of stopping Macintosh loops), but this stops your handler dead, and nothing else will be done. To terminate it from within a script, and still retain control, we can use the **exit repeat** instruction described below, with an **if** structure to test for the termination condition.

```
repeat expression times
    commands
end repeat
```

The *expression* is evaluated before the loop is entered and must produce an integer. The repetition occurs a fixed number of times, regardless of any assignments in the *commands*.

```
repeat with variable = expression to expression
    commands
end repeat
```

The two *expressions* must evaluate to integers, and the second one be equal to or greater than the first. The *commands* is repeated with the variable taking on each integer between the values of the expressions. The *variable* is initialized to the first expression and then incremented by 1 after each iteration of the loop. Assignments to the *variable* within the *commands* have no effect on the number of repetitions.

If you don't use the variable i, then the following two commands have identical effects:

```
repeat with i = 1 to 10          repeat 10 times
  beep                             beep
end repeat                       end repeat
```

Rather than counting up, you can count down:

```
repeat with variable = expression down to expression
  commands
end repeat
```

This is the same as the previous form, except that the first expression must be greater than or equal to the second, and the *variable* is decreased by 1 after each iteration.

Rather than counting, repetition can continue while some condition holds:

```
repeat while expression
  commands
end repeat
```

The *expression* here is evaluated before each iteration and the result must be **true** or **false**. The *commands* is executed until the result is **false**. The **until** form of **repeat** works the other way around, that is, it will repeat executing the commands so long as *expression* evaluates to false:

```
repeat until expression
  commands
end repeat
```

In both the **while** and the **until** forms, *expression* is evaluated before each iteration and the result must be **true** or **false**.

Here is an example of **repeat...while** in use, to delete trailing blank lines from a field:

```
repeat while number of words in last line of field x = 0
  delete last line of field x
end repeat
```

You have to use **repeat while** or **repeat until** if you want a **repeat with**-style loop, but one where the number of repetitions may change as you go along. For example, if you want to work through a field deleting certain lines (or through a string deleting certain characters), then the number of lines in the field will decrease and would be unsuitable as a limit for **repeat with i = 1 to number of lines in field 1**. Often, you can rewrite such a loop to run in the opposite direction, as in **repeat with i = number of lines in field 1 down to 1**. The advantage is that, as i decreases, the deleted lines were all at higher values of it; and however many lines are deleted, one always stops at line **1**.

So far, all of these loops have been controlled by their first line: they may repeat for ever, or for a controlled number of times, or until something goes true or false. Nevertheless, often it's convenient to control a loop from within. There are two ways to do this in HyperTalk.

The **exit repeat** command, which can only occur within the *commands* of a repeat loop stops the loop immediately, and whatever command after the **end repeat** is run next. You can also use **exit to HyperCard**, which can be used inside the loop or even inside any handler called by the commands in the loop. Of course, **exit to HyperCard** stops everything, and no commands after the loop will be run.

Part way through a loop, you often want to get on to the next iteration. Often this can be done by ingenious use of **if**s, but it is often easier and clearer to use the **next repeat** command. The **next repeat** command, like **exit repeat**, can only occur within the *commands* of a repeat loop, and its effect is to terminate the current iteration and to continue immediately with the next iteration (with a new value of the *variable* where appropriate).

It is useful to remember that the expressions in the **while** and **until** forms can be functions that you write. You can use functions to make the tests quite complex, or – just as useful – to print out in a field or message box what is going on, and whether the **repeat** is making progress.

4.4 Defining handlers and functions

Handler definitions are stored in *scripts*. A script is a string and is one of the properties of a HyperCard object. A script may include several handlers. Scripts are always stored in textual form and can be viewed or edited at any time. Like the other properties of objects, they can also be changed by HyperTalk programs. The results of editing a script take effect immediately the script is saved. (Technically, handlers are compiled just before execution, not when a script is saved; the compilation is automatic and transparent to the user.)

The following commands are concerned with handler and function definitions:

on *name* [*parameters*]	*-- starts a handler*
function *name* [*parameters*]	*-- starts a function*
end *name*	*-- ends the text of a function or handler*
exit *name*	*-- stops a function or handler running*
return *expression*	*-- stops and returns a value from a function (or handler)*
global *names*	*-- declares global variables*

Defining handlers

The **on** command introduces a handler definition. The name of the handler and (optionally) a parameter list follows, on the same line. The body of the handler follows on the subsequent lines, up to the matching **end**, which must be followed on the same line by the name of the handler (the name given in the **on** command).

```
on wakeUp n
  repeat n times
    beep
  end repeat
end wakeUp
```

This handler would be invoked by a command such as:

    wakeUp 12

provided that the definition for the wakeUp handler appears in the script of an object that is in the CMP when the command is executed. If not, the **send** command would have to be used (see the discussion of **send** below).

Parameters are always evaluated before the handler is called. So, even if we have modified the definition for the wakeUp handler to:

```
on wakeUp n
  put 22 into card field "Alarm duration"
  repeat n times
    beep
  end repeat
end wakeUp
```

we will always get exactly 12 beeps on executing:

    put 12 into card field "Alarm duration"
    wakeUp card field "Alarm duration"

By the way, if you had wanted to get the sort of effect that this handler almost gets, you would have had to pass the field name as the parameter. Once the handler knows the field name – rather than the field's value when it was called – it can do what it likes with the field. The following example therefore beeps 22 times (after defining wakeUp in the card script, you could type the last two lines into the message window):

```
on wakeUp n
  put 22 into card field "Alarm duration"
  repeat card field n times
    beep
  end repeat
end wakeUp
```

We might use wakeUp by passing it a parameter in a field:

    put 12 into card field "Alarm duration"
    wakeUp "Alarm duration"

This sort of programming is extremely useful when you want to do the same sort of thing to several objects.

Terminating a handler

Execution of a handler is terminated by an **exit** command or when control reaches the end of the handler (there is effectively an implicit **exit** before the **end** in every handler).

Defining functions

The handlers that we have described so far can only be used like procedures – they are invoked when a command with a matching name is executed. There are also handlers that behave like functions – they are invoked when an expression containing a function call with a matching name is evaluated. The message-passing mechanism and the current message path that we have described for binding commands to command handlers is also used to bind function calls to function handlers. As we have already noted, the expressions in a HyperTalk command are evaluated just before the command is executed.

The word **function** is used to introduce function definitions. Function definitions are exactly like to handler definitions except for the use of the keyword **function** instead of **on** to introduce them, and the use of **return** to terminate execution and to deliver the result. Note that, for consistency with handler definitions, parentheses are not used to delimit the parameters in function definitions, even though the parameters of functions *are* parenthesized in function calls. It is an error for a function not to have a **return** line – unless it does an **exit to HyperCard!**

The function:

```
function sum aList
    put 0 into theTotal
    repeat with i = 1 to number of lines of aList
        if line i of aList is a number then
            add line i of aList to theTotal
        end if
    end repeat
    return theTotal
end sum
```

could be used to produce the **totalUp** handler described earlier in this chapter. Using this function, the **totalUp** handler would then be:

```
on totalUp fieldName
    answer "The total is" && sum(field fieldName)
end totalUp
```

Return has two quite different meanings in HyperTalk; it is a keyword standing for a command in functions and it is a constant standing for the ASCII return character. In the function **sum**, **return** is used as the control structure, terminating the execution of the function and delivering the result. Although this is strange, no confusion arises, even when a function returns **return**!

Handlers versus functions

The **return** command can be used in handlers as well as functions. Its effect is very similar to that in functions; terminating execution of the handler and delivering a result, but since handlers cannot be called as part of an expression, the result has to stored in an anonymous container that is accessed using the built-in function **the result** or **result()**. Many built-in HyperTalk commands do this; the disadvantage is that, in consequence, the value in **result()** gets changed rather often, and may therefore not be what you expect it to be.

Variables in handlers

Handlers and functions can have local and global variables. A variable is storage container for a number, string or any other value. All of the values stored and manipulated in HyperTalk programs are actually strings of characters, and these may be interpreted as integers, real numbers, character strings, sequences of words or any other data format for which there are operations in HyperTalk (for example, dates).

Local variables in HyperTalk are very similar to those found in procedural languages, but they need not be declared. For example, i is a local variable in:

```
on wakeUp n
  put n*3 into i
  repeat i times
    beep
  end repeat
end wakeUp
```

If a local variable is used in an expression before it has been given a value, its 'value' will be its name! Generally, but not always, an error will be reported when the expression is evaluated, so the following would produce an error indication when the expression i*3 is evaluated, because i has not been given a value:

```
on wakeUp n
  repeat i*3 times
    beep
  end repeat
end wakeUp
```

On the other hand, **put i into x** would make **x** equal to the character i.

As in most procedural languages, local variables are created afresh each time the handler is executed. Their use is restricted to the handler in which they are created, and they are destroyed when the handler terminates. There is no conflict between local variables with the same name used in different handlers. Each local variable refers to a separate container.

Global is used to create variables that can be accessed in handlers other than the one that created them. A global variable is created and initialized to contain the value **empty** whenever the first **global** command that mentions the variable is executed. It continues to exist as long as HyperCard is running (even if a different stack has been opened) and can be accessed by any handler that executes a **global** declaring the same name. Thus:

```
on wakeUp n
  global noOfAlarms
  repeat n times
    beep
  end repeat
  add 1 to noOfAlarms
end wakeUp
```

keeps a tally in the global variable **noOfAlarms** of the number of times **wakeUp** has been called. (Our example depends on HyperCard's slightly quirky extension of arithmetic by which **empty + 1 = 1**.) NoOfAlarms can be used in any other handler that declares it. For example:

```
on ShowAlarms
  global noOfAlarms
  put "No of alarms: " & noOfAlarms into line 1 of card field "Status"
end ShowAlarms
```

Global variables can be useful even in a single handler. Here is a version of **wakeUp** that ensures that only one alarm is given, no matter how many times we may call **wakeUp**:

```
on wakeUp n
  global woken
  if woken = empty then
    repeat n times
      beep
    end repeat
    put true into woken
  end if
end wakeUp
```

Global variables can be used to enable handlers to cooperate in two stacks that are open together or one after the other.

Global variables should not be confused with objects (such as buttons, fields, cards and backgrounds). Objects are created when a **doMenu** command that creates a new object is executed (such as **doMenu "New Card"**) and continue to exist as long as the stack that contains them. Global variables are created when **global** is executed and (unlike objects) they are destroyed when HyperCard is shut down (as when the **Quit HyperCard** menu item is selected).

Global variables should be used with caution; the same name can accidentally be used for (what are intended be) different global variables in the same stack, or even in different stacks where both stacks happen to be used during the same activation of HyperCard. There can only be one global variable with a given name, so clashes of this sort can lead to incorrect programs, and this kind of error is not easy to detect. One approach to avoiding this kind of problem is to append a few characters to the name of each global that make the name unlikely to appear in other stacks; for example by including the initial letters of the name of the stack.

4.5 Messages

We have described the role of message-passing as a mechanism for the execution of program commands, but messages can also be generated as a result of mouse events (mouseUp, mouseEnter, mouseLeave, and so on) and changes in the state of the current stack (openCard, closeCard, openStack, and so on). A stack receives these messages from the system whenever the associated events occur. It is this feature of HyperCard that enables stacks to behave as interactive programs, detecting relevant actions by the user without any special effort, other than having handlers to catch the messages and do the actual work.

Some system messages are generated as a consequence of user actions, or even by a script 'pretending' to be a user, such as:

- A key press – which generates a keyDown x message, where x is the key. A script can use keyDown to simulate what would happen if the user typed.

- A menu selection – which generates a doMenu i, m message where m is the selected menu and i is the menu item that was selected. Scripts use doMenu to select HyperCard menu items.

- A mouse click – which generates a mouseDown message followed, if the mouse button is held down, by some number of mouseStillDown messages and, finally, a mouseUp message. Rather than send mouseDown and the other messages, scripts more often use the command click at x,y to send a mouseDown and mouseUp to whatever object is at position x,y on the card.

Other system messages are generated as a result of program or user actions that change the state of the current stack, such as going to a new card – which generates a closeCard message followed by an openCard message; the old card is sent the closeCard message, and the new card being opened is sent the openCard message. The message idle is sent when HyperCard is doing nothing else.

System messages are sent to a specific *target* object. If the target object's script does not contain a handler for it, the CMP is scanned in the usual way until a matching handler is encountered. The target for a system message is the object most directly affected by the associated event. For example, if the mouse is pressed while the cursor is within the area of a card button, a mouseDown message is sent to that button, but if the cursor was not in any button or field, the mouseDown is sent to the current card.

Messages generated by the system fall into two classes: those that make HyperCard work, and those that are ignored by HyperCard but are sent so that your scripts 'know what is going on'. (See Appendix A for a list of them. Again, the HyperTalk Reference stack contains full details on each of them.)

Thus most user actions generate *system messages* that are normally handled by the HyperCard system, but can be intercepted and handled specially when necessary by handlers placed in the CMP. There are nearly twenty such commands. For example, when the user selects a menu item, the system message **doMenu** is generated (with a parameter giving the menu item selected); when the user types a character on the keyboard, a **keyDown** message is generated (where the parameter is the key). If you provide handlers for **doMenu** or **keyDown**, you can make menu selections or key presses do other things.

System commands that are not intercepted by any scripts as they pass along the CMP are interpreted by the HyperCard system, which takes the appropriate default action – to execute the menu command in the case of **doMenu** or to insert the character typed into the text of the target field in the case of **keyDown**.

Many messages are simply ignored by HyperCard. These system-generated messages are generated solely for the purpose of activating handlers in the current stack, somewhere along the CMP. There over thirty forms. Examples include **mouseDown** and **mouseUp** (sent to the object within which the mouse button is pressed and released, respectively), **idle** (sent to the current card approximately every 10th of a second when no handlers are executing) **openStack** (sent to the current card when a stack is first opened), **openCard** (sent to the current card when it is opened) and **newCard** (sent to a new card when it is created).

The current message path in detail

The purpose of the current message path is to enable commands and system messages to be routed to the appropriate handler. The choice of an appropriate handler is strongly dependent on the user's current focus of attention – the stack, background and card that are currently open and, in the case of system messages, the field or button that the cursor is in.

So how is the structure of the CMP determined? Let's start by considering the first and last objects in the CMP. The first object in the CMP of a message is the target object, defined as follows:

1. For system messages deriving from mouse actions (such as: **mouseUp**, **mouseDown**, **mouseStillDown**, **mouseEnter**, **mouseWithin**, **mouseLeave**) the target is the top-most object containing the mouse cursor – this may be a button, a field, or if the cursor is not in a button or field, the current card.

2. For system messages deriving from other actions on a field or a button (**openField**, **closeField**, **exitField**, **keyDown**, **newField**, **deleteField**, **newButton**, **deleteButton**), the target is the relevant field or button.

3. For system messages deriving from keyboard actions (**keyDown**, **returnKey**, and other keyboard-derived system messages), the target is the relevant field if the text cursor is in a field, otherwise it is the current card.

4. For all other system messages (**openCard**, **openStack**, **idle**, **suspend**, **resume**, etc.) and commands (**doMenu**, **help**) the target is the current card.

5. For messages generated as a result of doing a **send**, for example, in **send "wakeUp" to card "Alarm clock"**, the first object in the CMP is the target object specified in the **send**, that is, the object named after **to**. When no target is specified (as in **send "wakeUp"**) the implicit target is the object containing the **send** command (so **send "wakeUp"** is equivalent to **send "wakeUp" to me**).

6. For messages generated by the execution of a script command, the first object in the CMP is the object whose script contains the handler currently being run. If there is a handler for the message in the same script, it will be handled by it.

As we have already stated, the *last* object in every CMP is the HyperCard system itself. This ensures that built-in commands can be received and handled by HyperCard; it is also how undefined messages are intercepted and reported as errors.

a button	a field	the current card	the current bg	the current stack
↓	↓	↓	↓	↓
the current card	the current card	the current bg	the current stack	the stacks in use
↓	↓	↓	↓	↓
the current bg	the current bg	the current stack	the stacks in use	the Home stack
↓	↓	↓	↓	↓
the current stack	the current stack	the stacks in use	the Home stack	HyperCard
↓	↓	↓	↓	
the stacks in use	the stacks in use	the Home stack	HyperCard	
↓	↓	↓		
the Home stack	the Home stack	HyperCard		
↓	↓			
HyperCard	HyperCard			

Now that we know how to determine the first and last objects in the current message path, let's consider the rest of the CMP between them. The rest of the current message path is based on the structure of HyperCard stacks and the nesting of HyperCard objects that comprise the current hierarchy, as described in Chapter 2.

In most cases (when no **go** to a card or **send** has been executed) the current message path is the most direct route from the target object to the HyperCard system through the current hierarchy. The table above shows the paths followed by messages whose initial targets are the objects shown at the top of each column in the table. The stacks 'in use' that are shown in the table are a feature of HyperCard that enables the stack scripts of other stacks to be included in the current message path. This is useful for organizing collections of general-purpose handlers and making them available to several stacks. The stacks in use feature is described more fully later in this chapter.

The table can also be represented diagrammatically:

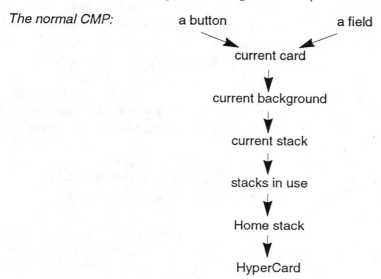

The normal CMP: a button   a field

current card

current background

current stack

stacks in use

Home stack

HyperCard

Messages can be initially targeted at any object in the diagram (by HyperCard in the case of system-generated messages, by executing a handler or function call, or by using the **send** command). Each message follows the arrows until it reaches an object that has a script containing a handler with a matching name.

Commands for sending messages

Messages are normally sent simply by executing commands. If a handler contains the command **flyByNight**, then (putting it pedantically) executing the command **flyByNight** causes the message **flyByNight** to be sent along the CMP. But HyperTalk is much more flexible than this, since it is possible to redirect messages other than along the CMP.

The following commands are provided for doing interesting things with messages:

> **send** *expression* **to** *object*
> **do** *expression*
> **pass** *name*

Send and do

Send is used for running a command somewhere other than in the current handler or, when it is used from the message window, **send** can be used for running commands in any object. It is very easy to use:

> **send "wakeUp 12" to card "Alarm clock"**

calls the handler **wakeUp** in the script of the card called **"Alarm clock"**, no matter where the **send** command occurs, and no matter whether the current card is **Alarm clock**.

Send is particularly useful when you want to make certain that you are using HyperCard's standard operations and not something that has been reprogrammed, either by you or someone else. For example, a stack might have a handler to intercept **doMenu** to stop the user quitting HyperCard; but if a script wants to quit, it could say **send "doMenu quit" to HyperCard**. Nothing can override this. (Send without a destination doesn't necessarily send messages to HyperCard; always say **to HyperCard** if that's where you want your message to go.)

If you send commands to another stack – which is a useful thing to do – you can only send them to the stack script, not to any card, background, button or field. Since **send** does not **go** to the other stack, make sure that the handler in the other stack does not refer to any objects in that stack (unless it does a **go** itself).

Do *command* is a bit like **send** *command* to this card, except that it can run several lines of commands, as well as control structures. The following therefore beeps three times:

```
put "repeat 3 times" & return & "beep" & return & "end repeat" into wow
do wow
```

Curiously, although the parameters of **do** and **send** are normally put in quotes, and you might therefore think you are sending the string itself, a simple string is evaluated *as if* it were a call to a handler. In other words, **send "x y" to this card** sends the message **x** with whatever the value of **y** happens to be; if you wanted to send **x** with the parameter being the letter **"y"**, then you would have to use the more tedious **send "x" && quote & "y" & quote to this card**.

Pass

Most often handlers do not want to redefine a message completely, they just want to modify it. Thus, we might have a handler **doMenu** in the current card to catch **doMenu** messages – not so that we re-do all HyperCard's menu stuff, but just so that **Delete Card** is changed to ask if the user really wants to delete a card. We can write such a handler as follows:

```
on doMenu m
  if m = "Delete Card" then
    beep
    answer "Do you really want to delete this card?" with "OK", "Cancel"
    if it is not "OK" then exit doMenu-- don't do anything
  end if
  send doMenu && m to HyperCard
end doMenu
```

This is fine, so far as it goes. But perhaps the current background script has its own **doMenu** handler to make some modification to some other menu? It would be better for the card **doMenu** handler to send the **doMenu** message to the current background. We could write **send doMenu && m to this background**, but HyperTalk provides an alternative, more reliable way to do it. We write **pass doMenu**. This not only sends all the parameters of the current handler (had you forgotten that **doMenu** actually has two parameters? The handler above loses the second one!) but also correctly follows the CMP.

To stress this, the following handler does *absolutely nothing*:

```
on x
   pass x
end x
```

It is very sophisticated. If some script executes the command **x**, this handler may be on the current message path, which means it will catch the message. The handler **x** passes the message **x** (along with any parameters it might have had) to continue down the CMP, *as if it had never been intercepted.*

Pass is rather like **exit**, it stops execution of the current handler, but it sends the entire message back along the CMP. Since it stops execution of a handler, any overriding you want to do must be done *before* pass. If you need to do things afterwards, you'll have to use **send** carefully.

The current message path after a send or a go command

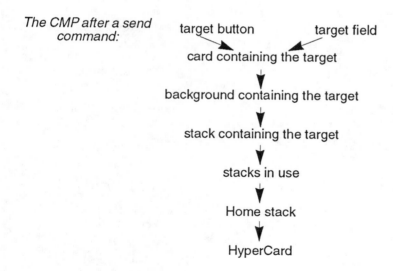

The CMP after a send command:

target button   target field

card containing the target

background containing the target

stack containing the target

stacks in use

Home stack

HyperCard

The current message path becomes more complex when the target is not in the current card, background or stack. This arises in two cases: first, when the **send** command is used, and the target of the **send** is an object that isn't in the current hierarchy, then the message is handled in the hierarchy of the target object. **Send** can be used to send a message to any object in the current stack (and for some very limited purposes to other stacks). It is most commonly used to activate handlers in objects on the current card, as in:

```
if the hilite of card button "Help" then
    send "mouseUp" to card button "Help"
end if
```

which sends a mouseUp message to a button called Help on the current card, regardless of where the handler executing this send command is in the current hierarchy. We can also send a message to an object not in the current hierarchy. For example: send "Wakeup" to next card or send "Wakeup" to card field "alarm" of next card. So our CMP diagram on page 85 has to be modified to the one shown on the previous page.

Secondly, when a handler contains a command that goes to a card in another stack (by the execution of a go command or a pop command), messages sent by the commands that follow the go are interpreted with respect to *both* the previous hierarchy and the new hierarchy of the card that is the destination of the go command. This change to the CMP is temporary and applies only until any currently executing handlers have finished execution. The informal effect of this is that the search for a matching handler is extended after a go command – when a handler for a message can't be found in the environment in which the currently running script was invoked, the new current environment is checked for a matching handler.

The CMP after a go command:

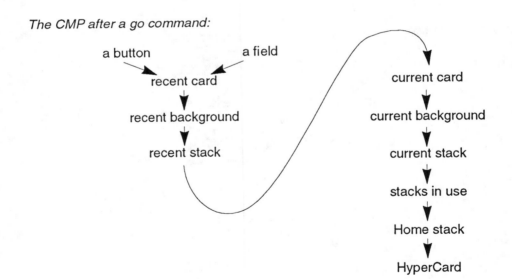

The CMPs for messages sent from a handler after executing a go command are shown in detail in the diagram above for the case where a go command results in change to a new current card in a different stack. (The 'recent card', 'recent background', 'recent stack' refer to the card that was the current card (or background or stack) before the go command was executed).

Object references and using the target

Using the current message path and **send**, you can easily lose track of where messages originated from. For example, you may want to have a handler in the stack script that does something to the button that was clicked on: this is called the *target* button. HyperTalk provides the function **the target** to get the name of that first object in the CMP.

A typical application of **the target** is in a **mouseUp** handler in a card, background or stack script. It will provide some standard behaviour for buttons or fields that do not have their own **mouseUp** scripts. We use **the target** to find out the name of the original object getting the **mouseUp**. The target gives you the full name; **the short target** gets the short name of the target; **number of the target** gets the target object's number.

For example, suppose that we want all of the buttons on a card to act as radio buttons – whenever any card button is clicked, it is highlighted and all others are de-highlighted (The radio button style doesn't do this, it just gives the button the *look* of a radio button). Normally, each button would have to have its own script:

```
on mouseUp -- handler for radio buttons
  set hilite of me to true
  repeat with i = 1 to number of buttons
    set hilite of button i to false
  end repeat
end mouseUp
```

Instead, and much more directly, we can handle each button's **mouseUp** with a handler in the card or background script. The first part of the **mouseUp** handler simply checks that this is a **mouseUp** whose target was a button, so that we don't try and set **hilites** on fields or the card itself!

```
on mouseUp -- card/background/stack handler for radio buttons
  if word 2 of the target = "button" then
    repeat with i = 1 to number of buttons
      set hilite of button i to i = number of the target
    end repeat
  end if
end mouseUp
```

The inner loop of the **mouseUp** handler sets the **hilite** of all buttons except the one the user clicked on to **false**. Usually you'd have plenty of buttons on a card that are not radio buttons, for example a Home button and the usual go next, go previous card buttons. You don't have to do anything to get this to work, since those other buttons will normally have their own **mouseUp** handlers, so **mouseUp** will never progress along the CMP and reach the radio button **mouseUp** handler in the card script.

You may want some of the radio buttons to execute their own individual **mouseUp** handlers as well as the standard radio button handler in card script. This can be done by including a **pass mouseUp** command in each individual handler. For example, the following handler could be included in script of one radio button, to play the sound resource **channel 1 signature tune** and alter the **hilites** of all of the radio buttons:

```
on mouseUp -- handler for musical radio buttons
    play "channel 1 signature tune"
    pass mouseUp
end mouseUp
```

It's worth a brief digression to suggest a way of having more than one 'family' of radio buttons. To do this, we need some way to identify the different groups. The **Print Report** dialog box is an example of a built-in dialog using three families of radio buttons: one family chooses to print from all cards or just marked cards; one family chooses fixed or dynamic height; and the last family chooses a view, margins, size or spacing. Now you know how to implement it.

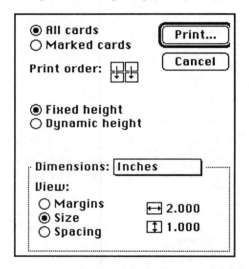

How can we do the same sort of thing with radio buttons on cards? A convenient way is for the script of each radio button to be given a standard first line, just a comment like -- **GroupA**. Note that **GroupA** will be the second word of the first line of the script. Every button starting with that comment is in the same family, and their **hilites** will be mutually exclusive.

```
on mouseUp -- handler for several families of radio buttons
    if word 2 of the target = "button" then
        if style of the target = "radioButton" then
            put word 2 of line 1 of the script of the target into family
            repeat with i = 1 to number of buttons
                if word 2 of line 1 of the script of button i = family then
                    set hilite of button i to i = number of the target
                end if
```

```
        end repeat
      end if
    end if
  end mouseUp
```

Another use for **the target** is when the current card changes as a result of a **go card**. The interpretation of references to objects after a **go card** changes in the currently running handler to reflect the new context. For example, in the following command sequence using a handler defined in the current background:

```
totalUp "Expenditure"
go next card
totalUp "Expenditure"
go back
```

the two fields to which the **totalUp** handler is applied are clearly on different cards. To achieve the same effect as the above sequence of commands using **send** instead of **go card**, we might try to write:

```
totalUp "Expenditure"
send "totalUp" && quote & "Expenditure" & quote to the next card
```

But when a handler is executed as a result of a **send** operation, the context for the interpretation of its object references doesn't change. So the second script has quite a different interpretation. The **field "Expenditure"** referred to by the **totalUp** handler is the one on the current card, and not the one to which the message is sent.

The only remedy is to modify **totalUp** to make it context-independent by appending **of the target** to the field reference. Since this would make the handler more complex, we use **get** to store the field's contents in the variable **it** to save writing out **the target** several times:

```
on totalUp fieldName
  put 0 into total
  get value("field fieldName of" && the target)
  put number of lines of it into n
  repeat with i = 1 to n
    if line i of it is a number then
      add line i of it to total
    end if
  end repeat
  put total into message box
end totalUp
```

The target (or target()) gives us the first recipient of the message that is currently being handled. The original **totalUp** simply said **field fieldName**, leaving HyperCard to decide which card that field was to be found on depending on what **go** commands had been used. By writing **field fieldName of the target**, we are specifying that only the field on the target card will do. Moreover, we have to use **value** because **the target** could return **card ID 345, bkgnd field** "xxx" or some such, and HyperCard can't parse field fieldName of something so uncertain – the parameter of value instead first gets the target evaluated and *only then* (when HyperCard knows what it is, say card ID 345) parses the expression field fieldName of card ID 345 (or whatever) to see what the value of that field is. It's much easier to use go; besides, if you don't have the screen locked, you can actually watch HyperCard change cards as the script goes to cards with the go command.

All the quotes in the send commands *are* necessary to get quotes around the name in the message; the command sends a message totalUp "Expenditure" to the next card. Sometimes you will be tempted to get around the quotes, as in send "totalUp Expenditure" to next card, which will sometimes work. It won't work when you have a variable called expenditure. If you have just put 5 into expenditure, this send would send totalUp 5, not totalUp "Expenditure" which is what you wanted.

The target, then, enables very powerful HyperTalk programming. In the following sub-sections we describe a few other HyperTalk functions that make programming easier at this level.

Using stack scripts from other stacks

Looking at the CMP diagrams, if you want to provide handlers that several stacks can use (because they are so useful!) you might put them in your Home script. Handlers in your Home script are available for all stacks *you* run, but any stack of yours that you want to give away won't work with anyone else's *Home* stack, because the handlers it needs won't be in their *Home* stacks. Rather than keep track of the handlers you need, and rely on your friends cutting-and-pasting these handlers into their *Home* stack script (and then remembering to delete the handlers when they're not needed any more – assuming you have chosen handler names that aren't already taken!) there is, fortunately, a much easier and more reliable way.

You can insert stack scripts in the CMP just prior to the *Home* stack script by using the start using s, where s is the stack whose stack script you want to include in the CMP. When you want to stop using s's stack script, say stop using s. The global property stacksInUse gives you an item list of the stacks currently in use (it is empty at the start of a HyperCard session). Each time you start using a stack, its name gets put after the last item of stacksInUse; if the stack is already in use, its name gets moved to the end. You can have up to ten stacks in use at any one time. The CMP works backwards through the stacksInUse, looking for handlers in the stack script of the last item of the stacksInUse first, working back to the *Home* stack's script. You may have developed handlers for doing invoicing and stock control. Put these handlers in a stack stock control. Any stack that needs to use these handlers could include the following openStack and closeStack handlers:

```
on openStack
  start using stack "stock control"
  pass openStack
end openStack
```

```
on closeStack
  stop using stack "stock control"
  pass closeStack
end closeStack
```

The stack **stock control** itself may have handlers:

```
on openStack
  start using this stack
  pass openStack
end openStack

on closeStack
  stop using this stack
  pass closeStack
end closeStack
```

No message is sent when a stack is taken out of use, though the command **stop** itself can be handled. Here is one way to know when your stack stops being used: it would typically remove any menus it has added – this example simply calls a handler **stopUsing**:

```
on stop
  get word 2 of long name of me
  if char 1 of it = quote then
    delete first char of it
    delete last char of it
  end if
  if param(3) = it then
    stopUsing -- this stack has stopped being used (so delete its menus or whatever)
  end if
  pass stop
end stop
```

Since this handler looks so unreliable, the best way of stopping using a stack is explicitly to send a **stopUsing** message as well (you can't use **closeStack**, because the stack should handle **closeStack** in any case in case the user explicitly closes it – stacks in use don't have to be open). Here's how you'd stop using *all* stacks using this method:

```
repeat for number of items in the stacksInUse times
  send stopUsing to item 1 of the stacksInUse
  stop using stack item 1 of the stacksInUse
end repeat
```

Another good use of using stacks is to help stack development: you can have a stack with handlers for doing useful operations like showing all hidden buttons (in case you lose them), for locking and unlocking fields, and so on. By not using your tools stack, you will be able to check that the stack works correctly without any handlers in the tools stack.

There is more discussion in Chapter 9 about using stacks for implementing menus.

Special object names

There are several useful names that add nothing to what you can do, but make it easier to say.

me – this is the object containing the script of the handler. In principle you know what that object is! But **me** is a handy way of writing **this button, this field** – which for some reason you are not allowed to write! It's also a bit faster than writing the legal **this stack, this card** and **this background**. Here's an example: **set the hilite of me to true**. As you would expect, you can use **name of me, ID of me**, and so on. For fields, **me** also refers to the text in the field, so in a field handler you can write **put empty into me**.

recent – this is the card that was current prior to the present one. It's useful if you do a lot of **go**s. As usual, you can write **name of recent card** and so on.

last, middle, any – just as you can use the ordinal names **first, second, third** ... **tenth** to specify objects (**the first button** is equivalent to **button 1** and to **button one**), you can also use **last, middle**, and **any**. If the object is a card, you can say **previous, next, back, recent, forth** as well. Unfortunately you cannot do sums with these descriptors: thus **go to last-1 background** won't take you to the penultimate background, which you'd have to do with **go to background (number of backgrounds-1)**.

4.6   The moral

Having described HyperTalk in detail but, even so, not completely, it's obvious that it is deep-down a very complicated language. Writing this chapter we've found that complexity and arbitrariness frustrating, and at times we've wondered; if we had problems explaining it clearly – do the implementors of HyperCard really understand it? Will the next version of HyperCard be subtly different? For example, we didn't give all of the forms of the **go** command – **go forth** was one variant we omitted – because we wanted to give you the principles rather than all of the variations, which in themselves aren't very edifying.

On the other hand, in practice HyperTalk is very easy to use. It's very easy to type commands into the message window, or to make little scripts in buttons to experiment and find out exactly what some command does or exactly how to achieve some effect. And, besides, when you write complicated scripts and begin to wonder about the issues we've raised in this chapter, your scripts are anyway going to need thorough testing, and when you do *that* testing you'll be simultaneously finding out how HyperCard's quirks affect what you want to do. Getting around HyperCard's quirks won't be any harder than getting around or fixing your own bugs. It all goes to make HyperTalk an exciting interactive language – certainly one that should fascinate computer scientists.

The remainder of this book brings all the features of HyperTalk together and shows how it can be used to make impressive and useful systems quickly.

CHAPTER 5

Graphics Programming

Using handlers to
implement general-purpose functions

Turtles are little creatures that can draw pictures. They were made famous by the success of the children's programming language LOGO. The idea of turtle graphics is to make drawing fun and easy, indeed, to make writing programs to control the turtle fun and easy. The original turtles were real mechanical devices that rolled around on a large sheet of paper with a pen, but it was soon realized that the turtle could simply be a 'virtual' device that simulates the turtle's movements on the screen and the same programs that controlled the mechanical turtle to draw on the paper would draw the same pictures on the screen. We will see that it is easy to build a simulated turtle graphics system in HyperCard: this may well be your – or your child's! – easiest way into understanding topics like recursion and fractals.

LOGO was popular for school use, particularly because it made it possible to draw some pictures on computers that didn't have a mouse. In HyperCard, which has a mouse and good painting tools, the advantage of LOGO-like programming is that it is a good, visual way of teaching programming concepts such as iteration and recursion. Like other methods for programming graphics, turtle graphics enables us to produce pictures quickly that would be very tedious to produce manually. This makes it a good way to get into fractals, as we shall soon see.

5.1 Graphics in HyperTalk

Graphics in HyperCard, whether you are a user working interactively or working from within HyperTalk, follows a *paint model*. This means that when you draw things on the screen, pixels are made black or white rather as if you were using a paint brush and eraser on a sheet of paper (actually, two sheets of paper, since in HyperCard you have a background picture as well). Turtle graphics is a form of painting where the so-called turtle drags the paint brush around the screen, like you would have dragged the mouse by hand. Instead, you program the turtle to do the painting for you.

For example, the command **fd** (**fd** is short for 'forward') moves the turtle forward about an inch, and draws a straight line in the direction the turtle is heading. We will soon define **fd** as a handler in HyperTalk, but right now we'll show you what can be done with it. If we then say **rt**, the turtle turns right – **rt** is another handler we'll write below. A further **fd**, **rt**, **fd**, **rt**, **fd**, **rt**, **fd** will finish off drawing all four sides of a square, which of course is easiest to do with a **repeat** loop. Put together, this makes a turtle graphics programs like the following; we've shown the picture it draws to the right:

```
on square
  repeat 4 times
    fd
    rt
  end repeat
end square
```

Next we can do neat patterns:

```
on pattern
  repeat 8 times
    square
    rt 45
  end repeat
end pattern
```

We see that **rt** can take an optional parameter, here 45 degrees, to override the default of 90 degrees. Likewise, **fd** can take a parameter, the distance the turtle is to move when it should move some distance other than an inch.

We can easily draw a triangle with three straight lines.

```
on triangle
  repeat 3 times
    fd 90
    rt 120
  end repeat
end triangle
```

If we replace each line drawn here by **fd 90** with a bent shape, like ‿⌃‿, we get a far more interesting shape, a star. Of course, each of the bits of the bent line is also a straight line. We could replace *them* by a still smaller version of the bent line. If we keep on doing this until we get lines that are too short to worry about, the result is a pleasing picture, a fractal called the Koch snowflake. We'll now work out how to draw it.

The little bent line can be drawn by the turtle using: **fd 10**, **lt 60**, **fd 10**, **rt 120**, **fd 10**, **lt 60**, **fd 10**. We make a handler **line** to do this:

```
on line
  fd 10
  lt 60
  fd 10
  rt 120
  fd 10
  lt 60
  fd 10
end line
```

Now replace each call to **fd 10**, which is a straight line, by a recursive call to **line**, but asking for a shorter line. There needs to be some way to stop this process going on for ever, drawing shorter and shorter lines, getting nowhere. Obviously, **line** needs a parameter to say how long a line is wanted, and when it is too short, we should use **fd** instead and be done with it. In the handler shown here, we've stopped at lines of 10 pixels length:

```
on line n
  if n ≥ 10 then
    divide n by 3
    line n
    lt 60
    line n
    rt 120
    line n
    lt 60
    line n
  else
    fd n
  end if
end line
```

Now use this fractal line handler in another handler to draw the three sides of the 'triangle' and we have our snowflake:

```
on snowflake
  repeat 3 times
    line 90
    rt 120
  end repeat
end snowflake
```

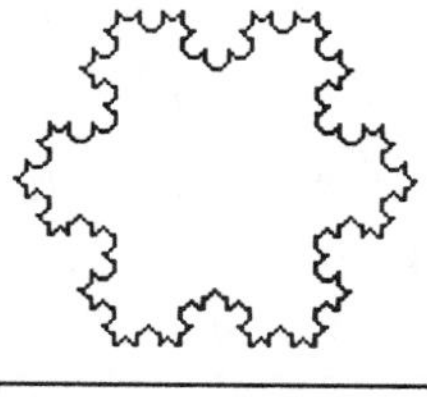

The basic idea of drawing fractals with turtle graphics is to replace one or more uses of **fd** (which gets the turtle to draw a straight line) with a recursive call to the same handler, to draw a smaller version of the same picture, the same length as the line **fd** would have drawn. (There are other sorts of fractal as well.)

5.2   Turtle graphics in HyperTalk

We shall define handlers for the turtle graphics commands (**fd**, **rt**, and so on) and put these in the background script of a stack. We can then write turtle graphics commands in the card script. That means that when you write turtle graphics commands you can't see and be distracted by the 'innards' (the implementation) of the turtle graphics: you have a clean script to program in that looks as simple as LOGO. When HyperCard runs your card script, messages such as **fd** will be sent back towards HyperCard, via the background where we will have defined them to do turtle graphics.

Global variables for the turtle

At any moment, the turtle is somewhere on the card screen and is facing some direction. The turtle has to keep track of where it is going between calls to **fd**, **rt** and so on, and this means that we need some global variables to keep track of the various numbers required.

One way is have three global variables: **xcor**, **ycor** and **heading**. These variables give the position of the turtle in pixels from the top left of the card and the heading of the turtle in degrees clockwise from vertical. (In fact, HyperCard works in radians, not degrees, but part of the point of a turtle graphics system such as the one we are writing is to make life easier! So we shall have to convert degrees to radians every so often.)

The simplest handler to write first is **rt**, which turns the turtle right:

```
on rt a
    global heading
    subtract a from heading
end rt
```

Here, **rt** takes a parameter **a** and changes the heading by **a** degrees. We want to make **rt** more 'user friendly': to turn a right angle if no parameter is supplied by the user. To do this, we use the paramCount to see whether **a** was in fact given; if not, we set **a** to 90, as follows:

```
on rt a
    global heading
    if the paramCount = 0 then put 90 into a
    subtract a from heading
end rt
```

The handler **lt** is exactly the same, except we **add a to heading**.

```
on lt a
  global heading
  if the paramCount = 0 then put 90 into a
  add a to heading
end lt
```

If you want lt and rt spelt out in English as left and right, that might apparently be done by something like:

```
on right a
  rt a
end right
```

except that this would *always* provide a parameter for rt, even though right's a might be missing! You'll therefore need to repeat the paramCount bit. The best way is as follows:

```
on right a
  if the paramCount = 0 then rt
  else rt a
end right
```

since this keeps the decision about what to do with no parameters in one place (namely in rt), rather than repeating the decision in rt, right and droit, and perhaps not being consistent.

Moving forward with fd is a bit more complicated, but only because trigonometry is difficult anyway, not because of HyperTalk. Suppose we want to go forward a distance d. Given that the turtle is at position xcor, ycor on the card, we need to move it horizontally to xcor plus something and ycor plus something. The somethings are d*sin(heading*pi/180) horizontally and d*cos(heading*pi/180) vertically. If we put these values in two variables newxcor and newycor, then to draw the line we choose HyperCard's line tool and drag from xcor,ycor to newxcor,newycor. However, drag requires whole numbers (because you can't drag from part way through a pixel), not the real numbers our trigonometric calculations have given us. We must round the coordinates to whole numbers and use drag round(xcor), round(ycor) to round(newxcor), round(newycor).

The last step of fd is to update the global variables xcor and ycor to the new position for the turtle. It's important that we keep the variables xcor and ycor as accurately as possible so that we keep track of *exactly* where the turtle is supposed to be, even if HyperCard needs it to be drawn spot on a pixel – that's why we don't round them, but only use round in drag.

Putting everything together, complete with a default 50 if no distance parameter is given, results in the following handler for fd:

```
on fd d -- move foreward
  global xcor, ycor, heading
```

```
      if the paramcount = 0 then put 50 into d
      put xcor+d*sin(heading*pi/180) into newxcor
      put ycor+d*cos(heading*pi/180) into newycor
      choose line tool
      drag from round(xcor),round(ycor) to round(newxcor), round(newycor)
      put newxcor into xcor
      put newycor into ycor
    end fd
```

We can add a similar handler for **bk** (to move the turtle backwards) or define **bk d** as **fd -d**. Unlike the method we used for **right** and **rt**, if no parameters are given to **bk**, we can't call **fd** with no parameters, since **fd** would simply move in the right distance in wrong direction! So **bk** has to be written out:

```
    on bk d -- move backwards
      if the paramCount = 0 then fd -10
      else fd -d
    end bk
```

That is all there is to turtle graphics. We can add various utilities, and allow the turtle's marking pen to be up or down (so that we can control whether it draws or not). Since HyperCard has lines of different thicknesses, we can also easily change the thickness of the turtle's lines.

Before the turtle can work, we must initialize the global variables (**xcor**, **ycor** and **heading**). There's quite a nice way of doing this, but we'll talk about it later, after discussing some useful turtle utilities.

Useful turtle utilities

It is useful to have a handler to clear the card and put the turtle in the middle facing upwards. In fact, it's essential – it initializes all the turtle graphic globals! Here's one way to do it:

```
    on draw
      reset paint
      clear
      home
      setheading -- point upwards
      pendown
      pen -- thinnest pen
    end draw
```

Clearing any graphics from the card is straight forward scripting that mirrors exactly what you'd do as a mouse-operating user:

```
on clear
   choose select tool -- any paint tool
   domenu "select all"
   domenu "clear picture"
   choose browse tool
end clear
```

For the turtle to go home (which is LOGO's name for the centre of the card – we don't mean HyperCard's Home!) we simply set the global variables **xcor** and **ycor** to put the turtle in the centre of the card. It will be good programming practice to implement a more general handler **setpos** to put the turtle anywhere, and then **home** will use that to 'home' the turtle. We may as well arrange for **setpos** (which normally takes two parameters) to default its parameters to the centre of the card. Then **home** is quite trivial:

```
on home
   setpos
end home
```

Before we implement **setpos**, the fact that you can *set* a position suggests that you should also be able to *get* a position. A function **getpos()** is easy:

```
function getpos
   return round(xcor) & "," & round(ycor)
end getpos
```

We tell the user rounded positions, but inside the turtle graphics system we keep the coordinates as accurately as possible.

An interesting HyperTalk issue is this. Suppose the user saves the turtle's position by saying **put getpos() into here**. Then later he might want to get the turtle back to that place by saying **setpos here**. The thing is that **here** is only one parameter, but it looks like two! If you wrote out **here** (by saying **put here**) you'd see it was **0,0** but **setpos 0,0** has two parameters, whereas **setpos here** has only one: it's exactly as if you had said **setpos "0,0"**.

We therefore use **the paramCount** to see how many parameters **setpos** has. If it has only one, then, we may have to 'take it apart' and pretend it had two, the first and second items of its single parameter. If **the paramCount** is one, we see how many items are in the first parameter, if there are two, then make them the actual parameters. Finally, if there really is only one parameter, then we will default the missing parameter to the horizontal centre line (consistent with missing both parameters out, when we default to the centre point, which is on the centre line).

The centre of the card is not **0,0**, which is the top left. Because **setpos** and **getpos** completely hide how we want to handle the globals **xcor** and **ycor** (we've already seen that they are actually reals, but we tell the user they are integers), we can, if we wish, make the centre of the card 0,0 for the turtle graphics world and simply make **setpos** and **getpos** convert between turtle-world and HyperCard-world.

Unfortunately, it's not obvious which is best to do: if we are building a child's turtle environment, then 0,0 should be the centre, but if we are building a stepping block for learning about HyperCard graphics then 0,0 should be the top left, otherwise we will get confused about where the centre 'really' is! Some decisions clearly depend on who you are programming your stacks for, and there is no one right answer, unless we add a handler to move the turtle origin (then we can put it in the top left, the centre, or anywhere else that takes our fancy). If you get to this stage, you should turn to any graphics programming book, since this is only just the beginning of the possibilities.

If we settle for 0,0 being in the top left of the card, **setpos** will turn out something like this:

```
on setpos x, y
  global xcor, ycor
  if the paramCount = 1 and number of items in x = 2 then
    put item 2 of x into y
    put item 1 of x into x
  else if the paramCount ≤ 1 then
    get the rect of this card
    put item 4 of it div 2 into y
    if the paramCount = 0 then put item 3 of it div 2 into x
  end if
  put x into xcor
  put y into ycor
end setpos
```

The **rect of this card** (or the **rectangle of this card**, written in full) returns a list of four items, for the top left (horizontal, vertical) and bottom right (horizontal, vertical) coordinates of the card window. The standard card size gives 0,0,512,342. The centre of the card is then at **512 div 2** and **342 div 2**. We use **div** rather than / to get an integer (whole number) value: it just happens that cards have sizes that are divisible by 2, but there is no reason why we should rely on it when it is so easy to program more carefully.

5.3 Making a turtle demonstration stack

Now we have implemented a turtle graphics stack, it needs packaging so that other people can use it. We need to make a stack that presents turtle graphics nicely, complete with the relevant documentation. What we describe here is supplied in full on the book disk.

One way to arrange the stack is to have a first, introductory card (saying what the stack is about, who its author is, and so on) and then a second card giving details of what turtle graphics functions are available. Maybe there should be some simple demonstrations that take the user through turtle graphics step-by-step. Additional cards can be nice demonstrations, pretty pictures, plus an invitation to the user to experiment and add his own cards.

Given that the turtle background has all the handlers to implement turtle graphics, we may as well make running turtle graphics automatic as each card is opened. We will assume that the user's (or demonstration) cards have a handler turtle that has been written to draw the turtle graphics on that card. The background handles openCard and sends turtle to the card script, hence starting the turtle graphics scripts on that card.

If, however, the user has not yet put a turtle handler in the card script, the turtle message will fall back, through the background script on to Home and HyperCard. We therefore place our own turtle handler in the background script: if it gets called, it reminds the user that he needs to provide the turtle handler for the card. Thus, each card runs its turtle graphics as soon as it is opened, or reminds the user to write a turtle handler to do so.

We add the following two handlers to the turtle background:

```
on openCard
    draw -- in case someone forgets
    unlock screen -- so that we can see what's happening (in case it was locked)
    send "turtle" to this card -- start the turtle handler in the card
    choose browse tool
end openCard

-- if the card hasn't got a turtle handler, complain!
on turtle
    answer "Please add a turtle handler to the card"
end turtle
```

When the card's turtle handler returns, the opencard handler continues, and we make sure that the user is left using the browse tool. We may or may not want to pass openCard.

After the introductory card, the second card of the stack lists all of the turtle graphics handlers we've provided (see illustration on next page).

The '?' button is a gimmick to encourage the user to explore: it runs an interesting bit of turtle graphics or pop-up a field that says something useful. How do you think the horizontal and vertical lines are drawn, given that the turtle graphics draws on the card image and the background is shared with all other turtle cards? They must be done some other way! They are narrow fields. We set their style to rectangle (in the field info dialog box), then used the message window to say set the width of field narrow to 2 and set the height of field short to 2. As fields (or buttons) they are unaffected by HyperCard's paint operations, so the turtle cannot affect them, and as card fields they don't appear on any other cards sharing the same background.

Since the righthand column doesn't say very much – it's only a brief reminder – we need to do some scripting so that the user can click on lines in the first column and get more information.

The first column is two fields. The instructions at the bottom (*Click on any of these lines*

Primitives:	Meaning:
turtle	name of user's turtle handler (put in card script)
clear	clear the screen; turtle unaffected
home	put turtle in centre of screen; turtle heading unaffected
setpos x, y	put turtle at (x,y); turtleheading unaffected
getpos()	get x,y pair of where turtle is
setheading x	set the direction the turtle is facing
getheading()	get the direction the turtle is already facing
turtlevisible()	return true if the turtle is in the HyperCard card area
fd x	move forward x (approximately x/72 inches)
bk x	move backwards x
rt x	turn right x degrees
lt x	turn left x degrees
pen x	choose a pen of thickness 1 to 8
penup	stop drawing
pendown	start drawing
draw	initialise the turtle's playground
Click on any of these lines to get more information.	— the same as saying clear; home; setheading; pendown

to get more information) is a separate, small field that has no script. The other field contains the text: **Primitives**, turtle, … draw. It is a locked field so that when the user clicks on it, rather than being able to edit the text (as with an unlocked field), the field is sent **mouseDown**, **mouseUp** and so forth. We then handle **mouseUp** in the field's script and see what is on the line the user clicked on.

The HyperTalk function **the clickLine** gives us an expression (like **line 2 of card field 1**) from which we work out the line the user clicked on. Line 4, say, is the word 'turtle'; we then use line 4 somehow to get more details about the turtle handler. One way is to change the field number (1, here) and get a line of text from another field that we have already filled in with the help texts. Here's how to do it.

First, **get the clickLine**, which puts (for example) **line 2 of card field 1 into it**. Next, replace the last word of it with the name of the field that has got the help text in, **info**, say, by doing: **put "Info" into last word of it**. Now it is an expression that we can use to get the right help text. We could simply say **answer value(it)**. (If we had said **answer it**, the user would see **line 2 of card field info**, not what **line 2 of card field info** *was*; we want the user to see the value of it!)

If you do this, you'll soon agree that it would be nice if the help text contained blank lines so that the answer dialog box was more legible. But we are using lines to separate our entries in the **info** field. To get around this problem, we use * (or any other symbol we choose) to indicate blank lines; then, of course, we have to work out a way of converting stars to return characters! That looks like hard work, so before launching forth, it is worth reviewing whether we are going about the problem the right way at all.

First, the advantage of lines of help in the info field is that this is very easy to organize. It takes just one field, and we can align it against the other field to get the help text on the right lines. Secondly, going from the clickLine to the corresponding line in the other field is fast and efficient. That could be important.

Alternatively, we could have 16 fields, with names like turtle, rt, draw and so on. We would then do something like, show card field value(first word of the clickLine). Each of these 16 fields would be locked and have a script to catch mouseUp: simply doing a hide me to conceal the field again. This sort of scheme is quite neat. It allows us to use various fonts and text styles easily, but it has a few minor problems. First, we must make sure that openCard hides all of the 16 fields (it would be confusing if they had got left showing from last time). Secondly, we'd have fun creating all those fields, naming them and editing them. Indeed, if we change the name of a turtle command from (say) setpos to setxy, we run the risk of losing track of the old help in field setpos!

For our present purposes, lots of fields seems like overkill. We'll write some script to convert stars to returns. We could go through the help text character-by-character, but that can be slow. Better is to use the built-in function offset which can be used to find strings, like stars, quickly.

Offset("*", text) will either return 0 (in which case there is no * in text) or it will return the character position (1, 2, 3...) of the first star. We simply replace that star with a couple of returns, and then repeat to see if there are any more stars left. The complete handler is given below.

```
on mouseUp
  get the clickLine
  put "Info" into last word of it
  put value(it) into text
  if text ≠ empty then
    get offset("*", text)
    repeat while it > 0
      put return & return into char it of text
      get offset("*", text)
    end repeat
    answer text
  end if
end mouseUp
```

This handler allows for us not providing help text for some lines in the field (for example, its blank lines!).

The next idea for the help card is to provide a simple demonstration. Handling openCard, we can ask whether the user wants to have an interactive introduction to turtle graphics.

```
on openCard
    answer "Do you want a simple demo?" with "No" or "Yes"
    if it is "yes" then demo
    put "Try typing your own turtle commands into the message window"
    pass opencard -- so the background will get it
end openCard
```

If the user doesn't want a demo, he is still invited to try the turtle commands out from the
message window. Since this openCard puts stuff in the message box that may not be
appropriate for other cards, we provide a closeCard handler to clear it and then hide it.

```
on closeCard
    put empty
    hide message
    pass closeCard
end closeCard
```

All that's left is the handler for the simple demonstration.

When you can program things it's always a bad idea to hand-craft something
complicated – because then it would be more difficult to change and improve later. Instead
we'll use a simple, flexible idea. A handler say will take several lines of HyperTalk and tell the
user what the lines are just before it executes them.

We'd write something like: say "draw" & return & "fd 150" & return & "setheading
135" to get a demo of draw followed by fd 150, followed by setheading 135. Now we see
that our idea, though flexible, is a bit tedious (especially if we anticipate a long demonstration
spread over many lines)! Instead, we can make say insert all those returns itself if we choose
something else that is easier to type. Indeed, if we use commas, then HyperTalk's items will
work very nicely (we are now restricting the demonstration to use only commands that have
no commas in them). Here's how we imagine demo:

```
on demo
    say "-- this is what the turtle does,draw,fd 150,setheading 135"
    repeat with i = 1 to 3
        say "-- then this,fd,rt"
    end repeat
    say "-- and finally this ...,fd,beep,wait 2 seconds,draw"
end demo
```

The handler for say is simple. We convert the items in its parameter to be lines in a variable
code, then answer code so that the user can see what it is about to be run, then do code to
get HyperCard to actually do it:

```
on say whatsit
  put empty into code
  repeat with i = 1 to number of items in whatsit
    put item i of whatsit into line i of code
  end repeat
  answer code
  do code
end say
```

5.4 Nice turtle demonstrations

After all that work, we ought to be able to get some nice demonstrations for the turtle graphics stack. (We gave the handler for a snowflake earlier.) Here are some more ideas.

A tree

A tree has branches. A fractal tree is a tree whose branches are smaller versions of itself. To give our tree a pleasant 'lean into the wind' we define left and right branches slightly differently; furthermore, as we go up the tree we draw with a finer and finer pen. Thus the trunk is thick and sturdy, but the highest branches are slender.

With this fairly complicated drawing, you'll need to do some fiddling with the 'magic numbers' 20 and 18 and the others to start the tree growing in the right place and to fit nicely on the card. The numbers shown here are for the standard 512 by 342 card size.

```
on turtle
  setpos 320, 341
  tree 20, 18, 8 -- draw tree
end turtle
```

Recall that our turtle graphics package in the background script automatically calls the handler turtle on getting the openCard message; just by writing this handler in the card script ensures that the turtle will be initialized and our handler will be called automatically when the card is opened.

A tree has left and right branches which are recursively defined to be smaller trees:

```
on tree len, ang, level
  if level = 0 then exit tree
  lt ang
  lbranch len, ang, level-1
  rt 2*ang
  rbranch len, ang, level-1
  lt ang
end tree
```

```
on lbranch len, ang, level
   pen level
   fd 2*len
   tree len, ang, level
   pen level
   bk 2*len
end lbranch

on rbranch len, ang, level
   pen level
   fd len
   tree len, ang, level
   pen level
   bk len
end rbranch
```

If you want to simplify the script, it's not difficult to make a single handler that does the work of both lbranch and rbranch by using another parameter to indicate which you want.

A Pythagorean tree

We got the following beautiful drawing after 42 minutes on a Mac IIx. It is based on a 3:4:5 right-angled triangle, where (as in the theorem of Pythagoras) a square is drawn on each side. Each square has a smaller triangle drawn on its opposite side, which in turn has two more squares on it, and so on and on, getting smaller and smaller, until we're just drawing dots.

The diagram on the left shows the base shape; the one on the right is the fractal version.

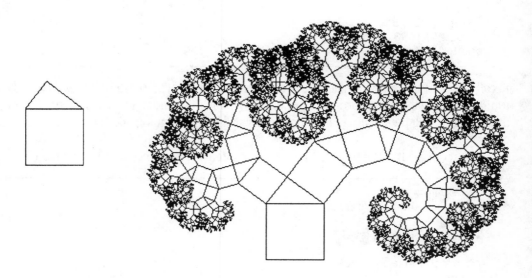

```
on turtle
  global a
  rt
  put 180*atan(3/4)/pi+90 into a
  setpos 200,330
  pythag 60
end turtle
```

The lines marked with the four dots (••••) in the handler below are the recursive calls. If they are replaced by calls to fd, then pythag does not recurse and instead draws the base shape. Pythag recurses with n decreasing (by a factor of 3/5 or 4/5), and it stops when n=1 because it would be pointless (literally) to try to draw something smaller than one pixel! By changing the condition n > 1 to something larger (say n > 4) the drawing process is considerably speeded up, though with a corresponding loss of fine detail.

```
on pythag n
  global a
  if n > 1 then
    fd n
    lt
    fd n
    lt
    fd n
    rt a
    pythag (3*n)/5 -- ••••
    rt
    pythag (4*n)/5 -- ••••
    rt 270-a
    fd n
    lt
    fd n
    lt
    fd n
  else fd n
end pythag
```

We use a global variable a for the relevant angle of the 3:4:5 triangle. You can change the atan(3/4), used in the handler turtle, to other values, say atan(u/v): when u = 1 and v = 1, the angle a will be 45° and the drawing will be symmetrical. You would also have to modify the recursive calls to pythag accordingly, changing the 5 to sqrt(u*u+v*v). Originally we wrote 5 directly, knowing it was sqrt(3*3+4*4), the length of the longest side of a right-angled triangle with other sides 3 and 4.

Polyspirals

Polyspirals are rather like polygons but they are drawn with each side getting longer and longer. Unlike ordinary polygons, they don't 'join up' but grow bigger and bigger. Very pretty pictures can be made when the lines cross over (which happens when the angle between sides is acute).

The script for polyspirals keeps on drawing until the turtle 'drops off the card'. We need a new function, turtleVisible() to find out whether the turtle is visible on the card. It's easy to implement in the turtle background, and it can become one of our turtle utilities:

```
function turtleVisible
    return turtlepos() is within the rect of this card
end turtleVisible
```

Being within the rect of this card doesn't always mean the turtle is visible to the user! The menu bar may be in the way; you can hide it by putting hide menubar in the script somewhere, for instance in the openCard handler.

Make a card field help (positioned near the bottom of the card, say, out of the way of the main drawing area), and then put the rest of the polyspiral script into the card script:

```
on turtle
    put "To stop hit" && numToChar(17) & "+. then choose browse tool," ¬
    && "but let it run a few times!" into card field "help"
    repeat forever
        draw
        polyspi 10+random(40), random(179)
    end repeat
end turtle
```

We use a script to construct the text in the help field rather than typing it in directly! Normally one would type it in, but since it's hard to type the command symbol, it is easier to get HyperTalk to get the symbol from its numeric value: numToChar(17) gets the character in question.

The call to polyspi in the turtle handler above asks for polyspirals with sides initially randomly between 11 and 50, turning an angle of somewhere between 1 to 179 degrees. (180 would result in a straight line, a degenerate polyspiral.)

The handler for polyspi is simple: just persevere drawing the polyspiral until the turtle goes outside the card window. It's important to note that this repeat ... while loop will eventually stop since side gets longer and longer and eventually would be longer than the sides of the card, so the turtle will eventually (perhaps after 511 steps!) get outside and turtleVisible() will then definitely be false.

```
on polyspi side, angle
  repeat while turtleVisible()
    fd side
    rt angle
    add 1 to side
  end repeat
end polyspi
```

The **idle** message is sent whenever HyperCard isn't doing anything else. In this case, it will be sent if the user types **command–.** to stop polyspi and then changed over to the browse tool. (**Idle** is not sent when any tool other than browse is selected.) We use **idle** to move the user onto the next card's turtle graphics demonstration.

```
on idle
  choose browse tool
  go next card
end idle
```

Here are some typical polyspirals it will draw:

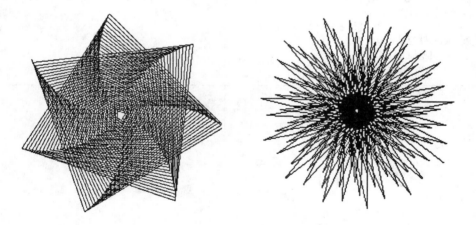

Combining turtle and HyperCard graphics

Finally, overleaf is a quick example of the sophisticated effects that can be achieved combining turtle graphics (used to draw the snowflake outline) with standard HyperCard paint graphics, used to fill successive snowflakes with patterns.

Snowflakes were drawn in increasing sizes, each one filled. A snowflake is drawn, filled, and then cut (hence held on the clipboard). The next snowflake is drawn and filled with a different pattern. Then the clipboard is pasted back, placing the previous, smaller, snowflake 'on top of' the current snowflake. You'll have to work out how to get all the snowflakes drawn

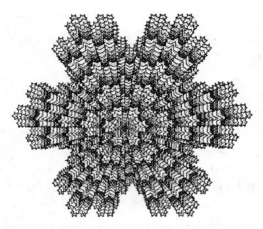

from the same centre, but basically the following code is placed inside a **repeat** loop, with **n** increasing to draw the snowflakes with successively increasing sizes. (You can't draw the bigger snowflakes first, since their fillings would mix up and the bucket tool would not get the desired effects – but do try it to see what happens!)

```
doMenu select
doMenu cut picture
snowflake n
set the pattern to 11-2*(n div 10 mod 6)
choose bucket tool
click at 256,171
doMenu paste picture
```

CHAPTER 6

Timing Scripts

Making things more efficient

Sometimes it is important to make HyperCard run as fast as we can. It's therefore a good idea to make a stack to find out exactly what styles of HyperTalk programming are faster and which slower. Saying get 5 is about 30% faster than saying put 5 into it, even though both do exactly the same thing. Generally, using it is faster than using a variable, though if you need to use variables, global variables are slightly faster than local variables (not allowing for the housekeeping you need: globals may be faster, but they may not do exactly what you want). Both are faster than fields.

6.1 Timing: just how efficient are scripts?

In HyperTalk it is fairly easy to time something:

```
put the ticks into startTime
something
put the ticks into endTime
answer "It took" && (endTime-startTime)/60 && "seconds"
```

If the HyperTalk code being timed is pretty fast, say a single put, then we need to start worrying about the time taken to do the sums, like the put the ticks into endTime. Things are worse than this, since although dividing the ticks by 60 appears to give us a time to within $1/60$ of a second, we might have just missed a tick at the start and end of the timing: that means that we can be out by as much as $1/30$ second, even assuming that the ticks is running accurately to sixtieths of seconds. On a 20 MHz 68030 Mac put statements have timings around 0.001 s, so being somewhere within 0.03 s is not good enough. We'll have to do better.

To be more accurate, the something that is being timed must be done more than once. If we do it ten times, say, then we can divide the total number of ticks taken by 10, and hence improve the accuracy to $1/300$ of a second, that is, to within 0.003 s. Running a put 100 times our timing figures may be out by 30%; running it 1000 times we can get timing to within 3% or so.

Still there is a subtle problem: the following script does not time **something** running 1000 times:

```
put the ticks into startTime
repeat 1000 times
  something
end repeat
put the ticks into endTime
answer "It took" && (endTime-startTime)/60000 && "seconds"
```

It includes the time taken to run around the **repeat** loop, and that can be a considerable fraction of the time taken for the something itself. But doing this sort of thing you can discover that **repeat 1000 times** is about 70% faster than **repeat with i = 1 to 1000** (i.e., it takes 30% of the time).

HyperCard compiles scripts the first time they are run: this means that the first script timing may be awry because it includes the compilation time. On a slow Mac with a stack of many large scripts we may want to find out about compilation times to make them as fast as possible! However, the compiler is probably going to be revised with future releases of HyperCard and it's not clear much would be gained by trying to compile more quickly. We should take all these points into consideration when designing a HyperTalk-timing system.

Let's now turn to consider what we want the user interface to look like. It's going to be useful to be able to compare the timings of at least two ways of scripting something. We might therefore have two fields that we can type HyperTalk into, and buttons to time the scripts therein. A nice frill will be for the stack to indicate clearly which is the faster script, and by how much. Here is our design:

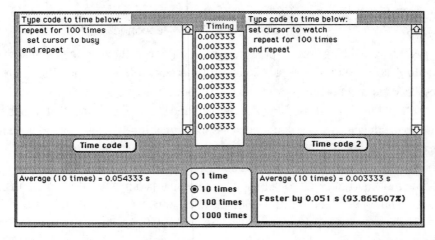

Imagine a user typing a script into one field, timing it, and then trying a supposedly faster version in the other field. With two fields it is easy to find which is fastest. The user would probably copy the fastest script to the other field, then try and improve one copy of it, and so forth, gradually getting the script faster and faster – and hopefully keeping it doing the same thing, not introducing any bugs!

We want to be able to find out such facts as:

```
repeat for 100 times
   set cursor to busy
end repeat
```

is *much* slower (about 13 times slower) than:

```
set cursor to watch
repeat for 100 times
end repeat
```

and by how much.

There is a trade-off between accuracy and how long we take over the timings. We saw above that if something is timed just once, our times can be out by 1/30 s (0.03 s) and that this error decreases the more repetitions we time – but this takes longer to do. Yet we don't know whether the user wants 'quick and dirty times' or 'slow and accurate times'; we should therefore provide a convenient way of controlling the number of repeats, say choosing 1, 10, 100 or 1000 repeats using radio buttons.

6.2 Implementing the timer

Let's create two fields to hold the scripts to be timed; call them **"code1"** and **"code2"**. Each will have a button that runs the timing system on the HyperTalk code in that field:

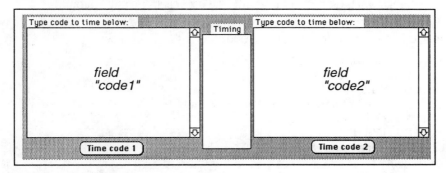

Since each field must be timed in exactly the same way, and because we don't want to write out tricky code twice, the two buttons will use a common handler, simply telling it which field to get the test code from:

```
on mouseUp                    on mouseUp
   doTime 1                      doTime 2
end mouseUp                   end mouseUp
```

We need a group of radio buttons to set the number of times a test in run for. We'll have four buttons:

Each button needs to highlight itself and, of course, unhighlight the others. If a handler **unsetTimes** unhighlights all four buttons, then each button can have a **mouseUp** handler like this:

```
on mouseUp
  unsetTimes
  set the hilite of me to true
end mouseUp
```

where unsetTimes is:

```
on unsetTimes
  set the hilite of card button "1 time" to false
  set the hilite of card button "10 times" to false
  set the hilite of card button "100 times" to false
  set the hilite of card button "1000 times" to false
end unsetTimes
```

This approach is 'fail safe' since if, accidentally, more than one button somehow gets highlighted, things will be sorted out next time the user clicks on any button.

Within the timing handler, which we'll call **doTime**, we'll need to convert which button is highlighted into numbers for the timing code and for the timing calculations:

```
if the hilite of card button "1 time" then
    put 0 into r
    put 60 into d
else if the hilite of card button "10 times" then
    put 1 into r
    put 600 into d
else if the hilite of card button "100 times" then
    put 2 into r
    put 6000 into d
else
    put 3 into r
    put 60000 into d
end if
```

Another way of doing this would be for r and d to be globals and for the buttons to set their values accordingly. Although it may be 'neater' so far as **doTime** is concerned, it will make the code of **doTime** more obscure: we need to use the values of r and d, and it will be handy to see in a single script how they are initialized. Here d is the number to divide the ticks with to get a value in seconds; **r** is the power of ten that gives the number of repetitions, that is 10^r is 1, 10 or 100 depending on how many repetitions we want. We use **r** to make 10^r copies of the script to be timed.

If **f** is the parameter of **doTime**, then we can get the script from field **code1** or **code2** by **get card field ("code" & f)**. Next, we need to repeat the script in it once, ten times or one hundred times. The best way to do this is to have a repeat loop that increases the size of it by a factor of 10. To do this, the variable **a** is made to be twice as long as it, then the variable **b** is made to be four times as long as it (by using **a** twice). Finally, getting two copies of **b** and one of **a** makes it 10 times longer:

```
repeat r times
    put it & return & it into a
    put a & return & a into b
    get b & return & b & return & a -- the script in it is now ten times longer
end repeat
```

We need to put the script in it somewhere where it can be run and timed. We could write **do it**. This idea has two problems: logically, the script in it might change some of our variables (for instance, it might **get 5**, in which case we lose our script that is supposed to be in it!), and, since we want accurate timings, we need to separate compilation time from running time. It is probably better to put the script we've built in it into a handler (say, in the script of the field it came from): this solves the variable clash problem (the handler will have its own it and own local variables). It also means we can force HyperCard to compile the script by sending it a message, then subsequently we can time actual runs of the script without HyperCard recompiling it. So we sandwich the script between 'on x' and 'end x', and then, having stored the script in the field, run it by **send "x" to field "code1"** or field **"code2"**.

We want to get accurate timings, without timing how long **send "x"** takes as well. We use a global variable **results** in the **x** handler to time the script. The following diagram shows how timing **get 5** ten times works. First, it is repeated ten times, then it is bundled into a handler **x** that puts the total time taken into the global variable **results**.

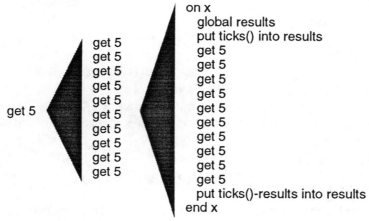

```
                                          on x
                                              global results
                                              put ticks() into results
                        get 5                 get 5
                        get 5                 get 5
                        get 5                 get 5
                        get 5                 get 5
                        get 5                 get 5
            get 5       get 5                 get 5
                        get 5                 get 5
                        get 5                 get 5
                        get 5                 get 5
                        get 5                 get 5
                                              put ticks()-results into results
                                          end x
```

Doing this is just routine tacky HyperTalk:

```
put "on x" & return & "global results" & return ¬
& "put ticks() into results" & return before it
put return & "put ticks()-results into results" & return & "end x" after it
set script of card field ("code" & f) to it
```

If a script is expanded a thousandfold to time it very accurately, there is a danger that the handler that is constructed will exceed HyperCard's limit on the size of scripts, which is currently 32000 characters. If a user tries timing a long script, there's a danger that HyperCard will come up with the obscure error message "can't set that field property" – meaning we've tried to set the script property of the field to something so long that HyperCard can't cope with it. Since HyperCard may be changed one day to be more generous, the best way of scripting is:

```
if number of chars in it > 32000 then
    put it into temp -- because answer is about to lose it
    beep
    answer "Warning! Probably too difficult for this version of HyperCard"
    get temp -- restore old value of it
end if
set script of card field ("code" & f) to it
```

We next get HyperCard to compile the script:

```
send "x" to card field ("code" & f) -- to compile the handler
```

Once we have a compiled script, we can run it to get the timing results. If we run it a few times, our timings will be more accurate:

```
-- repeat the timings 10 times and average the results
put return into card field "timings"
repeat with i = 1 to 10
    send "x" to card field ("code" & f)
    put results/d & return after last line of card field "timings"
end repeat

put 0 into s
repeat with i = 1 to 10
    add line i of card field "timings" to s
end repeat
divide s by 10
```

We put the individual timings into a field so that the user is kept informed of progress (if any!). You can also work out the standard deviation if you want to.

We want to display the timing like 'Average (10 times) = 0.008 s' or 'Average (1 time) = 0.005 s'. We carefully say 'times' or 'time', and it's easiest to invent a function (plural) to get the English grammar right:

```
-- display the results
put "Average (" & d/60 & " time" & plural(d/60) & ") = " & s && "s" ¬
into card field ("results" & f)
```

The function plural is trivial (but very handy – like the version given in Chapter 1):

```
function plural n
  if n = 1 then return empty
  return "s"
end plural
```

Incidentally, the two fields **results1** and **results2** are not locked: that makes it easy for people like the authors of this book to cut-and-paste timing results into a book about HyperTalk timings!

Finally, we want to show the user which script is the fastest (it's not likely, but the two scripts might also be the same speed):

```
-- which is faster?
put s into line f of card field "bothresults"
get card field "bothresults"
if line 1 of it < line 2 of it then
  put line 2 of it - line 1 of it into d
  put "Faster by" && d  && "s (" & d*100/line 2 of it & "%)" ¬
  into line 3 of card field "results1"
  set the textStyle of line 3 of card field "results1" to bold
  put empty into line 3 of card field "results2"
  set style of card field "results1" to shadow
  set style of card field "results2" to rectangle
else if line 1 of it > line 2 of it then
  put empty into line 3 of card field "results1"
  put line 1 of it - line 2 of it into d
  put "Faster by" && d && "s (" & d*100/line 1 of it & "%)" ¬
  into line 3 of card field "results2"
  set the textStyle of line 3 of card field "results2" to bold
  set style of card field "results2" to shadow
  set style of card field "results1" to rectangle
else
  repeat with i = 1 to 2
    put "Same speed" into line 3 of card field ("results" & i)
    set the textStyle of line 3 of card field ("results" & i) to bold
    set style of card field ("results" & i) to rectangle
  end repeat
end if
```

Setting the **textStyle** helps highlight the improvement, for example:

```
Average (10 times) = 0.003333 s

Faster by 0.051 s (93.865607%)
```

6.3   Accessing objects and using 'go'

The stack we developed above (just one card) is suitable for finding out about the timings of simple HyperTalk scripts; it is intended for **repeats**, **ifs**, and so on. It shows its limitations if we try timing a **go**, since we may well end up somewhere else! To be precise, we should know where we are before sending **x** to the script, and then come back afterwards.

There are several ways of going from one card to another. Which is best? As with referring to objects generally it is fastest to refer to cards by their ID, then by their number, then by their name. This is a shame, if not perverse, since from a programming point of view the ID, though fastest, is the most obscure; and the name, which is clearest, is the slowest!

Since HyperTalk is compiled this result is very surprising! The compiler doesn't take advantage of converting nice programming (using object names) into something it can run fast (like IDs). Probably the designers were worried that some scripts might change the names of objects: for example, if we have a button X with number 3, then we rename button 1 to be X, references in the script to button X should now change from number 3 to 1. Buttons are renumbered when they are brought closer or sent further back, on the other hand their IDs remain constant. This is all confusing (and makes HyperTalk slow): the best solution would have been to redesign HyperTalk so that it simply didn't work this way and so that it could be compiled efficiently — such a move would also have solved the ambiguity about referring to buttons and other objects whose name is a number but not necessarily the HyperTalk number of the object.

6.4   How to speed up stacks generally

It takes effort to work out how to write fast and reliable HyperTalk, as it does to write fast and reliable programs in any language. It's not always a case of making your scripts go as fast as possible: if you aren't going to use them often, don't forget that you should include the time you take to write the scripts. If you are writing scripts for other people, however, it is always worth seeing if you can find any improvements.

This section gives several hints for improving the speed and reliability of HyperTalk scripts.

Stopping HyperCard's extra activities

As well as running your HyperTalk script, HyperCard is probably busy sending messages (like **openCard**) as your script goes from card to card; it is probably drawing on the Mac screen, redrawing the tool and pattern palettes; and so on. You don't always need HyperCard to be doing this unless you like watching it.

In a complicated stack, you will want to switch off all superfluous HyperCard activities before embarking on anything complex; contrariwise, afterwards you should restore things to normal (so that **Back** and **Recent** in the **Go** menu work properly for the user). This suggests that you should have two handlers for general use – either put them in the stack script (where they will stay with the stack that uses them) or put them in Home or in a stack you always use (as with **start using "tools"**). We call the handlers **toComputer** and **toUser** respectively:

```
on toComputer
  set cursor to busy
  set lockScreen to true
  set lockMessages to true
  set lockRecent to true
end toComputer

on toUser
  set cursor to normal
  set lockScreen to false
  set lockMessages to false
  set lockRecent to false
  send openCard to this card
end toUser
```

HyperCard keeps track of how many times you try to **lock** and **unlock** the screen, and only really unlocks it when it has been unlocked at least as many times as it has been locked, or when it returns to the idle state (see Appendix A). This is usually what you want in stacks, but if you are writing general purpose handlers like **toComputer** and **toUser**, you need to decide what *you* want to happen. Either **toUser** should *really* unlock the screen (because it is called 'to user', and the user wants to see the current screen, which can only be seen if the screen is really unlocked) or, following HyperCard's view, you don't want to unlock the screen if it was already locked when **toComputer** was first called.

For the first view, you need a handler like:

```
on toUser -- really unlock everything
  set cursor to normal
  repeat while not the lockScreen
    unlock screen
  end repeat
  set lockRecent to false
  set lockMessages to false
  send openCard to this card
end toUser
```

For the second view, we shouldn't necessarily **unlock** the other properties. There are various solutions, most reliably using global variables to save the values of the properties in **toComputer** and then restore them in **toUser**. But this is the simplest approach:

```
on toUser -- don't unlock if any handler wants it still locked
   unlock screen
   set lockMessages to the lockScreen
   set lockRecent to the lockScreen
   if the lockScreen then set cursor to busy -- spin the busy ball again
   else set cursor to normal
   send openCard to this card
end toUser
```

On returning things to normal (with **toUser**) whichever way, we send an **openCard** message to the current card. In some stacks (that don't do things with **openCard**!) this won't be necessary, but having **set lockMessages to true** in **toComputer**, we may have landed on a new card without opening it properly. Conversely, you may want to check that you are not sending **openCard** again to the card you started on: to do this, simply use a global variable that you set to the card ID in **toComputer**, then, in **toUser**, use **if cardID ≠ the ID of this card then send openCard to this card**. It's important to use the card ID (not its number or name) since card IDs are unique; if your scripts have moved cards around, by sorting them perhaps, you could easily end up on a card with the original number but which, however, was actually a different card.

Efficient scripting

A rule of thumb is that each line of your script takes time, and each word on a line takes time. So although it is faster to use **it** than a variable, the two lines **get a**, **put it** will be slower than **put a**. Also, referring to a field will take longer than referring to a variable; referring to a field in another stack will take even longer. Try and do it once if you need to. The same rule – making your scripts shorter speeds them up – correctly suggests that **add 1 to x** is faster than **put 1+x into x**.

HyperTalk lets you write names without quote marks; you can say **field fred** and **field "fred"**, and they mean the same thing unless **fred** is a variable. Nevertheless, HyperCard has to decide whether **fred** is a variable or not, and this takes time that you can save by using quotes: **"fred"** is *never* a variable. So: using quoted names is faster, as well as safer.

When you call standard HyperCard functions you are allowed to use **the** or **()** forms: as in **the time** or **time()**. Since the form **the time** cannot be a user-defined function (there is no way you can write functions to intercept **the abbreviated time**) HyperTalk sends it directly to HyperCard. To speed scripts up, then, you can write all standard HyperCard functions using the **the** form. This saves the time of having a look in all the card, background and various stack scripts to see if the functions are otherwise defined.

Exploiting HyperTalk's script compiler

Very often it's necessary to test that two values are both true, as in, **if interesting() and worthwhile() then something**. If, however, **interesting()** is false, then there is no way that something will get done! But HyperTalk will still waste time deciding if it's **worthwhile()**. HyperTalk always evaluates both sides of an **and**. You can do better by writing: **if interesting() then if worthwhile() then something**, since here the function **worthwhile()** is only called if **interesting()** is found to be **true**.

  Handlers are compiled when they are first used (this may change in subsequent versions of HyperCard; maybe scripts will be compiled when any handler in them is used). The consequence of this is that careful design of handlers can reduce the time they take to compile. A handler may have a **repeat** loop whose body may or may not be executed, or there may be an **if** statement, that may be true or false. If the condition is false, HyperCard is not going to run

Slower to compile, faster to run:	Faster to compile, slower to run:

if decision then
 line1
 line2
 ...
end if
	if decision then doit
	
	 :
	
	on doit
	 line1
	 line2
	 ...
	end doit

the commands in the **if** statement, and it would have been a waste of time compiling them. In such cases, replace scripts that may not be executed with calls to handlers. The calls can be compiled fast, and the original code will only be compiled when – if – the handler gets called. Or imagine a handler with an **if** command, with two big branches. When HyperCard compiles this, it has to compile both alternative branches of the **if** before it can do anything. Instead, if both branches are replaced with their own handlers, there is only one word to compile for each (very fast). Then, when the original handler is run, at most one of these handlers need be compiled.

Doing explicit calculations

Despite HyperTalk being compiled, the compiler doesn't attempt to do calculations to speed up scripts. For example, if you need to work out the area of a card you might write **get 512*342**. Although the compiler could in principle replace this by **get 175104** (it can in principle do sums at least as well as you can!) it doesn't. That means that if you are desperate for speed improvements, you can work out and simplify all of your commands. You may get the scripts to go faster, but you run the risk that you will make mistakes working out the **512*342** and other sums – you may also forget what **175104** was supposed to be if you ever need to change the size of the card (so at least you should leave a comment, as in **get 175104 -- 512*342**).

  If a sum is only worked out once, there is generally little reason to speed it up, but if it is in a repeat loop it may be worked out lots of times, then it can be worthwhile to 'take it out,' as we explain how to do next.

In the following example, we have taken the sum **512*342** out of the lefthand repeat loop. In the righthand script, the sum is only worked out once, as against the lefthand script which does 9999 times more multiplications than necessary! With more complex examples you can get dramatic improvements.

```
repeat for 10000 times          put 512*342 into area
    something 512*342           repeat for 10000 times
end repeat                          something area
                                end repeat
```

Compacting stacks

A good way (good because it's so easy) of speeding a stack up is to compact it. An uncompacted stack, especially if it is a big one, can be rather slow. Compacting a stack speeds it up (it also takes up less disk space which is useful too). Unfortunately compacting a stack – which you do by saying doMenu "compact stack" – is slow in itself, so you won't want to do it too often! Typically, you might look at the freeSize of this stack and if this seems excessive, say over 8000, then compact the stack; alternatively look at the ratio of freeSize to the total size of the stack and compact if it is more than 20%.

```
if the freeSize of this stack/the size of this stack > 0.2 then
    get visible of the message window
    put the message into oldMessage
    beep
    put "Please wait while stack is compacted ..."
    doMenu "compact stack"
    put oldMessage into msg
    set visible of the message window to it
end if
```

This approach is not intrusive; but if compacting the stack in question tends to take a lot of time, in deference to the user, you should ask as well:

```
answer "Now's a good time to compact this stack ... do you want to wait?" ¬
with "Cancel" or "OK"
if it = "OK" then doMenu "compact stack"
```

Another important way to save space is to put empty into any global variables you've finished with. Global variables stay around throughout a HyperCard session, even after the stack that created them has long since been closed. Yet the globals that a closed stack created will still be around, consuming valuable space. Chapter 11 shows you how to find out what globals your stack uses: use a similar method and write a closeStack handler that puts empty into each one (or, better, also put empty into each global at the earliest opportunity when you have done with it).

Making a stack look faster

If you can see what HyperCard is doing, time seems to pass much faster! In other words, if you are doing some complex drawing the user may prefer to watch it happen, rather than wait with nothing else to do than get impatient for some action – however much you have managed to speed it up. If something takes an awfully long time, tell the user that HyperCard will beep when it has finished: then the user can stop watching the screen and do something else more useful. If a script involves both producing results and doing some complicated work, try and show the results first, as this will give the user something to look at and ponder while the stack gets on with the other work. Set the cursor to busy from time to time, as this reassures the user that something is still happening.

Versions of HyperCard

All of the preceding discussion was based on the version of HyperCard we were using when we wrote this. Later versions may change; indeed, you may even be working with an older version. When you make a stack fast and efficient, you must be aware that your experiments are done on the particular version of HyperCard you have, and other versions may be subtly different. It is possible to put a lot of effort into making some script beautifully efficient, only to discover that HyperCard's next version works out a detail you have relied on in some completely different way. In the worst case, your stack may not work as you expect.

A stack should check that the version gives a value it expects. Stacks should include this sort of check in their openstack script:

```
if the version < 2.1 then
    answer "This stack was designed for HyperCard Version 2.1" ¬
    & return & "You have HyperCard version" && the version ¬
    & return & "Proceed with caution, if at all." with "Abort" or "OK"
    if it = "Abort" then
        doMenu "Quit HyperCard" -- or go to stack Home to be lenient
    end if
end if
```

(The final if command is written on two lines and has, therefore, an end if. If we had written it on one line, as is generally possible, the end if required for the *second* if would have been parsed as an end if for the *first* if statement. This is the so-called dangling else problem, which actually refers to the confusion – also present in HyperTalk – of which if some elses should be associated with.)

6.5 Plotting results

Very often the speed of a script isn't enough to decide whether it is faster or slower than another script. It may just happen to be faster for the number of cards (number of lines in a field, or whatever) you tested it on; but with a different number of cards it might get *much* slower, or even faster. In general, we need to know how the timings vary with the amount of work the script is supposed to be doing. If we double the number of cards in the stack, will the speed halve or quarter? These sorts of question are essential when you go from a prototype stack with perhaps ten cards in to a full-blown database with several thousand cards in: you may be disappointed how speed deteriorates as the stack is scaled up. Indeed, a small stack may be impressively fast, but completely different HyperTalk 'tricks' (algorithms) may be necessary to get it to work well enough when it is enlarged to its working size.

A first step in finding out how your scripts behave is to plot graphs of their times: you plot time against number of cards (or whatever varies with the data, perhaps the size of fields). The next chapter describes in detail how we can get HyperCard to plot graphs, but here it is worth discussing a few of the common timing graphs to look out for. They are shown in the table on the last page of this chapter.

The *Timing Graphs* stack that was used to plot these standard graphs is illustrated below. Horizontally, we measure the number of cards, and vertically the time the script takes.

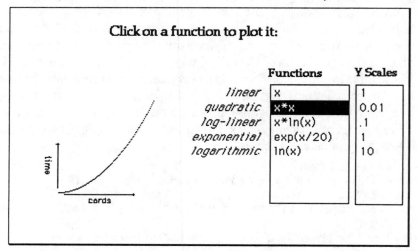

Of course, we have some scaling to do to get the lines plotted to stay within the graphing area. We plot the graphs on the card picture. The axes and the various labels are drawn in the background picture so that they will remain when the card picture is cleared. The names, expressions and Y scales for the various functions are in card fields. The user can add more functions by unlocking the fields.

The graphs are plotted by the **mouseUp** handler in the **Functions** field:

```
on mouseUp
    get the clickLine -- 'it' now contains, e.g. "line 2 of card field 1"
    select it
    hiliteSelection -- hiliteSelection is defined below
    put value(it) into aFunction -- aFunction now contains, e.g. "x*x"
    if aFunction ≠ empty then
        put line word 2 of it of card field "Y Scales" into yScale
        -- yScale now contains the corresponding line from
        -- the "Y Scales" field
        put 1 into xScale
        put 50 into xOffset
        put 200 into yOffset
        choose pencil tool
```

```
        doMenu "Select All"
        doMenu "Clear Picture"
        repeat with x = 1 to 100
            click at xOffset+xScale*x,  yOffset-round(yScale*value(aFunction))
        end repeat
        choose browse tool
    else
        beep
    end if
end mouseUp
```

The xOffset and yOffset values are included to plot the graph neatly, away from the edge of the card. The expression round(yScale*value(aFunction)) gets the nearest integer to the value of the function, x*x or whatever the user has selected, scaled by the required factor; x, of course, will be a value taken successively from 1 to 100 because of the repeat loop. (Since HyperCard's vertical coordinates increase coming downwards from 0 at the top of the card, but we want to plot graphs with 0 at the bottom, we subtract the function's value from 200.)

The hiliteSelection handler places a transparent card button (with its hilite property set to true) over the selected line in the Functions field:

```
on hiliteSelection
    put left of me into item 1 of theRect
    put item 2 of selectedLoc() - textHeight of me into item 2 of theRect
    put right of me into item 3 of theRect
    put item 2 of selectedLoc() into item 4 of theRect
    set rect of card button "hiliter" to theRect
end hiliteSelection
```

6.6 Summary

We have described many of the factors that affect the performance of HyperCard stacks. We don't recommend using the optimization techniques described in this chapter all the time; the clarity of your scripts is often a more important consideration, especially when the script is not used frequently enough for its performance to be an issue.

We began by discussing the timing of scripts and we described a general-purpose stack that can be used to time scripts, overcoming many of the pitfalls of using a less systematic approach.

In the last section, we discussed the need to consider the performance of scripts over a range of sizes of stack (or whatever determines the amount of data that the script has to process). This can be examined by collecting timings over a range of stack sizes and plotting a graph. In the next chapter we show how to plot a graph from a set of data values.

Another way to examine the performance of scripts is by analyzing their algorithms (the methods they use to do their tasks). This approach characterizes the performance of a program (time to execute it) as a function of the data size. We have provided a table showing the kinds of results that emerge from such an analysis, and we have shown how to write a script to plot the graphs of functions such as those described in the table.

The proper analysis of algorithms is a complicated business, and for further information we do best to refer you to standard books on the subject – see the *Further Reading* section of this book.

Commonly-occuring timing graphs:

time / cards	A *linear* script. The time it takes increases linearly with the number of cards. This is the sort of timing you'd expect from a script that has to look at each card once or twice.
	A *quadratic* script. The time it takes increases with the square of the number of cards. This is the sort of timing you'd expect from a script that has to look at each pair of cards. Simple sorting scripts will be quadratic, though sorting can often be done better, as in the next graph.
	A *log-linear* script. You can see the upward curve in this plot: it gets slower and slower in comparison with linear, but it isn't as bad as quadratic. Good sorting scripts will be roughly log-linear. Depending on the scales of the graphs, there may be cases (in the early part of the graph) where a quadratic performance is better than a log-linear performance!
	An *exponential* script. The time it takes increases with a power of the number of cards. This is the sort of timing you'd expect from a script that has to look at each subset of cards. You might get this sort of timing from a stack that tries to find all possible matches (say, fitting groups of applicants to jobs) between cards. It's not good news, since the timing goes through the ceiling very quickly, and you may find that you literally have to wait years for the script to process 100 cards!
	A *logarithmic* script. The time it takes increases with the logarithm of the number of cards. This is the sort of timing you'd expect from a script that efficiently searches an ordered stack of cards.

CHAPTER 7

Graphical Techniques

Charts, graphs and diagrams

7.1 Introduction

Bar charts, pie charts and graphs are often used to display business and technical information in graphical form. It's easy to program such graphical presentations in HyperTalk. Having learned the graphical programming techniques described in this chapter you will be able to build stacks that can draw charts directly from the data stored in their fields, and you can apply the same graphical techniques to develop other applications of your choice.

This chapter also describes how to make interactive programs using mouse input to enable a user working interactively to produce block diagrams, electrical circuits and other graphical work.

7.2 HyperCard graphics

Although the painting tools are normally used interactively to place graphics or text in a card or background picture, they can also be used in HyperTalk programs. The graphical techniques introduced in this chapter depend on using HyperCard's painting tools from within HyperTalk programs. This is an example of an important characteristic of HyperTalk – you can do almost anything in HyperTalk that can be done by the user interactively in HyperCard.

If you haven't used the painting tools in HyperCard, try doing so before attempting to write graphical programs in HyperTalk. It's a good idea to be familiar with the straightforward way in which you can produce simple pictures. Remember that the pictures and everything you draw are added to the card picture (or background picture) as pixels – there are no graphical objects or characters in HyperCard's graphics. (HyperCard is like MacPaint rather than MacDraw.) If you want graphical objects as such, these can sometimes be simulated using buttons and fields, see the block diagram editor described in Section 7.5 on page 149 for an example that makes good use of fields as graphical objects and Chapter 8 for a way to produce simple animations using button icons.

Drawing tools are selected in HyperTalk using the **choose tool** command. The currently selected tool itself is manipulated using **click**, **drag** and other mouse-like operations, just as a user would. These operations enable the tools to be controlled from HyperTalk.

The painting tools are only available at user level 3 (*painting*) or greater, so unless you are sure that the user level is already set to 3 or above, type **set userLevel to 3** into the message window before trying to access a painting tool from HyperTalk. (Typically a stack that does graphics will have a **set userLevel to 3** (or more) in its **openStack** handler. We will talk about **openStack** and related issues at length in Chapter 9.)

Click and **drag** are HyperTalk operations that take card coordinate positions as arguments. Coordinates are specified by a pair of integers separated by a comma. Remember that the coordinates are specified relative to the current card window with the first (x) coordinate representing the horizontal offset and the second (y) coordinate representing the vertical offset (down the screen from the top of the card). Thus **"5, 8"** specifies a point that is 5 pixels from the left edge of the card and 8 pixels from the top of the card. Pixels are approximately $1/70$ inch or 0.3 mm across on most Macintosh screens. Standard cards are 512 pixels across and 340 pixels high; the card size, for every card in the stack, can be adjusted to size **x** (wide) by **y** (high) (within certain limits) by **set the rect of this card to 0,0,x,y**.

One way to design a graphical program in HyperTalk is to work out the best way to draw the picture that you want using the HyperCard painting tools in the normal way and then to program the same set of operations in HyperTalk. You may find it useful to draw a template for what you want by hand on the background and then try to get your program to work by drawing on the card picture: this way you will be able to clear the card picture and start again without losing the template or other guidelines you drew on the background. The bucket tool can be used for filling the background with tartan patterns (graph paper) that can be used to help with alignment when you are drawing the template.

A simple graphical program

Suppose that our aim is to produce an oval with an inset cross (a gun sight!) as illustrated below. It doesn't take long to work out how to draw such a picture using the **oval** and **line** painting tools.

Here is a script that uses those tools together with the **drag** operation to produce the required picture:

```
on mouseUp
    choose oval tool                    -- select the oval tool
    drag from 100,100 to 200,300        -- draw the oval
    choose line tool                    -- select the line tool
    drag from 100,200 to 200,200        -- draw a horizontal line
    drag from 150,100 to 150,300        -- draw a vertical line
    choose browse tool
end mouseUp
```

If you can't remember the HyperTalk names for tools, you can select the tool whose name you

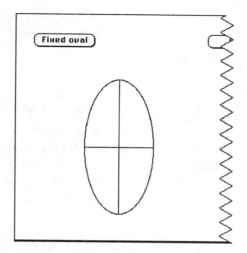

want from the tool palette and then type **the tool** in the message window: this gives you the current tool name; you can then cut and paste the name from the message window into your script. Likewise, you can find out the current painting pattern number by typing **the pattern**.

You may wonder why we would go to the trouble of writing this script when we can do the job more quickly by using the painting tools directly by hand! But this simple graphical program can be generalized to do more things. Here is a general-purpose **drawOval** program derived from the **mouseUp** handler given above:

```
on drawOval p1, p2            -- p1 and p2 should be points:
                              -- each is a pair of integers separated by a comma
    put p1 && p2              -- put the values of p1 and p2 into the message box
                              -- to help debugging
    put item 1 of p1 into x1  -- separate the x and y coordinates of each point
    put item 2 of p1 into y1
    put item 1 of p2 into x2
    put item 2 of p2 into y2
    -- Get the mid-points:
    put x1+trunc((x2-x1)/2) into midx   -- we use trunc to ensure that the coordinates
    put y1+trunc((y2-y1)/2) into midy   -- supplied to drag are whole numbers
    choose oval tool
    drag from p1 to p2        -- draw the oval
    choose line tool
    drag from x1, midy to x2,midy   -- draw the 'gun sight' lines
    drag from midx,y1 to midx,y2
    choose browse tool
end drawOval
```

drawOval takes parameters specifying two points and draws an oval, as before, with an inset cross. Given the **drawOval** handler, the following script is what we need to produce the same picture as our original **MouseUp** handler:

```
on mouseUp
  drawOval "100,100", "200,300"
end mouseUp
```

Each of the points, the pairs of integers, that are the parameters of **drawOval** has been put in quotes – because each parameter must be a separate string. If we hadn't used quotes, HyperCard would think we were passing four parameters to **drawOval**, not two.

The **drawOval** handler can be used to produce ovals in other programs. Here is a simple button script that prompts users to make an oval at any position and with a size of their choice:

```
on mouseUp
  --prompt the user in the message box:
  put "Please click at top left of oval..." into msg
  set cursor to cross          -- show the user that they are now in drawing mode
  wait until mouseClick()              -- wait until the user clicks the mouse button
  put clickLoc() into p1               -- save the top left point
  put "Please click at bottom right of oval..." into msg
  beep                                 -- prompt the user to click again
  wait until mouseClick()              -- wait until the user clicks the mouse button
  put clickLoc() into p2               -- save the bottom right point
  put empty into msg                   -- clear the prompt
  drawOval p1, p2                      -- do the drawing
  choose browse tool
end mouseUp
```

7.3   Graphical presentations of data

Now that we know how to produce simple drawings in HyperTalk, let's see what is involved in producing more sophisticated graphical displays of data such as the bar charts and pie charts that are commonly used in business and line graphs used to present scientific and technical data.

A bar chart script

Bar charts (also known as histograms) provide a simple way to present tabular data in graphical form. Suitable data tables have two columns, one column providing the *labels* to be assigned to the bars and the other column providing the values that determine the heights of the bars.

The illustration on the next page shows a bar chart displaying a set of sales figures sampled at two-year intervals over a twelve-year period. Since our stack will be general purpose, all of the data needed to draw the graph, including the names that identify the types

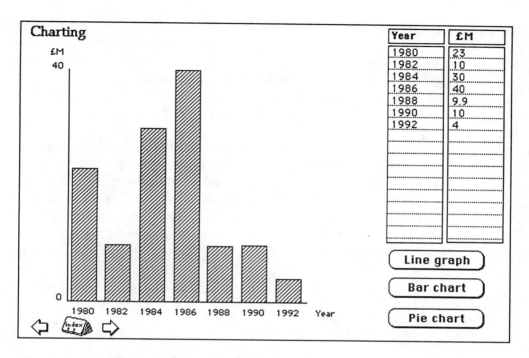

of the data, are held in unlocked fields, allowing users to enter the two columns of data and their names and then click on the **Bar chart** button to produce their chart.

In our stack the two columns of the table are represented by two fields called **X-values** and **Y-values**. The Y values (righthand column) must be numbers (integer or real); the X values (lefthand column) may be any text (not necessarily numeric). The names of the X and Y values are used to label the axes of the chart, and are held in the two fields above, called **label** and **value**.

Here is the **MouseUp** handler for the **Bar chart** button:

```
on mouseUp
   startGraphics                        -- get ready for graphics ...
   put maxLine(fld "Y-values") into YMax-- find the largest Y value
   --draw the axes (drawBarAxes is defined below):
   drawBarAxes fld "X-values", YMax
   set filled to true                   -- set the global drawing property "filled"
   choose rectangle tool                -- prepare to draw rectangles
   set pattern to 14                    -- diagonal stripes
   repeat with i = 1 to number of lines in fld "X-values"-- one bar for each X value
      drawBar i, line i of fld "Y-values" --draw each bar (drawBar is defined below)
   end repeat
   endGraphics                          -- revert to browse mode
end mouseUp
```

The startGraphics handler is a general-purpose handler we've written to make graphics in HyperTalk easier; it does things like hiding the tools palette so that the user is not distracted by it flickering (nor is HyperCard slowed down by refreshing it) and clearing the card so that new graphics can start from scratch. We'll describe it and its twin endGraphics when we have discussed all of the drawing routines – we want startGraphics to be general enough to help with many routines (here, bar charts, pie charts and line graphs) otherwise it wouldn't be worth calling a handler!

The drawBarAxes handler is defined below[†]. We've used our own handler TypeStringAt to save having to choose the text tool, set textAlign and a click at X, Y: each call to TypeStringAt represents four lines of script. On the other hand TypeStringAt chooses the text tool even if it is already chosen, so this represents a bit of wasted time that we could improve on. A section at end of this chapter (Section 7.6 on page 154) discusses optimizations for speeding this sort of operation up – we'll worry about all optimizations together when we've seen all of the scripts that might need improving, rather than worrying right now about what might turn out to be minor details.

```
on drawBarAxes XValues, YMax
    --these globals are initialized in startGraphics:
    global theLeft, theBottom, theRight, theTop
    global Xorigin, Yorigin, XScale, YScale, Barwidth
    -- Set up the WC to DC mapping parameters:
    -- scale factor for x = width of graph/(number of bars)
    put (theRight-theLeft)/(number of lines in XValues) into XScale
    -- scale factor for y = height of graph/maximum y value
    put (theBottom-theTop)/YMax into YScale
    put theLeft+trunc(XScale/2) into XOrigin
    put theBottom into YOrigin
    put max(trunc(3*XScale/4),5) into BarWidth
    choose "Line tool"
    drag from theLeft, theBottom to theRight, theBottom
    drag from theLeft, theBottom to theLeft, theTop
    TypeStringAt "Right", theLeft-5, theBottom, "0"
    TypeStringAt "Right", theLeft-5, theTop, YMax
    TypeStringAt "Right", theLeft-5, theTop-15, bg fld "Value"
    TypeStringAt "Left", theRight+10, theBottom+15, bg fld "Label"
end drawBarAxes
```

maxLine is a function that returns the largest numeric value amongst the sequence of text lines

[†]   In computer graphics terms, the drawBarAxes handler sets up a mapping between a world coordinate (WC) space that is defined by the ranges of x and y values to be presented and a device coordinate (DC) space that is the card space available for the chart. The parameters that define this mapping are computed and placed in global variables by drawBarAxes. DrawBar and any other handlers that may be needed to present the data will accept values in WC, transforming them to DC values for use in the display operations (click and drag).

that is passed as the argument. There are all sorts of ways of defining such a function, but as HyperTalk provides its own **max()** function (which is therefore very efficient), we'll use it. The problem is that **maxLine** takes a list of *lines* but **max** takes a list of *items*:

```
function maxLine theLines          -- return the maximum value
   repeat with i = 1 to number of lines in theLines
      put word i of theLines into item i of it
   end repeat
   return max(it)
end maxLine
```

In the **drawBarAxes** handler we calculate the scale factors and origins to be used in our graph and draw and label the axes, leaving the x and y scale factors and origins in global variables. Now we will define a pair of functions **XTransform** and **YTransform** that will transform x and y coordinate values from World Coordinates to Device Coordinates so that we can write the handlers that actually draw the bar graph entirely in terms of the World Coordinate values in the data fields:

```
function XTransform X               -- transforms X to Device Coordinates
   global XOrigin, XScale
   return trunc(XOrigin + XScale*X)
end XTransform

function YTransform Y               -- transforms Y to Device Coordinates
   global YOrigin, YScale
   return trunc(YOrigin - YScale*Y)
end YTransform
```

These two handlers will be useful not only for drawing bar charts, but also in the construction of line graphs, so we place them in the background script, to enable handlers anywhere in the cards of this background to access them.

In bar graphs the x values are assumed to be labels and the bars are drawn with equal spacing between them and with each bar labelled by one of the x values. To arrive at a width for the bars, we divide the width of the space available for the chart by the number of bars required (that is, the number of separate y values to be presented) allowing a quarter bar width spacing between the bars.

The **drawBar** handler draws rectangles to represent the bars filling them with a suitable pattern selected from the pattern palette using the **select pattern** command. Our global parameters XOrigin, YOrigin, XScale, YScale, BarWidth provide all of the information needed to produce the bar at the right position and with the correct width and height:

```
on drawBar X, Y
   -- draws and labels a single bar in the chart at position X, with height Y
   global YOrigin, BarWidth
```

```
    put xTransform(X-1) - BarWidth div 2 into barLeft
    put yTransform(Y) into barTop
    -- draw the bar:
    choose "Rectangle tool"
    drag from barLeft, YOrigin to barLeft+BarWidth, barTop
    -- label it:
    TypeStringAt "Center", xTransform(X-1), YOrigin+15, line X of fld "X-Values"
  end drawBar
```

A pie chart script

Pie charts present a set of proportions or numeric values as different sized segments of a circle, providing a useful way to visualize items of numeric data in proportion to the total of all the items. Each *y* value is now represented by a segment of the circle whose angle is directly proportional to that value and the segment is labelled with the corresponding *x* value. The illustration below shows a pie chart presenting the same set of sales data that was presented as a bar chart above. The pie chart presentation here helps to show, for instance, that the combined sales for 1984 and 1986 are more than half of the total.

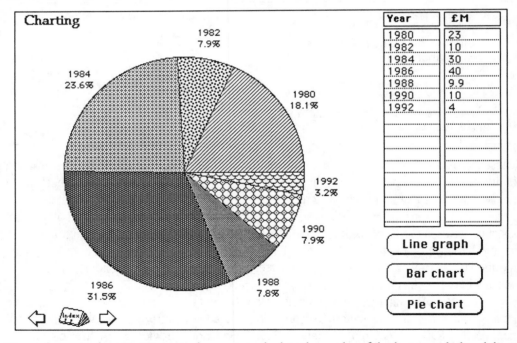

To produce pie charts in HyperCard we must calculate the angles of the lines needed to delimit each segment and then calculate the coordinates of the end-point of the lines from those angles. We will use the **cos** and **sin** functions to perform the calculation. Though it may be unfamiliar, the computation of angles must be in radians, since HyperTalk's **cos** and **sin** functions expect their arguments in radians. The angle at the centre of a full circle of 360 degrees is 2π radians (π = 3.14159, but rather than remember what π is, we'll use HyperTalk's pi), and the angle of the segment representing any proportion y out of y_{total} is therefore $2\pi y$ divided by y_{total}.

Here is the MouseUp handler that contains the main script components. Several new handlers are used: drawPieCircle, drawRadius, SumLines, FillSegment and LabelSegment. We shall define drawRadius and FillSegment, leaving the others as an exercise for the reader (unless you have our disk!).

```
on mouseUp
  startGraphics                    -- Clear the graphics area and initialize
  put pi*2 into TwoPi              -- 360 degrees in radians
  put SumLines("Y-values") into TotalY -- get the total of the y values
  put 0 into CurrentAngle
  -- drawPieCircle initializes globals theCentreX, theCentreY, theRadius
  -- and draws a containing circle and an initial radial line:
  drawPieCircle
  -- draw a segment for each X value:
  repeat with i = 1 to number of lines in fld "X-values"
    -- compute the angle:
    put (line i of fld "Y-values")*TwoPi/TotalY into SegmentAngle
    -- draw a bounding line for the segment:
    drawRadius CurrentAngle+SegmentAngle
    FillSegment i, CurrentAngle+SegmentAngle/2 -- fill the segment
    add SegmentAngle to CurrentAngle
  end repeat
  -- prepare to label segments
  set numberFormat to "0.#"
  put 0 into CurrentAngle
  -- label each segment with its X value and its Y value as a percentage
  repeat with i = 1 to number of lines in fld "X-values"
    put (line i of fld "Y-values")*TwoPi/TotalY into SegmentAngle-- position for label
    LabelSegment CurrentAngle+SegmentAngle/2, line i of fld "X-values" ¬
    & return & 100*line i of fld "Y-values"/TotalY & "%" -- make the label
    add SegmentAngle to CurrentAngle
  end repeat
  endGraphics
end mouseUp


on FillSegment theSeg, theAngle    -- theSeg is the number of the segment
                                   -- theAngle is angle of the mid-line of segment
  global theCentreX, theCentreY, theRadius
  -- compute X,Y for a point on the mid-line and just inside the circumference
  put theCentreX + trunc((theRadius-2) * cos(theAngle)) into X
  put theCentreY - trunc((theRadius-2) * sin(theAngle)) into Y
  choose "bucket tool"
  -- choose a different pattern for each segment:
  set pattern to 12 + ((2*theSeg) mod 27)
  click at X,Y                     -- using the bucket tool, this does the fill
end FillSegment
```

```
on drawRadius theAngle          -- theAngle is in radians
   global theCentreX, theCentreY, theRadius
   put trunc(theRadius * sin(theAngle)) into Y
   put trunc(theRadius * cos(theAngle)) into X
   choose "Line Tool"
   drag from theCentreX, theCentreY to theCentreX+X,theCentreY-Y
end drawRadius
```

FillSegment relies on the use of the **Bucket tool** to fill each segment with a pattern. It is important to remember that the bucket tool fills the connected area of the picture surrounding the point at which it is clicked, and it will 'leak out' of any holes. So it is important to ensure that the boundary of each segment is complete, and that we click the bucket tool well within the boundary, even when the segment is very small. We ensure this by choosing a point to start pouring near the bounding circle and by not labelling any of the segments until all of the segments have been filled (since a label could intersect the segment boundary and thus make a hole for paint to leak out).

The patterns available for use by the bucket tool are those in HyperCard's **Patterns** menu. When we select a pattern by program we must specify it by number. So the command **set pattern to 12+((2*theSeg) mod 27)** selects alternate patterns (because adjacent patterns tend to be too similar) whose numbers are derived from the segment number, omitting the first twelve patterns. This produces a diverse range of patterns.

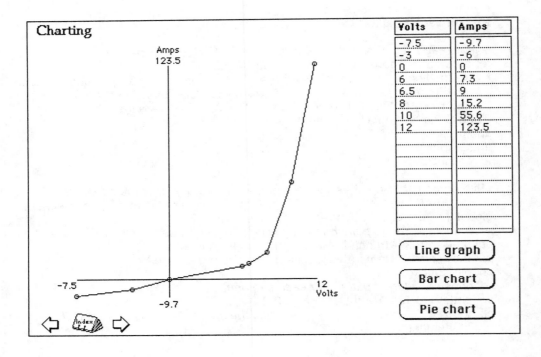

A line graph script

To complete the suite of graphical presentation tools, we'll add a facility to produce simple line graphs that can be used to present business, scientific or technical data.

Line graphs differ from bar and pie charts in several ways. A line graph presentation can be derived from any set of pairs of integers or real numbers. Both the x and the y values must be numeric and they need not be equally spaced. The pairs of numbers are plotted as points in an x–y space and a sequence of lines is drawn to join all of the points in ascending order of their x values. The x and y values may be positive or negative, so we must calculate a position for the origin that allows space for negative values if there are any. This will be done in the drawLineAxes handler.

Here is the mouseUp handler and associated functions for the **Line graph** button:

```
on mouseUp
  startGraphics
  -- sort the data to ensure that the number pairs are in ascending order of x values:
  sortFields "X-values", "Y-values"
  -- get the bounds on X and Y. bounds delivers a pair of items:
  get bounds(fld "X-values")
  put item 1 of it into Xmin
  put item 2 of it into Xmax
  get bounds(fld "Y-values")
  put item 1 of it into Ymin
  put item 2 of it into Ymax
  -- draw axes for a line graph (drawLineAxes is defined below):
  drawLineAxes Xmin, Xmax, Ymin, Ymax
  -- for each point, plot the point and connect it to the previous one (plotPoint and
  -- connect are defined below)
  repeat with i = 1 to number of lines in fld "X-values"
    put xTransform(line i of fld "X-values") into xi
    put yTransform(line i of fld "Y-values") into yi
    PlotPoint xi, yi
    if i > 1 then Connect xPrev, yPrev, xi, yii-- skipping the first point
    put xi into xPrev
    put yi into yPrev
  end repeat
  endGraphics
end mouseUp

on plotPoint x, y                    -- draws a circle of radius 2 at X, Y
  choose "Oval Tool"
  drag from x-2,y-2 to x+2,y+2
end plotPoint

on connect x1, y1, x2, y2            -- draws a line from X1, Y1 to X2 Y2
  choose Line Tool
  drag from x1,y1 to x2,y2
end connect
```

bounds works rather like **maxLine** above, except that it returns **min(it) & "," & max(it)**, finding both maximum and minimum values at once.

The handler for **drawLineAxes** is given below; it is a little more complex than **drawBarAxes**. It positions the origin appropriately when there are negative *x* or *y* values and labels the axes. Various global variables are set to the correct values, taking care not to allow them to be invalidated by negative *x* s and *y* s.

```
on drawLineAxes Xmin, Xmax, Ymin, Ymax
   global theLeft, theBottom, theRight, theTop
   global XOrigin, Yorigin, XScale, YScale
   -- adjust the minimum and maximum values so that they include the origin at (0,0)
   -- this will make drawing the graph's axes a lot simpler
   if Xmin > 0 then put 0 into Xmin
   if Xmax < 0 then put 0 into Xmax
   if Ymin > 0 then put 0 into Ymin
   if Ymax < 0 then put 0 into Ymax
   -- set up the World Coordinate to Device Coordinate mapping
   -- (to be used in XTransform and YTransform)
   put scaleFactor(Xmin, Xmax, theLeft, theRight) into XScale
   put scaleFactor(Ymin, Ymax, theBottom, theTop) into YScale
   put theLeft-trunc(Xmin*XScale) into XOrigin
   put theTop+trunc(Ymax*YScale) into YOrigin
   -- Label the axes with appropriate spacing:
   TypeStringAt "Center", XOrigin, theTop-14, bg fld "Value"
   TypeStringAt "Center", XOrigin, theBottom+12, Ymin
   TypeStringAt "Center", XOrigin, theTop-2, Ymax
   TypeStringAt "Right", theLeft, YOrigin+10, Xmin
   TypeStringAt "Left", theRight, YOrigin+10, Xmax
   TypeStringAt "Left", theRight, YOrigin+20, bg fld "Label"
   -- draw the axes. We do this after the labelling so that the white edges
   -- of text left by the text tool do not damage the lines.
   choose "Line tool"
   drag from theLeft, YOrigin to theRight, YOrigin
   drag from XOrigin, theBottom to XOrigin, theTop
end drawLineAxes

function scaleFactor min, max, bottom, top
   -- computes the WC to DC scale factor required to fit the top and bottom World
   -- coordinates into the max and min Device coordinates
   return abs((top-bottom)/(max-min))
end scaleFactor
```

Plotting requires the *x* values to be in increasing order, otherwise the plot could loop back on itself. A simple insert sort gets the field **keyField** into order:

```
put number of lines in fld keyField into n
   repeat with i = n-1 down to 1
      put line i of fld keyField into a
```

```
        put i into j
        repeat while j < n and a > line j+1 of fld keyField
          put line j+1 of fld keyField into line j of fld keyField
          add 1 to j
        end repeat
        put a into line j of fld keyField
    end repeat
```

As an exercise you might like to modify this text-book sort to use **put after**, so that HyperTalk does the insertion more efficiently – but be warned that you will have fun with **returns** getting lost (because **line i** of a field *excludes* the **return**, but when you insert a new line, it requires the **return**). Since the script operates on fields, we can speed it up much more easily by locking the screen (so the changes to the field can be done without refreshing the screen). Better, we should copy the fields into variables, sort, and then put the variables back into the fields. Whatever, we modify the outline to make the same changes to the *y* values field, so the pairs of values move are sorted together:

```
on sortFields keyField, otherField
    put number of lines in fld keyField into n
    repeat with i = n-1 down to 1
        put line i of fld keyField into a
        put line i of fld otherField into b
        put i into j
        repeat while j < n and a > line j+1 of fld keyField
          put line j+1 of fld keyField into line j of fld keyField
          put line j+1 of fld otherField into line j of fld otherField
          add 1 to j
        end repeat
        put a into line j of fld keyField
        put b into line j of fld otherField
    end repeat
end sortFields
```

Object-oriented programming for checking graph types

Different sorts of graph have different sorts of restriction. Thus a pie chart cannot be used to plot negative values, and a line graph cannot be used to plot non-numeric data, which, however, both a bar and pie chart can handle. How should we best modify our button scripts to check for the various conditions?

Each button starts with a call to the handler **startGraphics**. If this is placed in the stack script, the message **startGraphics** will go via the background of all the charting cards. We can intercept it, check the data is suitable for the chosen graph, and then **pass startGraphics** so that it continues to the stack script. This is good programming, and is one of the advantages of object-oriented languages: we are extending the meaning of **startGraphics** but leaving its original script unchanged – we are not likely to be introducing any bugs into whatever it does.

We easily find out which graph we are trying to draw by looking at the name of the target (where the mouse originally clicked); the first word of the short name of the target will be the word "Bar", "Line" or "Pie" accordingly.

```
on startGraphics -- goes in background script
    put first word of short name of the target into graphType
    -- do the various checks
    pass startGraphics -- continue with the initialization in the stack script
end startGraphics
```

Here are the sorts of things we need to fix up and check for:

```
-- fix Label and Value fields
if number of words in field "Label" = 0 then put "Label" into field "Label"
if number of words in field "Value" = 0 then put "Value" into field "Value"

-- fix blank lines
fixLines "X-values"
fixLines "Y-values"

-- if X and Y values don't match, can't draw a graph of any sort
if number of lines in field "X-values" ≠ number of lines in field "Y-values" then
    answer "You need the same number of entries in '" & field "Label" & ¬
    "' and '" & field "Value" & "' to draw any graph."
    exit to HyperCard
end if

-- if X-values are not all numeric, cannot be Line graph
if graphType = "Line" then
    repeat with i = 1 to number of lines in field "X-values"
        if not (line i of field "X-values" is a number) then
            answer "Some '" & field "Label" & "' entries are not numbers." ¬
            & return & "You can only draw Bar and Pie charts."
            exit to HyperCard
        end if
    end repeat
end if

-- if some Y-values less than zero, cannot be Bar or Pie graph
if "Bar Pie" contains graphType then
    repeat with i = 1 to number of lines in field "Y-values"
        if line i of field "Y-values" < 0 then
            answer "Some '" & field "Value" & "' entries are less than zero." ¬
            & return & "You can only draw Line graphs."
            exit to HyperCard
        end if
    end repeat
end if
```

FixLines deletes trailing blank lines (so that fields end up being exactly the length they look) and replaces any other blank lines with zero:

```
on fixLines f
   get number of lines in field f
   put true into trailing
   repeat while it > 0
      if number of words in line it of field f ≠ 0 then
         put false into trailing
      else
         if trailing then delete line it of field f    -- trailing blank lines
         else put 0 into line it of field f            -- other blank lines
      end if
      subtract 1 from it
   end repeat
end fixLines
```

7.4 Drawing mazes

One sort of maze (mathematically called a *spanning tree*) has exactly one route from everywhere to everywhere else; this means it has no loops, which would permit more than one way to get between some two points. A maze like this is easy to draw, but needs some recursive thinking: you might like to skip the next paragraph and get straight to the HyperTalk!

First draw a border wall around where we intend the maze to be. Draw entrance and exit holes on the border anywhere. If we can get in and out of the maze the design of the maze will guarantee exactly one route from the entrance to the exit, wherever they are placed. To draw the inside of the maze, we have to draw the walls within. If we draw a wall across the maze anywhere, we then have two smaller regions, which we can connect with a gap in the wall. Interestingly, where ever we draw the wall and its gap, there will still be exactly one route from the original entrance to exit, possibly going through the gap we have just drawn. Having split the large box into two, we now have two smaller regions, and in these we can repeat the process: draw any wall with a gap. Each time we draw a wall we split the remaining region into two, and we still preserve the single route through the maze (though probably complicating it). We stop when the regions are smaller than the walls themselves. The pictures below will make this process much clearer.

We initialize things then call **maze** to draw the maze the size and place we want. The numbers given here happen to be suitable for the standard HyperCard card size. We'll use the line tool to draw all the maze's walls, so we set the lineSize to be 8 pixels wide.

```
reset paint
set lionizes to 8
choose line tool
```

```
doMenu "select all"
doMenu "clear picture"
maze 1, 1, 29, 19
```

The handler **maze** draws the four walls (the two vertical walls will have gaps) and then cuts the maze in half. The handler **vgap** draws a vertical line with a gap in it; **hline** draws a horizontal line (as we shall see, and **vgap** uses **vline** to draw its lines).

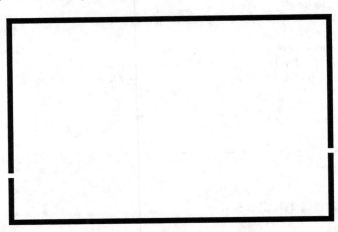

```
on maze x1, y1, x2, y2
    vgap x1, y1, y2                  -- left border and entrance hole
    vgap x2+1, y1, y2               -- right border and exit hole
    hline x1, y1, x2                -- top border
    hline x1, y2+1, x2             -- bottom border
    horizontal x1, y1, x2, y2      -- cut maze in half
end maze
```

Horizontal is given four parameters, the top left **x** and **y**, and the bottom right **x** and **y**

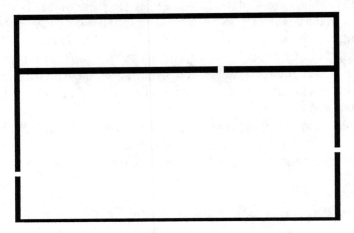

coordinates of the region we are drawing in. If the region is not too narrow to split, we think of somewhere between y1 and y2, that is, a vertical position within the region, and draw the horizontal dividing wall using hgap.

```
on horizontal x1, y1, x2, y2
  if x2 > x1 then
    get somewhere(y1, y2)
    hgap x1, it, x2
    vertical x1, y1, x2, it-1
    vertical x1, it, x2, y2
  end if
end horizontal
```

Next, the top and bottom regions will require division, and for contrast, we divide them with a vertical line.

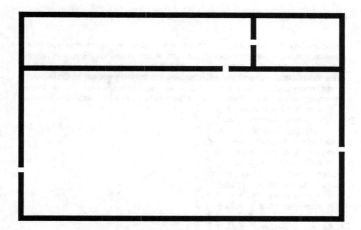

The handler vertical does exactly the same as horizontal, but draws a vertical wall:

```
on vertical x1, y1, x2, y2
  if y2 > y1 then
    get somewhere(x1, x2)
    vgap it, y1, y2
    horizontal x1, y1, it-1, y2
    horizontal it, y1, x2, y2
  end if
end vertical
```

We can let vertical recurse and then look at the drawing just after horizontal's second call to vertical.

Vertical will call horizontal to divide the lower left hand region into two, then

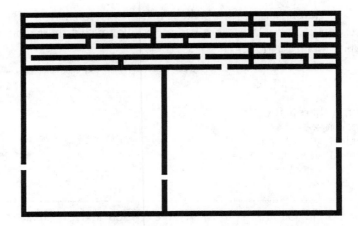

horizontal will recurse, and so on, until the left region is completely drawn. As we hoped, there is only one route through this region, which you can check in the figure below.

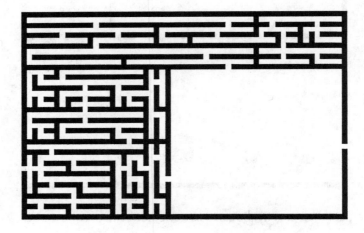

Walls with gaps, done with hgap and vgap, are straightforward if we assume we have handlers hline and vline to draw the horizontal and vertical lines!

```
on hgap x1, y1, x2
  get somewhere(x1, x2)
  hline x1, y1, it-2
  hline it, y1, x2
end hgap

on vgap x1, y1, y2
  get somewhere(y1, y2)
  vline x1, y1, it-2
```

```
    vline x1, it, y2
  end vgap
```

We need the support handlers to draw lines. It is tedious to sort out the arithmetic to ensure lines are drawn properly aligned (allowing for the thickness of the line we are drawing with), and to arrange for the complete maze to be symmetrically placed on the card. Although the arithmetic is tedious, this is the only place the maze scripts convert from world (maze) coordinates to device (HyperCard) coordinates.

```
  on hline x1, y1, x2
    drag from 16*x1+7, 16*y1+4 to 16*x2+23, 16*y1+4
  end hline

  on vline x1, y1, y2
    drag from 16*x1+7, 16*y1+4 to 16*x1+7, 16*y2+20
  end vline
```

Lastly, we need a function to give us random positions between two extremes:

```
  function somewhere a, b
    return a+random(b-a-1)
  end somewhere
```

A '3D' effect

Some HyperCard graphics operations can make the maze look more impressive, as if it is carved in relief as illustrated on the next page. The handler **shadow** developed now is almost self-explanatory.

We first cut the picture (it could be any picture we make a shadow for, but here it will be of the maze we've just drawn). Fill the blank card that's left with a grey pattern (pattern number 22).

Having got a grey card, the picture is pasted back successively in three positions: up a bit and to the left in white, down a bit and to the right in black, and finally back in the original place in grey. The final pasting goes over the black and white images, so their edges sort of peep out round the grey original, giving us the effect we want. Making 3D reliefs is only one of the interesting effects you can get by messing around with HyperCard's graphics; tracing outlines, inverting, rotating and so on all do interesting things ... .

```
  on shadow
    choose select tool
    drag from (topLeft of this card) to (bottomRight of this card) with optionkey
                                -- selects just the black
    doMenu "cut picture"
    doMenu "select all"
```

```
    set pattern to 22
    doMenu "fill"                    -- make grey background
    doMenu "paste picture"           -- the shadow
    drag from 100, 100 to 101, 101    -- move down right
    doMenu "paste picture"
    doMenu "invert"                  -- make it white
    drag from 100, 100 to 99, 99     -- move up left
    doMenu "paste picture"           -- the thing itself
    doMenu "fill"                    -- made grey
  end shadow
```

How to get the same random numbers again

Although we could have messed around with HyperCard's painting tools to make the maze
illustrations by hand, it was far easier to modify the scripts so that we could repeatedly draw
exactly the same maze. We then commented out various lines in the handlers so that the
drawing could stop at suitable places to cut and paste into this book.

Here is one way to do it: somewhere (the handler that generates the random numbers
used) is modified to save them in a global variable numbers. When we want to replay the
drawing of a maze, the commented lines (see below) are uncommented, and the original
random numbers are picked out one by one from numbers. Count has to be initialized to 0
each time, of course, and numbers is initialized to empty just before running maze when
numbers are being collected.

```
function somewhere a, b
  global numbers, count
  add 1 to count
  -- return word count of numbers
  get a+random(b-a-1)
  put " " & it after last word of numbers
  return it
end somewhere
```

If you want to repeat the exact maze drawings from this chapter, **numbers** started off like this: 16 14 6 20 22 4 4 8 13 2 2 8 7 3 3 5 3 10 2 20 16 3 3 14. Since the maze takes 294 random numbers to draw, it's a safe bet that the world has never seen the same maze before, and never will again.

7.5 A block diagram editor

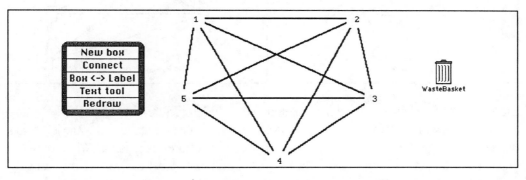

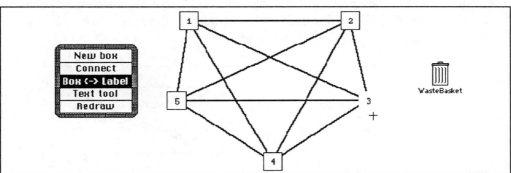

So far we have shown how to do some useful kinds of graphical output. Of course there are many other applications for graphical output. It can be applied to produce presentations of non-numerical information such as simple block diagrams, electrical circuits or even road networks, and it can be used for animation (see Chapter 8). But in many of these, the positioning of the parts of pictures cannot be determined without user involvement, and we have not yet discussed the inclusion of mouse input in HyperTalk scripts. (Actually, if you look back to the first graphical example you'll see that our second **MouseUp** handler for drawing ovals does use mouse input.)

The block diagramming editor is designed to draw pictures involving blocks, text labels and connecting lines, as in the first picture on the previous page.

In the second picture, the Box-to-Label tool has been selected (the tool button is highlighted and the cursor has changed to a cross hair), and we are about to click on the third label on the pentagon to change it into a box.

The powerful thing our editor does can be seen from the next two pictures. We have

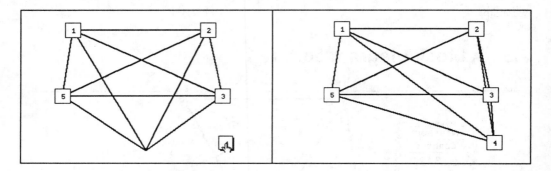

clicked on the box labelled 4 and have started to drag it (left picture), but when we let go the connecting lines are redrawn automatically (right picture). A box is highlighted while it is being dragged – this gives the game away, as you can see boxes are really fields! When they are highlighted, they are changed to **shadow** style. (The box-to-label tool works by changing **opaque** to **rectangle** styles or back again.) If we continued dragging box 4 to the wastebasket, the wastebasket would highlight (just like the Macintosh!) and we can drop the box (left picture below), and the lines disappear (right picture below):

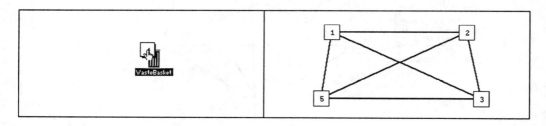

Labels are entered by using the text tool. All fields become selected by the text tool by having their **showlines** property set: this also shows up for labels. Fields use a **closeField** handler to adjust their sizes automatically to the width of the label typed in them. The next picture shows a box adjusted in size for a longer label name.

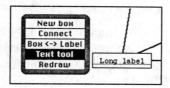

You've got the entire script for the block diagramming editor on the book disk, so here we'll only describe the ideas behind the editor.

How boxes and connections work

Boxes are fields, normally with their lockText property set so that they can intercept mouseDown messages used for dragging them. When they are dragged within the rect of the button **wastebasket**, we highlight the button. If we get a **mouseUp** at this stage, the field is deleted. MouseDown calls dragObject "cd fld id" && id of me giving the ID of the field being dragged; dragObject selects the object and then loops until the mouse is released up:

```
selectObject object
repeat until the mouse is "up"
  set loc of object to the mouseloc
  set hilite of bg btn "WasteBasket" to ¬
  the mouseloc is within the rect of bg btn "WasteBasket"
end repeat
```

When the user releases the mouse, we decide whether to delete the field.

```
if hilite of bg btn "WasteBasket" then
  lock screen
  choose field tool
  click at the loc of object
  doMenu "Clear field"
```

We then have to get rid of any lines that used to connect to this box. We've stored details of all connections drawn in a field Connections, as lines of two items (like cd fld id 123,cd fld id 86): the IDs of the starting and ending fields. So, having deleted the field, we go through the list of connections and delete any lines that contain the deleted field's ID. The mouseDown handler redraws all the connections – it has to, even if a field is not deleted since the connections also need redrawing when a field has been moved.

```
get number of lines in bg field "Connections"
repeat until it = 0
  if line it of bg fld "connections" contains object then
    delete line it of bg fld "Connections"
  end if
  subtract 1 from it
```

```
      end repeat
      set hilite of bg btn "WasteBasket" to false
   else deselectObject object -- only need to deselect object if it hasn't been deleted
```

We use field IDs throughout as a convenient way of referring to the card fields involved. Since fields can be deleted (by dragging them to the wastebasket) it is important to use a form of reference, namely IDs, that does not change! Had we used numbers, which might have seemed easier, then when a field was deleted the numbers of other (higher numbered) fields would change. This would make a mess of the data in the list of connections.

Making new boxes

New boxes are made by copying a background box that has been set up the right size and with all the relevant scripts. Like startGraphics and endGraphics used for the charting scripts, the tool buttons use utility handlers, radio and endRadio to sort out which ones stay highlighted.

```
   on mouseUp
      radio
      choose field tool
      show bg field "Box template"
      click at loc of bg field "Box template"
      doMenu "Copy field"
      hide bg field "Box template"
      doMenu "Paste field"
      set name of last card field to "rectangle"
      endRadio
   end mouseUp
```

When a new box is created, its name is set to rectangle. This may seem strange, but we use the field's name to remember whether it is a box (rectangle) or label (opaque) style. When we drag a field, its style is changed to shadow – whether it is a box or label – and when we deselect an object the easiest thing to do is set its style back to its short name (which will be rectangle for boxes and opaque for labels).

Since all the fields share the same script, it seems a better idea to have their handlers, like mouseDown, in the background (or card) script. The mouseDown handler then needs to work out that it has been sent from the right sort of object, a field, not a card or a button:

```
   on mouseDown                         -- in background script
      if "rectangle opaque" contains short name of the target then
         dragObject "cd fld id" && id of the target
         redraw
         choose browse tool
      end if
   end mouseDown
```

Likewise **closeField** (which is only sent to fields) adjusts the field's size:

```
on closeField
  put id of the target into object
  get 13+8*number of chars in cd fld id object
  if it < height of cd fld id object then get height of cd fld id object
  set width of cd fld id object to it
end closeField
```

Connecting boxes

Connecting two boxes requires noting when a box is clicked on: since we have to do this several times in the block diagram editor (for example, also when converting boxes to labels) we have used a function **hitBox()**. Either the function returns the ID of the field the user has selected and changes the style of the field to make it look selected, or it returns **empty** if the user has clicked into blank space. The script for the connect boxes tool button then looks surprisingly straightforward:

```
on mouseUp
  radio "cross"                          -- let's have a cross-shaped cursor
  put hitBox() into firstBox
  if firstBox ≠ empty then
    put hitBox() into secondBox
    if secondBox ≠ empty then
      if firstBox = secondBox then beep
      else
        choose line tool
        drag from loc of firstbox to loc of secondbox
        put firstbox & "," & secondbox & return after bg fld "Connections"
        deselectObject secondBox
      end if
    end if
    deselectObject firstBox
  end if
  endRadio
end mouseUp
```

The function **hitBox()** decides which box (field) has been clicked on by the user, or returns **empty** if the user misses. If we ever call **hitBox** when there aren't any fields that the user can click on (for example, the user is trying to connect boxes but there aren't any), then we **beep** and suggest that some boxes are first created.

```
function hitBox
  if number of card fields < 1 then
    beep
```

```
        answer "Make some boxes first."
    else
        wait until the mouse is "down"
        get the mouseloc
        repeat with i = 1 to number of cd fields
            if it is within the rect of cd fld i then
                get "cd fld id" && id of cd fld i
                selectObject it
                unlock screen
                wait until the mouse is "up"
                return it
            end if
        end repeat
        beep                        -- missed
    end if
    return empty
end hitBox
```

Exercise: generalizing the editor

The diagram editor uses fields as the boxes or blocks. Buttons, instead of fields, have their own advantages: icons can be used for different symbols, such as transistors, resistors and capacitors – then the block diagramming editor becomes an electric circuit editor. Other sorts of editor can be similarly designed for central heating design, chemical apparatus, metabolic pathways, and so on. We designed the block diagramming editor to send box names to handlers in the form **cd fld ID 4562**, which is easy to change to **cd btn ID 234**, and then with a new tool to change button icons, and perhaps a fancier way of drawing lines with the connect tool (for example, only using vertical and horizontal lines) one obtains a new block diagramming editor.

7.6 Optimizing graphics

There are various ways of speeding up graphical programs. No technique is worth using when you are developing a stack, since it will tend to make debugging harder: you might even want to slow scripts down so that you can see what they are doing!

The two simplest methods to speed up scripts are to hide both palette windows (tools and patterns), and then to lock the screen, so that no graphical changes are visible. Hiding the menu bar doesn't save as much time, but it avoids distracting flicker. You may want to be able to see the drawing as it occurs – especially if it is slow and there is a risk the user might think nothing is happening. Alternatively, you can briefly unlock the screen 'every so often' to make a compromise between speeding up the drawing and letting the user see that something is going on.

Like many complex HyperTalk scripts, graphics scripts should start and end with calls to a pair of handlers like **startGraphics** and **endGraphics**, to which you may add **doMenu select all** and **clear picture**, and other stuff like **set lockRecent** and **lockMessages** to true:

```
on startGraphics
  global oldState
  reset paint
  put visible of "tool window" && visible of "pattern window" && ¬
  the userLevel into oldState
  hide tool window
  hide pattern window
  hide menubar
  lock screen
  if the userLevel < 3 then set userLevel to 3
end startGraphics

on endGraphics
  global oldState
  set visible of tool window to word 1 of oldState
  set visible of pattern window to word 2 of oldState
  set userLevel to word 3 of oldState
  show menubar
  choose browse tool
end endGraphics
```

All of our example programs will run an order of magnitude faster if we minimize the number of tool changes. Suppose you want to set the tool to the line tool. If it is already the line tool, you'd be wasting time. It happens that finding out what the tool is faster than setting it, so the following will generally be faster: **if the tool ≠ "line tool" then choose "line tool"**. Of course, it would be *even* faster if you can work out (by thinking about it!) what the tool is just at this point in your script, and either using a direct **choose line tool** or doing nothing, whichever is needed. To emphasize: if you do write optimizing code like this, and certainly if you hide the tool palette, you may never notice that you are perhaps wastefully choosing tools you don't need, or you may not notice that a slight reorganization could mean all the line tool stuff is done before all the brush tool stuff – a more radical optimization that would save *all* of the tool swapping around. The simple technique we gave here (and any other) obtains the most impressive speed improvements when it is disguising poor scripting!

The reasons for writing **the tool** rather than (the two keystrokes shorter) **tool()**, and for using the 'unnecessary' quotes for the parameter of **choose** were explained in Chapter 6, which also gave more general recommendations for speeding up scripts: one of its main suggestions, that is worth repeating here, is that you first need to find out where a script is running slow before putting much effort into trying to speed it up – otherwise you will waste *your* time.

CHAPTER 8

Animating Things

Moving HyperCard graphics,
animating algorithms, direct manipulation

HyperCard is ideal for any application that falls naturally into the card metaphor. Animation is
not always easy, but it makes stacks look far more attractive.

8.1   Forms of animation in HyperCard

The main thing in trying animation is to find ways to temper your ambition as a stack designer
with what can reasonably be achieved without enormous effort in HyperTalk. A lot of
animation in HyperCard, then, comes down to knowing the right tricks for the specific effects
you want to achieve. On the other hand, writing animation programs in any language not
specifically designed for it is tedious: some simple animation in HyperTalk is quite easy, so long
as you don't want to write arcade games.

A word of advice. If you have seen a HyperCard stack do a nice animation that you like,
you'll find it a lot easier to copy its scripts than start from scratch, but remember that the
animation you saw may rely on XCMDs, the exact values of global variables, and other
idiosyncrasies like the icon or button numbers. Indeed, if you are keen on animation, and you
need it to be done really flashily, you are advised to look at some of the many proprietary
extensions for HyperCard for animation. The techniques in this chapter should be adequate for
simpler animations of the kind that we have illustrated. They will also give you some interesting
programming ideas even if you don't want to use HyperTalk directly for animation.

The *HyperCard Tour* stack provided with HyperCard is a good demonstration of many
of these techniques, combined with good graphics. (Use **set userLevel to 5** to be able to
examine all of the scripts in it.)

Visual effects

A range of visual effects are possible when HyperCard changes the current card. One way to
learn about them is to create a new button, link it to another card, and then use the button

dialog box to set its visual effect; resulting in a button with a **mouseUp** script like this:

```
on mouseUp -- icon is "next arrow", which points to the right
    visual effect wipe left slow
    go to next card
end mouseUp
```

If you imagine a stack's cards placed on a table, with you looking at them through a camera, then when you move the camera right, the cards will seem to move to the left. Thus, if you have a button whose icon is a *right* arrow, the visual effect you want will be a wipe *left* or scroll *left*. Similarly, if you want to give the impression of a two-dimensional layout of cards, up arrow buttons will need downward visual effects.

You can use visual effects with **unlock**, as in **unlock screen with visual iris open to grey**. As usual, **unlock** will have no effect if the screen is not locked or if it is locked more than once. A screen locked several times needs as many unlockings for the user to see any change – a scheme that ensures that if we **lock screen**, we can safely call any handlers that **lock** and **unlock** the screen themselves: they will only unlock 'their' locking.

Trivial animation

What do you want animation for? Some very trivial animation can be achieved by using existing features directly. You can animate the message passing operations of HyperCard simply by saying **show message watcher**; you can animate all the variable assignments by saying **show variable watcher**. A script can animate simple things by using **put** to put text into the message window, or putting text into fields. For example, we can use the message window for a (rather fast!) count-down:

```
repeat with i = 10 down to 1
    put i && "and counting."
end repeat
put "0 Blast off!"
```

When HyperCard is not doing anything else, it sends the **idle** message to the current card about 60 times a second. If you write a handler for this message, you can change anything that is displayed. This is the basis of most animation.

A button with a 'rolling' name that rolls past is quite eye catching, and is easily programmed. Here are two examples:

```
on idle                          -- flashing spots
    get the short name of button 1
    if it = "•" then get "• •"
    else get "•"
    set the name of button 1 to it
end idle
```

```
on idle                              -- rolling message
  global i
  add 1 to i
  get "A rolling message ... "
  if i > number of chars in it then put 1 into i
  set the name of button 1 to char i to i+10 of (it & it)
end idle
```

The second example makes the button name 'A rolling message ...' roll by (changing the button name to '**A rolling** ', then ' **rolling m**', then '**rolling me**' and so on). Although it is written so that the length of the message is calculated, it does assume that the message is at least ten characters long, otherwise **char i to i+10** won't work. If the rolling message isn't long enough you'll need to reduce the **10** to something smaller or change the expression (**it & it**) to make a string long enough, say, (**it & it & it**) if it happens to be between 5 and 9 chars long. It is as well to set the **textFont** of the button to a fixed-width font such as Courier, since the width of the rolling message will otherwise vary in a slightly distracting way (because the widths of letters such as i and m are different in variable-width fonts).

A self-explanatory rolling message, such as 'click here for help', is particularly useful for stacks designed for strangers to the Macintosh or HyperCard.

The message **mouseWithin** is sent continuously, rather like **idle**, to the target object when the mouse is over a button or field. If you want some activity within a button (or field), it is easier to use **mouseWithin** than **idle**.

Gradual revelation

If you are explaining something in English, a very easy and straightforward way is to reveal fields gradually, each containing a sentence or two of the explanation. You can do this a field at a time (which is a bit tedious: you have to keep track of each of the fields), or you can copy one field to another. If you do a lot of it, consider devising a script so that the fields have a uniform structure and that they are easier to edit (you edit the 'master' field, and let the script construct the 'slave' fields). The *Animation* stack on the *HyperProgramming* disk does this. Another way is for a script to generate the field contents, line by line.

Animating by using cards

Cards have pictures, and by using **show all cards** you can make an animation out of them. **Show all cards** displays each card in turn; you can use **show marked cards** after marking some cards, or a **repeat** loop with a **wait** instruction in it to show extracts of your stack, so that you can have several animations in one stack, or so that a stack can contain an animation part and a conventional part. For example, the *Animation* stack includes a short sequence of cards shaking a cup and rolling some dice.

Cards you want to animate often get out of order as you cut and paste and create new cards. One way to get them back together is to say **sort numeric by cardPlace()** where cardPlace returns a number corresponding to where you want the card to go. Here, we define cardPlace to put the cards on the **animation sequence** background next to each other at the end of the stack:

```
function cardPlace
   get number of this card
   if short name of this background = "animation sequence" then
      return it + number of cards
   end if
   return it
end cardPlace
```

Animating by numbers

Any object property that is a number can be used for animation purposes. We'll show in later examples in this chapter how to use an object's position to make it move, but you can also use properties like the **scroll of the card window**, as follows:

```
get the scroll of card window
put it into msg                        -- to help you debug
set the scroll of card window to item 1 of it+16, item 2 of it
```

to move the entire card image under script control. If you have a card window smaller than the card itself, you can achieve a pleasant panning effect, ideal for flying aircraft over rocky terrain.

Animating by dragging

Inspired by John Barnett's game *Cannon Fodder*, here is a scene of destruction: a cannon shooting cannon balls at an enemy's house. The picture was taken while a cannon ball was on its parabolic trajectory towards the house.

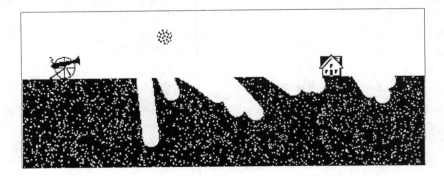

A handler drawGround is used to restore the cratered ground after a shoot-out. The script here is straight forward, and follows what you would do with the menus and mouse by hand. Both the cannon and house are buttons and don't need to be redrawn; they might instead have been drawn on the background. **Reset paint** is done to ensure all the paint brushes and paint patterns are as normal. The portion of the card representing the ground is filled with black and then the **lighten** menu operation is used to produce a mottled effect:

```
on drawGround
    lock screen
    reset paint
    set brush to 5                    -- for a big ball
    choose line tool
    doMenu select all
    doMenu clear picture
    drag from 0,200 to 512,200
    choose bucket tool               -- default pattern is black
    click at 1,201
    doMenu select all
    doMenu lighten
    doMenu lighten
    choose browse tool
    unlock screen
end drawGround
```

We use several numbers to calculate the path of the cannon ball. Getting the firing parameters from a field meant that we could experiment with different numbers and then hide the field when everything worked satisfactorily – there was no need to go into the mathematics of parabolas! The cannon **mouseUp** handler first of all gets these parameters from a random line in the data field:

```
function trajectory
    put random(number of lines in card field "trajectory data") into path
    return line path of card field "trajectory data" & "," & path
end trajectory

on mouseUp                           -- shoot the cannon
    drawGround
    put empty into depth
    repeat forever

        -- get firing data
        get trajectory()
        put item 1 of it into range
        put item 2 of it into speed
        put item 3 of it into climb
        put item 4 of it into path

        put item 1 of loc of me into x1
        put item 2 of loc of me into y1
```

Each cannon ball flight path has a number **path**, and for each path we record the depth of crater last made by using **line path of depth**. At first, all lines of the variable **depth** will be empty, so the first time a particular path is fired, **line path of depth** is initialized to **y1**, which is the vertical position of the cannon button.

```
put line path of depth into thisdepth
if thisdepth is empty then put y1 into thisdepth
```

At this stage, it's time to fire the cannon and to make a suitable noise. Having added a sound resource **Bang** to the stack, we can make bangs, but it is more realistic to make several sorts of bang, depending on the firing path. HyperCard can't parse **play "Bang" tempo 20 char path mod 4+1 of "aceg"**, apparently because it tries to play the notes **char**! This bug can be avoided by using **do** to evaluate the rest of the line, which selects a note from **aceg**, then plays it.

```
-- fire into the air
do play "Bang" tempo 20 char path mod 4+1 of "aceg"
```

The flying cannon ball is created by painting a shot (initially just underneath the cannon) and then dragging it on a series of straight paths, together giving the impression of moving along a parabola.

```
-- draw the shot
choose brush tool
set pattern to 16              -- for a gritty ball
click at x1, y1

choose select tool
drag from x1-8, y1-8 to x1+8, y1+8 -- pick up the ball

put x1 into x2
put y1 into y2
repeat while y2 ≤ thisdepth
   put x2 into x1
   put y2 into y1
   put x1+speed into x2
   if x2 ≥ 500 then exit repeat     -- shot off the card!
   put y1+trunc((x2-range)/climb) into y2
   drag from x1, y1 to x2, y2
end repeat
```

Since the method of dragging the selected picture won't work if the selection box hits the side of the card, there is a special check in the repeat loop to drop out when **x2** is about to go off the card. The loop otherwise terminates when the cannon ball gets to ground level. It might have hit the house, and the easiest way to find out would be to click at this location and see whether the house button **mouseUp** handler gets activated, but that would mean changing to the browse tool, and that causes a noticeable delay. Thus, the script has to work it out for itself!

```
-- have we hit the house?
if x1 & "," & y1 is within the rect of card button "house" then
    send mouseUp to card button "house"
end if
```

To simplify the cannon handler, the **mouseUp** handler of the house exits to HyperCard, so we don't have to worry what to do when the **mouseUp** message has been handled.

If the house hasn't been hit, the craters in the ground are created by dragging a white paint brush, using the same parabola algorithm as when flying through the air. The crater for the path is made 20 pixels deeper.

```
-- dig the crater
add 20 to thisdepth            -- each crater goes deeper into the ground
choose brush tool
set pattern to 1               -- white, to delete the ground
repeat while y1 < thisdepth
   put x1+speed into x2
   put y1+trunc((x2-range)/climb) into y2
   drag from x1, y1 to x2, y2
   put x2 into x1
   put y2 into y1
end repeat

put thisdepth into line path of depth
wait until the sound is "done"
end repeat

choose browse tool
end mouseUp
```

At the end of the repeat loop, **wait until the sound is "done"** (it's Bang while we're waiting) so that the sounds and shooting don't get out of step. Finally, the **mouseUp** handler for the house:

```
on mouseUp
  repeat 4 times
    set hilite of me to not hilite of me
    wait 5
  end repeat
  choose browse tool
  answer "House hit - shooting over!" & return & ¬
  "Click on cannon to start again."
  exit to HyperCard
end mouseUp
```

Animating by using icons

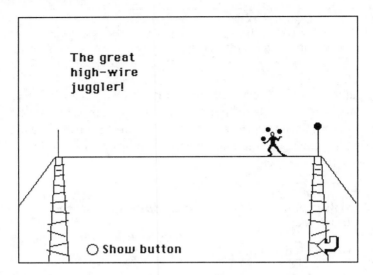

This and the next section will develop the reasoning behind this **idle** handler, one which you can find in the animation stack. We give you the whole handler here to make it easier to understand how the various bits fit together.

```
on idle
  global step
  get the icon of button "juggler"
  set the icon of button "juggler" to 21573+(it+1) mod 4
  get the loc of button "juggler"
  add step to item 1 of it
  set the loc of button "juggler" to it
  if it is not within rect of button "rope" then
    put -step into step
  end if
end idle
```

The **idle** handler makes the juggler walk back and forth along the dangerous high wire and juggle the balls at the same time.

We'll consider juggling the balls first: it's made up from a simple sequence of four icons. The four icons of the juggler make a sequence, with foot-tapping and the three balls in slightly different positions:

If we named the icons "juggler 1", "juggler 2", "juggler 3" and "juggler 4", we could change the icons easily by **set the icon of button "juggler" to "juggler" && i**, where i counts **1, 2, 3, 4** on each call to the **idle** handler. We would need a global variable:

```
on idle
  global juggler
  add 1 to juggler
  if juggler = 5 then put 1 into juggler
  set icon of button "juggler" to "juggler" && juggler
  :
```

We can dispense with the global variable by getting the current icon, and working out what the next one should be. It happens that their icon IDs in our stack are 21573, 21574, 21575, 21576, so the juggler icon can be set by using

```
get the icon of button "juggler"
set the icon of button "juggler" to 21573+(it+1) mod 4
```

The *Animation* stack also illustrates some rolling dice, which are accompanied by a sound.

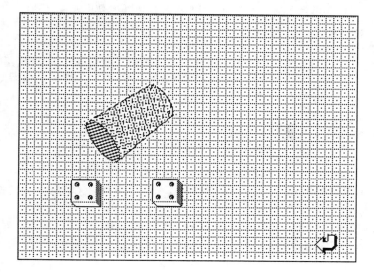

After **play "roll"**, the animated rolling continues until the sound is done:

```
play "roll"
go last card of bg "roll"
repeat until the sound is done       -- synchronizes with end of the "roll" sound
  get throw()                        -- puts two numbers into 'it' (see below)
  -- there are six 'dice' icons in HyperCard, named "dice,1" to "dice,6"
  set icon of bg button "die 1" to "dice," & item 1 of it
  set icon of bg button "die 2" to "dice," & item 2 of it
end repeat
:
```

```
function throw -- returns two items containing random numbers (1-6)
    return random(6) & "," & random(6)
end throw
```

Using buttons to position objects

HyperTalk's programming language requires coordinates, for example in the **drag** command, to make animation work. You can easily write a **mouseUp** handler for the card script that says where you are clicking: this is an easy way of finding the exact coordinates of points you need for the animations. See Chapter 3 for an example script to do this. (You may find that your home stack already has one; try typing **xy** into the message box. See Chapter 11 to find out what else is in the home script.)

You have to make a note of the coordinates and then edit them by hand into your programs. This is tedious, and makes changes in the future harder: what do you do when you want to move a graphical object? A better solution is to program in the coordinates, and we can use the locations and sizes of buttons to do this. The button tool provides a very easy way of resizing and moving buttons, so if our animation uses button positions, everything is easy to modify as the whim takes us.

The animation stack provides a simple example: a moving clown icon is walking backwards and forwards on a high wire, and juggling at the same time. Having got the icon to juggle, we want him (or her) to walk backwards and forwards. If **speed** is +1 or -1 (or whatever distance we want the juggler to take each 'step'), then

```
get the loc of button "juggler"
add step to item 1 of it
set the loc of button "juggler" to it
```

is one way of making it walk. But when the juggler gets to the end of the high wire, it should turn around – that can be done by **put -step into step**, but how do we know when to turn around? We make a new button covering the high wire graphic, then when the location of the juggler is not within the rectangle of this button, we should change direction:

```
if loc of button "juggler" is not within rect of button "wire" then
    put -step into step
end if
```

If we think the juggler goes too far or not far enough, we simple choose the button tool and adjust the position or size of the **wire** button. The relevant open handler (**openCard**, **openBackground** or **openStack**) can initialize the position of the juggler with

```
set the loc of button "juggler" to the loc of button "wire"
```

It is also possible to use **drag** to move a button (or field), but with the disadvantage that the normal button (field) tool's outlining of objects is distracting. On the other hand, if the outlines are no problem (perhaps all buttons have their **rectangle** style set, or their icons anyway blacken their outline) the dragging can be done smoothly.

The hazards of arcade games

For more complex animations – say an arcade game with a skier zooming down a slope and many hazards for her to avoid, or a car racing around a dangerous circuit – what seems like a good solution (moving the skier or the car using button locations in the **idle** handler, with other buttons representing the hazards) starts to have its own problems: the handler soon gets too complicated; requiring checking whether the skier (or car) is on top of any one of the many hazards. Worse, as more hazards are added the **idle** handler has to be kept up to date.

A far better approach is to make HyperCard do the work. If, after each move, the skier clicks (that is, the script contains the instruction **click at the loc of me**); this will send a **mouseUp** message to any button she happens to be over. The nature of the hazard and its effect on the skier can be programmed naturally in the **mouseUp** handler of the relevant button itself.

Revealing the card image

The animation stack animates a hand raising and lowering its finger, apparently bouncing a small ball (an animated button).

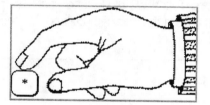 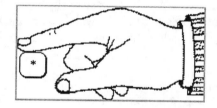

The card picture is shown on the left, and it completely obscures the background picture. Hence the first line of the **mouseWithin** handler appears to make the hand's finger flick up; the repeat loop then makes the button float up to it (the distance 20 was found by experiment). Then the card picture is shown, and the button jerked back 20 pixels down.

```
on mouseWithin
  hide card picture
  get the top of me
  repeat with i = it down to it-20
    set the top of me to i
  end repeat
  show card picture
  set the top of me to it
end mouseWithin
```

There is a problem with the handler: if a user interrupts it, the button can be left at any position on its 20 pixel journey, so next time it will start rising from there! Furthermore, the card picture may be left hidden. Type **top of button "*"** into the message box to find out where the top should be: it happens to be **173**, but rather than read that, cut it and add these lines to a suitable handler in the card script:

```
set the top of button "*" to 173
show card picture
```

These lines could go in **openCard**, but fixing errors only once per card opening may not be often enough with some users! They can go in an **idle** (or **midle**) handler, so the animation is reset whenever nothing else is happening; otherwise, the **mouseWithin** handler should do its own initialization.

8.2 Hints

A few simple ideas can make a lot of difference to your animations, their reliability and the ease with which you can develop them.

Your own **idle** handler can get in the way of developing the stack. In particular, you'll find that you cannot type into the message window. It's a good idea, then, to start the **idle** handler with a 'get out' clause, so that you can stop your animation working while you work on other details of the card or stack. For example the following **idle** handler can be stopped by setting **stop_idle** to true; you will then be able to type in the message box and do other things without the handler taking over from you.

```
on idle
   global stop_idle
   if stop_idle then exit idle
   ...
end idle
```

Since you can't type much in the message window, you either need a menu item that sets **stop_idle** directly, or a single-letter handler that sets it, on the basis that typing **s** *return* (say) can be done fast enough. Rather than introduce a global variable (**stop_idle**), you could use the value of **the userLevel**: certainly if **the userLevel** is less than **5**, you can't work on the scripts anyway, so you may as well let **idle** take over!

HyperCard continues to send **idle** messages even when it is not being used: your animations can slow down other applications. It's generally polite, then, to switch off your animations. The most reliable way of doing this is as follows:

```
on idle
   if the suspended then exit idle
   :
```

All these suggestions change what is in your **idle** handler. If your stack has several **idle** handlers (say, one in each background, and perhaps some special ones on particular cards), then putting the same code in all of these handlers is not the way to program well. It's asking for troublesome bugs: you may accidentally program one **idle** handler one way, and another way.

There are two better approaches. First, you can define a stack function **animate()** that returns **true** when you want an **idle** handler to do its work. This solution means that each **idle** handler must start something like: **if animate() then** ..., but at least there is now only one place in the stack (the body of the **animate** function) where you have to debug the conditions where you want **idle** to run. A more elegant solution is to have only one **idle** handler, in the stack script. This handler decides whether animation is appropriate, and if so, sends the message **midle** (i.e., my idle) to the current card. No card or background has an **idle** handler (that has to decide whether to animate anything) but has a **midle** handler that is only called when the stack script decides animation is required. Here's how to do it in the stack script, assuming you want to do it with a checkmark in a menu:

```
on idle
   if the suspended then exit idle
   if there is a menu "Animation" then
      if checkMark of menuItem "Run" of menu "Animation" then
         send "midle" to this card
      end if
   end if
end idle

on midle
   -- put original code from stack idle handler here
end midle
```

A checkmark can be controlled by a simple menu message (**set checkMark of menuItem "Run" of menu "Animation" to not checkMark of menuItem "Run" of menu "Animation"**) and does not require any special handlers. See Chapter 9 (next) for full details of using menus.

You can add 'speed control' code here: for example, so that the message **midle** is only sent when **the sound is "done"**, or you might want to animate until the sound was finished, then you would have a repeat while loop:

```
repeat while sound is not done
   send "midle" to this card
end repeat
```

If you want to slow down animation, you can **send midle** when **the ticks mod 3 < 2** (which slows it by a third). And so on: there are very many possibilities. What, then, if different cards or backgrounds require different treatment? The trick mentioned in Chapter 2 of using names of cards to hold useful information can be used very effectively here: put different characters into the name of each card (or background) depending on what effects you want to happen, for example:

```
if char 1 of the short name of this card = "•" then
  repeat while sound is not done
    send "midle" to this card
  end repeat
else send "midle" to this card
```

Stopping run-away animations

An animation run by an **idle** handler can be brought under control if you can select a tool other than the browse tool: this stops HyperCard sending **idle**. Alternatively, you can edit the script of a run-away animation from another stack. Unfortunately, you can't type a command like **edit script of background 1 of stack "demo"**, since HyperCard doesn't like referring to objects in other stacks. Instead, create a new button and give it a script like this:

```
on mouseUp
  lock messages
  go stack "demo" in a new window
  edit script of this background      -- or whatever
end mouseUp.
```

In the editor, you can select all the script (or the bit causing problems) and comment it out using **Comment** from the **Script** menu. When you return to the stack, the animation will be dead. This technique will work even if the run-away stack has **set the cantAbort of this stack to true**.

If there are no other stacks open that you can click on, and the run-away stack has fiendishly hidden the menu bar and handles the ***command-space*** command so you can't restore it, then you must get to the Finder and launch another HyperCard stack, and there add the button with the script above. You will of course need to add a **show menubar** command, and possibly a **reset menubar**, in case the problem stack has ruined the standard menubar as well as hidden it!

Animations can go disastrously wrong if the buttons, graphics or other things start off in the wrong place: this happens most often when the user interrupts an animation then restarts it. The first card of an animation sequence should start with an **openCard** handler that puts everything in its right place. You can either have a script that sets the **loc** of buttons and fields (and any other properties affected by the animation) or, useful if you have dragged paint around, delete the current card, make a copy of a previously-prepared backup card (say, the last card of the stack) and paste it in place – this restores all the objects and gets the graphics copied nicely.

In a sequence of cards used for an animation it's important that each card gets the user to the right card to start the sequence. Typically, you'll have all the cards on the same background, so the background's **openCard** handler can say **go first card of this background**. The **openCard** handler of the first card on the background can then animate the cards in the background, a method that does not send any more **openCard** messages.

8.3 Animating algorithms

Combining programming language and graphics facilities, HyperCard makes an ideal system for animating algorithms and showing what they do. Animation helps people understand how algorithms work and helps debug bad code. One of our aims will be to produce a general-purpose approach to animation, so that you are not restricted to our particular algorithms. You will be able to add your own ideas easily.

The examples of animation we'll describe in this section show how simple sorting algorithms work. Typically, a sorting algorithm takes an array of numbers and sorts them into increasing (or decreasing) order. Thus 3, 7, 6 would be sorted to 3, 6, 7.

The first rule of animating algorithms is to make the problem visually interesting. In this case, simply showing numbers move around is not exciting. Instead, a better representation for the numbers is to use a bar chart, where each number is represented by a bar of appropriate size. The bars then move around as the sorting algorithm puts them into order.

How best can we show bars (of varying sizes) in HyperCard? It may be as well to experiment here: for instance, lines of a field (with so-many characters, such as '–', in them) might do; graphics done with HyperCard's painting tools might do; or we could use an existing HyperCard object, such as buttons, and control their size properties. We decided on this last choice: we'll use buttons, and use their **rect** (short for **rectangle**) property to control their size. Buttons have the advantage that they can easily be highlighted (i.e., black or white) simply by setting their **hilite** property. (However, we have designed the HyperTalk scripts so that if you want something other than buttons it would be easy to organize.) Our final design is shown below.

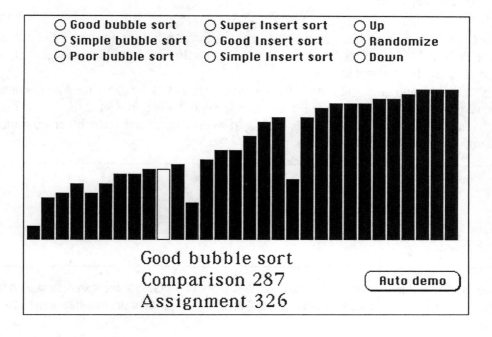

The idea

A card will show a selection of algorithms (bubble sort, insert sort, and so on), the main animation display and a field showing interesting facts about how efficient the chosen algorithm is. Cards will look like the picture on the previous page.

The main features can be seen: a selection of buttons at the top of the screen that activate various algorithms (three each of bubble and insert sort) together with three buttons on the righthand side to set up the data, randomly or in increasing or decreasing order. The bars at the bottom show a bubble sort in progress: it has already done 287 comparisons and 326 assignments. The white bar (an un-highlighted button) shows where the bubble sort has got to.

The scripts

One of the first things to do is to position 30 (or how many you want) buttons in the right place. With anything that's so repetitive, it's best to write a one-off handler to do this. The buttons need to be put in the right place and set to some sensible sizes. Since we're anyway going to need a button to do this (called Randomize), the makeButtons script can click that button.

```
on makeButtons
  repeat with i = 1 to 30
    doMenu "New Button"
    set style of card button i to rectangle
    set the showName of button i to false
  end repeat
  click at the loc of card button "Randomize"
end makeButtons
```

Once the buttons have been created, we can reuse makeButtons to ensure the buttons' properties are correct. Thus, once we have run makeButtons from the message box, we comment out the doMenu line.

How should randomize work? Its mouseUp handler sets the size of the 30 card buttons we've just created to a random size. The best way to do this is to put all of the button-sizing code into its own handler; not only is it going to be used again and again, but if we want to change it, it'll be best to have it in one place.

```
on mouseUp
  repeat with i = 1 to 30
    hi i, random(30)
  end repeat
  reset_animation
end mouseUp
```

The handler hi is in the card script, and sets the size of card button i to the specified size, in this case random(30). If we want increasing sizes, hi i, i will do, and for decreasing sizes, hi i,31-i.

The final line, **reset_animation**, is to make sure that all the buttons are black (some might have been left white from an aborted sort) and to do any other tidying up necessary.

```
on reset_animation
  global comparisonCount, assignmentCount
  repeat with i = 1 to 30
    black i                    -- in case left white
  end repeat
  put 0 into comparisonCount
  put 0 into assignmentCount
  put empty into card field "steps"
end reset_animation
```

We're using a handler to set buttons black: should we wish to change how the stack works (say, to use painting tools instead of buttons) we only have to change the **black** and **white** handlers, rather than the code of all the algorithms that we want to animate. Note **reset_animation** also resets the two global variables for counting how efficient each algorithm is.

The functions for changing the colour of a button are straightforward:

```
on white b
  set the hilite of card button b to false
end white

on black b
  set the hilite of card button b to true
end black
```

We change the size of a button by using the **rect** property:

```
on hi b, h
  assignment
  set the rect of card button b to 20+15*b, 250-5*h, 34+15*b, 260
end hi
```

If we had used the button property **top**, then the top of the button would move, but the button's height would be unchanged; if we had used the property **height**, then the centre of the button would not move (so the bottom of the button would have moved down symmetrically). The animation might look better if the buttons are positioned along the centre line of the card, and we used the **height** property, but by using the **rect** property we can also fine tune the horizontal spacing of the buttons at the same time as adjusting their height – so this is a better solution for while we are developing the stack.

The handler **hi** makes the buttons 14 pixels wide, separated by one pixel. The bottom of each button will be at 260 and the height will be **250-5*h**: that is the higher **h** the taller the button (remember that the top of the button is measured from the top of the card). Since every call to hi is an assignment, we'll call the handler **assignment** to count it and update the field monitoring the algorithm's progress. Also, we'll have a similar handler to count comparisons. (There other things that can be counted: assignments and comparisons are enough for now, but other algorithms may need other sorts of measurement or animation.)

The algorithms need to know how high each button is, or rather not its height but the number it is representing. The function hival returns the height of the button:

```
function hival b
   return (250-top of card button b)/5
end hival
```

We could have used the button property **height**, but since we set the top position of the button explicitly (when we set the **rect** property), it's easiest to work out the size from the **top** property (which is also **item 2** of the rect). We might have wanted the height of the button to be a slightly different number than the algorithm itself is using (it might be double the number or its logarithm or something), and using a function like hival keeps such worries in one place.

We need to write an algorithm to try out and to animate. The conventional bubble sort algorithm will do:

```
-- simple bubble sort
on mouseUp
   init
   -- now sort
   put true into sorting
   repeat while sorting
    put false into sorting
    repeat with i = 1 to 29
       put hival(i) into a
       put hival(i+1) into b
       comparison
       if a < b then
         white i
         hi i+1, a
         white i+1
         black i
         hi i, b
         black i+1
         put true into sorting
       end if
    end repeat
   end repeat
end mouseUp
```

The first line of the handler calls **init** to make sure that all buttons start out being black, in case the user interrupted another animation and left some buttons white. **Comparison** is called each time we compare two values, and calls to white and black are used to animate the algorithm. Calling hi calls assignment to keep track of how many assignments are performed.

What use is animation? Here is a slightly different version of bubble sort:

```
-- poor bubble sort
on mouseUp
  init
  -- now sort
  put true into sorting
  repeat while sorting
    put false into sorting
    repeat with i = 1 to 29
      comparison
      put hival(i) into a
      put hival(i+1) into b
      if a <= b then
        white i
        hi i+1, a
        white i+1
        black i
        hi i, b
        black i+1
        put true into sorting
      end if
    end repeat
  end repeat
end mouseUp
```

The only difference between this and the last is that the comparison is <= rather than <. This makes the algorithm wrong in some cases, and it takes *much* longer when it does work. If you animate it, it is easy to see why! It is useful to compare bubble sort with a better algorithm, like insert sort:

```
-- simple insert sort
on mouseUp
  init
  -- now sort
  repeat with i = 29 down to 1
  put hival(i) into a
  put i into j
  white j
  repeat while j < 30 and a < hival(j+1)
    comparison
    hi j, hival(j+1)
    black j
    add 1 to j
    white j
  end repeat
```

```
      comparison
      hi j, a
      black j
      end repeat
    end mouseUp
```

Try these three algorithms out on random, increasing and decreasing sequences. You should find that the bad bubble sort is terrible, and insert sort is much better than either of the bubble sorts.

The remaining handlers to define are init, **assignment** and **comparison**. They are all straightforward:

```
  on init
    reset_animation
    put short name of target into line 1 of card field "steps"
  end init

  on assignment
    global assignmentCount
    add 1 to assignmentCount
    put "Assignment" && assignmentCount into line 3 of card field "steps"
  end assignment

  on comparison
    global comparisonCount
    add 1 to comparisonCount
    put "Comparison" && comparisonCount into line 2 of card field "steps"
  end comparison
```

If you run an open day or demonstration day, it may be useful for animations to run endlessly and automatically. A button **Auto demo** does this. It loops for ever, clicking on various buttons on the card. You will be able to devise your own quite easily, perhaps clicking buttons at random.

```
  on mouseUp
    repeat forever
      click at the loc of card button randomize
      click at the loc of card button "good bubble sort"
      click at the loc of card button randomize
      click at the loc of card button "good insert sort"
    end repeat
  end mouseUp
```

8.4   Direct manipulation

All the examples we've covered so far in this chapter have been depressingly automatic; they have required no interaction with the user. Direct manipulation, in contrast, is animation done directly with the mouse. As the user moves the mouse, so the graphics move directly. Another example of direct manipulation, a simple 'window manager', was discussed in Chapter 2.

Many situations where a HyperCard stack wants the user to give some numbers can be better done by direct manipulation. An example is a stack that introduces a student to spreadsheets or matrices, which are being simulated by a grid of fields. The first thing the student is supposed to do is specify what size the grid is to be. We could use two **ask** commands, one to get the number of columns, and one to get the number of rows. This is certainly the easiest to program, and can be used to provide helpful, if condescending, instructions along with the **ask**, as in ask "Type number of rows (1 to 5):". Another approach is to have two fields: this has two advantages, the fields can easily display what numbers the user chose last time, and the user is not forced to fill in one field before the other: they can do it in either order.

These two methods require the user to count and to type. Children may be able to do neither, and anyway when it is possible to avoid typing using the mouse is always preferable. Unfortunately programming HyperTalk to provide a direct manipulation alternative is somewhat harder than two **ask** dialogs! But we will learn a few useful techniques along the way.

We must decide how to make the grid of fields work: we can either have the right number of fields or we could *show* the right number of fields, secretly having enough for the largest sized grid the user is allowed. The latter is far more efficient, since changing a field from hidden to visible takes far less time than choosing the field tool, making a new field, moving it into position, and so forth.

The first problem is to arrange a grid of, say, 5 by 5 fields of the appropriate size regularly on a card. It is best done by a script:

```
on mouseUp
   get number of fields
   set cursor to watch
   set editbkgnd to true
   repeat with x = 1 to 5
     repeat with y = 1 to 5
       doMenu new field
       add 1 to it
       set the width of field it to 50
       set the height of field it to 20
       set the loc of field it to 60*x+40, 30*y+20 -- field 5x+y-5
     end repeat
   end repeat
```

```
      set editbkgnd to false
      choose browse tool
    end mouseUp
```

If these fields are for a spreadsheet or mathematical matrix, then you'd probably also **set the textAlign of field it to right**, so that numbers in the fields are right-adjusted. The figure (below) shows the 25 fields as they might appear when right-adjusted and initialized by using **random(100)**. We've drawn a simple grey background to make them look better.

12	13	52	28	72
69	59	100	71	5
25	95	11	99	98
24	35	91	24	98
69	100	61	74	20

The numbers in the script (like 60, 40, 30, 20) can be adjusted to get the grid proportions that you want for the application. You run the script, see where the fields end up, adjust the numbers and then have another go. So it is a good idea to add some script to get rid of the fields, so that creating fields can start from scratch. The following will do, and should be inserted just before the first repeat loop:

```
choose field tool
repeat with i = 1 to number of fields
  show field 1                        -- a hidden field can't be clicked
  click at the loc of field 1
  doMenu "clear field"
end repeat
```

The idea of direct manipulation is that the user chooses a tool (like HyperCard's line tool) and then uses the mouse to apply that tool. The tool either gets 'put down' when the user releases the mouse or when a different tool is selected. If the user only ever does one thing, it might be easiest to have a card **mouseStillDown** handler to do the work, but the tool metaphor suggests clicking on a button (perhaps one of several) to select the tool.

The tool button's script will therefore look something like:

```
on mouseUp
  set cursor to cross               -- a cursor symbol chosen for this tool
  toolwork
end mouseUp
```

Very often the action of direct manipulation, say dragging a graphic around the card window, only occurs while the mouse button is held down. But the handler is for **mouseUp**. Do we need another handler for **mouseDown** (and **mouseStillDown**) that uses some technique to tell when they are supposed to be activated? Rather than use global variables (or the **hilite** property of the tool button), it is far better to stay under the control of the tool button's own script. We wait, within the **mouseUp** handler, for the mouse to be clicked down again, then while the mouse is still down, we do the work the tool is supposed to do. Here is the scheme:

```
on mouseUp
  set the cursor to cross
  wait until the mouse is down
  repeat while the mouse is down
    get the mouseloc
    -- now do the work at location it
  end repeat
  set cursor to normal
end mouseUp
```

This scheme gives the user the impression that the tool is automatically deselected after he releases the mouse. The last line, **set cursor to normal**, is not required, since HyperCard does that as soon as an **idle** message is processed.

The final **mouseUp** handler also contains two **answer** commands to give the user some additional help. Notice the commented-out **put** lines: these helped debug the handler (the numbers used here should correspond to the numbers used in the field setting-up handler described above, otherwise the mouse position won't coincide with the field positions whose visibility it is changing). A few lines of script make sure that x and y are between 1 and 5, so we only refer to the 25 fields we created: code like this is really important to make sure HyperCard doesn't fall over on the user!

```
on mouseUp
  answer "Click and drag the mouse within the grey area" && ¬
  "to adjust visible fields."
  set the cursor to cross
  wait until the mouse is down
  repeat while the mouse is down
    get the mouseloc
    put trunc((item 1 of it-10)/60) into x
    put trunc((item 2 of it)/30) into y
    if x < 1 then put 1 into x
    else if x > 5 then put 5 into x
    if y < 1 then put 1 into y
    else if y > 5 then put 5 into y
    -- put x && y                    -- check we've done the right arithmetic
    get 5*x+y-5
    -- put it                        -- check we've worked out the right field
    if it > number of fields then put number of fields into it
    repeat with i = 1 to it
      set the visible of field i to ((i-1) mod 5) < y
    end repeat
    repeat with i = 1+it to number of fields
      hide field i
```

```
      end repeat
   end repeat
   answer "You have selected" && x & "x" & y && "=" && x*y && "fields."
end mouseUp
```

A small point here is that we set the cursor shape *after* calling **answer**, since **answer** itself changes the cursor to an arrow, which isn't what we want.

12	13	52
69	59	100
25	95	11
24	35	91

Like many interactive programs, the way this script works is best understood by trying it out: it works far more naturally than it appears from reading it! How does it work? The user clicks on the tool button, the answer dialog box appears and tells him what to do. While holding the mouse down, he can adjust the size of the grid of fields. If he releases the mouse over the field showing 91, he'd be left with the fields shown in the illustration visible.

Outline direct manipulation

Hiding and showing lots of fields (up to 25 in the previous example) can get too slow for effective direct manipulation, and often we may want to do even more sophisticated things. There are ways of speeding up the script (for example only changing the visibility of affected fields, rather than all of them, as the script above does), but sometimes there is no faster way of working. In this case, direct manipulation should work by animating a suggestive outline of what is wanted. You will have noticed that the Macintosh user interface does this, for example, when a window is moved: just the outline of the window moves, and this can be done faster than moving the whole contents of the window.

We'll redo the previous example by using an outline method. A rectangular button ('outline') is the easiest way to generate an outline that can be adjusted without lots of drawing operations; buttons are easy and efficient to move and resize.

So, simply, when the outline drag tool is selected, the rectangle of the outline button is adjusted to follow the mouse cursor. In our example, we want to keep the top left of the button fixed, and move the bottom right. To provide helpful feedback to the user, we make the name of the button say what size it is.

Almost all of the handler works the same way as before. The repeat loop only changes the size and name of the outline button. When the repeat loop terminates, because the user released the mouse button, the grid size is set by calling a handler **setsize**: it works exactly as before, and it's too boring to write out twice. Calling handlers like **setsize** is clearer programming but a bit slower; but in the outline direct manipulation handler we needn't be worried about the time taken to call a handler since it is only called once.

```
on mouseUp
  set name of bg button id 336 to "4x4"
  set rect of bg button id 336 to 75,40,305,150
  show bg button id 336
  answer "Drag bottom right of 4x4 outline with mouse."
  set cursor to 3 -- a sort of cross
  wait until the mouse is down
  repeat until the mouse is up
    put trunc((mouseh()-10)/60) into x
    put trunc(mousev()/30) into y
    if x < 1 then put 1 into x
    else if x > 5 then put 5 into x
    if y < 1 then put 1 into y
    else if y > 5 then put 5 into y
    set rect of bg button id 336 to 75, 40, (x+1)*60+5, (y+1)*30
    set name of bg button id 336 to x & "x" & y
  end repeat
  setsize x, y
  hide bg button id 336
end mouseUp
```

The outline button has to be referred to as **bg button id 336** since we keep changing its name! We use the button's ID since this won't change, even if we bring the button closer or send it farther away: we might want the button to be behind the fields it is controlling, or in front of them. For our example, since we change the button's name, it obviously should be in front of the fields (otherwise its name might be obscured behind some fields). The field creation button therefore needs changing to ensure that the outline button is in front of the new fields we make – new objects are always created 'on top', so for each new object, we should bring the outline button closer by one. So add the following to the field creation handler:

```
choose button tool
show bg button id 336
click at the loc of bg button id 336
repeat for 25 times
  doMenu "Bring closer"
end repeat
hide bg button id 336
```

How does the method work? As before the user chooses the tool by clicking on the button. The outline button appears, and as the user drags the mouse, the bottom right of the button tracks the mouse. When the user releases the mouse, the grid of fields is adjusted to the size of the button. The figure below shows the button with its name (4x4) and the cross cursor.

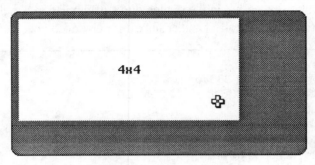

Direct manipulation with more than one tool

If we want more than one tool for direct manipulation, the best way to do this is by using a palette, just like the HyperCard paint tools palette. However, the problem with palettes is that they are a bit trickier to design than menus (and, indeed, you can't do them unless you have the power tools stack). The best approach is to decide how you want the palette to work by first putting the operations into a menu, and getting it to work properly. When it works to your satisfaction, make a palette and get it to send the messages sent by the menu; you can then delete the menu. Chapter 9 tells you more about palettes and menus.

About Menus

Menus and programming their operations

The menus in the HyperCard menu bar can be created and modified, and their operations can be programmed in HyperTalk.

Menus provide another way for you to make operations available to the users of your stacks, as a useful alternative to buttons. The main advantages of menus is that they do not take up space in the card design and they remain available even when you change backgrounds and stacks, yet they can do most things buttons do. On the other hand, buttons are more readily visible to the user and can be much more help for new HyperCard users who might not think of browsing around menus looking for what they can do! The choice is really one of expectations: unless you add new menu titles, users may not think of looking in what – at first sight – appear to be HyperCard's standard menus.

HyperCard 'looks after' buttons in stacks; as you go from card to card, or from stack to stack, buttons *automatically* disappear and appear, depending on whether they are card buttons or background buttons. HyperCard does not do this for menus or menu items – once put in a menu, a menu item stays there until a script takes it out. The main challenge that this chapter addresses is how to program menus to behave the way you want them to.

Since changes to menus are completely under your control, menus are particularly useful for 'tool' operations that remain accessible when the user goes from card to card, background to background or stack to stack. Menus are therefore especially useful for stacks that are used by other stacks. They are also useful for operations that are likely to be used only occasionally, for example, operations to analyse or modify the behaviour of a stack – the operations in the **Home** menu of the *Home* stack being a good example.

The standard *Power Tools* stack provides a simple mechanism for creating menus, but it is probably more confusing than it is worth. The Power Tools stack also provides a mechanism for creating palettes – rather like the HyperCard tool and pattern palettes. So far as their programming is concerned these behave in a very similar way to menus, and we won't dwell on them in this chapter, except for a brief discussion at the end.

9.1 Using menus

If you want your stack to resemble a conventional Macintosh application as closely as possible, you should follow the usual conventions. Menu operations ending in **...** ask the user for more interaction: **Print...** being a typical example, where a dialog box appears asking how many copies you want to print. You can achieve the same sort of effect in HyperCard by making menu items go to a card that shows a picture of the dialog box, and of course, the (simulated) dialog box's buttons and text fields will be normal HyperCard buttons and text fields. With a bit of effort, you can ensure the background picture is the same, and perhaps copy the card image (without messing up the dialog box drawing)! If you want a dialog box to be used on only one card, you can keep it in the card image and use **hide** and **show card picture** to control whether it is visible.

HyperCard provides the following basic facilities for manipulating menus from HyperTalk:

```
create menu name
delete menu name
```

These two commands respectively create an empty menu and delete a menu title in the menu bar. A newly created menu will be at the far right of the menu bar. It is an error to create a menu that is there or to delete a menu that isn't there. Fortunately, the **there is** operator can be used, as in:

```
if there is a menu m then delete menu m
```

Also, **the menus** provides a return-separated list of the names of the menus in the menu bar. You might like to type **answer the menus** in the message box to see it easily.

The operations on items within a menu are handled a little strangely by HyperTalk. To **set** menu items (**menuItems** in HyperTalk), you can use an item list (a comma-separated list) or a sequence of lines (a return-separated list); when you **get** menu items, however, you get a return-separated list. Furthermore, you cannot change a menu item by using **put "thing" into item 3 of menu x**, instead you have to write **menuItem** in full: **put "thing" into menuItem 3 of menu x**. You can use the other prepositions **before** and **after** (instead of **into**) as usual. **Delete** works as usual (as a general deleter): you can use it (as above) to delete the entire menu, or by specifying particular menu items, you can delete just those from the menu.

Once a menu has been created it can be used immediately. For example:

```
create menu "My Fonts"
put "Courier,Helvetica,Times" into menu "My Fonts"
```

gives you a menu that can be used to change fonts, perhaps faster than the standard, larger, **Font** menu. The menu will work in exactly the same way as HyperCard's existing **Font** menu because HyperCard automatically sends a doMenu message when the user selects a menu item.

For example, HyperCard would send the message, doMenu "Courier", "My Fonts" if you selected the first item of the **My Fonts** menu, and if there is no handler for it in the current path, it will be handled in HyperCard just as though you had used the **Courier** entry in the normal **Fonts** menu.

But the message can also be caught in a normal doMenu handler in a card, background or stack script, depending on where you want it to take effect. If you handle doMenu messages, you'll also get doMenu messages whenever the user selects operations from the standard HyperCard menus, so you should use **pass** to pass those messages to HyperCard (see Chapter 4 for an explanation of **pass**). Otherwise you could get in a position where **Quit** won't quit from HyperCard (which, looked at the other way, would be useful if you want to leave HyperCard running with no easy way of stopping it)! The following handler is the sort of thing that is required:

```
on doMenu mitem, m
  answer the params -- just to see what's going on
  if mitem = "Courier" then
    beep
    put "Courier font selected"
    exit doMenu
  else if m = "Font" then
    -- and so on
  end if
  pass doMenu
end doMenu
```

This handler will *stop* you from using Courier, indeed, whether Courier came from our **My Fonts** menu or the original **Font** menu! Of course, we would have done something more substantial than beeping and putting "Courier font selected" into the message window in a *real* handler! But we can also use handlers like this to convert HyperCard's *existing* menu items to our own purposes. For example, this would be useful if we had provided a **Find** button, and we wanted the **Go** menu's existing **Find...** to work in exactly the same way:

```
-- this code makes both menu selection and command–F click a button
if m = "Find..." then
    click at the loc of button "Find"
    exit doMenu
end if
```

The **Find** button might bring up a dialog box, for instance. Alternatively, the button's mouseUp handler could doMenu "Find...", then the script to do the actual finding could be more localized, say, on a background or stack script, and hence shared with several backgrounds that maybe don't even have a button called **Find**.

Menu messages

DoMenu handlers soon become messy since there are very many cases that have to be considered. HyperTalk therefore allows you to 'do your own thing' rather than automatically generating a doMenu message: with each menu item you can attach a message, a so-called *menu message*. So, when the user selects a menu item its **menuMessage** is sent – unless you have a doMenu handler (in the current card, background, stack, any stack in use, or the *Home* stack) that intercepts it first. That is, menu messages are sent by HyperCard *only* after it has got the doMenu message, not as soon as the user selects the menu item.

You use **set** to set a menu message. For example, to set the menu message of a menu item **beep** in the menu **test** actually to do a beep, do this:

> set the menuMessage of menuItem "beep" of menu "test" to beep

You can place any message in place of **beep** in this example. (We will give a realistic example making full use of menu messages later in this chapter.) Hence the simple doMenu handler we gave above can be dispensed with. In the doMenu handler we actually wanted to do several things when **Courier** was selected – since menu messages are only single messages, we have to define a new message and a handler for it:

> set the menuMessage of menuItem "Courier" of menu "My Font" to courier

Having done that, a possible handler for **courier** would be:

```
on courier
  beep
  put "Courier font selected"
end courier
```

You find out what a menu message is by using the menuMessage of menuItem *i* of menu *m*, for instance in a **get** or **put** command. The menu item description *i* may either be the actual name of the menu item, or a number (1 for the first item). Menuitem *i* of menu *m* should be used in preference to line *i* of menu *m* – since line *i* only gives you the *name* of the menu item, not the menu item itself. (There is further confusion since you can't use menuitem to refer to more than one menu item, unlike item which can be used in expressions like item 1 to 4 of x.)

Since menu messages are so useful, it is possible to set them in other, possibly more convenient ways. If you are using **put** to set up a menu's menu items you can also set up the menu messages at the same time, so long as you provide the same number of menu messages! The following form does both at once:

> put "a,b,c" into menu "test" with menuMessages "x,y,z"

You can use the usual **put** prepositions: **before** and **after**, if you want to put the new menu items before or after an existing entry.

Menu styles and properties

As well as menu messages, menu items can have command characters (so the user can type **command–Q** instead of selecting **Quit** from the **File** menu) and check marks. Also menu items can be enabled or disabled. HyperCard does not (yet!) let you provide icons, change the font of menu items, or (unfortunately) have hierarchical menus: if you want to do these things you'll have to write – or better, find one that's already written! – an external command (XCMD), which involves programming out of HyperTalk, probably in Pascal.

Like menu messages, command characters are set by using a property: the commandChar property: set the commandChar of menuItem n of menu m to c, where c is a character. Similarly, a menu's checkmarks are set (or unset) by set the checkmark of menuItem n of menu m to b, where b is (or evaluates to) true or false; the check mark is usually a tick (✓), but you can set the markChar property to use other characters (see the example below).

Enabling is done by setting the enabled property: set the enabled of menuItem n of menu m to b. Enabling/disabling can also be done with menu names in the menu bar, effectively enabling or disabling the entire menu. The style of menu items can be changed to any combination of text styles (plain, *italic*, **bold**, etc.) – but this feature is normally only used for text style menus (again, see example below). The final feature of menu styles is the grey dividing line between menu items: this is created simply by using - (a minus sign) as the menu item. When you get menu items that represent dividing lines, a number is appended to make the entries unique, so that they can more easily be deleted. (HyperCard 2.0v2 and later versions give -1, -2 and so on, for the dividing lines of the standard HyperCard menus, but not for the dividing lines that you create yourself!)

There is an alternative way of enabling and disabling, not using set, which you may find more convenient:

```
enable menuItem n of menu m
enable menu m
disable menuItem n of menu m
disable menu n
```

The following picture shows all the possibilities used in a single menu:

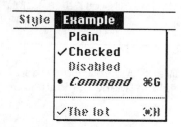

And the HyperTalk scripting to get the menu effects shown:

```
on aMenu
  disable menu "Style"
  create menu "Example"
  put "Plain,Checked,Disabled,Command,-,The lot" into menu "Example"
  set the checkMark of menuItem 2 of menu "Example" to true
  disable menuItem 3 of menu "Example"
  set the commandChar of menuItem 4 of menu "Example" to "G"
  set the checkMark of last menuItem of menu "Example" to true
  disable last menuItem of menu "Example"
  set the commandChar of last menuItem of menu "Example" to "H"
  set the textStyle of menuItem 4 of menu "Example" to italic
  set the markChar of menuItem 4 of menu "Example" to "•"
end aMenu
```

The advantage of disabled menus and menu items is that users can see what they *might* be able to do. Sometimes the reason for disabling a menu is that users simply *cannot* do something at the moment, in that it doesn't make any sense (such as a **Cut** when nothing is selected to cut). You can also use disabled menus and menu items for helping users learn about your stack. Beginning users still like to know what they will be able to do, but by disabling menus and menu items you can easily protect them from making mistakes with features that they don't yet know about. However, a disabled menu won't let users look at its menu items; so it may be more helpful to learners to do the following, rather than **disable menu "X"**:

```
repeat with i = 1 to number of menuItems in menu "X"
  disable menuItem i of menu "X"
end repeat
```

You will often want to set the style, check marking or enabling of menu items in **openCard**. Here is a simple example: we assume we've got a menu item **Mark** in the menu **Card**:

```
on openCard
  set checkMark of menuItem "Mark" of menu "Card" to the marked of this card
  pass openCard
end openCard
```

Better to make no assumptions (this works even if there is not a menu **Card**, whether or not it contains the menu item **Mark**):

```
on openCard
  if there is a menuItem "Mark" of menu "Card" then
    set checkMark of menuItem "Mark" of menu "Card" to the marked of this card
  end if
  pass openCard
end openCard
```

9.2   Showing whether objects have scripts

HyperCard's **Objects** menu has menu items for getting information about the stack, background and card. You often have to select these (holding down the shift key to be faster) to see whether there are scripts in the objects. It would be nicer if HyperCard checked the menu items for objects that had scripts. Here we see the **Objects** menu with checkmarks showing that the current background and stack have scripts, but the current card does not:

```
 Objects
   Button Info...
   Field Info...
   Card Info...
 ✓ Bkgnd Info...
 ✓ Stack Info...

   Bring Closer    ⌘•
   Send Farther    ⌘-

   New Button
   New Field
   New Background
```

The following handler, check_menus, sets the check mark of each menu item if the corresponding object has a script.

```
on check_menus
    if there is a menuItem "Card info..." of menu "Objects" then
        set checkMark of menuItem "Card info..." of menu "Objects" to ¬
        script of this card ≠ empty
    end if
    if there is a menuItem "Bkgnd info..." of menu "Objects" then
        set checkMark of menuItem "Bkgnd info..." of menu "Objects" to ¬
        script of this background ≠ empty
    end if
    if there is a menuItem "Stack info..." of menu "Objects" then
        set checkMark of menuItem "Stack info..." of menu "Objects" to ¬
        script of this stack ≠ empty
    end if
end check_menus
```

We need to arrange that check_menus is called whenever any details may have changed. We need a few handlers like the following, perhaps in the Home script or in a tools stack that can be used (see Chapter 4 for a discussion of *stack using*, and below for techniques for scripting the feature).

```
on openCard
  check_menus
  pass openCard
end openCard

on openBackground
  check_menus
  pass openBackground
end openBackground

on openStack
  check_menus
  pass openStack
end openStack

on resumeStack
  check_menus
  pass resumeStack
end resumeStack
```

Simplifying menus

Delete can be useful if you want to make an 'easy to use' stack with as few irrelevant menu items as possible. In the following script, we delete the (possibly confusing) **Compact Stack** menu item from the **File** menu. Once deleted, there will be two adjacent dim grey lines if the userLevel is 1 or 2, and we should delete one of them:

```
delete menuItem "Compact Stack" from menu "File"
if the userLevel < 3 then delete menuItem "-1" from menu "File"
```

We could have deleted menuItem 5, if we are certain it *was* the fifth item; instead we had to discover (perhaps by typing answer menu "File" into the message window) that the grey lines are '-1','-2', rather than the expected '-'. Since we are real programmers, we should write scripts that don't depend on this curious feature which may be changed later – indeed, it is good practice to check for some other possibilities, as does the following script:

```
on removeCompact
  removeMenuItem "Compact Stack", "File"
end removeComp

on removeMenuItem mitem, m
  -- reset menubar -- (this line was used when we debugged the code)
  get menu m
  repeat with i = 1 to number of lines in it
    if line i of it = mitem then
      delete menuItem i of menu m
      if number of menuItems in menu m > 0 then
```

```
            -- deleting menuItem m may have left two adjacent dim lines
            if i > 1 and i ≤ number of menuItems in menu m then
                if char 1 of menuItem i of menu m = "-" then
                    -- if so, delete first one
                    if char 1 of menuItem i-1 of menu m = "-" then
                        delete menuItem i-1 of menu m
                    end if
                end if
            end if
            -- may have left a line at the top
            if char 1 of first menuItem of menu m = "-" then
                delete first menuItem of menu m
            end if
            -- may have left a line at the bottom
            if char 1 of last menuItem of menu m = "-" then
                delete last menuItem of menu m
            end if
        else
            -- we may want to delete an empty menu
            delete menu m
        end if
        exit removeMenuItem
    end if
  end repeat
end removeMenuItem
```

This handler takes care to sort out dividing lines in the menu, but if you modify the handler to enable, disable, or check menu items (rather than to delete menu items), you should of course dispense with the code that deletes menu dividing lines.

Sometimes we may not be sure which menu the menu item is in that we want to delete (or enable or check), in which case we have to search each menu item of each menu in the menus. Some menus may not belong to HyperCard (they might have been put up by DAs or other Macintosh utilities). For obscure reasons, such menus have names that are not empty but contain no words! The handler **removemitem** (which we write below) only needs a menu item name, but it does not check whether HyperCard will actually let you remove the menu item – the **Font** menu, for instance, is fussy.

```
  -- handler that looks for the rightmost menu to remove menuItem m from
on removemitem m
    repeat with i = number of lines in the menus down to 1
        get line i of the menus
        if number of words in it ≠ 0 then -- check it's not a nonstandard menu
            get menu it
            repeat with j = 1 to number of lines in it
                if line j of it = m then
                    removeMenuItem m, line i of the menus
                    exit removemitem
```

```
        end if
      end repeat
    end if
  end repeat
end removemitem
```

For example, calling removemitem "Quit HyperCard" will stop anyone quitting HyperCard by using the menu or by typing **command–Q**. If you then remove the keyboard from the Mac, you have a pretty safe environment for running HyperCard demonstrations in a public place.

When you get menus in a mess, **reset menubar** restores HyperCard's normal menu bar – though you will lose any menus placed there by other stacks (unless they notice that their menus have vanished)! It's a good idea to reset the menu bar if you delete menu items by specifying their item numbers rather than their names.

Handling menus (and palettes) in several stacks

Although menus are conceptually objects, HyperTalk does not treat them like other objects. Whereas buttons are on cards or backgrounds, you don't have card or background menus, or even stack menus. The consequence of this is that some thought has to go into making sure your stack displays the right menus at the right time!

HyperCard sends the message **openStack** when a stack is first opened, and you'll probably use a handler for this message to initialize anything the stack requires, such as global variables, palettes and menus. When HyperCard sends **closeStack**, the stack is closed and you'll tidy up by deleting the menus and palettes so that they don't clutter up the Macintosh screen. This is all straightforward, but things get more complicated when the user has more than one stack open at a time. When several stacks are open, it is important not to leave menus and palettes on the screen when they no longer work.

Whether or not you intend your stack to be used together with other stacks, it's as well to follow the guidelines this section describes.

The **openStack** handler should initialize things for your stack. For concreteness, we'll assume that the stack puts up a menu created by a handler **createMenu** (we give the script for **createMenu** later). An initial attempt at an **openStack** handler that does this could look like:

```
on openStack
  createMenu
end openStack
```

Likewise, **closeStack** would call **deleteMenu**. But this is inadequate as it stands: the menu might be left on the menu bar even when this stack is not running. It's therefore important to handle **suspend** and **resume** messages that are sent when the user clicks on other stacks. Also, you may be using stacks that need to handle messages for their own purposes (for instance, in deciding whether *they* will display menus); we should **pass** all messages on to them. We can improve the stack script as follows:

```
on openStack
  createMenu
  pass openStack
end openStack

on closeStack
  deleteMenu
  pass closeStack
end closeStack

-- sent when the user clicks on this stack (when it wasn't on top)
on resumeStack
  createMenu
  pass resumeStack
end resumeStack

-- sent when the user clicks on another stack (when this one was on top)
on suspendStack
  deleteMenu
  pass suspendStack
end suspendStack
```

This scripting (which is usually put in the stack script) is correct, so far as it goes. However, we may also want to provide handlers – or menus – that can be accessed from other stacks when they are on top. This is done by using the HyperTalk command **start using**, and, simply, we start using this stack in the **openStack** handler. Once a stack is in use, messages that the current stack either passes on or does not handle will be passed through this stack (because it is being *used*). That means that we can leave menus up that have messages to be handled by this stack. To avoid the risk that the top stack handles them, we can make them **send** messages to a specific stack where they should be handled.

A new problem arises when we **start using** a stack: we may get **openStack**, **resumeStack** and other messages that do not refer to *this* stack being opened or resumed (or anything else). So the handlers given above would create and delete menus when another stack was opened and closed! There are several ways to avoid this (final!) problem. Some stacks we have seen use the function **the stacks** to see which is the top-most stack. **The stacks** returns a list of open stacks, one per line, with the current stack as the first line. Thus, by looking at the first line it is possible to tell if the current stack is the one where messages such as **openStack** were originally addressed.

There are simpler ways to do it. First, we could place the **openStack**, **closeStack** and other handlers for system messages in the first card of *our* stack. Thus, when the stack is opened or closed it will get these messages, since HyperCard sends them along the current message path starting with the current card. Later, when our stack is in use, stack messages that originated from other stacks' activities would go through our stack script, and not be handled in the card script. However, we can't always put **openStack** and **closeStack** handlers in the stack's first card (or first background) because of the way the stack needs to be designed (see below). In this case a sensible approach is illustrated below, using **the long name** property in a simple function **notMe()**:

```
-- return true if the stack getting the messages is not this one
function notMe
    -- the top most stack is line 1 of the stacks
    return long name of this stack is not long name of me
end notMe
```

Recall from Chapter 4 that the **name of this stack** will be the stack that is currently running, whereas **name of me** is the name of the object where the handler is defined. We've used the **long name** property, which gives the full file pathname, because this ensures **notMe** is correct even if we have several stacks with the same names, but of course they'll have to be in different folders or on different disks – and then their long names will be different.

We modify all the other handlers we've written (**openStack**, **closeStack**, **resumeStack**, **suspendStack**) to **pass** their message when **notMe()** returns true. In all cases, if **notMe** is true then we **pass** the relevant message (either to another stack or to HyperCard itself), otherwise we handle the message as above. We now have:

```
on openStack
    if notMe() then pass openStack
    createMenu
    start using this stack
    pass openStack
end openStack

on closeStack
    if notMe() then pass closeStack
    deleteMenu
    stop using this stack
    pass closeStack
end closeStack

on resumeStack
    -- when this stack is clicked
    if notMe() then pass resumeStack
    createMenu
    -- note that resumeStack might want to check which background we
    -- have resumed to, in case different backgrounds provide different
    -- menus or, for example, to set different checked or enabled menu items
    pass resumeStack
end resumeStack

on suspendStack
    -- sent when another stack is clicked
```

```
      if notMe() then pass suspendStack
      deleteMenu
      pass suspendStack
   end suspendStack
```

A typical occasion when it is helpful to use the **notMe()** approach – rather than putting simple handlers in the first card's script – is when we want to adjust menus to relate to whichever stack is open, as would be the case when one provides menu items to go to each card or background of the currently open stack. Below is shown how **openStack** might operate: it has to adjust the menus if it is not this stack that is being opened, otherwise it must create the relevant menus (or menu items).

```
   on openStack
     if notMe() then adjustMenus
     else createMenus
   end openStack
```

It's worth devoting a word about the handlers for creating and deleting menus: they ought to take care that they don't create menus that are already there, and don't delete menus that aren't there! In the following code, we've given the menu a rather boring name – something like **first word of short name of this stack** might have produced something more imaginative.

```
   on createMenu
     if there is not a menu "X" then
       create menu "X"
       put "Y" into menu "X" with menuMessage "Z"
     end if
   end createMenu

   on deleteMenu
     if there is a menu "X" then
       delete menu "X"
     end if
   end deleteMenu
```

Handlers for setting the **userLevel** should be called in the same places as **createMenu** and **deleteMenu**. Here we assume that we want the **userLevel** to be **5**, and the handlers are straightforward – though **resetUserLevel** works even if we forget to call **setUserLevel** first:

```
   on setUserLevel
     global savedUserLevel
     put the userLevel into savedUserLevel
     set the userLevel to 5
   end setUserLevel
```

```
on resetUserLevel
  global savedUserLevel
  if savedUserLevel is a number then
    set the userLevel to savedUserLevel
  end if
end resetUserLevel
```

9.3   CantAbort and aborted handlers

The greatest problem with menus is that you can never quite be certain what menus are actually displayed, and with their menu messages, exactly what they are doing. Problems can arise from poorly written handlers (such as **suspendStack**) in other people's stacks leaving unwanted menus and menu items in place when your stack is running. This problem is exacerbated by menu messages sending messages that may have accidental effects in your own scripts.

Here are some useful suggestions:

- In your handlers **openStack** and **resumeStack**, unless there is a good reason not to, **reset the menubar**. (But you probably won't want to reset the menu bar in stacks that merely provide themselves for use by other stacks.)

- Use menu messages sparingly. You are probably better off using **doMenu**. Menu messages have to do something, but menu items without menu messages are harmless if you forget to process them in a **doMenu** handler.

- Use the **cantAbort** stack property sparingly – and only once you are certain everything works – in your **openStack**, **closeStack**, **suspendStack** and **resumeStack** handlers.

- Make certain that your stack has the menus it expects, and that you don't leave other stacks with menus they don't want. (Notwithstanding HyperCard quirks: there are ways of 'resuming' stacks without being sent a **resumeStack** message! If you are really worried, you will have to check things in an **idle** handler.)

9.4   Examples using menus

Like buttons, menus can be used for practically anything. We'll give three examples of their use.

An overhead talk stack

If you are able to use a screen projector connected to your Macintosh you can use HyperCard for presenting talks. Unless you want colour, HyperCard is as good as any other presentation program, better perhaps, because you can program it easily to get just the sort of eye-catching effects you want.

For a typical talk, you will have a stack of 30 or so cards, possibly many more if you have animation sequences (see Chapter 8). Your talk will progress card-by-card as you press the right arrow key on the keyboard. This all sounds very systematic, but giving talks is an unpredictable business. What happens if nobody wants to hear about your introduction (they already know it)? What happens if you need to go over a whole section again? And so on.

Menus can come to your rescue as follows. We will assume that each new topic in your talk starts with a card that you have named. When the stack is opened, we build a **Talk** menu by searching the stack for any named cards. The card names become menu items, and we arrange the menu so that selecting a menu item goes to that card, namely, the first card in the talk about that topic.

It's wise to add a completely blank card (called **Blank** – you might want a black one and a white one, to suit the projector and lighting) which you can put at the end of your stack: then you can easily use the **Talk** menu to blank out the projection screen if you want to.

Here's one way to do it:

```
on talkmenu
  if there is no menu "Talk" then
    create menu "Talk"
    getcardnames
  end if
end talkmenu

on getcardnames
  put empty into menu "Talk"
  repeat with i = 1 to number of cards
    get the short name of card i
    if first word of it ≠ "Card" then
      put it after menu "Talk"
      set the menuMessage of last menuItem of menu "Talk" to ¬
      "go card" && i && "of" && name of this stack
    end if
  end repeat
  put "-,Update menu" after menu "Talk"
  set the menuMessage of last menuItem of menu "Talk" to ¬
  "send getcardnames to" && name of me
end getcardnames
```

Note that by using send *message* to name of me as the menu message (see the last line of the getcardnames handler), we avoid the complication of using stacks – the message will be sent to the correct stack (me), even if it is not in use.

You can use **mark** to remember cards that people raise questions on, so that you can easily go back and deal with them later. You can use various sorts of highlighting and visual effects too. A useful trick is to cover text to be highlighted with a transparent button, with a script as follows:

```
on mouseEnter
   set the hilite of me to true
end mouseEnter

on mouseLeave
   set the hilite of me to false
end mouseLeave
```

Highlighting inverts everything under the button: text or pictures – normally black on white – become white on black. By using **mouseEnter** and **mouseLeave** handlers, you can highlight the important parts of the card as you move the mouse around to point them out to the audience.

An object-property tool

Buttons and fields have properties, such as whether they are visible, whether they auto-highlight, whether they have locked text. We'll now make a simple menu that allows you to change any true/false property of a button or field.

The menu has menu items for each property, and a final item for removing the menu when you are finished with it.

```
ObjTools
   Button tools:
   AutoHilite
   Hilite
   SharedHilite
   ShowName
   Visible
   ...........................
   Field tools:
   AutoTab
   DontWrap
   LockText
   SharedText
   ShowLines
   Visible
   WideMargins
   ...........................
   Remove this menu
```

A handler **makeMenu** constructs the menu using a utility handler **ToolMenu** that we'll describe in a moment:

```
on makeMenu
  set cursor to watch
  if there is no menu "ObjTools" then create menu "ObjTools"
  put empty into menu "ObjTools"
  put "Button tools:" after menu "ObjTools"
  disable menuItem "Button tools:" of menu "ObjTools"
  ToolMenu "AutoHilite", "btn,bg btn", "arrow,cross", true
  ToolMenu "Hilite", "btn,bg btn", "arrow,cross", true
  ToolMenu "SharedHilite", "bg btn", "arrow,cross", true
  ToolMenu "ShowName", "btn,bg btn", "arrow,cross", true
  ToolMenu "Visible", "btn,bg btn", "arrow,cross", false
  put "-" after menu "ObjTools"
  put "Field tools:" after menu "ObjTools"
  disable menuItem "Field tools:" of menu "ObjTools"
  ToolMenu "AutoTab", "cd fld,fld", "arrow,cross", true
  ToolMenu "DontWrap", "cd fld,fld", "arrow,cross", true
  ToolMenu "LockText", "cd fld,fld", "locked,unlocked", true
  ToolMenu "SharedText", "fld", "arrow,cross", true
  ToolMenu "ShowLines", "cd fld,fld", "arrow,cross", true
  ToolMenu "Visible", "cd fld,fld", "arrow,cross", false
  ToolMenu "WideMargins", "cd fld,fld", "arrow,cross", true
  put "-" after menu "ObjTools"
  put "Remove this menu" after menu "ObjTools" ¬
  with menuMessage "unmakeMenu"
  start using me
end makeMenu
```

If you prefer, a simpler and shorter menu can be constructed since some properties are common to both buttons and fields, and the ToolMenu handler can do both at once:

```
ToolMenu "AutoHilite", "btn,bg btn", "arrow,cross", true
ToolMenu "Dontwrap", "cd fld,fld", "arrow,cross", true
ToolMenu "Hilite", "btn,bg btn", "arrow,cross", true
ToolMenu "LockText", "cd fld,fld", "locked,unlocked", true
ToolMenu "SharedHilite", "bg btn", "arrow,cross", true
ToolMenu "SharedText", "fld", "arrow,cross", true
ToolMenu "ShowLines", "cd fld,fld", "arrow,cross", true
ToolMenu "ShowName", "btn,bg btn", "arrow,cross", true
ToolMenu "Visible", "cd fld,fld,btn,bg btn", "arrow,cross", false
ToolMenu "WideMargins", "cd fld,fld", "arrow,cross", true
```

ToolMenu constructs menu items in the **ObjTools** menu; its first parameter (such as Autohilite) is both the property to be controlled and the menu item itself. The remaining properties say what sort of object this property applies to, what sort of cursor to use when controlling that property, and whether you can change the property if the object is hidden. (These parameters should become clear when we explain how properties are changed.) After constructing the menu, the last line of the makeMenu handler starts using this stack so that the menu messages that ToolMenu constructed will work from any stack. The simplest part of makeMenu makes the last menu item, **Remove this menu**, which has menu message unmakeMenu. This handler removes the menu and stops using the stack:

```
on unmakeMenu
  set cursor to watch
  if there is a menu "ObjTools" then delete menu "ObjTools"
  stop using me
end unmakeMenu
```

ToolMenu is the most interesting handler: it looks deceptively simple!

```
on toolMenu aProperty, objectTypes, cursorPair, visibleOnly
  get the params
  put "propertyTool" into word 1 of it -- replace handler name with propertyTool
  put aProperty after menu "ObjTools" with menuMessage it
end toolMenu
```

Given a property name (such as AutoHilite) it makes a menu entry **AutoHilite** which will send the menu message propertyTool with parameters that are toolMenu's own parameters. Thus toolMenu "AutoHilite", "btn,bgbtn", "arrow,cross", true makes a menu item **AutoHilite** and makes it send the message propertyTool "AutoHilite", "btn,bg btn", "arrow,cross", true.

Finally, we get on to the real 'work' of the **ObjTools** menu. When the menu sends the message propertyTool, we go into a repeat forever loop and wait until the user presses the mouse down. Hopefully this will be over a button or field (as appropriate for the property we are trying to change) – the function AnObjectAt will tell us what.

```
on propertyTool aProperty, objectTypes, cursorPair, visibleOnly
  set cursor to "plus"
  put the message into oldMessage
  put aProperty && "tool: click to escape"
  repeat forever
    put empty into prevObject
    repeat until the mouse is "down"
      repeat with i = 1 to number of items in objectTypes
        put AnObjectAt(item i of objectTypes, the mouseLoc, visibleOnly) ¬
        into theObject
        if theObject ≠ empty then exit repeat
      end repeat
```

If the object the user has clicked (theObject, possibly empty) on is a different object from the last one clicked on (prevObject), then something needs doing. Note how, as the user changes a property, we change both the cursor and the message displayed in the message window:

```
            if theObject ≠ prevObject then -- something needs changing
              put theObject into prevObject
              if theObject = empty then
                -- we're not now over an object
                set cursor to "plus"
                put aProperty && "tool: click to escape" into msg
              else
                -- change property of the object we're over
                get value(aProperty && "of" && theObject)
                put "Click to set the" && aProperty && "of" ¬
                && name of theObject && "to" && not it
                if it then set cursor to item 1 of cursorPair
                else set cursor to item 2 of cursorPair
              end if
            end if
          end repeat
          if theObject = empty then exit repeat
          else
            get aProperty && "of" && theObject
            do "set" && it && "to not" && it
          end if
          wait until the mouse is "up"
        end repeat
        put oldMessage
      end propertyTool
```

The function for finding objects at the mouse position is straightforward.

```
      function anObjectAt objectType, aLoc, visibleOnly
        repeat with i = 1 to value("number of" && objectType & "s")
          get objectType && i
          if visibleOnly and not visible of it then next repeat
          if aLoc is within rect of it then return it
        end repeat
        return empty
      end anObjectAt
```

All that remains are two utility handlers so that the **ObjTools** menu is installed by the
makeMenu handler when this stack is opened. We've used a function rightStack rather than
notMe this time:

```
      function rightStack
        return the long name of this stack is long name of me
      end rightStack
```

```
on openStack
  if rightStack() then makeMenu
  pass openStack
end openStack
```

RightStack is, of course, **not notMe()**, which sounds obscure.

A handler tool

Often you want to know just what handlers are available from any card within a stack you are developing. Suppose the **mouseUp** handler of a button calls the handler **x**. Now where is **x**? Is it in the card, background, or where?

We'll use HyperCard's menus and *stack using* features to make a simple, but useful, developer's tool: a menu that shows all current handlers, and which can find and let you edit the relevant scripts. We'll have some fun, since each menu item of the **Handlers** menu (as we shall call it) is going to work from whichever stack it is used.

First, let's get some of the routine scripting out of the way, so that we can quickly get on to the hard work. When the stack is opened, it creates its menu and tells HyperCard to start using it (so that it can intercept the menu messages from the menu it creates). Initially, the Handlers menu is empty but for a single menu item, **New Menu**. When the user selects this, HyperCard will send the menu message **processScript**, which will put all the current handler names into the menu.

```
on openStack
  if notMe() then pass openStack
  start using this stack
  if there is not a menu "Handlers" then
    create menu "Handlers"
    put "New menu" into menu "Handlers" with menuMsg processScript
  end if
end openStack

on closeStack
  if notMe() then pass closeStack
  stop using this stack
  if there is a menu "Handlers" then delete menu "Handlers"
end closeStack
```

So **processScript** will do all the work. But first, it's best to decide what sort of menu messages are required. Imagine that the menu item is **mouseUp**; its menu message will have to edit whichever script contains that **mouseUp** handler. We could simply have **edit the script of ...** as the menu message, which would certainly be efficient, but this will be harder to debug and we also want to be more useful. The menu message, instead, can send a message **editHandler** with the details of the object containing the handler. We'll also use **editHandler** to initialize the standard script editor's global variable **ScriptFindString** so that the user simply has to type ***command–G*** to locate the handler itself within the script.

Here is editHandler; we are fussy about which stack the script may be in, and that we distinguish between 'on' handlers and 'function' handlers. Notice the commented-out **answer** commands – vestiges of earlier debugging attempts!

```
on editHandler theHandler, theObject, theStack, theType
  global ScriptFindString
  -- answer thehandler && "in" && theobject && "in" && thestack

  -- get to the right stack where the script is
  if theStack ≠ short name of this stack then
    -- answer "In:" && short name of this stack
    -- answer "Go to:" && theStack
    go to stack theStack
  end if

  -- initialize ScriptFindString
  if theType is "h" then put "on" && theHandler into ScriptFindString
  else put "function" && theHandler into ScriptFindString

  edit script of theObject
end editHandler
```

If the menu item **mouseUp** is selected, you can see that we intend to send a menu message something like: editHandler "mouseUp","cd btn id 67","bars","h". Here we've selected a **mouseUp** in a card button (with ID 67) in the stack **bars**. The "h" indicates that this is a handler (on mouseUp) rather than a function. (We could have sent a message editHandler "on mouseUp" ... , without the final parameter. Apart from saving a little space when the handler is a function, there is a lesson to be learnt later on from doing it this way!)

How is the menu created in the first place? ProcessScript is called (without any parameters) when the user selects **New Menu** from the **Handlers** menu. ProcessScript then collects all the handler names from the stack script, the current background script, the current card script and the button and field scripts (on both the background and card). This job is most easily done recursively. ProcessScript, then, has a parameter which is the object whose script it is collecting handler names from; if no object is given, it is to use the current stack – and, incidentally, this is a new call to processScript, so the menu has to be re-initialized.

```
on processScript theObject
  -- answer theobject
  if the paramcount = 0 then
    put "stack" into theObject
    put "New menu" into menu "Handlers" with menuMsg processScript
```

The next step is to recurse, to process the current background:

```
        processScript "bg id" && id of this bg
    else
```

Otherwise, we are on a background, card, background field, background button, card field or card button. We recurse as necessary, and in the case of fields and buttons, recurse on each one:

```
        get first word of theObject
        if it = "bg" then
          processScript id of this cd
        else if it = "card" then
          repeat with i = 1 to number of fields
            processScript "fld id" && id of fld i
          end repeat
          -- note that we don't use "bg" as background abbreviation
          repeat with i = 1 to number of background buttons
            processScript "bkgnd btn id" && id of bg btn i
          end repeat
          -- note that card fields are called "cd" so we don't recurse!
          repeat with i = 1 to number of card fields
            processScript "cd fld id" && id of cd fld i
          end repeat
          repeat with i = 1 to number of card buttons
            processScript "cd btn id" && id of cd btn i
          end repeat
        end if
      end if
```

It's time to show we are doing something:

```
    set cursor to busy
```

Now get the script of whatever object we are looking at. If the script is **empty** there is nothing further to be done, so we **exit processScript**:

```
    put the script of theObject into theScript
    if theScript is empty then exit processScript
```

For convenience and speed, put the stack's name and the object's name into variables:

```
    put word 2 of the name of this stack into theStackName
    put quote & theObject & quote into theObjectName
```

We scan this object's script to find its handlers. These will be lines with their **word 1** being either **on** or **function**. Since this scanning takes some time (depending on how long the script is), we repeatedly **set the cursor to busy**. (Had the script been **empty** we have already **set the cursor to busy** once, so it's already spinning.)

The inside of the **repeat** loop is messy, as it builds the menu messages. We've taken care to quote menu message parameters correctly, including the **"h"** and **"f"** that distinguish **on** handlers from functions. (Had we used simply **h** or **f**, there would have been a risk of big surprises if **h** or **f** were global variables.)

```
-- scan for handlers and functions
repeat with thisLine = 1 to the number of lines in theScript
  set cursor to busy
  get word 1 of line thisLine of theScript
  if it = "on" or it = "function" then -- got one
    put word 2 of line thisLine of theScript into handlerName
    put handlerName & return after theHandlers
    put "editHandler" && quote & handlerName & quote & "," & ¬
    theObjectname & "," & thestackname after theMenuMsgs
    -- note we quote h and f in case they are global variables
    if it is "on" then -- handler
      put "," & quote & "h" & quote & return after theMenuMsgs
    else -- function
      put "," & quote & "f" & quote & return after theMenuMsgs
    end if
    -- the next line helps debug things
    -- answer last line of themenumsgs
  end if
end repeat
```

Finally, we put a line between groups of handlers from each script, then put everything we've collected from this script into the **Handlers** menu. If this is the very first group of handlers, the dim line will come just after the **New menu** menu item that was created with the menu at the beginning of **processScript**.

```
put "-" after menu "Handlers"
put theHandlers after menu "Handlers" with menuMsgs theMenuMsgs
end processScript
```

That's it. (We'll leave it to you as an exercise to decide what to do when there are more than 64 menu entries, the limit imposed by HyperCard. You may also like to use **the long names** of stacks to avoid any name conflicts in case you have same-named stacks open but in different folders.)

We've said ... **quote & something & quote** ... rather a lot. If you do much more of this, it'll be worth writing a function:

```
function q a
    return quote & q & quote
end q
```

Then you can write more concisely, for example:

    put "," & q("f") & return after theMenuMsgs

Why is processScript a long handler? Why isn't it split into several parts? One reason is that we happened to write it like this, and it just grew! The real reason, though, is that the more handlers you have in stacks that are in use the greater the chances of accidentally calling one of them when you don't mean to. Chapter 11 shows how we could have used more advanced scripting techniques to have constructed our menu with more panache.

9.5   Palettes

Programming with palettes is a bit like programming with menus: when the user clicks on a palette button, it executes a single line of HyperTalk, typically sending a message. For the user, palettes have the advantage over menus that they can be moved around to convenient positions, they use pictures or icons rather than words (menu items), and they can be hidden or permanently displayed according to what the user wants. A permanently displayed palette is useful since it can show one of its buttons highlighted, whereas a menu only shows a menu item checked when the user has the mouse actually over the menu. For the programmer, palettes are a bit more inconvenient than menus since they must be constructed using the palette maker, found in the HyperCard *Power Tools* stack. (We won't describe how to construct palettes, since your *Power Tools* stack may be a different version; it anyway has detailed instructions.)

A typical palette is shown below. There are 13 buttons, used for navigating the stack. The top row moves to the first card, the previous card, marks the current card, moves to the next card, and (at the far right) goes to the last card. The bottom row allows the user to move to various positions through the stack roughly proportional to where the user clicks on the arrow.

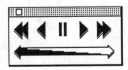

A useful feature of palettes is being able to get all the commands that have been put in. Typing answer the commands of window "Controller" (if Controller is the name of your palette) will give a list of the commands: of course, you should now make sure you have provided handlers for all of the commands!

CHAPTER 10

Finding Things

Making large stacks easier to use

Large stacks contain lots of interesting things – but how do you find them again? HyperCard has a basic find capability, and this chapter will show how we can use HyperTalk to build much more powerful search capabilities on top of it. The chapter ends by showing how to script 'find by example', a powerful way of finding text in a stack, especially for searching in stacks with many fields. Find by example is extremely easy to use.

10.1 Improving HyperCard's find command

If you type **command–F** HyperCard selects **Find...** from the **Go** menu and puts find "" into the message window. The cursor is conveniently positioned so that if you start typing, what you type goes between the quotes; when you hit **return** HyperCard tries to find a card with a field containing the text you typed.

Perhaps more in keeping with the Macintosh user interface would be to display a dialog box and to invite the user to type what they wanted to find, which is easily done by **ask "What text do you want to find?"**:

```
┌─────────────────────────────────────────────┐
│  What text do you want to find?               │
│                                               │
│  ┌─────────────────────────────────────────┐ │
│  └─────────────────────────────────────────┘ │
│            ┌────────┐   ┌──────────┐          │
│            │   OK   │   │  Cancel  │          │
│            └────────┘   └──────────┘          │
└─────────────────────────────────────────────┘
```

We can also save what the user looks for so that it can be offered as a default for the next find. Before rushing to change the menu message of the **Find...** menu item, we should write and test a handler to do this.

```
on my_find
  global my_find_text
  ask "What text do you want to find?" with my_find_text
  if it ≠ empty then
    put it into my_find_text
    find it
  end if
end my_find
```

Ask puts the text that the user typed into it. If the user types nothing or clicks **Cancel**, ask puts empty into it. Otherwise, the script does a find for the typed text. Next time this handler is called, the **ask** dialog suggests the text the user last looked for, **my_find_text**. In other words, just hitting return (or clicking **OK**) will conveniently repeat the find with the last text we searched for.

Finding the next one

Very often there is more than one card in a stack that we may be looking for. In the example above, there may be several friends of ours called Lester, or several people whose address is in London. Having found one, we may want to find another, but find will find the *current* card again – we won't get anywhere. A more useful find, then, is one that looks starting with the next card.

The following handler, next_find does just this. We retain the basic idea from **my_find** of keeping a default find text in the global variable **my_find_text**. We start the find from the next card. The screen is locked so that the user is not distracted by the card changing just before the search starts. Finally, if find does not succeed, we must go back to the card the user started from.

```
on next_find
  global my_find_text
  ask "What text do you want to find?" with my_find_text
  if it ≠ empty then
    put it into my_find_text
    lock screen
    go next
    find it
    if the result = "not found" then
      beep -- because nothing was found
      go back
      end if
    unlock screen
  end if
end next_find
```

There are variations on this theme: perhaps you want something like next_find, but to go ahead and do the find if my_find_text is defined, otherwise to ask for it. A handler find_again repeatedly finds the last thing you looked for:

```
on find_again
  global my_find_text
  if number of words in my_find_text = 0 then
    ask "What text do you want to find?" with my_find_text
    if it ≠ empty then
      put it into my_find_text
      exit find_again
    end if
  else
    lock screen
    go next
    find my_find_text
    if the result = "not found" then
      beep -- because nothing was found
      answer "Couldn't find '" & my_find_text & "'"
      go back
    end if
    unlock screen
  end if
end find_again
```

All that remains to be done is to fix up the **Go** menu with our improvements:

```
set the menuMessage of menuItem "Find..." of menu "Go" to next_find
put "Find again" after menuItem "Find..." in menu "Go"
set commandChar of menuItem "Find again" in menu "Go" to "A"
set the menuMessage of menuItem "Find again" in menu "Go" to find_again
```

This can easily be done in an openStack handler, perhaps in Home or in one of your tool stacks. Don't forget to start using this stack if you want to use these menu items from another stack.

More ways to find

The find command is more versatile than we've so far indicated.

Find "word" looks for fields containing words starting with word; if you look for several words (find "word1 word2 word3"), find searches for a card where each of these can be found starting a word. If you want to find exact word matches, use find word "test", which will only find a card with fields containing the word test, but not ones with testing; alternatively, if you want to find text anywhere, not just at the beginning of a word, use the chars qualifier, as in find chars "test". This would find not only a card containing test and testing but retest as well.

These examples treat each word of the search text as a separate string to search for. In the example find "word1 word2 word3", HyperCard finds – or tries to find – a card containing the three words **word1**, **word2**, and **word3** in any order. If you wanted to find a card with the *exact* text word1 word2 word3 (that is, a single string containing two spaces), you need to use **find string "word1 word2 word3"**.

The last form, **find whole "text"** finds text matching from the beginning of words. None of the **find** variants worries about upper- and lower-case letters: **find "a"** and **find "A"** are the same. Likewise, HyperCard ignores accents: **"á"** and **"a"** work the same, just looking for **a**.

If we simply try **find "Lester"** we might find a Mr. Lester or someone living in Lester Avenue. If we just want to look for someone's surname, then **find "Lester" in field "name"** would be the way to be more specific: it only searches for words in the field **name**. If we've already marked cards we're interested in, then **find** can be restricted to search just those cards. In total, the following combinations are possible:

find *text* in field *f*	look only in field *f* (possibly a card field), rather than all fields
find *text* of marked cards	look only at marked cards
find *text* in field *f* of marked cards	look only in field *f* on marked cards

If you want to experiment, type a **find** command in the message window. **Find** will show you exactly what text has been found by leaving it enclosed in a little box (or rather, if more than one piece of text has been found, only the first bit will be boxed). The expression **the foundText** can be used in HyperTalk to do something with that text. But as typing into the message window loses **find**'s box, it is worth experimenting with a handler that uses an **answer** dialog box to show the various values of the found expressions:

```
on test
  global my_find_text
  ask "What text do you want to find?" with my_find_text
  if it ≠ empty then
    put it into my_find_text
    find it
    answer the result & return ¬
    & the foundChunk & return ¬
    & the foundField & return ¬
    & the foundLine & return ¬
    & the foundText
  end if
end test
```

Note that the first part of this handler is the same as **my_find**, but we couldn't call **my_find** because we want to see what **the result** is after find. If we had simply called **my_find**, then **the result** would have been the result of calling **my_find**, not the result of the find.

Use expressions like **word 2 of the foundChunk** to find the starting character of the found text. All the values will be **empty** in the case that no card was found. **The result**, rather than being **empty** (the blank top line in the dialog box opposite!), will be **Not found**.

```
char 292 to 295 of card field 3
card field 3
line 3 of card field 3
fish

                              [   OK   ]
```

10.2 Flexible searches

Suppose we have a large stack of clip art. Each card has a picture that has been scanned in (or that we've collected by cutting-and-pasting from other stacks), and a field that has a brief description of the picture. We want to be able to find a picture, say a horse's head, for a story we are writing.

If find "horse" is used we will find only the first card with a horse, and it is perhaps tedious to keep reissuing the find command (typing **command–F**) to get more. In particular, after finding the first horse, we don't know whether there are any more horses, so is it worth doing another find? It would be better if, somehow, HyperCard told us whether there are more horses that we can look for in case we aren't satisfied with the first one.

The idea we need to work out is that when the user does a find, they really want to find any one of the many cards that the find command would find. Here we want to find all of the cards with the word horse on. Suppose the user does a find (for horse) which finds the first card with horse, the idle handler could silently keep looking for another horse. If we find another, then we highlight a button **Find Next**. That would mean that the user could click **Find Next** to get to the next card with horse in it. This idea might be useful for some special sorts of stack, but it sounds too complex!

As is often the case, the designers of HyperCard have anticipated this sort of need, and it is done in a special way. This will have the advantage that it can be done very fast, but perhaps not with the exact design details we might have wished for.

The approach we will use is to mark the cards we want to find.

Marking cards

HyperCard can mark cards. Each card is either marked or unmarked, and whether a card is marked or not is easily found using the marked property of the card. Thus, the marked of this card will be either true or false, depending on whether this card is marked. Since marking is a card property, we can conveniently mark or unmark a card by using set; alternatively we can use the special commands mark and unmark.

Thus, set the mark of this card to x is equivalent to, but faster than,

```
if x then mark this card
else unmark this card
```

However, the **mark** commands have useful variants, such as **mark all cards**, which is vastly more efficient than you using a **repeat** loop going over each card and marking it individually with **set**!

Here are the full possibilities:

mark *card*
mark all cards
mark cards by finding *text*
mark cards where *expression*

If you want to unmark cards, just use **unmark** instead of **mark**; all the various forms for **mark** work with **unmark** too.

Marking cards by finding text can be qualified in exactly the same way as the **find** command itself:

mark cards by finding *text* **in field** *f*   find *text* in field *f*
mark cards by finding chars ...
mark cards by finding word ...   as for the qualifiers in the **find** command
mark cards by finding whole ...
mark cards by finding string ...

The command **mark cards where** *expression* goes to each card and evaluates the expression in that card, then sets the mark of the card accordingly. You can do things like, **mark cards where field 3 contains "fish"**, which is a far more efficient way of doing:

```
repeat for number of cards times
  go next card
  if field 3 contains "fish" then mark this card
end repeat
```

or even:

```
repeat with i = 1 to number of cards
  if field 3 of card i contains "fish" then mark card i
end repeat
```

The line in the **repeat** loop is *not* set the mark of card i to field 3 of card i contains "fish" because this would unset the mark of cards where field 3 does not contain fish. The **mark** command does not affect cards that are already marked (and **unmark** does not affect already unmarked cards). If you wanted to set the mark so that it indicated whether field 3 contained fish so that if the card is marked it *does* contain fish, and if it is not marked it *does not* contain fish, then you would first need to **unmark all cards** (so that there are no marked cards not containing fish in field 3), then mark those cards containing fish. This sounds complicated, but it is arranged so that you can keep on adding (or removing) marks as you interactively find out more about what you want.

In summary, rather than the inefficient:

```
repeat for number of cards times
  go next card
  set the mark of this card to field 3 contains "fish"
end repeat
```

you should:

```
unmark all cards
mark cards where field 3 contains "fish"
```

The advantages of the **mark** command become more apparent when you want to do more advanced work. Suppose that having found cards containing fish, you now also want to mark cards that have pictures of fish *or* dolphins. If you use the **set** command, you will have to remember to look for fish as well as dolphins; with the **mark** command you simply mark cards containing dolphins, and the existing marks on fishy cards remain without you doing any special work. The result is that marked cards now have fish or dolphins, possibly both.

Having marked the cards we're interested in, we can look at **number of marked cards** to see if we have found a sensible number (say no more than **10**) out of our hundreds of clip art pictures. We could then **show marked cards**, which is rather like **show all cards**, but which only shows the cards we have marked as containing fish or dolphins; likewise **print marked cards** will print the same cards. We could also step through the cards one by one using **go next marked card** or **go previous marked card**.

Finding interactively

Overleaf is a card from a clip art stack. The stack has hundreds of scanned pictures and each card has a description in **background field 1**: in the picture above, the clip art picture is a swordfish, and its description is a few words (swordfish, fish, sea) so that we can locate it by using keywords. Five of the bottom buttons are the conventional buttons that many stacks have: left and right arrows, go home, show all (using **show all cards**) and the bent arrow, which does a **visual effect iris close** and a **pop card** to get back to wherever we came from. The other six buttons support a flexible interactive search, which we'll now describe. Maybe we will want to put the buttons into a couple of menus: this would certainly get us some more space on the card for bigger pictures.

The **Show all** button shows all the cards, which is probably rather tedious. Above it the button **Show 13** is similar, but shows only thirteen cards – ones that we are looking for. The user has already said that they are looking for cards with fish in their description: 13 such cards have been found. Of course, if we had found 16 cards, then the button's name would have been **Show 16**! The idea is that **More** lets the user add more cards that are interesting; **Less** lets the user remove cards they don't want. Having seen swordfish and some of the other fish, we might decide to look for some dolphins as well: click **More** and type dolphin into the dialog box. The **Clear** button unmarks all of them.

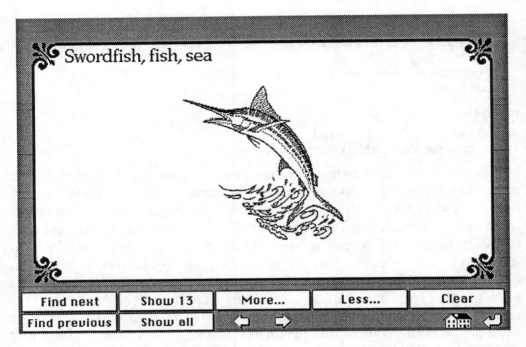

The **Find next** and **previous** buttons are the simplest to start with. If there aren't any cards marked yet, then we save the user the trouble of clicking the **More** button by doing it from the script. If there is only one marked card, and it happens to be this one, then there isn't a next or previous card to show: so we say so.

```
on mouseUp -- find next
  if number of marked cards = 0 then click at loc of bg button "More..."
  if the marked of this card and number of marked cards = 1 then
    answer "This is the only card you've found so far."
  else go next marked card
end mouseUp


on mouseUp -- find previous
  if number of marked cards = 0 then click at loc of bg button "More..."
  if the marked of this card and number of marked cards = 1 then
    answer "This is the only card you've found so far."
  else go prev marked card
end mouseUp
```

Show is used to show all of the currently marked cards. Again, we check whether there are 0 or 1 marked cards, and handle these cases specially. Since the user may enter commands such as **mark this card** into the message window, we need to keep checking that the number shown in the name of **Show 13** (or whatever) is correct. The simple handler **new_show** corrects the name of the button if necessary.

```
on mouseUp -- Show N cards
  new_show
  if number of marked cards = 0 then
    answer "Click 'More...' to find cards."
  else if the marked of this card and number of marked cards = 1 then
    answer "This is the only card you've found so far."
  else show marked cards
end mouseUp
```

New_show also has to be called when the stack is opened, so the stack script should have the following handlers:

```
on openStack
  new_show
end openstack

on new_show
  set name of bg button id 13 to "Show" && number of marked cards
end new_show
```

Clear could simply unmark all marked cards, which would be easy. We should call new_show to update the name of the **Show** button to **Show 0** since there are now no marked cards left.

```
on mouseUp -- clear
  unmark all cards
  new_show
end mouseUp
```

In case the user has clicked on **Clear** by accident, we ought to ask if the user really wants to unmark the cards. Again, we treat the cases of 0 and 1 marked cards individually: if no cards are marked, maybe the user needs a hint about how to use the **More** button, whereas if only one card is marked we should say 'it' rather than 'them,' to get the English grammar right.

```
on mouseUp -- clear
  if number of marked cards = 0 then
    answer number_found() & "Click 'More...' to find some."
    exit mouseUp
  end if
  if number of marked cards = 1 then get "it?"
  else get "all of them?"
  answer number_found() & "Forget" && it with "OK" or "Cancel"
  if it is "OK" then unmark all cards
  new_show
end mouseUp
```

The function number_found says how many cards are currently marked, and is used because the other two buttons (**More** and **Less**) also want to show the user the number of marked cards. By using a common function, which therefore should be in the stack (or background) script, we can ensure the user interface is consistent across the three buttons.

```
function number_found
   if number of marked cards = 1 then get "One card"
   else if number of marked cards = 0 then get "No cards"
   else get number of marked cards && "cards"
   return it && "found so far." & return
end number_found
```

The handler for **More** can work in the way we described above for improving find: it uses a global variable (last_find) to keep the last words the user wanted to look for and uses these as the default text for ask.

```
on mouseUp -- more...
   global last_find
   ask number_found() & "Find more cards with what words?" with last_find
   put it into last_find
   mark cards by finding it in bg field 1
   new_show
   go next marked card
end mouseUp
```

There is a limitation with this script which only became apparent to us after using the clip art stack for a little while. On some cards, we had forgotten to put in any description text at all! This script can't mark such cards, so we haven't made it easy enough to find cards that need descriptions adding. We thought of adding a special button (say, **Find cards with no description**) but it's a bit long-winded, and rather special-purpose to waste screen space with. Instead it is neater to recognize when the user enters nothing in the **ask** dialog **of the More** button, and ask if this means the user wants to find cards with no description:

```
on mouseUp -- more...
   global last_find
   ask number_found() & "Find more cards with what words?" with last_find
   if it ≠ empty then
      put it into last_find
      mark cards by finding it in bg field 1
      new_show
      go next marked card
   else
      answer "Add cards with no words?" with "OK" or "Cancel"
      if it is "OK" then
         mark cards where number of words in bg field 1 = 0
```

```
        new_show
        go next marked card
      end if
    end if
  end mouseUp
```

The script for **Less** is almost the same, except we **unmark** cards rather than **mark** them. We
also need to change the English accordingly, and to warn the user that if no cards are marked,
then none can be unmarked!

```
  on mouseUp -- less...
    global last_find
    if number of marked cards = 0 then
      answer "First find some cards:" & return ¬
      & "Click on 'More...' to look for things."
      exit mouseUp
    end if
    ask number_found() & "Ignore those containing what words?" with last_find
    if it ≠ empty then
      put it into last_find
      unmark cards by finding it in bg field 1 in marked cards
      new_show
      go next marked card
    else
      answer "Remove cards with no words?" with "OK" or "Cancel"
      if it is "OK" then
        unmark cards where number of words in bg field 1 = 0
        new_show
        go next marked card
      end if
    end if
  end mouseUp
```

10.3 Finding by using search expressions

The examples so far have all looked for simple text. More generally we might have a HyperCard
stack that contains more complex information, and we may want to search for cards that satisfy
numerical conditions. Here is one way to bring the generality of HyperTalk into searching.

We have a field (called **search**) into which the user can type HyperTalk expressions,
one per line. On pressing the search button, HyperCard will look for cards where all lines in
the field are **true**. In the following example, that would mean finding cards where the sex is
female or the age is greater than 40 and the address field contains Glasgow. We will mark the
cards using the command **mark cards where** *expression*, and then let the user find them by **go**

next marked card. Of course, the fact that we are marking cards can be concealed: the search button can both mark appropriate cards and go to the next marked card itself, making it look to the user like a single operation. A problem to solve is how to get mark cards to work with a field of several lines.

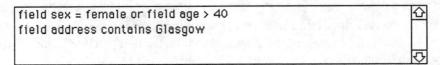

```
field sex = female or field age > 40
field address contains Glasgow
```

The idea is simple: by asking mark to mark cards where a function returns true, we can work out anything; thus, we define a function found that does what we want with the field for any one card, and then give it to mark: as in mark cards where found(). Since found will be called on each card separately, it is important that it uses the right field to get the HyperTalk expressions from! We can't refer to card field search of this card, since 'this card' will keep changing as mark works its way through the stack. On the other hand, it would be inefficient to say card field search of card ID 23145, since this too would have to be worked out repeatedly, once for each card. Rather, it is most efficient to put the value we want, the value of card field search, into the container it: this will be the same on every card it is evaluated in, and it will be efficient:

```
on mouseUp -- search
  unmark all cards
  get card field "search"
  mark cards where found(it)
  if number of marked cards > 0 then go next marked card
end mouseUp
```

Once cards have been marked, the last line of the handler goes to the next one – if no cards got marked we don't try and go next marked card because this would be an error. You might want to add another line, else beep or use answer to explain why nothing appears to be happening.

The function found evaluates the search field (that has been passed in its parameter s). It does this by using value(line i of s) for each line, which, as its name implies, works out the value of its parameter taken as a HyperTalk expression. If any line is false, we know that the overall value of found should be false, so we may as well return false immediately. The last line of the handler assumes that if no line of the field evaluated to false, then all were true, so found returns true. Since this is a bit complicated, when we developed the function, we needed to follow what was going on by using an answer dialog box: as is good practice, we've still left it in (but commented it out) in case we ever forget or have some bugs to deal with!

```
function found s
  repeat with i = 1 to number of lines in s
```

```
        -- answer line i of s & return & value(line i of s)
        if value(line i of s) = false then return false
     end repeat
     return true
  end found
```

We can add a couple of frills. We may want to narrow searches, searching amongst only those cards we have already found; this can be done by adding a check-box button (with autoHilite). It is also good manners to say how many cards we've marked. Here is the result:

```
on mouseUp -- search
   get card field "search"
   if the hilite of card button "Narrow search further" then
      unmark cards where not found(it)
   else
      unmark all cards
      mark cards where found(it)
   end if
   if number of marked cards = 1 then get "card found"
   else get "cards found"
   put number of marked cards && it into card field count
   if number of marked cards > 0 then go next marked card
end mouseUp
```

10.4 Finding 'by example'

The last example might have been very powerful, but it was nasty to use. You have to know HyperTalk to know how to make best use of the search field. One of the reasons for using HyperTalk is so that HyperCard stacks can be made easier to use, not harder! The last finding method of this chapter is finding by example: rather than provide expressions (in HyperTalk), we ask the user to provide examples of what he is looking for. Then HyperTalk comes into its own looking for cards that match the examples the user has provided.

Most HyperCard stacks have more than one background field. An address list will have fields for names, phone numbers and other personal details. A power user might want to type find "Lester" in field "Name", but it would be easier for an ordinary user, even a power user in a hurry, to be able to type 'Lester' directly into the appropriate field. If we arrange the position of the find fields (as we shall call them) so that they are in the same places as the fields we want to search, we don't even have to remember their names.

The address list that comes with HyperCard is an example: there are many fields (called Name, Company, Street, CityState, Zip, Phone 1, Phone 2, Phone 3, Phone 4, Notes). How is a user supposed to remember that the person's town is kept in the field CityState?

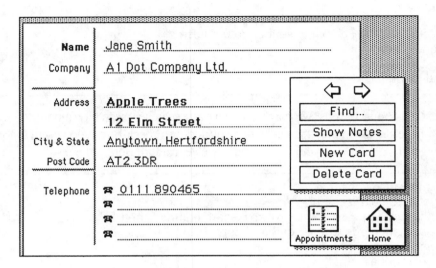

You can find out what the fields are called by running a handler like this, which (as shown here) puts the field names into the message window where you can easily cut and paste them:

```
on whatFields
  get empty
  repeat with i = 1 to number of fields
    if not lockText of field i and not dontSearch of field i then
      put short name of field i & ", " after it
    end if
  end repeat
  put it
end whatFields
```

So, rather than typing find Smith in field Name, it would be easier to type Smith into the right field, as in the picture opposite, where, as it is shown, clicking the **Find...** button will find a card with Smith in its name field.

We can obviously spend more time designing the appearance of the card: so far all we've done is change all the field labels to Find Name, Find Company, and so on; we've changed the background (to lots of little **f**s) and added two help buttons (top right). The thing that is really interesting is how to get our 'find by example' to work properly.

Basic find by example

The basic method of find by example is simple: we scan the fields, and for those that aren't empty (or better, don't contain any words) mark the cards that contain that text for those fields. The result is that we have marked cards that contain the examples in the right fields. The next little script extract shows how it might be done.

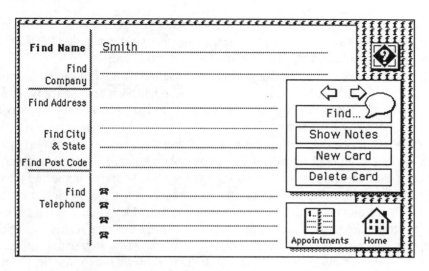

This script shows the general idea, but has several problems that we will need to iron out:

```
unmark all cards
repeat with i = 1 to number of fields
   get field i
   if number of words in it ≠ 0 then
      mark cards where field i contains it
   end if
end repeat
go next marked card
```

To explain how to solve the problems, we'll write out the **Find** button's handler line-by-line below and explain what additions and changes need to be made for a more thorough solution.

```
on mouseUp -- find by example
```

At the beginning of the handler we should check whether the user has actually given us any examples to look for, and suggest that they do.

```
get 0
repeat with i = 1 to number of fields
   add number of words in field i to it
end repeat
if it = 0 then
   answer "Enter something to look for in some of the fields"
   exit mouseUp
end if
```

The simple example above provides an *OR* search: that is, it finds cards whose fields matched the first example *OR* the second example *OR* the third. One might want an *AND* search: in other words, to be able to search for a Smith in New York, rather than people called Smith *OR* in New York. If you wish you can provide a button that lets the user choose whether to *OR* or *AND* the examples, but for simplicity we'll just deal with the *AND* case here.

The most efficient form of marking will be to use the **mark** commands, rather than us going through each card one-by-one and using **set**. (We might want to use **set** if we had several backgrounds and had to go through the chosen background explicitly: the **mark** command scans all backgrounds whatever we want!)

If there is only one field with an example in it, things are rather easy. We just mark those cards that contain it. Suppose the field with the example is number **1**. We cannot **mark cards where field 1 contains field 1**, since we want one field **1** to be the example and the other to be the field searched for! We have to put the example somewhere constant, such as in the container **it**. Hence **get field 1**, then **mark cards where field 1 contains it** will work correctly, supposing that the **field 1** of the example and **field 1** of the searched cards correspond (for example, they are both the **Name** field). But, in fact, we won't want to search all fields (such as the constant field **labels** in the address list), so there is no reason for the field numbers to correspond; instead, we should use the field names. This is how to do it:

```
unmark all cards
get field 1
put short name of field 1 into fieldname
mark cards where field fieldname contains it
```

But that only copes with one example. If there are several examples to find, we will want to mark the cards that contain *all* of them. Having marked the cards containing the first example, there will be *fewer* cards that *also* contain the second example; in other words we will need to unmark some of the cards marked by looking for the first example. Of course, we should unmark those cards that don't contain what we want. If we had just two fields, **1** and **2**, this is how it would be done:

```
unmark all cards
get field 1
put short name of field 1 into fieldname
mark cards where field fieldname contains it
get field 2
put short name of field 2 into fieldname
unmark cards where not (field fieldname contains it)
```

In general, we'll have more than two fields, so a **repeat** loop is called for. We introduce a flag first_field that is **true** for the first field, and **false** subsequently. This enables us to choose whether to **mark** or **unmark** cards. So we continue with the handler:

```
put true into first_field
unmark all cards
repeat with i = 1 to number of fields
   get field i
   if number of words in it ≠ 0 then
      -- we have to be careful since field numbers don't correspond
```

```
        put short name of field i into fieldname
        if first_field then
           mark cards where field fieldname contains it
           put false into first_field
        else
           unmark cards where not (field fieldname contains it)
        end if
     end if
  end repeat
```

You can see that if first_field is kept **true** (if we never **put false into** first_field), then all examples will add more marking (rather than do unmarking): this is what we would want for OR-ing examples. The easiest way to do this would be by looking at **the hilite** property of a button:

```
  put the hilite of button "OR examples" into first_field
```

Now there is a bit of fun: this card, the one with the examples on, necessarily has the examples on it! But we don't want to find it.

```
  unmark this card -- it will get marked anyway!
```

At this point we have marked those cards that contain all of the examples in their respective fields. We may have found no cards, in which case we should say so. This last detail brings us to the end of the **Find...** mouseUp handler.

```
     if number of marked cards = 0 then
        answer "No cards found with this example"
        exit mouseUp
     end if
     go next marked card
  end mouseUp
```

Fixing a bug: female contains male

There is a bug: we use contains to locate text from examples, but contains doesn't know about words. Thus, it finds female using male as an example, since "female" contains "male" is true. If we used is (=) as the comparison operator, then we wouldn't be able to find fields with example fields that weren't *exactly* equal – we'd like to be able to use examples that only give one word, and we certainly don't want to have to worry about trailing spaces that HyperTalk's is would worry about, but which the user wouldn't be able to see.

A solution is to define our own 'contains' function, that does exactly what we want; we then replace field fieldname contains it with calls to this function, as containsExample(field fieldname, it). Here's one approach, which returns **true** if any word in the example matches any word in the field:

```
function containsExample f, example
    repeat with i = 1 to number of words in f
        repeat with j = 1 to number of words in example
            if word i of f = word j of example then return true
        end repeat
    end repeat
    return false
end containsExample
```

We pay a penalty of speed in making the example searching more powerful. Maybe it would have been easier – certainly faster – to use M and F instead of male and female; however, an important point is to use HyperTalk's **contains** first since we know it works, though with limitations that we can live with while we develop the rest of the script.

In general: use HyperTalk's built-in operators, functions and commands whenever possible, even if they are only approximations to what you want in the end. You then debug the simple scripts, making allowances for HyperTalk's way of doing things. Only then, when you know the structure of your script is correct, replace the limited HyperTalk bits with your own handlers or functions to get exactly the functionality the script requires. If you want to extend a HyperTalk function or command, write a handler with the same name in the stack script (or wherever is appropriate); if you need to modify an operator (such as **contains**) you will have to rewrite everywhere it is used, as we did in fixing the male/female bug. If you don't take this approach to developing stacks, you have to debug everything at once, which is far harder.

Building the example card automatically

The most tedious part of the find by example programming is collecting the relevant fields together. We could use a 'spare' card on the same background that we want to search: this would ensure everything looks exactly right, but we then have the problem that we can't make all the modifications we really want; certainly the idea is no good if you want to be able to search on more than one background (perhaps your address list has two backgrounds, one for childrens' details and one for adults'). Another problem is to ensure that the card really is 'spare', and is never confused with a real address.

Another approach is to have a special *find by example* background and have exactly what we want on it, including the background script. This way will be more reliable, but we will have to do a lot of field copying-and-pasting and so forth to set it up properly. In fact, this is just the job for HyperTalk!

The *find by example* card in the *Finding Things* stack on the *HyperProgramming* disk has a **Setup** button that is used to do just this. It first scans the stack to find eligible backgrounds (one that don't have **the dontSearch** property set to **true**) and makes a menu out of them. The user chooses the background out of the menu for which they want to make a find by example card, and this then runs a script that copies the fields (and all of their properties) onto the current card. It also writes the names of the fields above them, so that the user can see what they are supposed to mean. Here is how it looks after setting up from the **Data** background in the *Finding Things* stack on the *HyperProgramming* disk, having provided a few examples. (The fields are arranged in exactly the same places and with the same styles as in the background we are going to search, and the names of the fields have been written just above them.) Here, we're looking for a man called Newton whose favourite colour is blue, but we are not interested in what pets he has, or where he lives:

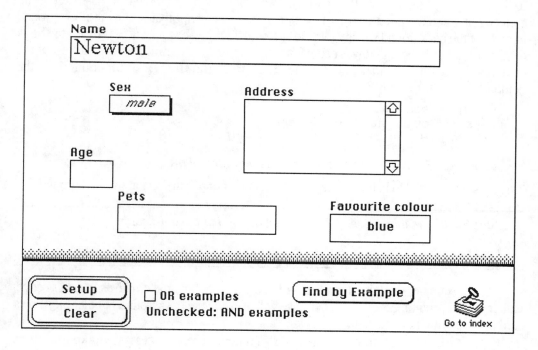

The **Setup** button makes the menu as follows:

```
on mouseUp
  if bkg() ≠ 0 then
    answer "You have already set the fields up!"
    exit mouseUp
  end if
  if there is a menu "Background" then
    answer "You may want to click Clear to clear the card"
  else
    -- find out which background
    create menu "Background"
    repeat with i = 1 to number of backgrounds
```

```
      if not the dontSearch of background i then
         put short name of background i after menu "Background" ¬
         with menuMessage "make_query" && i
      end if
   end repeat
end if
answer "Choose a background from Background menu"
end mouseUp
```

The only strange thing here is the first few lines, calling a function bkg(). The idea is that the background script defines bkg() to return 0, but if the find by example card has been set up correctly, it will have put a handler for bkg() in the card script that returns the background number of the background we are going to search. This scheme is only necessary for the book disk, since it would be unlikely for someone to try **Find by Example** before the rest of the card has been finished in a tailor-made card. The **Find by Example** button in the demonstration stack simply starts with:

```
if bkg() = 0 then
   answer "You haven't set up the fields yet!"
   exit mouseUp
end if
-- answer "Search:" && short name of background bkg()
```

This exits the mouseUp handler when the definition of bkg is the one in the background:

```
function bkg -- this is called if bkg is not defined in the card script
   return 0
end bkg
```

It's a good example, though, of overriding handlers by defining alternatives in other scripts earlier in the current message path: here, we will override the background handler bkg() by a card handler with the same name.

The **Setup** button arranges for each menu item to send a message make_query b, where b is the number of the background. The make_query handler checks that the user has indeed selected the right background, and then proceeds to copy the background fields from that background to the search card.

```
on make_query b
   answer "Make the Find by Example card for searching background '" ¬
   & (short name of background b) & "'?" with "Cancel" or "OK"
   if it is "OK" then
      go background b
      put 0 into copied
      -- now copy the fields to this card
      set editBkgnd to true
      reset paint -- resets textAlign, textSize, textStyle, textHeight
```

```
      set the textFont to Chicago
      repeat with i = 1 to number of fields
        if not the dontSearch of field i then
          select field i
          put short name of field i into fieldname
          doMenu copy field
          go back
          doMenu paste field
          show_name fieldname, topLeft of field fieldname
          -- ensure fields are visible (on our white background)
          get the style of field fieldname
          if it = "opaque" or it = "transparent" then
            set the style of field i to "rectangle"
          end if
          set the visible of field fieldname to true
          go background b
          add 1 to copied
        end if
      end repeat
      set editBkgnd to false
      if copied = 0 then
        answer "There are no background fields here worth looking for!" ¬
        & return & "Choose another from the Background menu."
        go back
        exit make_query
      end if
      go back
      delete menu "Background" -- not needed anymore

      -- make sure we know which background to search!
      set script of this card to "function bkg" & return ¬
      & "return" && b & return & "end bkg"
      choose browse tool

      get "field"
      if number of fields > 1 then get "fields"
      answer "Now type something to look for in the " & it ¬
      & ", then click the Find by Example button to look for it."

    end if
  end make_query
```

The final handler is a utility to print the name of a field, using the text tool, just above where it's positioned:

```
on show_name name, where
   -- answer name && where
   choose text tool
   click at item 1 of where, item 2 of where-4
   type name
end show_name
```

10.5 Summary

HyperCard has a basic find command (with lots of options for finding different sorts of text, words, substrings). But HyperCard's find is hardly interactive – at best you can get HyperCard to type find in the message window, to save you typing it! However, HyperTalk enables you to embed the basic command into extremely useful interactive tools that are fully integrated into stacks.

This chapter has shown how to find things, finding things one at a time. The next chapter shows how you might collect everything in a stack that satisfies some criterion: you might want to find everything about Newton, for example, and collect all the text together from cards that mention him.

CHAPTER 11

Collecting Things

Gathering data from fields and data from scripts

Stacks usually contain a lot of information, and it is easy to loose track of what's there. The last chapter showed how to find *individual* cards, but this chapter is about collecting *all* the information into one place so that you can read it, check it (perhaps automatically), or process it in other ways. A most powerful feature of HyperTalk is that we can easily collect information from a stack and then process it again – for example to check its spelling, to print it or to save portions to a text file (perhaps to use in a DTP system) – still within HyperTalk.

11.1 Spelling checking

A stack with lots of fields with text in them is bound to have some spelling mistakes. Which words are spelt wrongly, and how do you find them?

To find out, start by creating a new button to collect words from all the stack's fields. Its **mouseUp** handler will have to look at every field on every card, both card and background. The background shared text field case is easiest – we need only the text of one field, since, being shared, it will be the same on each card in that background:

```
repeat with i = 1 to number of backgrounds
   go background i
   repeat with j = 1 to number of fields
      if the sharedText of field j then put space & field j after it
   end repeat
end repeat
```

We repeat for each background, looking at each background field. If the **sharedText** of a field is **true**, then the text in that field is the same on every card in that background; we therefore append its text to the variable it. If the **sharedText** property is **false**, however, then the field can have different text for each card. (**SharedText** means that the text in the field is shared between all cards on the same background.)

Having collected background text, we need to collect all the text on each card. For a card i, we might think we can get all the card field text by:

```
repeat with j = 1 to number of card fields of card i
   put space & card field j of card i after it
end repeat
```

... except that number of card fields of card i isn't acceptable HyperTalk (just as it wouldn't have been correct to say number of fields of background i). Instead, we have to go to card i, then ask for the number of card fields once we are there:

```
go card i
repeat with j = 1 to number of card fields
   put space & card field j after it
end repeat
```

Then there are all the background fields on each card that have the sharedText property false; their text is unique to each card:

```
repeat with j = 1 to number of fields
   if the sharedText of field j = false then
      put space & field j after it
   end if
end repeat
```

These two repeats, scanning within cards, need to be put inside a loop running over *all* the cards:

```
repeat with i = 1 to number of cards
   go card i
   repeat with j = 1 to number of card fields
      put space & card field j after it
   end repeat
   repeat with j = 1 to number of fields
      if the sharedText of field j = false then
         put space & field j after it
      end if
   end repeat
end repeat
```

As we described in Chapter 6, we can speed these repeat loops up considerably by switching off various HyperCard functions, such as the saving of card pictures for the **Recent** dialogue box. Indeed, as the script stands it is *incorrect*: each go will send openCard, openBackground (and closeCard, and so on) messages that could have unfortunate consequences for us! The very first go stack "the stack?" *must* be preceded by set lockMessages to true. This will stop all the messages being generated, and the script will do exactly what it says, rather than some extra things we don't want. We could use a pair of handlers, toComputer and toUser, to switch off and on (respectively) all such HyperCard activities conveniently.

At the end of the repeat loops, we have got all the text from all fields on all cards, plus some extra spaces to separate the end of one field from beginning of the next.

If we are looking for spelling mistakes, we are not interested in repeated words. Removing repeated words will be easiest if we first sort the list of words, but since HyperTalk's **sort** can only sort items and lines, we need to convert word separators into **returns** (or commas). Here's an easy way of doing so:

```
-- convert words to word-newline
put empty into x
repeat with i = 1 to number of words in it
   put word 1 of it & return before x
   delete word 1 of it
end repeat
```

Some of these words will start or finish with punctuation (the words might be in quotes, or come before periods). We strip off leading and trailing punctuation from each line (each return-separated word) in x:

```
-- remove leading/trailing punctuation
repeat with i = 1 to number of lines in x
   get line i of x
   repeat until "abcdefghijklmnopqrstuvwxyz" contains first char of it
      delete first char of it
      if it is empty then exit repeat
   end repeat
   repeat until "abcdefghijklmnopqrstuvwxyz" contains last char of it
      delete last char of it
      if it is empty then exit repeat
   end repeat
   put it into line i of x
end repeat
```

Then sort it:

```
sort x
```

Then delete any repeated words (this script will also delete null words as a special case):

```
put 1 into i
get x
repeat for number of lines in it-1
   if line i of it = empty then delete line i of it
   else if line i of it = line i+1 of it then delete line i of it
   else add 1 to i
end repeat
```

Having got it into a column of unique words collected from all the fields in the entire stack, we can put it into a file and leave it up to your favourite word processor to find the spelling mistakes:

```
open file "word list"
write it to file "word list"
close file "word list"
answer "File word list has " & number of words in it & " words."
```

Before writing this code, which could create enormous files if it went wrong, check that the basic script works. Writing **answer it** is an easy way to do this (though it loses the value in **it** by making it **OK!**), or you may prefer to set a breakpoint and use HyperTalk's variable watcher. Another way, more versatile, is to say **ask "It="** with **it**, as this not only displays the value of **it** but also allows you to change its value easily. Remember that a variable (such as **it**) can have a value that is too big to fit into a field.

At this stage you may realize that an incorrectly spelt word is probably spelt the same way several times. So that you can fix every place where you spelt (say) 'banana' wrongly as 'bannana', you need to know how many times it was spelt that way. We may also note that the test inside the loop for empty lines can be taken outside; since it has been sorted, the empty lines must now all be at the beginning of it. We therefore don't need to waste time seeing if *every* line in it is empty once the initial empty lines have been deleted.

```
put 1 into i
put 1 into count
get x
repeat while line 1 of it = empty
   delete line 1 of it
   if it = empty then exit repeat
end repeat
if it ≠ empty then
   repeat for number of lines in it
      if line i of it = line i+1 of it then
         delete line i of it
         add 1 to count
      else
         put count & tab before line i of it
         add 1 to i
         put 1 into count
      end if
   end repeat
end if
```

We compared the last line of the field with the notional line 'after it'! Of course, it will be different (unless it is completely **empty**, which – note! – we checked wasn't the case before we started): this is a convenient way to get the script **put count & tab before line i of it** executed for every line in the field, *including* the very last.

Don't forget that, with the word counts added, the number of words is now half what it used to be.

> **answer "File word list has " & number of lines in it & " different words."**

Here, we mean *words*: but HyperTalk's idea of words doesn't know about tabs as separators (it uses spaces and returns) so the fact that we have made a list of things separated by tabs has not doubled the number of words. To make sure, the **answer** command uses the line count: this will be correct, even if someone changes what HyperCard thinks about words and tabs! (HyperCard also thinks that any number of words between quotes (") can be counted as just one word.)

Getting back to where you came from

Most operations, like collecting all words from every field, leave a script 'somewhere else' than where it started off. Before going on an excursion through a stack (or stacks), then, you can save the ID of the current card in a variable (say, put the ID of this card into thiscardID), then later say go thiscardID. Using the ID is safer that using the name (which may not be unique) or the number (which may change).

A better way, and one that can be used to bring you back to the right stack is as follows. The HyperTalk the long name of me in a card button handler gives a result like: card button "New Button" of card id 3033 of stack "Disk100:Work:HC:ideas". Taking word 7 of this gives us the ID of the card we started from, the card where the script containing the handler is. (We can't say number of this card, because running the script will have certainly changed the current card.)

Hence handlers that go around stacks do well to finish with:

```
go card ID word 7 of the long name of me
```

More generally, if you are not certain which stack you are in:

```
get the long name of me
go word 5 to number of words in it of it
```

This code is not universally reliable! If the button (or field) has a name, HyperCard gives the name in quotes, as we assumed above – that is, as one HyperCard word. (Things go awry if the name itself has quotes in it!) But if the object has no name, HyperCard gives its name as card field ID 14, or whatever, so its name then appears to be *two* words, ID and 14. Thus the magic numbers 5 and 7 in the examples above need to be checked for the particular case you are using them in, whether or not the object has a name, which of course you would know since you created the button in the first place, and you know whether it has a name or not.

What about push card and pop card? We don't recommend their use except within single handlers. If, between your push and pop, some other handler (or stack) has done a push without a pop, your pop will take you back *there*, not to where you last did a push. Likewise, go back may take your script somewhere unexpected.

11.2 Collecting global variables

HyperCard scripts often need global variables, but you shouldn't use variables that are already used for some other purpose. What global variables does a stack have? If we assume we already have a function globalsIn() that can find out what globals *one* script has got in it, then all we have to do is call this function on each script, throughout the stack:

```
on mouseUp
  put globalsIn("this stack") into globals
  repeat with i = 1 to number of cards
    go card i
```

```
      put globalsIn("this card") after globals
      repeat with j = 1 to number of buttons
         put globalsIn("button" && j) after globals
      end repeat
      repeat with j = 1 to number of card fields
         put globalsIn("card field" && j) after globals
      end repeat
   end repeat
   repeat with i = 1 to number of backgrounds
      go background i
      put globalsIn("this background") after globals
        repeat with j = 1 to number of fields
        put globalsIn("field" && j) after globals
      end repeat
      repeat with j = 1 to number of background buttons
         put globalsIn("background button" && j) after globals
      end repeat
   end repeat

   answer globals
end mouseUp
```

Of course, we don't yet have a globalsIn function! When you are debugging a complex script like this, it's not a bad idea to start with a simple globalsIn that is good enough for the rest of the script (nearly) to work, but simple enough for you to see whether the right sorts of things are going on. Here's one suitable suggestion:

```
function globalsIn object
   answer object
   get the script of object
   return number of lines in it & return
end globalsIn
```

Having got each script into it, we need to isolate the globals it uses. Some lines may be comments, but the general rule is that a line whose first word is global declares some global variables.

```
function globalsIn object
   put the script of object into s
   put empty into g
   repeat with i = 1 to number of lines in s
      get line i of s
      if first word of it = "global" then
         delete first word of it
         -- it is now a list of global variables
         :
      end if
```

```
      end repeat
      return g
   end globalsIn
```

A HyperTalk line may contain a comment: we obviously don't want to pick up any comments and think they are or define global variables. Having got a line of the script in it, does it contain a comment? Curiously the obvious HyperTalk: if it contains "--" then is not parsed correctly as the -- are treated as starting a comment even though they are in quotes. Instead you have to write if it contains "-" & "-" then. We remove the comment as follows:

```
   if it contains "-"&"-" then
      delete char offset("-"&"-", it) to (number of chars in it) of it
   end if
```

It's hypocritical to complain about HyperTalk's treatment of comments when we can delete them so easily! If, as might seem proper, "--" was not a comment when it appears in quotes, we'd have to take more care than we do here, though, fortunately, HyperTalk lines defining globals can't also contain quoted strings. As HyperTalk is, we can be certain that finding -- anywhere in a line indicates a comment. After stripping comments (even line continuations, like -- ¬ , can be commented out), we should also check whether the last character is a continuation, meaning that the next line has more globals on it (and the line after that may do too): we'll leave this detail as an exercise for you.

What now remains in it is an item list (comma-separated list) of global variables. We pick them off one-by-one and make a return-separated list to return to the mouseUp handler.

```
   repeat with j = 1 to number of items in it
      put item j of it & return after g
   end repeat
```

The reason for returning globals one-per-line is that you can then use the same script as the spelling checker did for words, but here to sort the global variable names, to remove punctuation, and to remove duplicate variables from the list. Our list of globals may contain spurious spaces before or after the variable names: this is removed the same way as punctuation (note that underline and digits need to be put in the alphabet). As a bonus, you can now find out which globals you have only used once in a stack – which is suspicious programming.

11.3 Collecting handlers

The problem of collecting handlers was covered in Chapter 9, as an example of uses of menus. You can, however, modify the function globalsIn described above to look for lines starting on or function, and this would then find handlers. As well as coping with comments, the modified function must (depending on what you really want to do) delete the parameters of the handlers. An idea of how useful this is can be seen from the *Home* stack handler collector that is described

•

below. This is a useful project because your *Home* stack script provides various short-cuts (that you can type into the message window) and which you'll find extremely useful – once you have used our script to find out what these handlers are!

What short-cuts does the Home script provide?

When you get the *HyperCard Developer's Kit*, the *Home* stack script provides a variety of useful short cuts. If you type hypertalk into the message window, the Home script will open the HyperTalk reference stack; you can also type hypertalk mark (here, providing a parameter, mark), and the *HyperTalk Reference* stack will be opened on a card telling you about marks.

How do you find out what other useful facilities your Home script provides? Obviously, you can simply open the stack script using **Stack Info...**, and have a direct look yourself. But there are a lot of handlers, and it would anyway be useful to get a more convenient summary. That is what we will do now: we'll write a utility designed to extract information about handlers and put the summary in a field.

First, create a new stack with a scrolling card field called handlers (or experiment with the *Shortcuts* stack on the *HyperProgramming* disk). Next, create a new button and make its script as follows:

```
on mouseUp -- get handler first lines
   put empty into card field "handlers"
   get script of stack "Home"
   repeat with i = 1 to number of lines in it
      if first word of line i of it = "on" then
         put line i of it into h
         delete word 1 of h
         put h & return after card field "handlers"
      end if
   end repeat
   delete last char of card field "handlers"
end mouseUp
```

The gist of the handler is to get the script we are interested in (here, the script of the *Home* stack) into the variable it, then we look for lines starting with the word on, and we put those lines (less the word on itself) into the handlers field.

We can also find lines from functions by writing: if first word of line i of it = "on" or first word of line i of it = "function" then, though it might be easier to write if "on function" contains first word of line i of it then.

So, when the handler is run (by clicking on the button, which sends the mouseUp message) we find out the handlers in the *Home* stack script. Some have comments of a rather useless nature (such as 'Δ type "b" into message box'): perhaps we should edit the script ourselves and put in more useful comments? Rather than edit the original comments (some might be worth keeping) we'll add our own comments on the *second* line of each handler we are interested in – some handlers may not be of any interest anyway (like **openStack**) and for these we simply don't add the second line. Unfortunately, some quite uninteresting handlers will already have comments on their second lines, and we have to devise a convention so that we don't pick them up as well: we'll start our special comments with an exclamation mark. For example, look through the stack script (using the editor) and find the **mw** handler and add a second line, shown in ***bold italic*** here, so that it looks like something this:

```
on mw -- Δ type "mw" into message box
--! mw: show message watcher
-- Requires XWindow: Message Watcher
show window "Message Watcher"
end mw
```

The **repeat** loop should now look for handlers (lines starting **on**) followed by a comment line, which will be the one we've added. This is easily done by:

```
repeat with i = 1 to number of lines in it
  if first word of line i of it = "on" then
    put line i+1 of it into h
    if first word of h = "-" & "-!" then
```

Note the now-familiar HyperTalk problem: had we written **first word of h = "--"**, this would have been taken as a comment! We have to disguise the --, which is done by writing "-" & "-" which has the same value, but isn't exactly a comment symbol. Having found our comment line, we remove any leading spaces and put the line after the end of whatever we've so far collected in the **handlers** field.

Since this script takes a few moments to do its work, the first line changes the cursor to **watch** – or **busy** if you prefer to show some activity (but remember to write **set cursor to busy** in the **repeat** loop so the cursor spins). When the handler finishes, we haven't set the cursor back to normal ourselves: HyperCard will do that automatically if nothing else is going on. We've also added a final line to put the field into alphabetical order to make it more useful.

```
on mouseUp -- get help lines from handlers
  set cursor to watch
  put empty into card field "handlers"
  get script of stack "Home"
  repeat with i = 1 to number of lines in it
    if first word of line i of it = "on" then
      put line i+1 of it into h
      if first word of h = "-" & "-!" then
        delete word 1 of h
        repeat while space = char 1 of h
          delete char 1 of h
        end repeat
        put h & return after card field "handlers"
      end if
```

```
        end if
      end repeat
      delete last char of card field "handlers"
      sort card field "handlers"
   end mouseUp
```

Here is what we might get (displayed in the handlers field) – notice the line for mw is as we expect:

```
   allowInterruption: can stop scripts while running
   b: get background info
   c: get card info
   disallowInterruption: can't stop scripts while running
   help [topic]: find topic in HyperCard help stack
   hypertalk [topic]: find topic in HyperTalk reference
   mw: show message watcher
   nav: bring up the navigator palette
   restoreuserlevel: restore user level (to before setuserlevelfive)
   s: get stack info
   se: change font of script editor
   setuserlevelfive: set user level to 5
   vw: show variable watcher
   xy: show coordinates (until mouse clicked)
```

The script can be made more useful if it can examine more than one stack script: we may want to make summaries of stacks that we are using (such as the *Power Tools* stack). Hence the script should ask us which stack script to examine. Here's how:

```
   ask "Get help lines from which stack script?" with the short name of this stack
   set cursor to watch
   put empty into card field "handlers"
   put empty into card field "form"
   hide card field "form"
   get script of stack it
```

The only change here is that we get the script from the stack it, having asked the user what it should be.

The stack provided on the book's disk is a bit more careful than this: it may be that the user cancels the ask dialog, in which case it would be empty. Therefore it's better to follow the ask command with a check that something sensible has been typed by the user:

```
   ask ...
   if number of words in it = 0 then
      if the result = "cancel" then get "You cancelled"
      else get "You typed nothing"
      answer it & ", so we'll get the text from this stack."
      put short name of this stack into it
   end if
```

Parallel scrolling fields

If you are really keen, you can make the handler information look much better by using two
fields. The form of the handler is put in the lefthand field, aligned right, and the rest of the
comment is in the adjacent righthand field, aligned left, as shown below:

```
                          c │ get card info                                        ⬆
     disallowInterruption │ can't stop scripts while running
            help [topic] │ find topic in HyperCard help stack
       hypertalk [topic] │ find topic in HyperTalk reference
                      mw │ show message watcher
                     nav │ bring up the navigator palette
          restoreuserlevel │ restore user level (to before setuserlevelfive)
                       s │ get stack info
                      se │ change font of script editor
         setuserlevelfive │ set user level to 5
                      vw │ show variable watcher                                   ⬇
```

The script for doing this is straightforward: go through the **handlers** field, removing characters
up to the first colon on each line, copying them into the other field, which we've called **form**:

```
on mouseUp -- make second field
  set cursor to watch
  put empty into card field "form"
  repeat with i = 1 to number of lines in card field "handlers"
    get line i of card field "handlers"
    repeat while char 1 of it ≠ ":" and it ≠ empty
      put char 1 of it after card field "form"
      delete char 1 of it
    end repeat
    delete char 1 of it -- the colon
    repeat while char 1 of it = space -- remove any following spaces
      delete char 1 of it
    end repeat
    put return after card field "form"
    put it into line i of card field "handlers"
  end repeat
end mouseUp
```

We want two fields that are both scrolling, but (as in the picture) we want only one scroll bar
and, of course, for that scroll bar to control both of the fields. We conceal the scroll bar of the
lefthand field by using **Send Farther**: choose the field tool, select the field and then select
Send Farther from the **Objects** menu, and then move the outline of the righthand field to
obscure the lefthand field's scroll bar. That gets us just one scroll bar (or, rather, it makes it *look*
like there is just one scroll bar), but how do we make the other field scroll properly?

The easiest way is to detect when the user scrolls the righthand field, and the set the

scroll property of the lefthand (form) field appropriately. The following **mouseWithin** handler does this, and it should be put in the script of the righthand field (which has to be locked so that **mouseWithin** is sent).

```
on mouseWithin
    get the scroll of card field "handlers"
    if it ≠ the scroll of card field "form" then
        set scroll of card field "form" to it
    end if
end mouseWithin
```

Unfortunately this has a bug: the message **mouseWithin** is only sent (of course!) while the mouse is within the field. So if the user scrolls the field and moves the mouse outside the field *before* releasing the button, no **mouseWithin** message will be sent. We can fix this simply by putting the script in the card and using an **idle** handler: **idle** being a message that is sent regardless. You can find out more about how the messages (including **mouseEnter** and **mouseLeave**) are treated by typing **mw** in the message window, which, as you know after working through the scripts here, brings up the message watcher window. Be sure to uncheck the message watcher's **hide unused messages** button.

(The **idle** method is used in the *About HyperProgramming* navigator stack. The alternative solution that the *Power Tools* stack gives for the same problem of multiple scrolling fields is to put buttons over each part of the scroll bar, so that the scripts know exactly what the user is doing.)

11.4 Collecting scripts

By changing **globalsIn** to a handler we can write out all the scripts in a stack to a file. You can then print the file using any word processor.

Although there are many ways you might want to collect a script, for instance, onto fields in another HyperCard stack, we shall simply save every script in a specified stack to a text file. We will change the order of looking at scripts to be more 'readable': when collecting globals it didn't matter what order the scripts were scanned in. After working out how to do this, we will improve the scheme to make use of the word processor's mail merge facility to get better formatting.

Start with two housekeeping questions: which stack's script do we want to save, and what file do we want to save it in? Since eventually we'll have written several handlers that dump scripts and bits of scripts to this file, we'll use a global variable **scriptfile**.

```
on mouseUp
    global scriptfile
    tocomputer
    get the name of this stack
```

```
go stack "the stack"
if the result = "No such stack" then
  beep
  exit mouseUp
end if
if the name of this stack = it then
  answer "Do you want to save the script of this stack?" ¬
  with "Cancel", "OK"
  if it = "Cancel" then exit mouseUp
end if

ask file "File to save scripts in:" with "Scripts"
if the result is "Cancel" then exit mouseUp

put it into scriptfile
open file scriptfile
```

At this stage we are in the right stack, and need to collect its scripts:

```
dumpscript "this stack"
repeat with i = 1 to number of backgrounds
  go background i
  dumpscript "background" && i
  repeat with j = 1 to number of fields
    dumpscript "field" && j
  end repeat
  repeat with j = 1 to number of background buttons
    dumpscript "background button" && j
  end repeat
end repeat
repeat with i = 1 to number of cards
  go card i
  dumpscript "card" && i
  repeat with j = 1 to number of buttons
    dumpscript "button" && j
  end repeat
  repeat with j = 1 to number of card fields
    dumpscript "card field" && j
  end repeat
end repeat
```

Close the file and get back to where we started from:

```
close file scriptfile

-- get back here, which ever stack we went to
get the long name of me
go word 5 to number of words in it of it
```

```
      touser
    end mouseUp
```

The handler **dumpScript** is called for each and every object in the stack. First, if the script is empty there's no point saving it, otherwise tell the user that we are saving a script by putting the object's name into the message window – this gives a sense of progress for an otherwise long and tedious operation.

```
    on dumpScript object
      global scriptfile
      get the script of object

      -- don't bother saving empty scripts
      if the number of words in it = 0 then exit dumpscript
      put "Saving script of" && object
```

We can easily get a description for the current object, like **button 5**, but since objects have names, IDs and numbers, perhaps we can do better? We can find out the name of an object by **value("the name of" && object)**, asking HyperTalk to find the value of the expression **"the name of" && object** (if we had merely written **the name of object**, HyperCard would have complained that **object**, being a container and not an object, didn't have a name).

```
      -- what's the name of this object?
      put value("the name of" && object) into objectname
```

Some objects, stacks, don't have IDs and numbers, and all other objects needn't have names. A problem at this stage is that if the user hasn't given a name in the **Info...** dialog box (or set it from HyperTalk by using **set name of ...**), then HyperCard gives it a 'default' name, like **card id 2123**. HyperTalk's **name of** returns a string like **card "Info"** if the card has an explicit name, otherwise something like **card id 2123**. We need to tell which is which. Fortunately, objects with explicit names always contain quote marks.

```
      -- has this object got a useful ID and number?
      if "card button field background" contains first word of object then
        if objectname contains quote then -- it has a user-supplied name
          put ", ID" && last word of value("the ID of" && object) after objectname
        end if
        put ", number" && value("the number of" && object) after objectname
      end if
      -- answer objectname -- just to check!
```

Finally we write out the name of the script and the script itself:

```
      write "Script of" && objectname & return to file scriptfile
      repeat while it ≠ empty and first line of it = empty
```

```
        delete first line of it              -- remove leading blanks
     end repeat
     repeat while it ≠ empty and last line of it = empty
        delete last line of it               -- remove trailing blanks
     end repeat

     write it & return & return to file scriptfile
  end dumpScript
```

If you intend to start dumping the scripts of *huge* stacks, it is worthwhile devising a few ways of saving paper. For example, many buttons will have trivial scripts like:

```
  on mouseUp
    visual effect dissolve very slowly
      go card ID 12312
  end mouseUp
```

… and it's not obvious that you need to see any of these when you are reading a printed version of the stack scripts. It is easy enough to ignore scripts whose only contents is a **mouseUp** handler and, apart from comments, lines with first word **go** or **visual** (**pass mouseUp, play, beep**, and so on, depending on what sort of things the stack does). You'll have to do some experiments: use the collector we gave above, look at the files it produces (by using a word processor), then modify the collection process to skip stuff you are not interested in.

Printing scripts using mail merge facilities

The last example dumped a plain text file and had no pretensions to looking pretty: no headlines, bold fonts or anything. Apart from dumping scripts to HyperCard fields (which can then be formatted from scripts), the most efficient idea is to make the program write a mail merge file.

Typically, a mail merge file consists of lines of data that can be merged with a master file – the 'letter master', or in this case, a script format master. The master provides the style details required for the scripts, and during a merge, each line of data is sucked in and merged with the master to make a 'form letter' – in this case, the formatted scripts.

In Microsoft's Word, the master file could be:

«DATA Scripts»

«Name»

Script:

«Script»

The first line gives the name of the data file that our script-dumping handler will write. Each line of the data file will be an object's name, a tab character and the script. You can see from the master file that the object name in the merged file will be in **bold** and the script's text in Helvetica, and that each script will be neatly separated from the previous one by a horizontal line.

The first line of the data file will specify the field names for mail merge:

write "Name" & tab & "Script" & return to file scriptfile

Subsequent lines will be in the form: *name* **tab** *script* – except that with Microsoft Word, we must replace each quote with two double quotes and enclose names and scripts inside double quotes:

write msw(objectname) & tab & msw(it) & return to file scriptfile

The function msw converts a string like card "Data" to "card ""Data""". It is easily defined:

```
function msw s
   put empty into t
   get offset(quote, s)
   repeat while it > 0
      put char 1 to it of s & quote after t
      delete char 1 to it of s
      get offset(quote, s)
   end repeat
   return quote & t & s & quote
end msw
```

If s contains a quote, the repeat loop copies s up to and including the quote into t adding the extra quote required, then looks for another quote in the rest of s. When there are no more quotes left in s (indicated by offset(quote, s) returning zero), we return t & s between the outer quotes.

11.5 Higher-order functions

We've just had three examples of handlers that do things with scripts: one to collect globals, one to collect scripts into a text file, and the last example, to put scripts into a mail merge file. HyperTalk lets us define a generic script processor, by passing the script-collecting handler as a parameter:

```
on scanObjects action
   tocomputer
   push card
   do action && q("this stack")
   repeat with i = 1 to number of backgrounds
```

```
        go background i
        do action && q("background" && i)
        repeat with j = 1 to number of fields
           do action && q("field" && j)
        end repeat
        repeat with j = 1 to number of background buttons
           do action && q("background button" && j)
        end repeat
     end repeat
     repeat with i = 1 to number of cards
        go card i
        do action && q("card" && i)
        repeat with j = 1 to number of buttons
           do action && q("button" && j)
        end repeat
        repeat with j = 1 to number of card fields
           do action && q("card field" && j)
        end repeat
     end repeat
     pop card
     touser
  end scanObjects

  function q s
     return quote & s & quote
  end q
```

The handler **scanObjects** applies its argument **action**, which is expected to be a handler, to each object name in the stack in turn. The standard HyperTalk command **do** does whatever its parameter tells it to (**do "b" & "eep"** would beep).

As an example of this method, if we want to learn about the size of each script, we could do this:

```
  on mouseUp
     scanObjects count
  end mouseUp

  on count object
     get the script of object
     answer object & return & return ¬
     & "Lines:" && number of lines in it & return ¬
     & "Words:" && number of words in it & return ¬
     & "Chars:" && number of chars in it
  end count
```

The handler **scanobjects** is called a higher-order function since its parameters are not ordinary values, like containers or values, but *other* handlers, such as **count**. Using higher-order functions is a very powerful way of programming, but is – in a language like HyperTalk – something that is not so much a method you first think of, but a method that becomes useful once you have written a lot of scripts and notice that you are doing many very similar things with different handlers (here, using them to look at every object in a stack). By then the stack probably works without you redesigning it to use higher-order functions! But if you do rewrite it, you gain the significant advantage that most of your scripting errors in the script will be concentrated in a single handler (here, scanobjects) rather than in many.

Scanobjects, in fact, can be thought of as a special sort of repeat statement. A call scanobjects x is a *bit* like:

```
repeat with i = first object to last object
  do x i
end repeat
```

Such handlers are called *iterators*, and are a powerful and flexible way of programming – you may be pleased to see that you can construct higher-order functions and iterators so easily in HyperTalk. HyperTalk iterators are especially useful when you want to do something to every card, or to every field, or to every button. Most books on functional programming will give you many more ideas on ways in which you can utilize such techniques; we'd recommend Peter Henderson's (see *Further Reading* at the end of this book).

Often you will want to do more than find out about each object separately. In our counting example, it would probably have been more use to know the total number of lines, words and characters for *all* scripts rather than for each one individually. We need action to feed its results into its next call. Change action from a handler to a function, so that we can get its results, and then rather than use do, we use value:

```
function scanObjects action, p
  tocomputer
  push card
  put value(action & q("this stack", p)) into p
  repeat with i = 1 to number of backgrounds
    set cursor to busy
    go background i
    put value(action & q("background" && i, p)) into p
    repeat with j = 1 to number of fields
      put value(action & q("field" && j, p)) into p
    end repeat
    repeat with j = 1 to number of background buttons
      put value(action & q("background button" && j, p)) into p
    end repeat
  end repeat
  repeat with i = 1 to number of cards
    set cursor to busy
    go card i
    put value(action & q("card" && i, p)) into p
    repeat with j = 1 to number of buttons
      put value(action & q("button" && j, p)) into p
```

```
      end repeat
      repeat with j = 1 to number of card fields
        put value(action && q("card field" && j, p)) into p
      end repeat
    end repeat
    pop card
    touser
    return p
  end scanObjects

  function q s, p
    return "(" & quote & s & quote & "," & p & ")"
  end q
```

In short, on each object, **scanobjects** applies the function **action** to the object and **p** (something else we want **action** to know), putting the new results into **p**. If you want to see what is happening, a good place to trace things is in the function **q** which constructs the nicely quoted parameters for **action**:

```
  function q s, p
    answer "put action(" & quote & s & quote & "," & p & ") into p"
    return "(" & quote & s & quote & "," & p & ")"
  end q
```

Even if you don't understand what's going on yet, seeing it work will help. Try it out with the example handlers given below.

If, for instance, we make **action** add up the number of lines, words and characters:

```
  function count object, l, w, c
    get the script of object
    return l + number of lines in it & "," ¬
    & w + number of words in it & "," ¬
    & c + number of chars in it
  end count
```

We can call **scanobjects** with some initial value for **count**'s parameters (three zeros); we will get all the information we want:

```
  on mouseUp
    get scanobjects("count", "0,0,0")
    answer "Script totals" & return ¬
    & "Lines:" && item 1 of it & return ¬
    & "Words:" && item 2 of it & return ¬
    & "Chars:" && item 3 of it
  end mouseUp
```

Scanobjects is such a useful sort of handler that it is best placed in a background, stack or tool stack's script, so that it can be used easily from many scripts, like buttons anywhere in the stack. Yet you'd probably want the definitions of the handlers scanobjects uses (such as count) to remain in those scripts. This causes a problem, since scanobjects will try to do action, but the action may not be defined in scanobjects's script. In this case, trying to do the action will just cause a '**Can't understand count**' error from HyperCard. Instead each do should send its parameter to the script where scanobjects was called from; this is probably where count (or whatever) is defined. Rather than rewrite each do line, you can change do to dot, and define dot as follows:

```
on dot s
   send s to the target
end dot
```

If you want to make the same improvement to the second scanobjects handler, which used value instead of do, you can use the following technique, and change the word function to on in the definition of the relevant action function that is used (send can't send functions, but on handlers can return results that the result picks up as if they were functions):

```
function valuet s
   send s to the target
   return the result
end valuet
```

11.6 Collecting go commands to check them

It's easy to make programming mistakes in large stacks. We can use the ideas of the previous sections to track down all dubious go commands. Maybe you have some buttons in your stack that were written a long time ago, and you have since deleted the card they used to go to? You should certainly find those obsolete gos and fix them.

We've just made a handler scanobjects, which can apply a handler to each and every object in a stack. We'll use this technique to search for lines starting go in each object's script. A handler findgo collects lines of go commands into a global variable gos; having found the go commands, we sort gos and remove duplicate lines (maybe there are lots of go 1), and then delete lines that go to cards we know exist. In the example here, we then use answer to display any remaining go commands; you may want to save them to a field instead if there are too many for an answer dialog box.

```
on mouseUp
   global gos
   set cursor to watch
```

```
        put empty into gos
        scanobjects findgo
        sort gos
        put 2 into i
        repeat while i ≤ number of lines in gos
            if line i of gos = line i-1 of gos then delete line i of gos
            else add 1 to i
        end repeat
        put 1 into i
        repeat while i ≤ number of lines in gos
            get line i of gos
            if value("there is a card" && it) then
                delete line i of gos
            else if it = "last card" or it = "back" then
                -- we could also add "next", "prev", "recent" and so on
                delete line i of gos
            else add 1 to i
        end repeat
        answer gos
    end mouseUp
```

Don't forget that it is worth putting **empty** into **gos** when you have finished with it; otherwise HyperCard will be wasting the memory that **gos** uses indefinitely.

Finding lines starting with **go** is easy:

```
    on findgo object
        global gos
        get the script of object
        repeat with i = 1 to number of lines in it
            if first word of line i of it = "go" then
                put line i of it into t
                delete word 1 of t
                if word 1 of t = "card" then delete word 1 of t
                repeat while char 1 of t = space
                    delete char 1 of t
                end repeat
                put t & return after gos
            end if
        end repeat
    end findgo
```

11.7 Summary

The user can only see a HyperCard stack one card at a time; the way HyperCard is designed it is not possible to see more than one card. Yet much useful information is spread about in a stack, and is more useful when it is collected together. This chapter showed various ways of doing that, and particularly gave some ideas for collecting and analysing scripts, which anyway are rather hidden from view. More generally, collecting text from a stack enables HyperCard to be integrated with other Macintosh applications, such as word processors. Chapters 12 and 14 show how to use collected information to make it easier to get from card to card.

The important programming concept of iterator was introduced. Iterators are handlers that take other handlers as their parameters, and apply these handlers to various objects, such as every card in a stack or on a background. They are an ideal way to collect material.

CHAPTER 12

Do-it-Yourself Hypertext

Making hypertext with HyperTalk

Hypertext enables an author to exploit the interactive nature of personal computers to present information in a manner that leaves each reader free to choose their own, rather than the author's, path through it: hypertext has no pre-defined reading sequence. Hypertext systems structure text through the use of *nodes* and *links*. Nodes are chunks of textual information and links are the routes between nodes. Nodes can be as short as a word or as long as several paragraphs. In conventional books, hypertext can be found as 'programmed learning' texts and in some childrens' adventure stories – in both of these forms you get text like, 'If your answer was *apple*, turn to page 234', which in HyperCard can be done automatically!

In HyperCard, hypertext *nodes* can be whole cards (containing any number of text fields) or they can be individual, possibly pop-up, fields within cards. The system HT, which we will describe in detail in the next chapter, supports both types. Pop-up nodes are analogous to footnotes in conventional documents; they are used for presenting small amounts of text without transferring the reader to a new visual context. Whole-card nodes are more like pages: they are separate visual contexts; users cannot view more than one card at a time and each card contains a separate piece of textual information.

Links connect a source node (or some words in a source node) to a destination node. Links can be implemented in HyperCard using buttons (in fact, anything that can execute a **go** command), or they can be constructed using mouse-sensitive pieces of text, also called *hot text*. The reader follows the links by clicking on them: they work like a powerful form of the cross-references in a conventional book. The advantage of constructing links from hot text rather than buttons is that the links move whenever the text moves, as for example when the surrounding text is edited, or when links are located in a scrolling field. In HyperCard, hot text is created by applying the style **group** to the text. If the **show groups** command is executed, text that has the **group** style is underlined with in grey like this: grouped text .

Hypermedia is similar to hypertext but the information in the nodes can be in media other than text. Macintosh computers are widely used in hypermedia applications because they can store and present information in many media, including speech, music and other recorded sounds, monochrome and colour images, as well as animation sequences. Most of the techniques for constructing hypertext that we'll describe can be extended to deal with information in other media.

A *hypertext system* is a system that enables authors and readers to create and access textual information structures. A complete hypertext system includes a user interface that enables authors to create nodes and links in a simple manner, avoiding the need for authors to write programs in order to implement links. HyperCard, then, is not a hypertext system; it is a toolkit from which hypertext systems can be built. Consequently, the user interface design and the representations and implementations of nodes and links are *not* built-in to HyperCard. This enables many different styles of hypertext and hypermedia application to be implemented. Except for some very simple cases, HyperCard does not provide the relevant operations for the creation of nodes and links, but it does contain some very useful components and operations for the construction of hypertext.

In Chapters 14 and 15, we will go in to the design and construction of a general-purpose hypertext system for HyperCard. In this present chapter, we introduce HyperCard's hypertext features with two systems that solve interesting problems; the hypertext features in HyperCard make the solutions much easier to use. You won't have to worry about writing a 'hypertext story' or even providing the links manually, which is why we call it do-it-yourself hypertext.

12.1 'Do-it-Yourself' hypertext

The big problem with hypertext is writing the text in the first place! Our first hypertext stack is therefore one that can write its own text. We'll have some fun, and on the way learn how to program hot text – text that works like buttons – in HyperTalk. Like most interesting stacks, explaining what it does takes a lot more effort than programming it!

The picture below shows a card from the *DIY HyperText* stack supplied on the book disk. It is a simple hypertext system, following the idea of cards as nodes, and uses both buttons and hot text for links.

The idea for writing the text is to generate it from a grammar, such as one might have learnt at school. The card shown below is saying that a sentence is made up from a noun phrase, a verb phrase and then another noun phrase, or by putting 'did you know that' in front of a sentence, or, lastly, by saying 'my' *adjective person* ('happy mother'?) followed by some adverb, then the word 'said', then a sentence, worked out by the same rules.

Thus we might get 'my happy mother rarely said did you know that cats eat dogs'. It would have been worked out as follows: we start with wanting a sentence. We choose a line from the possible forms of sentence, say, the last line (starting 'my'). At this stage, we have the first word of the sentence (and HyperTalk could write it directly to the field). Now we need an adjective: so, go to the card containing the choices for the adjective category, and following the same process, we might choose the line 'happy'. Since 'happy' isn't another category, we can write 'happy' down, and then look for a person – we chose 'mother'. And so it goes on – you can see how tedious writing is!

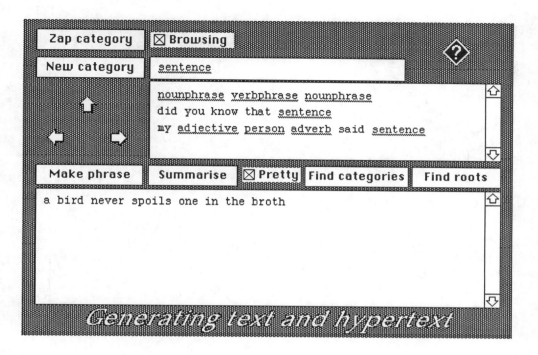

Before worrying about how to make the sentences (that's the easiest bit), what hypertext features does this stack provide? Take the card above: here, we've generated the sentence, 'a bird never spoils one in the broth'. If you click on bird, HyperCard immediately takes you to a card where the term bird was defined: as can be seen, it happens to be a noun.

There are three arrows on each card: if we click on the up-arrow on this card, we follow a hypertext link to the card that uses nouns. In this case, we go to the noun phrase card (we're only showing part of the card now):

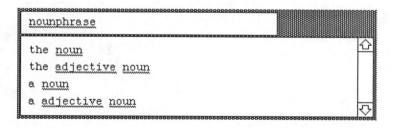

All of the underlined words in the fields can be clicked on, and doing so will take you to a card that defines that category, noun or adjective, or whatever. In fact, if a word is not underlined, this means that it is not a category, so instead we go to the card that has a category (like noun) using that word (like bird).

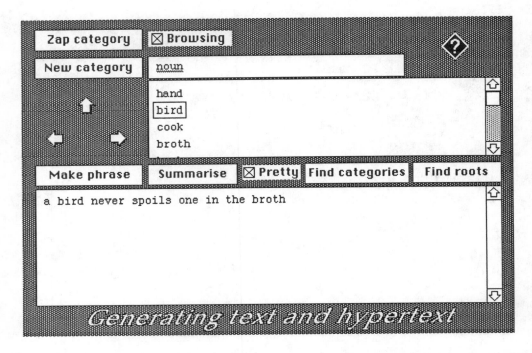

We can use the stack either for *browsing*, reading the hypertext and jumping around, or for *authoring* it, making new cards and links. A button at the top of the card changes mode from hypertext browsing to authoring. The button always seems to be checked: it simply changes its name each time it is clicked.

Sometimes it is frustrating that each card only gives a limited view on the hypertext and how each sort of category (sentence, noun phrase, adjective) links to each other category. We could draw a map, perhaps, but grammars like this have a standard representation called BNF (short for Backus Naur form) and this is the best way of representing them. If we click on **Summarise**, a conventional BNF grammar is worked out for the current card, some of which is shown here:

```
nounphrase ::= the noun | the adjective noun | a noun | a
adjective noun .

noun ::= hand | bird | cook | broth | bush .

adjective ::= small | spotted .
```

This text still works like hypertext: you can click on any word to find its grammar rules. Arguably, though, it looks a bit cramped: check the **Pretty** button and the grammar is redisplayed with a neat indentation (illustrated at the top of the next page). The actual grammar is shown in a scrolling field: we've only shown a bit of it here.

```
nounphrase ::= the noun |
               the adjective noun |
               a noun |
               a adjective noun .

noun ::= hand |
         bird |
```

Apart from the obvious features, like help and buttons for creating and deleting (zapping) categories, the last interesting feature to describe is the button **Find roots**. It finds all categories that are not used anywhere (except perhaps by themselves). We see here that bottle and sentence are two such categories; perhaps we have forgotten a sort of sentence (or noun phrase) that uses bottles? Alternatively, we could click on `bottle`, which would hyper-take us to the bottle card and we could delete it, to forget all about it. Or perhaps we want to make a new grammar for a bottle song (or something!). The stack will let you have as many grammars as you wish.

```
bottle
sentence
```

12.2 Browsing or authoring?

The simplest part of the stack lets the user edit text – usually called *authoring* in hypertext applications – by unlocking all fields. When fields are locked, clicking on them will generate **mouseUp** and other messages that activate the hypertext browsing features. The button at the top of the card is always checked and says whether the stack is in its authoring or browsing mode. It is implemented as follows:

```
on mouseUp -- Work as HyperText (browsing) or allow editing (authoring).
    if the short name of me is "Authoring" then
        set the name of me to "Browsing"
        get true
    else
        set the name of me to "Authoring"
        get false
    end if
    repeat with i = 1 to number of fields
```

```
        -- has no effect on the sharedText field
        set the lockText of field i to it
      end repeat
    end mouseUp
```

12.3 Help

The next simplest part of the stack is the help system. If you click the help button (the question mark, top right of the card), an **answer** dialog tells you to click what you want help on, but hold down the ***option*** key. Since many objects on the card have **mouseUp** handlers, we get in there first with a **mouseDown** handler! If the ***option*** key is down (the user does want help), we get the first line of that object's script to see what it has to say for itself, put up the helpful **answer** dialog box, and then **exit to HyperCard**. This last step stops HyperCard worrying about the outstanding **mouseUp**: the object's own handler never gets run. The **mouseDown** handler goes in the background script.

```
    on mouseDown -- provide help, by getting first line of script
      if the optionKey is down then
        if the first word of the target = "card" then
          beep
          answer "Click on any object, holding the option key down to get help."
        else
          get line 1 of script of the target
          delete char 1 to 3 of it -- remove the comment symbol
          answer "Help for " & second word of name of target ¬
          && "'" & short name of target & "':" & return & return & it
        end if
        exit to HyperCard
      end if
    end mouseDown
```

12.4 Underlining hot text

Category names (or 'non-terminals') are always underlined, and we use HyperCard's group text style for doing this. **CloseField** is sent by HyperCard when the user moves the cursor out of a field being edited, since this is the only time that grouping needs to be changed, we handle the message to ensure that the field's grouping is brought up to date just after any editing:

```
    on closeField
      hotText
    end closeField
```

The first part of **hotText** deletes any blank lines and is straightforward, though you have to be careful that if you **delete line i** of a field, the next line to look at is 'still' **line i**, not **line i+1**. The second loop in **hotText** scans each word in the field to see if there is a card of the same name; if so, it groups that word. This is done by the crafty test **if there is a card word i of field "phrases"**, which means take **word i of "phrases"** and succeed if there is a card with that name. If there is a card with that name, then **word i** should be underlined. The handler concludes by checking that the user can see the groups' underlining.

```
on hotText -- underline hypertext words
  put 1 into i
  repeat while i ≤ number of lines in field "phrases"
    set cursor to busy
    if number of words in line i of field "phrases" = 0 then
      delete line i of field "phrases"
    else add 1 to i
  end repeat
  -- make sure everything is ungrouped first
  set textStyle of word 1 to number of words in field "phrases" ¬
  of field "phrases" to plain
  repeat with i = 1 to number of words in field "phrases"
    set cursor to busy
    if there is a card word i of field "phrases" then
      set the textStyle of word i of field "phrases" to group
    end if
  end repeat
  put the secs into field "when underlined"
  show groups
end hotText
```

So grouping the text is easy, and no different than if we had wished to put category words in italic or bold text styles, except for the way in which the group underlining can be switched on or off with the **show groups** and **hide groups** commands. If had we really wanted hot text to be in a particular style, such as bold, we should set both **bold** and **group** styles, but **hide groups** so that the peculiar group underlining did not show as well.

It gets more interesting when fields are locked, however. When a field is locked (which this stack does by clicking the **Authoring** button – recall that this is the alternate name for the **Browsing** button), fields can respond to **mouseUp**, **mouseDown** and so forth just like buttons do. (If you are desperate, you can ***command–click*** over a field that is not locked to generate the messages.) Since the background has several fields all of which should provide the same hypertext features, we will handle all the **mouseUp** messages in the background script.

When the user clicks in a field various HyperTalk functions return interesting values: **the clickLine** gives the line number clicked (say, **line 5 of card field 3**); **the clickLoc** gives the screen coordinates of the click. Here, we use **the clickChunk** since this tells us precisely what the run of characters in the clicked group was; it returns a value like **char 3 to 6 of bkgnd field**

4. If we had not used groups, then the clickChunk would return the *word* clicked on: by using groups we can tell HyperCard to give us a larger chunk by grouping several words together. In our stack, either words are grouped, if there is a card with that name, or they appear as ordinary words ('terminals') in the field Phrases. The handler either goes to a card of the right name, or tries to find the word somewhere in the Phrases field.

```
on mouseUp -- provide the hypertext function; in the background script
    if the textStyle of the clickChunk = "group"
    then go to card the clickText
    else find word the clickText in field "phrases"
end mouseUp
```

Unfortunately, if we click in the field Phrases to start with, find may merely find what we clicked on! This isn't very interesting, so it is worth being more careful: if the last word of the clickChunk is 1 then the click was in the Phrases field (which is number 1), so we start the search from the next card. Starting on the next card guarantees to find the clicked text somewhere else in the stack if it is there on another card; furthermore, it means that repeatedly clicking a word will cycle through all of the appropriate cards. Here is the handler corrected:

```
on mouseUp -- provide the hypertext function
    if there is a bg button "Authoring" then exit mouseUp
    if the textStyle of the clickChunk = "group"  then
        get the clickText
        -- a precaution in case any cards are unnamed
        if first word of it = "card" then go it
        else go to card it
    else
        if the last word of the clickChunk is 1 then
            lock screen
            go next card
        end if
        find word the clickText in field "phrases"
    end if
end mouseUp
```

A small point of interest, the clickText gives you the actual text that was clicked, and we could equally have said value of the clickChunk, which would have worked it out from the expression that clickChunk gives.

   A few more refinements should be added to mouseUp. Our stack allows users to edit text, and in this mode hypertext jumping should be disabled. Secondly, there is a possibility (if the user has been fiddling with the **Card info...** dialog) that some card names have been lost. In this case, we may have the click text being something like card id 5322, and saying go card card id 5322 won't work! Here are all the details worked out:

```
on mouseUp -- provide the hypertext function
   if there is a bg button "Authoring" then exit mouseUp
   if the textStyle of the clickChunk = "group"
   then
      get the clickText
      -- a precaution in case any cards are unnamed
      if first word of it = "card" then go it
      else go to card it
   else
      if the last word of the clickChunk is 1 then
         lock screen
         go next card
      end if
      find word the clickText in field "phrases"
   end if
end mouseUp
```

12.5 Making hot text more accurate

An important point for hypertext stacks is that users (sometimes called 'authors') may add or remove cards that hot text refers to. So, somehow, we should make sure that the hot text underlining is always up to date. The simplest way to do this, of course, is to prohibit the user editing text or deleting, cutting, creating and pasting cards: we won't use this method!

Every time a card is opened, we could work out what text to underline. This is very reliable, but for most applications it would be too slow. It is a useful method to use when you are still designing the stack, because it is so easy and reliable to implement; then, when you think of a better method you can improve it. Or, every time a card is altered in any way, we work out what other cards to update; usually this method is unreliable, because we have to be very careful to find all of the possibly affected cards. It can also mean big delays when a small change is made.

The method we shall use is quite simple. We use a hidden shared text field, new underlines, to keep track of the last time anything changed. Each card has a hidden (background) field when underlined. On opening a card, if we find that field "new underlines" > field "when underlined", we simply refresh the underlining by calling hotText, which now also updates the when underlined field. Here's how:

```
on openCard
   set the scroll of field "phrases" to 0
   set the scroll of field "results" to 0
   if field "new underlines" > field "when underlined" then
      -- underlining may be out of date, so fix it up
      hotText
```

```
      end if
      show groups -- do this every-so-often in case it's off
   end openCard
```

We also have to make sure that cut card, and so on, **put the secs into field "new underlines"**.
Since we need to do this in many places, we have a background handler:

```
   on update
      put the secs into field "when underlined"
      hotText -- we've need to redo the hot text on this card now
   end update
```

We change the **closeField** handler too, making sure to calling **update** rather than **hotText**:

```
   on closeField
      update -- ensure we update all other cards too
   end closeField
```

12.6 Making new cards

Our stack lets the user add new cards, which will be automatically added into the hypertext. It's
important that new cards fit into the hypertext in 'the right way': for our stack that means that
their names must be unique, and (as it happens) a single word. On opening a new card, the
relevant script clicks on the category name field, to encourage the user to type a name there.
By using **closeField**, we check that the user enters a suitable name or we have to fix it up to
make it suitable.

```
   on closeField
      put short name of this card into oldname
      if number of words in me ≠ 1 then
         beep
         if there is a bg button "Browsing" then
            put return & return & "Click Browsing button to be able to edit it." into help
         else put empty into help
         if number of words in me = 0 then
            answer "There is no category name for this card." & help ¬
            with "Zap" or "Add one"
            if it is "Zap" then
               click at the loc of bg button "Zap category"
            end if
            put "?" into me
         else
            answer "Category names should be a single word; '" ¬
```

```
        & me & "' has " & number of words in me & "." & help
        -- we will make it into one word
        repeat with i = 1 to number of chars in me
           if char i of me = space then put "@" into char i of me
        end repeat
     end if
  end if
```

Whatever, if we find that there is already a card with the same name (possibly with one of our fixed up names, like ?), we modify the name of the current card and make it unique:

```
  set name of this card to empty
  if there is a card me then
     beep
     answer "There is already another card for '" & me & "'"
     get 2 -- think of a unique name for this card
     repeat while there is a card me & "-" & it
        add 1 to it
     end repeat
     put me & "-" & it into me
  end if
  set name of this card to me
  if short name of this card ≠ oldname then update
end closeField
```

Finally, we call **update** if we have changed the name of the card: this will ensure that we redo the hot text links on other cards (when they are next opened).

12.7 Making phrases

The **Make phrase** button is the simplest part of the stack! Of course, it starts off with a single comment line so that the help system has something to say for it.

```
-- Generate a random phrase from the grammar shown on this card.
```

The **mouseUp** handler starts with boring initialization, such as clearing the field results. We **set** the field's **textStyle** to **plain**, otherwise there might have been problems with groups 'merging' together as we added new words.

```
on mouseUp
  push this card
  lock messages -- because of openCard
  set textStyle of field "results" to plain
  put empty into field "results"
```

The first interesting bit is to choose a random line from the field phrases to start the process rolling:

```
get any line of field "phrases"
```

We work through it, repeatedly looking at the first word and deleting it when we are done with it. Each word is either a category name (non-terminal) or an ordinary word (a terminal). If it is a category, go to that card and replace the word with any line from that card's phrases field. (It looks more fun to actually go to the card and see things working, rather than to **put any line of field "phrases" of card word 1 of it into word 1 of it**, which is also a mouthful.) Otherwise, the word can be put in the field **results** and deleted.

```
        repeat while number of words in it > 0
          if there is a card word 1 of it then
            go card word 1 of it
            put any line of field "phrases" into word 1 of it
          else
            put word 1 of it & " " after field "results"
            scrollfield("results")
            delete word 1 of it
          end if
        end repeat
        pop card
        unlock messages
      end mouseUp
```

The utility **scrollfield** ensures that the user can always see the end of the field, by scrolling the field up so that its last line is in view. Unfortunately trying to work out how much to set the scroll (to **textHeight of field f * number of lines in field f**) won't work when lines are too long and wrap around, because **the number of lines** will be less than the number of lines displayed: the way to get around this limitation is to set the scroll to some huge number and HyperCard will courteously set it to be as large as it can be, which is what we want. Since other handlers calling **scrollfield** lock the screen for most of their work, **scrollfield** briefly unlocks the screen so that its job can be seen!

```
      on scrollfield f
        set scroll of field f to 10000
        unlock screen
        lock screen
      end scrollfield
```

Another way of making phrases would be by taking the *last* word of it, rather than the first. This would mean sentences were constructed backwards, so we would **put word 1 of it & " " before field "results"**. This would look fun, and we wouldn't need the call to **scrollfield**, since all the action would visible on the first word of the field!

Some phrases aren't worth waiting for. Here's an example: 'did you know that did you know that my spotted woman said did you know that my spotted man slowly said did you know that did you know that my small man slowly said did you know that my spotted woman quietly said my green woman said my small man said the small bush quietly is worth a bird'.

12.8 Finding categories

Categories are found by collecting the names of all cards and putting them into the **results** field. The field is then sorted, and has each line grouped to underline it. The user can then use the field as a hypertext index to any category listed.

```
on mouseUp
    set textStyle of field "results" to plain
    put empty into field "results"
    repeat with i = 1 to number of cards
        put (short name of card i) & return after field "results"
    end repeat
    sort field "results"
    repeat with i = 1 to number of lines in field "results"
        set textStyle of line i of field "results" to group
    end repeat
end mouseUp
```

In many hypertext applications, where the user cannot change any text, there would probably be a fixed card with the index on. This saves time for the user – but the author would still need a way of reconstructing the index card after any edits had been made.

12.9 Finding roots

Our hypertext stack lets you add any number of independent grammars (say, one for roman numerals, one for HyperTalk commands, one for English proverbs). Finding roots makes an index of the different grammars, which is itself a hypertext index that can be clicked on to find the root cards of each grammar.

More precisely a root is a non-terminal that is mentioned nowhere else. In HyperCard terms, it is a card that is not mentioned on any other card's phrases field. (The root of a grammar can mention itself, as does *sentence* in the examples above.)

To find roots, we have to look at each card in turn and see if any other card mentions it in its phrases field. We use HyperCard's **find** command, and check whether it finds a different card; otherwise we put the short name of the card at the end of the list of roots that is being constructed in the field **results**. (It is a shame that **find** can search for words, but it can't search for groups, but fortunately this stack never makes groups out of more than one word, so who would know?)

```
put empty into field "results"
repeat with i = 1 to number of cards
   set cursor to busy
   go card i+1
   find word short name of card i in field "phrases"
   if the result = "not found" or number of this card = i then
      put (short name of card i) & return after field "results"
      scrollfield("results")
   end if
end repeat
```

Having found the roots, we sort the field and group each line:

```
sort field "results"
repeat with i = 1 to number of lines in field "results"
   set textStyle of line i of field "results" to group
end repeat
```

12.10 Summarizing: writing grammars out

Generating the BNF form of a grammar is more tedious than worth explaining. We provide the full script here in case you want to work through it. The variable **summarised** is crucial to stop rules being repeatedly worked out, as could happen either when a rule is recursive (such as *sentence* being defined in terms of *sentence*) or when a rule is mentioned by several other rules (such as *adjective* which is used both by *nounphrase* and *sentence*); we still only want it worked out once.

```
-- Show the grammar generated by the phrases on this card.
on mouseUp
   push card
   lock messages
   lock screen
   set textStyle of field "results" to plain
   put empty into field "results"
   put empty into summarised
   put short name of this card into rules
   repeat while number of words in rules > 0
      put first word of rules into head
```

```
        put " " & head after last word of summarised
        go card head
        delete first word of rules
        put head & " " after field "results"
        set textStyle of last word of field "results" to group
        put "::= " after field "results"
        put return into indent
        repeat for number of chars in head + 5 times
          put space after indent
        end repeat
        repeat with i = 1 to number of lines in field "phrases"
          set cursor to busy
          put line i of field "phrases" into body
          if i > 1 then
            put "| " after field "results"
            if the hilite of bg button "Pretty" then
              put indent after field "results"
            end if
          end if
          put number of words in field "results" into k
          put body & " " after field "results"
          scrollfield("results")
          repeat with j = 1 to number of words of body
            get word j of body
            if there is a card it then
              set the textStyle of word k+j of field "results" to group
              if not wordin(summarised, it) then
                put " " & it after last word of summarised
                put " " & it after last word of rules
              end if
            end if
          end repeat
        end repeat
        put "." & return & return after field "results"
      end repeat
      pop card
      scrollfield("results")
    end mouseUp

    function wordin t, w
      repeat with i = 1 to number of words in t
        if word i of t = w then return true
      end repeat
      return false
    end wordin
```

12.11 Stable matching as hypertext

We will describe our second do-it-yourself hypertext much more briefly, just to give a flavour of its hypertext facilities. The stack is on the *HyperProgramming* disk, where you can easily find out how the rest of it works.

A common problem is to match people to activities, or people to partners. For example, in a classroom of eight students wanting to do eight projects from this book, several of the students wanted to do the same project, and (as the course tutors) we knew that some students would benefit from doing certain projects. We all have preferences. We need to find a way of allocating students to projects so that they have a so-called stable match, a match that will avoid arguments (of a certain sort!): we want to respect everyone's preferences as far as possible.

We won't go into the details of working out the stable matching here, as it is described well in many books on algorithms (where it is sometimes called the *stable marriage* problem); you can refer to the *Further Reading* section at the end of this book for suggested reading. The direct manipulation user interface to the stack and how hypertext linking helps – and how to implement it in HyperTalk – is of more interest. Unlike the last example, we won't use text grouping but will use text selection instead.

First, suppose the stack represents people and projects (or men and women, or whatever), one person or project per card. Each card, then, has a name which is who (or what) it is about. The central part of the user interface is the way that people express their preferences. We'll use a scrolling field, so that it can contain as many preferences as need be. The picture below shows the list of projects that someone prefers, with **Drawing mazes** favourite, and **Timing scripts** least favoured. In the illustration, the position of the cursor and the highlighting show that the user is about to reconsider the postion of the **Animating sorting** project:

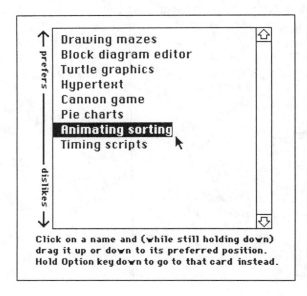

When the user clicks down on a line in the field, it is immediately highlighted. The mouse can then be dragged up or down, and the highlighted line will move with it, up or down – changing the preferences. It is a direct manipulation interface. If the **option** key is held down, when the mouse is released (sending a mouseUp message) HyperCard takes the user to the relevant card.

Thus the field provides two facilities: it can be used to reorganize people's preferences, and it can be used to follow hypertext links, to see more about the cards for each preference listed. Like all good do-it-yourself hypertexts, the field is constructed automatically from the names of cards that should be in it: in this stack, cards that are about people have projects in their preferences field, and cards that are about projects have people in their preferences field. The disk stack goes to a bit of trouble to check, for instance, that no two projects or people have the same names, and when a new card is added, that existing preferences aren't affected when each field is extended with the name of the new card.

The field must have its lockText property set true to enable it to handle the mouseDown, mouseUp and mouseStillDown messages. The following handlers are all in the field's script. For this stack, it is a background field since we want the same functionality on many cards, but the idea will work whether or not it is a background field. Indeed, the method makes a very good index card for a stack (see section 14.1 on page 289), and in that case there is no need for it to be a background field.

When the mouse is clicked down, the mouseDown handler works out what line in the field the user has clicked on, and saves it in a global lastline. The arithmetic is tricky, and has to allow for the user clicking beyond the last line of the text in the field, hence the function max. The function min ensures the arithmetic at least gives us a line number starting at 1!

```
on mouseDown
  global lastline
  set cursor to arrow
  get max(1, min(round((the mouseV-top of me+scroll of me) ¬
/textHeight of me), number of lines in me))
  put it into lastline
end mouseDown
```

The user may hold the mouse down and drag this line up or down. We therefore handle mouseStillDown and move the line up or down, by deleting it and inserting it back into the field on the new line the mouse is over. This process is a bit jerky, so it is best to lock the screen so that the user cannot see the intermediate stages of the operation.

```
-- While the mouse is still down,
-- repeatedly select (that is, highlight) the line
on mouseStillDown
  global lastline
  get max(1, min(round((the mouseV-top of me+scroll of me) ¬
/textHeight of me), number of lines in me))
```

```
select line it of me -- highlight the line
if it ≠ lastline then -- move it only if dragged to a new line
  lock screen
  put line lastline of me into a
  delete line lastline of me
  put a & return before line it of me
  put it into lastline
  unlock screen
  set hilite of bg button "Allocate" to true
end if
end mouseStillDown
```

Notice in the third line up we set the highlight of the button **Allocate**. This is because the user has dragged a line around the field, and therefore changed his or her preferences. The button is highlighted to remind the user to click it, which will recalculate a stable matching given the new preferences.

Finally, when the user lets go of the mouse, we should handle **mouseUp**. What is done depends on whether the **option** key is held down. If the **option** key is down, then we try to go to a card with the same name as the selected line of the field, which will be the one the mouse is over, thanks to our **mouseStillDown** handler. Otherwise we simply deselect the highlighted line – the user has finished adjusting preferences.

```
on mouseUp
  if the optionKey is down then -- try going to that card
    get the selection
    if it is empty then exit mouseUp
    if there is a card it then go card it
    else
      beep
      answer "There isn't a card for "" & it & ""." & return ¬
      & "Suggest you create a card with that name."
    end if
  end if
  select empty
end mouseUp
```

Sorting cards by direct manipulation

The direct manipulation method for adjusting users' preferences can also be used to solve a frequent problem – sorting a stack however the user wants it sorted. Here's one way to do it neatly: first, collect the card names in a scrolling field; second, allow the user to move lines up and down in the field (as described above); third, call a handler sortByPreferences to sort the cards in the stack into the order that the user has indicated. SortByPreferences uses **offset** to get the values to sort by – conveniently using the positions of the names of the cards in the text of our direct manipulation field:

```
on getCards
  put empty into field "preferences"
  repeat with i = 1 to number of cards
    put short name of card i into line i of field "preferences"
  end repeat
end getCards

on sortByPreferences
  get field "preferences"
  sort numeric by offset(short name of this card, it)
end sortByPreferences
```

You should ensure that card names aren't substrings of each other, else **offset** will give incorrect values, finding one card's name in another. (Consider cards called **York** and **Yorktown Heights**.) One way to fix this is to replace **short name of this card** everywhere with something unique like, **"[" & short name of this card & "]"**, but this may not look so good to the user who is adjusting the order of the cards in the field! Better, we should define our own **offset** that does *exactly* what we want – using HyperTalk's **offset** was a good way of starting the script and checking our ideas worked, but now we want to be more reliable.

There are two choices: either be slow or fast – but at the cost of enlarging the stack. Here is the slow solution. Recall that we only need **offset** to return an increasing value the lower the card name is found in the field; it needn't be a *character* offset as HyperTalk's **offset** returns:

```
function ourOffset a, b -- returns a line number, not a character position
  repeat with i = 1 to number of lines in b
    if a = line i of b then return i
  end repeat
  return 0
end ourOffset
```

Every time **sort** uses **ourOffset**, it has to search the field **preferences** (the parameter **b**). This will be slow. To be faster, we can work out what values **ourOffset** would have returned and store them in a field (**sort order**) on every card:

```
repeat with i = 1 to number of lines in field "preferences"
  put i into field "sort order" of card line i of field "preferences"
end repeat
sort numeric by field "sort order"
```

This illustrates a general rule: very often, you can speed a script up by using more space, typically by working things out to store in fields, to save working out the values repeatedly.

12.12 Conclusions

We usually think of a hypertext as some complicated written material containing links from idea to idea. HyperCard lets you create hypertext very easily: just make a background field and use a handler like:

```
on mouseUp -- simplest hotText?
  get the clickText
  if there is a card it then go card it
  else beep
end mouseUp
```

This would let you use (browse) a hypertext, but to help you to author text, you would need to extend it with script like:

```
on mouseUp -- simple hotText with authoring feature
  get the clickText
  if there is a card it then go card it
  else if the optionKey is down then
    set textStyle of the clickChunk to group -- group the new hot text
    doMenu "New Card"
    set name of this card to it
    answer "Write the text for the link: '" & it & "'"
    set lockText of me to false
  else beep
end mouseUp
```

With this small change, holding the **option** key down when you click on some text creates a new card to follow up on that link, and the linking text is automatically grouped.

Soon, however, life starts to get *very* complicated as you try to keep track of whether you have already written cards to follow up hot text links, whether you have deleted cards that used to be linked, whether you have changed the name of a card and should now go and revise all the text groups. The problem is that hypertext needs to be organized, and it is the organization of the text, rather than the linking machinery itself, that is the major obstacle to doing a good job. Hypertext needs organizing not just for the author creating the text, but also for the user who, in a large hyptertext, will not be able to keep track of where all the links are taking him. Clearly, for a worthwhile hypertext, a lot more will be needed than the trivial scripts shown above!

This chapter therefore got around the problem by generating hypertext automatically, from a grammar and by building a card index (used to set preferences). This ensured that the hypertext document was suitably organized to make the links work properly, and since HyperTalk generated the text itself it 'knew' what all the links should be and could look after them itself. This 'do-it-yourself' hypertext meant that we could learn about links, hot text and HyperCard's idea of groups, but the actual content of the hypertext as such was pretty dull! The next chapter starts the development of a serious hypertext system that is designed for linking real text; the chapter following it then extends the system with a suite of important tools that help you to organize hypertext and make it easier to use.

CHAPTER 13

A Hypertext Framework

Scripting a hypertext system in HyperCard

In this chapter, we'll show how to design and construct a general-purpose hypertext framework in HyperCard. The framework takes the form of a set of handlers that support hypertext facilities when placed in a stack, background or card script. The handlers enable hypertext nodes and links to be constructed by hypertext authors and accessed by readers using a simple and convenient user interface. Our framework can be extended to support simple hypermedia links to play recorded sounds, show colour images and run animations.

The framework that we'll describe is called *HT*. The purpose of the *HT* framework is to illustrate how it is possible to construct a unified set of scripts that will support all of the hypertext reading and authoring facilities needed for a wide range of hypertext applications. *HT* contains a set of scripts that support a particular style of hypertext interaction based on HyperCard's 'hot text' features. The generic *HT* scripts developed in this chapter can be installed in most existing stacks when you want to add hypertext features to them, without significantly constraining their design.

13.1 The design of *HT*

Here are our design decisions, you are free to change them:

User interface for browsing

HT supports two kinds of text link: links to pop-up fields on the current card – *pop-up links* – and links to other cards – *card links*.

Both kinds of link are activated by clicking on a piece of *grouped text* within a field. Grouped text is a HyperCard text style (like *italic* or **bold**) that is intended to be used for implementing hypertext links. Text that has the style **group** is displayed with a grey underline. (The underlining of groups is visible only after using the command **show groups** and can be hidden by using **hide groups**.) On the card illustrated overleaf, the word 'lost' and the words 'index card' are examples of grouped text.

In our *HT* framework, a piece of grouped text can have a pop-up link or a card link, or both, associated with it.

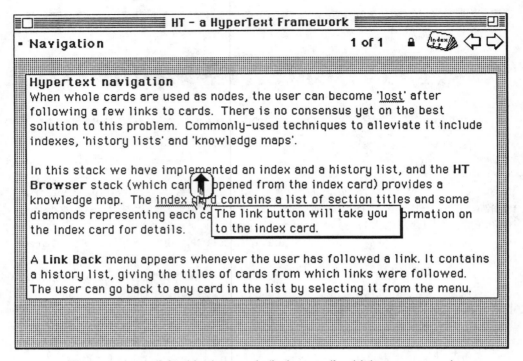

The user has clicked in the words 'index card', which are grouped.
This has revealed a pop-up link and a card link.

Pop-up links

Pop-up links provide a mechanism for displaying some extra information without leaving the current context. A pop-up link connects a piece of grouped text to a card field that is normally hidden; the field becomes visible whenever the mouse is clicked on the associated piece of grouped text and remains visible until the mouse is clicked in the field or until the card is closed.

Pop-up fields may contain more pieces of grouped text representing other links, so the information in an *HT* card can be structured as a hierarchy of pop-ups. Pop-ups are closed by clicking anywhere in the pop-up field except on grouped text. Clicking in the background of a card will close all of the currently open pop-ups.

Card links

Card links implement the concept of *hypertext link* more completely. A card link connects a piece of grouped text to another card, called the *target* card. When the user clicks on the grouped text, a button is displayed. If the button is clicked, the target card is opened. The choice of this indirect interface for access to the target is based on research which shows that immediate transfer to a new context (the target card in this case) can be disorienting for the user. Our design enables the user to decide whether or not to follow a card link after reading an explanation or description that is provided in an associated pop-up field.

Card links are implemented in *HT* by hidden buttons with a distinctive icon: ⬆. Whenever the mouse is clicked on a piece of grouped text that has an associated card link, its button appears under the mouse cursor. A second mouse click activates the link button, opening the target card. If the mouse cursor is moved away from the button without a click, the link is not activated and the button is hidden again.

If a card link and a pop-up link are both associated with the same piece of grouped text, then the pop-up field and the link button both become visible when the mouse is clicked on the associated piece of grouped text. This feature is useful because it enables a short piece of text to be attached to each card link, perhaps describing its purpose.

User interface for authoring

In many applications, hypertext is used to represent an evolving information structure. In general-purpose hypertext systems it is important to ensure that authoring and browsing (reading) can be performed together – they are often different aspects of the same activity. We have designed the *HT* interface to make adding links a direct extension of the reading interface so that pop-ups and card links can may be added at any time.

To create a new pop-up or card link, the user holds down the ***command*** key while dragging the mouse over the words that are to be grouped. As soon as the mouse button is released, the user is prompted to select the type of link that is to be created, as shown in the illustration below.

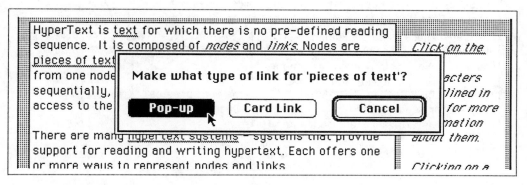

The user has dragged over the words 'pieces of text', with the Command key held down. This produces a prompt to select the type of link required.

When the user has selected the type of link, the link object (a pop-up field, or a button representing a card link) is created and a further dialog with the user takes place to produce a complete link (next illustration).

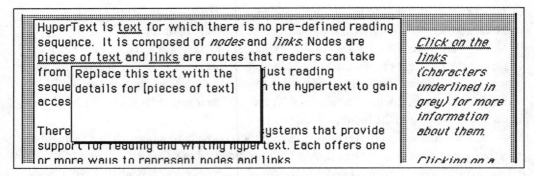

*A new pop-up field with its dummy message is positioned
just below the selected text.*

Completing a pop-up link

When a new pop-up field is created it contains a dummy message, as shown in the illustration above. Since we cannot predict how much text the user intends to type into the pop-up, as soon as the user clicks in the field, its style is changed temporarily to **scrolling**, enabling the user to type any amount of text without worrying about the size of the field. The user replaces the dummy text with the relevant information and closes the field using the Enter key or by clicking anywhere outside the field. When the user closes the pop-up, it is converted to a **shadow** field and its size is adjusted to fit the text as shown in the illustration below – the implementation of this last step is described in Chapter 14.

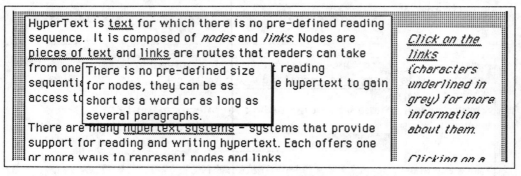

*When the user closes it, the style of the pop-up field is changed to 'shadow'
and its size is adjusted to fit the text in it.*

Completing a card link

The completion of card links requires a two-stage dialog. First a ⬆ button is created to represent the link; then the user indicates which card is to be the target of the link.

The second stage of this dialog raises a tricky design and implementation problem: how can we best enable the user to indicate the target of a card link? Users ought to be given full control of the stack so that they can use normal browsing and navigation methods to go to the target card, and we must provide an extra operation to complete the link and to remind the user that a link is incomplete until they indicate the target.

Our preferred solution to the design problem involves the use of a palette resource to produce an extra pop-up window containing two buttons that are used to indicate the target card or to cancel the creation of the current incomplete card link as in the illustration below.

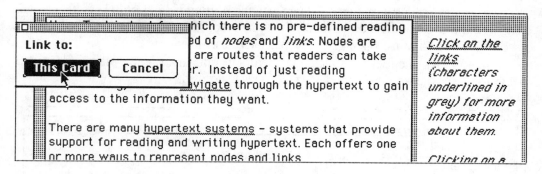

The 'windoid' at the top left is a suitable dialog device for the user to indicate the target of a card link, but it requires a 'palette' resource.

The implementation of this solution requires the addition of a suitable palette resource to the stack, which you can do with the *Power Tools* stack (or use the *HyperProgramming* disk stack, which already has the palette).

A second solution that is simpler to implement is based on the use of an extra menu called **Make Link**. The user interface design is similar, but instead of the palette window shown above, we add a temporary **Make Link** menu to the menu bar, shown in the illustration below. The menu is being used to create a card link to the current card, originating

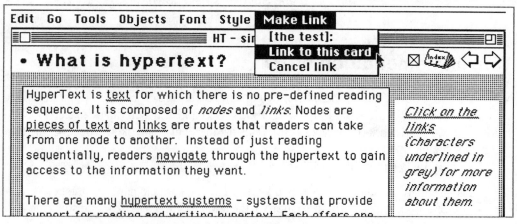

An additional menu is added to the menu bar for the user to indicate the target of a card link. The menu is removed when the link is complete.

from the words 'the test' on another card. We shall describe the implementation of this menu-based solution, since some readers may not be equipped to add Palette resources to their stacks.

Deleting links

It is sometimes necessary to delete a link when constructing a hypertext. This can be done in *HT* by clicking on the relevant grouped text with the ***command*** and ***shift*** keys held down. (The ***command*** key is held down for all authoring actions in *HT*, and the ***shift*** key is often used to denote an 'inverse' operation in the Macintosh user interface.)

In our stack, the user is prompted to confirm that the link is to be deleted (illustrated below) and if a confirmation is given, the deletion is performed.

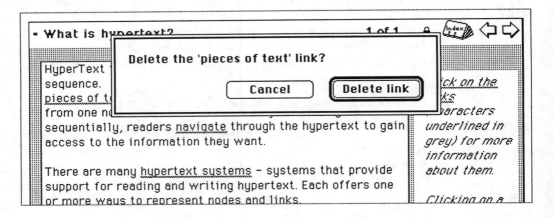

Deleting a link. The user has clicked on the 'pieces of text' grouped text with the Command and Shift keys held down.

13.2 Implementation of *HT*

Now we'll show how a generic script can be constructed to implement the design described above. Let's look first at a general-purpose *HT* mouseUp handler which can be placed in a card script, a background script or the stack script. This handler will be invoked whenever the user clicks on some grouped text.

Here is the key idea on which it is based:

- The grouped text that represents a link is used to generate the name for the field (in the case of pop-up links) or for the button (in the case of card links) that represents the link.

So the name of each pop-up field or card link button is derived from the text from which it provides a link. To make the names less likely to clash with names of the other objects in the stack, we enclose them in square brackets ([and]), and we truncate longer strings of grouped text to 29 characters (giving 31 including the brackets).

If our general-purpose mouseUp handler is placed in a card, background or stack script, it will receive a mouseUp message whenever the mouse is clicked anywhere in a card except in buttons or fields that have their own mouseUp handlers. This enables hypertext links to be added to and used in any fields that don't have mouseUp handlers. Here is a the main mouseUp handler, showing how the user's actions are detected and used to determine whether reading or authoring actions are required. MouseUp is constructed using popLinks, addLink, deleteLink, isaPopUp and closeAllPopUps handlers that are described later in this chapter:

```
on mouseUp                       -- handles hypertext reading and authoring actions
    -- check whether the click was in a field:
    if word 2 of name of the target is "field" then
        -- truncate the clickText and append brackets:
        put "["&truncate(clickText(), 29)&"]" into theName
        if the commandKey is down then -- command key indicates authoring actions:
            if the shiftKey is down then-- command and shift indicates 'delete link'
                deleteLink clickChunk(), theName
            else
                addLink clickChunk(), theName
            end if
            -- here we deal with reading action. Test for a click in grouped text
            -- uses "contains" because multiple textstyles are possible:
        else if textstyle of clickChunk() contains "group" then
            popLinks theName
        else                          -- user clicked on non-grouped text in a field:
            if isaPopUp(name of the target) then -- user clicked in a pop-up field, so hide it
                set lockText of the target to true
                hide the target
            else                      -- user clicked elsewhere, so hide all pop-ups
                closeAllPopUps
            end if
        end if
    else                              -- user clicked outside any field, so hide all pop-ups
        closeAllPopUps
    end if
end mouseUp
```

Reading actions

When the user clicks on some grouped text, our general-purpose mouseUp handler invokes the popLinks handler. PopLinks is the handler that shows the pop-up field or button associated with the selected grouped text, exploiting the fact that the name of the field or button is based on the content of the relevant grouped text.

We want the pop-ups to appear near the grouped text, so we set the position of the pop-up field or button each time it is shown, using the built-in functions clickH and clickV to discover where the user clicked. This ensures that pop-ups are always positioned near their associated text, even when the text is part of a scrolling field. We will deal in Chapter 14 with pop-ups that are too large, or too close to the edge of the card to fit when they are handled this way.

```
on popLinks aName                      -- called by mouseUp with the name of a pop-up
   if there is a card field aName then
      set topLeft of card field aName to clickH()+10, clickV()+10
      show card field aName
   end if
   if there is a card button aName then
      set loc of card button aName to clickH(), clickV()-12
      show card button aName
   end if
end popLinks
```

This simple handler is all that is required to implement *HT*'s pop-up fields. For card links, the remaining part of the implementation is contained in the script of the relevant button and is described in the section on following card links below.

Implementation of authoring actions

The authoring actions are the ones that enable users to create new links and delete existing links. These are implemented by the addLink and the deleteLink handler. AddLink is called whenever a user clicks with just the **command** key held down and deleteLink is called when they click with the **shift** key and the **command** key held down.

AddLink exploits a little-known feature of HyperCard – when the **command** key is held down and the mouse is dragged over some words in a field, the words that the mouse passes over are placed in the message box. We use this to identify whole words that constitute the hot text for the new link.

This simplifies the identification of the hot text, but it doesn't help us to determine the offsets of its initial and final characters within the field, and we need that information in order to assign the group style to the text. In the general-purpose mouseUp handler we have used the built-in function clickChunk() to assign a value to the parameter aChunk, but this only gives a reference to the first word that was clicked on and addLink has to extend this to refer to the end point of the hot text.

AddLink is rather long because it must deal with all possibilities. Both a pop-up field and a card link button may be associated with the same piece of hot text, so if we find that one link already exists, we must ask the user whether they want one of the other type. If no link exists, we ask which type of link is required. AddLink uses newPopUp, newCardLink and addStyle, which are described later:

```
    on addLink aChunk, aName     -- add a HT link to the current card.
     -- aName is the relevant link name. aChunk is the first 'hot text' word
     if "group" is in textStyle of aChunk then -- there are existing links:
       poplinks aName              --- show the links
       if there is a card field aName and there is a card button aName then
          -- there are already two links, so we can't add any more
          beep
       else if there is a card field aName then
          -- there is an existing pop-up link, so we can make a card link
          answer "Make a card link for '" & value(aChunk) & "'?" with ¬
          "Card Link" or "Cancel"
          if it is not "Cancel" then
            newCardLink aName
          end if
       else
          -- there is an existing card link, so we can make a pop-up link
          answer "Make a pop-up link for '"& value(aChunk) & "'?" with ¬
          "Pop-up" or "Cancel"
          if it is not "Cancel" then newPopUp aName
       end if
     else
       -- here we work out the offset of the start and end of the selected text in the field:
       if item 1 of mouseLoc() > item 1 of clickLoc() then
          put word 2 of aChunk+(length(msg)-1) into word 4 of aChunk
       end if
       -- validity check: if it's not the same, the user probably dragged the wrong way!
       if value(aChunk) ≠ msg then
          beep
          answer "Please try again. You must drag from left to right."
          exit addLink
       end if
       -- there are no existing links:
       answer "Make what type of link for '" & value(aChunk) & "'?" ¬
       with "Pop-up" or "Card Link" or "Cancel"
       if it is not "Cancel" then
          put "["&truncate(value(aChunk), 29)&"]" into aName
          addStyle aChunk, "group"
          if it is "Pop-up" then newPopUp aName
          else newCardLink aName
       end if
     end if
     hide msg window
    end addLink
```

The name msg is an abbreviation for **message** or **message box** – the text in the message box.

Deleting links

The deleteLink handler is quite straightforward. It deletes any pop-up fields or card link buttons associated with the grouped text that the user clicked on, exploiting the menu operations **Clear field** and **Clear button**, and removes the **group** style from the relevant text. DeleteLink uses a changeStyle handler that is described later.

```
on deleteLink aChunk, aName -- delete a HT link
    -- prompt the user for confirmation:
    answer "Delete the '"&value(aChunk)&"' link?" with "Cancel" or "Delete link"
    if it is "Delete link" then
        lock screen                    -- so that the user doesn't see intermediate stages
        set cursor to busy
        changeStyle aChunk, "group", "-"
        if there is a card button aName then
            show card button aName -- invisible objects can't be deleted!
            select card button aName
            doMenu "Clear button"
        end if
        if there is a card field aName then
            show card field aName
            select card field aName
            doMenu "Clear field"
        end if
        -- the 'select' operation changes the current tool, so revert to 'browse'
        choose browse tool
    end if
    hide message box
end deleteLink
```

Creating pop-up fields

The creation of new pop-up fields is done by the newPopUp handler, exploiting the **New Field** menu operation. This creates a new field at the centre of the card with **style rectangle**, measuring about 2 inches by 1 inch.

The **name**, **style** and contents of the field are set to appropriate initial values. The position and height of the field are left unchanged because they are reassigned whenever the pop-up is opened by the **popLinks** handler. Its height will be adjusted by the **closeField** handler (discussed in Chapter 14) to fit the text that it holds whenever its contents are edited.

```
on newPopUp aName
    lock screen                    -- so that the user doesn't see intermediate stages
    doMenu "New Field"
    choose browse tool
    set name of card field (number of card fields) to aName
```

```
         set style of card field aName to "shadow"
         put "Replace this text with the details for" && aName into card field aName
      end newPopUp
```

Creating card links

The creation of card links is more complex. The extra problem that arises is the identification of the target card by the user. As we have already discussed, a convenient way for the user to do this is to go to the required target card using normal navigation facilities and then to indicate that the current card is the link target by using a special menu operation.

The creation of a card link therefore has two stages. The handler that implements the first stage is called newCardLink. In the first stage, a card link button is created at the source card and a reference to it is placed in a global variable. The first stage concludes by creating a menu called **Make Link** and newCardLink then exits leaving the stack in the browse mode.

In the second stage, the user goes to the target card and then selects **Link to this card** from the **Make Link** menu. This invokes a handler called LinkToThisCard, whose effect is to insert an instruction of the form:

doCardLink n

into the script of the card link button, where n is the ID of the current card. The **Make Link** menu is then deleted.

Handlers for first stage of card link creation

Before examining the newCardLink handler, let's look at the handler it will use to create card link buttons. This is done by a newPopButton handler in a manner similar to the creation of a pop-up field, but in this case, the button must be given an icon, a width, a height and a skeleton script that will later be modified to contain the necessary instructions to implement the card link. The skeleton script is the same for all card links and is encapsulated as a string delivered by the function cardLinkScript. Here are newPopButton and cardLinkScript:

```
      on newPopButton aName        -- create a new card link button
         lock screen
         doMenu "New button"
         choose browse tool
         set name of card button (number of card buttons) to aName
         set style of card button aName to "roundRect"
         set width of card button aName to 25
         set height of card button aName to 29
         set icon of card button aName to "Fleet up arrow"
         set showName of card button aName to false
         set autoHilite of card button aName to true
         set script of card button aName to cardLinkScript()
      end newPopButton
```

```
function cardLinkScript          -- this is just a way to define a string constant
   return "on mouseUp" & return &¬
   "beep" & return &¬
   "end mouseUp" & return & return &¬
   "on mouseLeave" & return &¬
   "hideCardLink short name of me" & return &¬
   "end mouseLeave" & return
end cardLinkScript
```

The skeleton script delivered by **cardLinkScript** is as follows. The **beep** command in the second line is a placeholder for an instruction to go to the target card that will be inserted when the user identifies the target card:

```
on mouseUp
  beep
end mouseUp

on mouseLeave
  hideCardLink short name of me
end mouseLeave
```

NewCardLink is the next handler. It is invoked by **addLink** and uses the **newPopButton** handler described above and **deletePendingLink** and **createMakeLinkMenu** which will be discussed below.

After the execution of **newCardLink** the global variable **thePendingLink** contains a string of the form **card button id** *n* **of card id** *m* where *n* is the id of the newly created button and *m* is the id of the card that contains it, and a **Make Link** menu is present in the menu bar.

```
on newCardLink aLinkName -- initiates the creation of a card link
  global thePendingLink
  if there is a menu "Make Link" then -- can't have more than one new link pending
    get value("short name of"&&thePendingLink)
    answer "There is a card link pending for '"&it& ¬
    "', delete it?" with "Delete" or "Cancel"
    if it is "Delete" then
      deletePendingLink
    end if
  else
    newPopButton aLinkName -- make a new card link button
    -- put a reference to the button and the card into a global variable:
    get id of card button aLinkName
    put "card button id" && it && "of" && id of this cd into thePendingLink
    createMakeLinkMenu aLinkName -- install the "Make link" menu
  end if
end newCardLink
```

DeletePendingLink uses the contents of the global thePendingLink to remove the card link button in the case that the user decides to cancel a link before completing it:

```
on deletePendingLink
  global thePendingLink
  lock screen
  push card                    -- so that we can get back to this card
  go card id last word of thePendingLink -- go to card from which link was originated
  show thePendingLink
  select thePendingLink
  doMenu "Clear button"
  put empty into thePendingLink
  choose browse tool
  pop card                     -- return to the card we started on
end deletePendingLink
```

CreateMakeLinkMenu simply installs the **Make Link** menu. The menuMessages of its menu items refer to LinkToThisCard and linktoCancel handlers and these will be described below:

```
on createMakeLinkMenu aLinkName
  create menu "Make Link"
  put aLinkName&":" after menu "Make Link"
  put "Link to this card" after menu "Make Link" with ¬
  menuMessage "LinkToThisCard"
  put "Cancel link" after menu "Make Link" with menuMessage "linktoCancel"
end createMakeLinkMenu
```

Handlers for second stage of card link creation

The second stage, implemented in the LinkToThisCard handler, results in the replacement of the beep in the second line of the pending button's skeleton script with an instruction of the form:

doCardLink n

So when the second stage is completed, the skeleton script in the card link button is converted to:

```
on mouseUp
  doCardLink 6452          -- where 6452 is the identifier of the target card
end mouseUp

on mouseLeave
  hideCardLink short name of me
end mouseLeave
```

DoCardLink is described below; it is a general-purpose handler for use by all card link buttons. It is intended to be installed in the stack script, ensuring that card links can be followed from any card in the stack.

LinkToThisCard is invoked when the user selects **Link to this card** on the **Make Link** menu. It uses the contents of thePendingLink to access the incomplete link button and modify the second line of its script. When the second stage of link creation is complete, the user is returned to card from which the link was originated, to indicate the completion of the creation action.

```
on LinkToThisCard                    -- implements the second stage of card link creation
   global thePendingLink
   if thePendingLink ≠ empty then
      -- modify the script of the button referenced by global thePendingLink:
      get script of thePendingLink
      put "doCardLink" && short id of this card into line 2 of it
      set script of thePendingLink to it
      if there is a menu "Make Link" then delete menu "Make Link"
      get thePendingLink               -- save the reference so that we can return to the
                                       -- originating card
      put empty into thePendingLink
      go word 6 to 8 of it             -- return to the originating card
   end if
end LinkToThisCard
```

If the user selects **Cancel link** instead of **Link to this card**, the linktoCancel handler is invoked. LinktoCancel deletes the pending link button and hides the **Make Link** menu:

```
on linktoCancel                       -- cancels a pending link
   global thePendingLink
   if there is a menu "Make Link" then delete menu "Make Link"
   if thePendingLink ≠ empty then deletePendingLink
end linktoCancel
```

Following card links

The doCardLink handler is called by the **mouseUp** handler of any card link button when the user clicks on the button. The main task of **doCardLink** is simply to go to the target card, whose identifier is given as its parameter. In our design, **doCardLink** also invokes the handler called makeLinkBack. MakeLinkBack is described in Chapter 14; its purpose is to implement a 'history' mechanism in the user interface, enabling the user to retrace their steps.

```
on doCardLink aCardId
   if aCardId ≠ short id of this card then
      hide the target
      makeLinkBack
```

```
      visual zoom open slow
        go card id aCardId
      end if
    end doCardLink
```

Other handlers

We have used several handlers in the descriptions above that haven't yet been described.

The hideCardLink handler is invoked to hide the relevant button and any associated pop-up field whenever the mouse is moved away from a card link button or when a link is followed. Holding the **command** key down inhibits its action: this is necessary to enable the user to keep the button and any associated pop-up field visible so that they can be edited.

```
on hideCardLink aName
  if commandKey() is not down then
    if there is a card button aName then
      hide card button aName
    end if
    if there is a card field aName then
      hide card field aName
    end if
  end if
end hideCardLink
```

Truncate is the function to truncates names used in the general-purpose mouseUp handler described at the start of this section and in the addLink handler:

```
function truncate aString, aLength
  if length(aString) > aLength then
    return char 1 to aLength-1 of aString & "..."
  else return aString
end truncate
```

The Boolean function isaPopUp determines whether an object is a pop-up field. It is used in the general-purpose mouseUp handler:

```
function isaPopUp anObjectName
  get word 1 to 2 of anObjectName
  if it is "card field" or it is "card button" then
    get value(last word of anObjectName)
    if char 1 of it is "[" and last char of it is "]" then return true
  end if
  return false
end isaPopUp
```

CloseAllPopUps is also used in the general-purpose **mouseUp** handler. It closes all of the pop-up buttons and fields on the current card. Pop-up fields are locked, so that they can be clicked on to close them:

```
on closeAllPopUps
   repeat with i = 1 to number of card fields
      if isaPopUp(name of card field i) then
         set lockText of card field i to true-- in case it was unlocked for editing
         hide card field i
      end if
   end repeat
   repeat with i = 1 to number of card buttons
      if isaPopUp(name of card button i) then hide card button i
   end repeat
end closeAllPopUps
```

AddStyle is the handler used by **addLink** for adding the **group** text style to the selected sequence of characters. ChangeStyle is a more general-purpose procedure for adding or removing styles that is used in the **deleteLink** handler and by **addLink** in some cases.

Changing text styles is a bit messy because each character in a field can have several text styles. HyperCard doesn't deal with this case very cleanly. When the text style of a sequence of characters is requested, if the sequence contains characters with various styles, the value **mixed** is returned. The only way to add another style to the characters in the sequence is to do so character by character. For efficiency we treat the mixed case specially using **changeStyle** to deal with it:

```
on addStyle aChunk, theStyles
   get textstyle of aChunk
   if it contains "mixed" then       -- this is the slow and laborious case:
      changeStyle aChunk, theStyles, "+"
   else
      if it is "plain" then get theStyles-- this case is much simpler and quicker
      else put ","&theStyles after it
      set textStyle of aChunk to it
   end if
end addStyle
on changeStyle aChunkRef, aStyle, Op -- aChunkRef is of the form
                              -- "char 3 to 9 of card field 5"
                              -- Op is + to add aStyle, - to delete it
   put word 2 of aChunkRef into n -- n refers to first character of the chunk
   put word 4 of aChunkRef into m -- m refers to last character of the chunk
   delete word 3 to 4 of aChunkRef -- now aChunkRef refers to the first character
   repeat m-n+1 times
      get textStyle of aChunkRef
      if op = "+" then               -- adding a style
         if it is empty or it is "plain" then get aStyle
```

```
          else put ","&aStyle after it
        else                          -- removing a style
          if textStyle of aChunkRef is aStyle then get "plain"
          else
            repeat with j = 1 to number of items in it
              if item j of it is aStyle then
                delete item j of it
                exit repeat
              end if
            end repeat
          end if
        end if
        set textStyle of aChunkRef to it
        add 1 to word 2 of aChunkRef
      end repeat
    end changeStyle
```

13.3 Summary

We have described the design and implementation of a generic hypertext system for HyperCard – *HT*. The handlers described above implement the basic design features described in this chapter. We will describe some useful additional features in Chapter 14.

Our design is intended to enable existing stacks to be extended to include hypertext features. This can be done by adding the handlers here to the background or the stack scripts of the relevant stacks. In the form described here, card links can refer only to cards in the same stack as the one that contains the link. It is a relatively simple matter to extend the implementation to deal with multiple stacks.

CHAPTER 14

Hypertext Tools

Programming power tools for hypertext

Following a hypertext link can cause a change of visual context for the user – it does so in the case of *HT*'s card links – and the user can very easily become lost after following a few links to new cards. There is no consensus as yet on the best approach to this problem, except to call it the 'lost in hyperspace' problem. Commonly used techniques to alleviate it include the use of indexes, history lists and graphical browsers – also known as information maps, diagrammatic representations of some or all of the nodes and links in a hypertext.

In this chapter, we'll continue the development of *HT* by adding an index and history list. A separate *Browser* stack is also described. This constructs and displays an overview in the form of a graphical map of any *HT* stack, showing all of the cards and the card links. These schemes go a considerable way to alleviating the 'lost in hyperspace' problem; you'll be able to adapt our ideas and scripts to work with other stacks.

14.1 A hypertext index

The *HT* Framework stack includes an index card that can be included in any *HT* stack, as shown in the next illustration. The lefthand part of the index contains a list of the topics of cards in the stack. There may be several cards with the same topic, so the righthand part of the index contains a representation of each of the cards using the ◊ symbol. Clicking on a topic goes to the first card on that topic. Clicking on a ◊ goes to the corresponding card. For cards that have already been visited, the ◊ symbols are replaced by ♦ symbols.

The index is self-maintaining; there are operations to generate and update its entries so that authors can easily bring it up-to-date whenever cards are added or deleted in the stack and readers can reset the ♦s to ◊s whenever they want to start reading afresh. (In addition to its general uses, one can imagine a tool like this being used by teachers: the index will tell a teacher whether a pupil has completed all exercise cards. Maybe you'd want to show the pupil's marks on the index card as well.)

Cards that are to be included in the index should contain two background fields, called **Title** and **PageNo**. The contents of the **Title** field are used to produce the topics list – we have

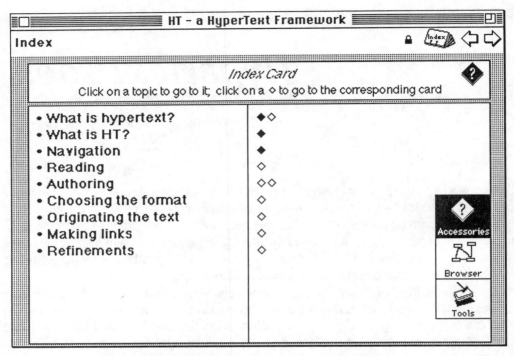

Typical index generated for a HT stack

made it a rule that titles are included in the index only if they begin with a '•' character – this enables authors of a hypertexts to control the contents of the index and ensures that the index card itself doesn't appear in the index. The contents of the **PageNo** field on each card are updated during the indexing operation to show the number of cards under the same topic and the 'page number' of the current card within the topic. The layout of these in the *HT* Framework stack is shown in the illustration below.

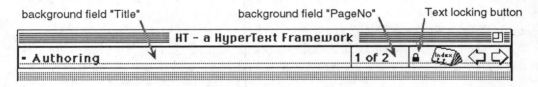

Index implementation

In normal operation, the index works like a simple hypertext. Let's assume that the names of all of the cards in our stack have been set the same as the contents of the **Title** fields. We can implement the index's basic operation with a simple **mouseUp** handler in the lefthand or **Topics** field. When the user clicks on a line in **Topics** field, the **mouseUp** handler highlights the line, then goes to the card with the corresponding name:

```
on mouseUp
  select clickLine()            -- highlights the line that the user clicked on
  get the selection             -- 'it' now contains the highlighted text
  if it is empty then exit mouseUp-- in case the user didn't click on a line
  visual iris open              -- just for the effect
  go card it                    -- the contents of 'it' should be the name of a card
end mouseUp
```

This implementation has two minor problems – it would be best if the highlighting could be done as soon as the user puts the mouse button down, to provide feedback and allow the user to change their mind before releasing the button; and the highlighting doesn't extend right to the end of the selected line. To fix these problems we need to implement a **mouseDown** and a **mouseStillDown** handler. We'll address these problems later, after describing the implementation of the righthand or **Blobs** field.

The user may click on the ◊ characters (we'll call them 'blobs') in the righthand field to go to any card. Here is how we handle the clicks in the righthand field:

```
on mouseUp
  get clickChunk() -- get a reference to the blob, e.g. "char 3 to 3 of card field 2"
  if value(it) = empty or value(it) = return then exit mouseUp
  select it                     -- highlights the blob
  put word 2 of it into theBlob -- puts position of the highlighted blob
                                -- relative to the start of the field into theBlob
  put word 2 of clickline() into theLine -- put number of the clicked line into theLine
  -- put the corresponding line from the topics field into topic:
  put line theLine of card field "Topics" into topic
  -- put the position of the 'blob' card relative to the first 'topic' card into n:
  if theLine>1 then
    get (number of chars in line 1 to (theLine-1) of me)+1 -- position of the last blob
                                         -- in the preceding line
  else get 0
  put theBlob - it into n       -- offset of the blob in the line
  visual iris open
  go card (number of card topic) + (n-1)-- go to the n'th card after the 'topic' card
end mouseUp
```

The **resetIndex** handler converts all of the ◆s to ◊s and, because it is intended to be used whenever a user wants to start from scratch, it calls **deleteLinkBack** to delete the history list (discussed in the next section).

```
on resetIndex
  repeat with i = 1 to number of chars in cd field "Blobs"
    set cursor to busy
    if char i of cd field "Blobs" is "◆"
    then put "◊" into char i of cd field "Blobs"
```

```
      end repeat
      disable menuItem "Reset HT Index" of menu "Edit"
      deleteLinkBack
   end resetIndex
```

The **disable menuItem** instruction greys-out the associated menu item; menus were discussed at length in Chapter 9.

The **reMakeIndex** handler is responsible for re-setting the contents of the **Topics** and **Blobs** fields to correspond to the current contents of the stack and entering page numbers on each card in the stack. It uses a function **doTopics** to step through all the cards with the same topic, assigning a page number to them and returning a count of them:

```
   on reMakeIndex
      lockEverything            -- (lockEverything is defined below)
      put empty into topics     -- will hold the topics list to go in card field "Topics"
      put empty into blobs      -- will hold the blobs list to go in card field "Blobs"
      push card
      go first card
      repeat until number of this card = number of cards
         set cursor to busy
         if there is no bg field "Title" then get space
         else get bg field "Title"
         -- we only index cards with a "Title" field prefixed with a "•":
         if char 1 of it is not "•" then
            go next card
            next repeat
         end if
         put doTopic(it) into n -- doTopics advances the current card to the next topic.
         put it & return after Topics -- append the current topic to the topics list
         -- append n blobs:
         put (char 1 to n of "◊◊◊◊◊◊◊◊◊◊◊◊◊◊◊◊◊◊◊◊" & return after blobs
      end repeat
      pop card
      put topics into card field "Topics"
      put blobs into card field "Blobs"
      deleteLinkBack
      disable menuItem "Remake HT Index" of menu "Edit"
   end reMakeIndex

   function doTopic aTitle
      put 1 into n
      push card
      set name of this card to aTitle
      repeat
         go next card
         if bg field "Title" ≠ aTitle then exit repeat
         add 1 to n
      end repeat
```

```
      pop card
      repeat with i = 1 to n
        if there is a bg field "PageNo"
        then put i&&"of"&&n into bg field "PageNo"
        go next card
      end repeat
      return n
    end doTopic

    on lockEverything
      lock screen
      set lockMessages to true
      set lockRecent to true
    end lockEverything
```

To keep the index card uncluttered, we add the operations to re-set and re-make the index to the **Edit** menu. Whenever the index card is open, the **Edit** menu contains two extra menu items: **Reset HT Index** and **Remake HT Index**. Here is how we add them to the menu:

```
    on openCard
      addIndexMenus
      pass openCard
    end openCard

    on closeCard
      deleteIndexMenus
      pass closeCard
    end closeCard

    on addIndexMenus
      if there is no menuItem "Remake HT Index" of menu "Edit" then
        put "Remake HT Index" before menuItem 7 of menu "Edit" ¬
        with menuMessage "ReMakeIndex"
        put "Reset HT Index" before menuItem 7 of menu "Edit" ¬
        with menuMessage "ResetIndex"
        put "-" before menuItem 7 of menu "Edit"
      end if
      if not (cd fld "Blobs" contains "♦") then
        disable menuItem "Reset HT Index" of menu "Edit"
      end if
    end addIndexMenus
```

And we have to get rid of the menu items on closing the card:

```
    on deleteIndexMenus
      if there is a menuItem "Remake HT Index" of menu "Edit" then
        repeat 3 times
```

```
        delete menuItem 7 of menu "Edit"
      end repeat
    end if
  end deleteIndexMenus
```

Now we'll deal with the problems in the **mouseUp** handler for the **Topics** field that we described above.

To highlight the selected line as soon as the user presses the mouse button, we use a **mouseStillDown** handler. This will be invoked repeatedly (50 times per second) whenever the mouse button is down. The following handlers should do the trick. They are designed to replace the **mouseUp** handler for the **Topics** field described at the beginning of this chapter:

```
on mouseStillDown                    -- highlight the line containing the mouse cursor
  -- compute the number of the line that contains the mouse cursor:
  get round((mouseV() - top of me + 4) / textHeight of me)
  if it > 0 and it ≤ number of lines in me and mouseLoc() is within rect of me then
    -- select the entire line that the mouse cursor is in:
    if it = 1 then put 1 into m
    else put (number of chars in line 1 to it-1 of me) + 2 into m
    put number of chars of line it of me into n
    select char m to m+n of me
  else select empty                  -- clear the selection
end mouseStillDown
```

The rather complex calculation following the comment: *-- select the entire line that the mouse cursor is in* is needed to ensure that the entire line containing the mouse cursor is selected, including the **return** character. This corrects the second problem mentioned above – making the highlighting extend to the righthand edge of the field.

```
on mouseDown                         -- to do the highlighting as early as possible
  mouseStillDown
end mouseDown

on mouseUp                           -- go to the card named in the current selection -
  get the selection                  -- there should be one, thanks to mouseStillDown
  if it ≠ empty then
    lock screen
    if last char of it = return then delete last char of it
    go card it
    unlock screen with visual iris open
  end if
end mouseUp
```

One small but irritating problem remains – occasionally a **mouseDown** occurs without a corresponding **mouseUp** – HyperCard simply sometimes loses the **mouseUp** event! If this happens, the user can click the mouse with no visible result. The following **mouseWithin** handler fixes that bug in HyperCard.

```
on mouseWithin              -- called repeatedly while the mouse cursor is
                            -- within the button and the mouse button isn't down.
    get the selection
    if it ≠ empty then mouseUp
end mouseWithin
```

14.2 A hypertext history list

A *history list* is another useful tool to help hypertext users to maintain a knowledge of their position and to avoid the 'lost in hyperspace' problem.

The history list for *HT* takes the form of a **Link Back** menu that appears whenever the user has used a card link. It contains a list, giving the titles of the cards from which links were selected. The user can go back to any card in the list by selecting it from the menu.

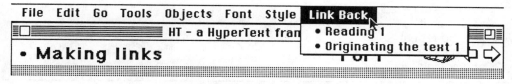

Pulldown menu for the history list

The **Link Back** menu shows the names of the cards from which a link was followed recently (the names of the last 20 different cards are retained), with the most recent card last. When the user selects an item from the menu, the selected card is opened and all of the items on the menu back to the selected one are deleted. The idea is that users should think of the menu as a way to retrace their steps. When they do so, the 'thread' that they have just retraced is removed. It's rather like Theseus's trip into the Minotaur's labyrinth: to stop him getting lost, he trailed a thread behind him. Obviously when Theseus used the thread to retrace his steps, he'd wind the thread up to get back to where he'd come from. Our **Link Back** menu works in a similar way; the thread is wound up so that the maze doesn't fill up with useless thread.

History list implementation

The details are a little messy, since two global variables are necessary. LinkBackItems is a global that contains all of the items currently in the **Link Back** menu and LinkBackMessages contains the **menuMessages** associated with the menu items.

When the **Link Back** menu is constructed, a `menuMessage` of the form golinkBack *id of card, menu item* is assigned to each menu item. So whenever the user selects a menu item the golinkBack handler is invoked with parameters giving the identifier of the card to go back to and the menu item that was selected. The handler for golinkBack is:

```
on goLinkBack anId, theItem   -- go to the card whose id is anID and
                              -- truncate the link back menu to theItem
   global LinkBackItems, LinkBackMessages
   if anId ≠ short id of this card then-- make sure we're not already at the card
      visual zoom close slow
      go card id anId
      -- now process the list of menu items to find the card name of the card
      -- we went to and delete all of the items back to it:
      put number of lines in LinkBackItems into n
      repeat with i = n down to 1
         if line i of LinkBackItems = theItem then
            delete line i to n of LinkBackItems
            delete line i to n of LinkBackMessages
            if number of lines in LinkBackItems > 0 then
               put LinkBackItems into menu "Link Back" with menuMessages LinkBackMessages
            else
               delete menu "Link Back"
            end if
            exit repeat
         end if
      end repeat
   end if
end goLinkBack
```

For all programs that create and use menus in HyperCard, there is a lot of housekeeping to be done to be sure that the special menus specific to a particular stack are only visible at the appropriate times. So whenever the stack is closed or ceases to be the currently open stack we must get rid of the menu from the menu bar. Unfortunately, HyperCard does not treat menus as *objects*. If it did, we could just say something like hide menu "Link Back". As it is, we must destroy the menu if we want to hide it, and we must then re-make it whenever we want to show it! These tasks are done by the following pair of handlers:

```
on deleteLinkBack
   global LinkBackItems, LinkBackMessages
   put empty into LinkBackItems
   put empty into LinkBackMessages
   if there is a menu "Link Back" then delete menu "Link Back"
end deleteLinkBack

on restoreLinkBack
   global LinkBackItems, LinkBackMessages
```

```
  if LinkBackItems ≠ empty and there is no menu "Link Back" then
    create menu "Link Back"
    put LinkBackItems into menu "Link Back" with ¬
     menuMessages LinkBackMessages
    set checkMark of last menuItem of menu "Link Back" to true
  end if
end restoreLinkBack
```

To complete our description of the history list mechanism, we must describe the 'hook' that connects the implementation of *HT* card links described in Chapter 13 to the history mechanism described here. The connections is through the makeLinkBack handler. As we noted in Section 13.2, makeLinkBack is called by doCardLink, the handler that is called whenever a user clicks on a card link button.

MakeLinkBack is installed in the background or stack script of *HT* stacks. Its task is to discover the id and the name of the card from which a link is being followed, and to install a new entry in the **Link Back** menu showing the card from which the link was activated.

There are several special cases, so the handler is fairly lengthy. In order to obtain the name of current card it starts by executing: send "getLinkBackEntry" to this card. This slightly strange method of invoking the handler getLinkBackEntry is used so that there can be different versions of getLinkBackEntry installed in different backgrounds, even though the makeLinkBack handler from which it is invoked is normally installed in the stack script.

A typical getLinkBackEntry handler is illustrated below, immediately following the makeLinkBack handler. Even though getLinkBackEntry isn't a function, it delivers a result, and this is accessed using the HyperTalk construct: the result.

```
on makeLinkBack              -- install the current card in the Link Back menu
  global LinkBackItems, LinkBackMessages
  send "getLinkBackEntry" to this card-- puts the card id and name into 'the result'
  put the result into theEntry
  if theEntry ≠ empty then
    -- if there is no Link Back menu, then create one:
    if there is no menu "Link Back" then
      create menu "Link Back"
    end if
    -- now remove any older occurrence of the current card from the menu:
    repeat with i = 1 to number of lines in LinkBackItems
      if line i of LinkBackItems = theEntry then
        delete line i of LinkBackItems
        delete line i of LinkBackMessages
        exit repeat
      end if
    end repeat
    -- add a new entry to the global variables that contain the menu contents:
    put theEntry&return after LinkBackItems
    get "goLinkBack"&&short id of this card&","&quote&theEntry&quote
    put it&return after LinkBackMessages
```

```
          -- restrict the length of the menu to 20:
          if number of lines of LinkBackItems > 20 then
             delete line 1 of LinkBackItems
             delete line 1 of LinkBackMessages
          end if
          -- update the menu:
          put LinkBackItems into menu "Link Back" with ¬
          menuMessages LinkBackMessages
       end if
    end makeLinkBack

    on getLinkBackEntry
       put empty into theEntry
       if there is a bg fld "Title" then put bg fld "Title" into theEntry
       if theEntry ≠ empty and there is a bg fld "PageNo" then
          put space&word 1 of bg fld "PageNo" after theEntry
       end if
       return theEntry
    end getLinkBackEntry
```

14.3 Operations on pop-up fields

Locking fields

Fields that contain *HT* links (grouped text) must be kept locked except when the text is being edited, so that the users' mouse clicks can be detected. To meet the needs of hypertext authors who are unfamiliar with Hypercard, we should provide a convenient operation to unlock and lock all of the hypertext fields on the current card. One way to implement this is with a button with the style checkBox. The button would have the following script:

```
    on mouseUp
       set hilite of me to not hilite of me-- hide or show the check mark
       setFieldLocks(hilite of me)    -- (setFieldLocks is defined below)
    end mouseUp

    on setFieldLocks aState
       select empty                     -- closes any field that's currently open
       repeat with i = 1 to number of cd fields-- look at all card fields
          if isHyperText(short name of cd field i)-- (isHyperText is defined below)
          then set lockText of cd field i to aState
       end repeat
       repeat with i = 1 to number of bg fields
          get short name of bg field i
          if it is "Description" or it is "Title"
```

```
        then set lockText of bg field i to aState
      end repeat
    end setFieldLocks
```

In our demonstration stack we have chosen to use a button with a pair of padlock icons (🔒 and 🔓) for this purpose. It has the following **mouseUp** handler in place of the one shown above. Note that the stack has two extra resources of type ICON (called **lock** and **unlock**) and two SND (sound) resources (also called **lock** and **unlock**):

```
on mouseUp
  if icon of me is 1413 -- number of icon called "lock"
  then
    set icon of me to "unlock"
    play "unlock"
  else
    set icon of me to "lock"
    play "lock"
  end if
  setFieldLocks(icon of me is 1413)
end mouseUp
```

Fitting fields to their contents

Pop-up and other hypertext fields would be still easier for hypertext authors to manage if they adjusted their size to accommodate the new text whenever their contents are edited. And whenever a field is opened for editing, we should ensure that the author can add text anywhere in the field. But for all field styles apart from **scrolling**, the text may extend beyond the bottom of the field's rectangle and therefore not be visible. The next set of handlers to be discussed deals with these problems.

Whenever a field is opened for editing, its style is changed to **scrolling** so that text can be added or edited anywhere in the field. When the field is closed, it reverts to its previous style (**rectangle** or **shadow** or whatever) and its height is adjusted to fit the new length of the text.

First we'll deal with making fields **scrolling** whenever they are opened. The **openField** message is sent to a field whenever the text cursor is placed in the field (this occurs whenever the user clicks in a field that is not locked). So if the following handler is placed in the card, background or stack script, it will be invoked whenever a field is opened.

The handler is straightforward. Note that in *HT*, we have defined *hypertext fields* to be card or background fields whose names are enclosed in [ ] brackets or contain the word description.

```
on openField
  global openFieldStyle
  put style of the target into theStyle
  if isHyperText(short name of the target) and openFieldStyle = empty then
```

```
      if theStyle ≠ "scrolling" then
        put selectedChunk() into theSelection
        setFieldStyle the target, "scrolling"
        select theSelection
      end if
      put theStyle into openFieldStyle
    end if
  end openField

  function isHyperText aName
    if aName contains "description" or (char 1 of aName is "[" and ¬
    last char of aName is "]") then return true
    else return false
  end isHyperText
```

When HyperCard changes the style of a field, the outside width of the field remains the same, but if the new style is scrolling or shadow, the usable width of the field's text box is reduced to allow for the scroll bar or the shadow. The task of the **setFieldStyle** handler is to change the style of a field while maintaining the size of its text box unchanged (so that any wrapped text in it doesn't change). The diagram below illustrates the differences in dimensions for fields of style shadow and scroll.

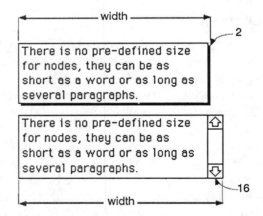

```
  on setFieldStyle aField, newStyle
    put style of aField into oldStyle
    put 0 into WidthChange
    if oldStyle is "scrolling" then subtract 16 from WidthChange
    if newStyle is "scrolling" then add 16 to WidthChange
    if oldStyle is "shadow" then subtract 2 from WidthChange
    if newStyle is "shadow" then add 2 to WidthChange
    lock screen
    set style of aField to newStyle
    if newStyle is "scrolling" then set scroll of aField to 0
```

```
      get rect of aField
      add WidthChange to item 3 of it
      set rect of aField to it
      unlock screen
   end setFieldStyle
```

Whenever a field is closed (when the text cursor leaves the field) HyperCard sends either a **closeField** message or an **exitField** message to the field. CloseField is sent whenever the contents of the field have been changed and **exitField** is sent when the contents haven't changed. We want the field to be restored to its original style in both cases, and if the text has changed we also want to adjust the position of the bottom of the field to include all of the text. So we have:

```
   on exitField
     global openFieldStyle
     if isHyperText(short name of the target) then
       if openFieldStyle ≠ empty and openFieldStyle ≠ "scrolling"
       then setFieldStyle the target, openFieldStyle
       put empty into openFieldStyle
     end if
   end exitField

   on closeField
     if isHyperText(short name of the target) then
       exitField
       fitText(the target)
     end if
   end closeField
```

Now we come to a problem that's trickier: the implementation of the **fitText** handler. If the number of displayed lines in the field has changed, how can we adjust the height of the field so that all of the text is certain to be visible? The difficulty is that there is no obvious way to discover the coordinates of the bottom line of a field. But there is a less-than-obvious way!

To solve the problem we note that:

- the text cursor can positioned after the last line of text in a field by an instruction of the form:

    select after text of card field 3

  and this is true even when the text is too long to fit in the field's text box, when the cursor would be positioned in the invisible portion of the field;

- the coordinates of the text cursor in a field can be obtained using the function **the selectedLoc**. If the cursor is in the invisible portion of the field, the coordinates returned by **selectedLoc** will lie outside the field's text box.

Here is a fitText handler that incorporates those ideas:

```
on fitText aField
    -- and adjust the bottom of the field to fit the text
    select after text of aField
    put item 2 of selectedLoc()+3 into theBottom
    get rect of aField
    put theBottom into item 4 of it
    set rect of aField to it
end fitText
```

FitText is called by the closeField handler, so it is used whenever a field is closed after a change to its contents.

Making pop-up fields fit on the card

The popLinks handler re-positions pop-up fields each time they are displayed, so that they always appear next to their associated hot text, even when the hot text has moved, as it might when it is in a scrolling field. Pop-up fields are normally positioned just to the right of, and below the mouse cursor. But if this makes the field fall partly off the card, the position should be adjusted to ensure that the field is visible.

The following popLinks handler used the width and height properties of the card window to check for this problem. If the popLinks handler described in Chapter 13 is replaced with this one pop-up fields won't fall off the card:

```
on popLinks aName          -- called by mouseUp with the name of a pop-up
    if there is a card field aName then
        set topLeft of card field aName to clickH()+10, clickV()+10
        if right of card field aName > width of card window-5 then
            set right of card field aName to width of card window-5
        end if
        if bottom of card field aName > height of card window then
            set bottom of card field aName to height of card window
        end if
        show card field aName
    end if
    if there is a card button aName then
        set loc of card button aName to clickH(), clickV()-12
        show card button aName
    end if
end popLinks
```

Adding links to other media types

The *HT* framework isn't intended to cater for hypermedia, but there are some easy ways to extend it to provide simple links to other media such as sounds, colour pictures and video sequences. The range of media available on Macintoshes is quite wide and rapidly expanding. In many cases, the data is stored in external files or in resources that can be copied into the resource fork of a HyperCard stack and accessed by XCMDs that are supplied by third-party developers (see Chapter 2 and *Further Reading*).

Probably the simplest way to extend *HT* to cater for links to other types of data is to extend the card link mechanism. In the simplest case the framework needn't be modified. The link buttons can just be 'subverted'. For example, to create a link to a sound resource – such as a piece of music or a voice recording:

1. Create a card link with any card as its target.

2. Edit the script of the card link button, replacing the **doCardLink** instruction in its **mouseUp** handler with an instruction to play the desired sound resource, for example:

    play "mySound"

    where **mySound** is the name of a sound resource that has been installed in the stack.

3. Modify the icon of the button to show the type of data to which it is connects; for example.

The link buttons can also be modified to play run animation sequences (using an appropriate XCMD) or to display images in other windows (using the **picture** XCMD).

14.4 A browsing stack

The navigation aid that is most often associated with hypertext systems is the graphical browser or information map. This provides a graphical representation of all or some of the cards and links in a hypertext and enables the user to view cards by clicking on their representations in the map. Our map-based browser is implemented as a separate stack containing a single card that shows an information map for a separate *HT* stack. That *Browser* stack operates on a target *HT* stack that is already open in another window, or if the *Browser* is opened first, the target stack can be opened using the **Open target stack** button.

The *Browser* stack can generate an information map for any *HT* stack. When the *Browser* stack is opened it creates an additional menu containing two items: **Local Map** and **Global Map**. The **Local Map** operation generates a map with representations of the currently open card in the target stack and the cards to which it is linked. The **Global Map** operation generates a map with representations of all of the cards in the target stack and the links between them. The next illustration shows the *Browser* stack with a global map of the *HT* framework stack. The map was generated automatically.

When the *Browser* stack is open, the user can go to any card in the target stack simply by clicking on the corresponding node in the information map. The node corresponding to the currently open card in the target stack is highlighted in the information map.

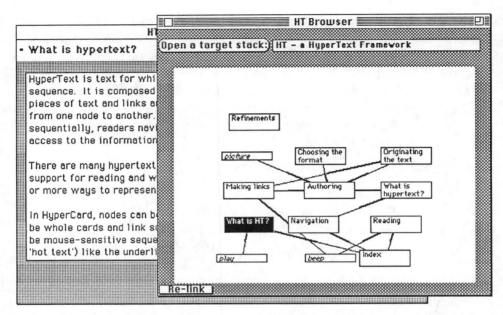

*The Browser stack is the front window, showing a map of the HT framework
stack, which is open in the window behind it.*

Implementing the Browser

The cards can easily be represented on the map by small fields showing the names of the cards and the links can be drawn by the line tool, using dual thickness to indicate their direction – they are thicker at the source end. But getting all of this to work may seem daunting – the *Browser* stack must process the target *HT* stack, identify all of the card links, and then use the information it has obtained to draw the map. In fact, the scripting is fairly straightforward, once a few problems have been resolved, and we describe the main components of the program below. Readers who have access to the book disk are referred to the card script of the map card in the *Browser* stack for those few parts of the script that are not given below. The script starts in the handler makeGlobalMap, which is invoked by the **Global Map** operation in the **HT Browser** menu.

First, a list of the cards in the target stack is made. The list contains a line for each card in the target stack giving the number of card links starting from the card, the id and name of the card, and the IDs of the cards that it is linked to. This involves visiting each card in the target stack and examining each card button to see whether it is a card link (or a link to data of a different media type – these result in nodes with labels such as 'play' and 'picture' in the map). The list provides all of the information needed for the *Browser* stack to draw the map.

Then the makeGlobalMap handler returns to the *Browser* stack itself and begins to draw the map. Note that makeGlobalMap is executed in the environment of the target stack while it is building the list of nodes and links.

MakeGlobalMap uses a handler clearMap to remove the old map from the *Browser* stack, a handler **drawNet** to do the actual drawing of the map and a handler **doHilite** to highlight the node in the map that represents the card that is currently open in the target stack:

```
on makeGlobalMap
   -- on entry, we are on the "HT Map" card of the Browser stack
   global HTCurrentTarget, HTBrowser
   lock screen                -- the user won't see anything until we're finished
   set lockMessages to true   -- saves time and unexpected events
   set lockRecent to true
   set cursor to busy
   go this card of stack HTCurrentTarget -- execute the following instructions in the
                              -- environment of the target stack:
   push card                  -- remember where we started in the target stack
   put empty into theMapList
   put empty into prevTitle
   -- build the list of cards and links:
   repeat with i = 1 to number of cards
      set cursor to busy
      go to card i
      put getTitle() into theTitle
      if theTitle = prevTitle or theTitle = empty then next repeat
      put theTitle into prevTitle
      put line 1 of getLinks() into theLinks
      put number of words in theLinks into n
      put short id of this card into cardId
      put n&&cardId&&theTitle&","&theLinks&return after theMapList
   end repeat
   pop card
   put short id of this card into currentId
   go this card of stack HTBrowser -- now we're back in the Browser stack
   clearMap                   -- delete the old map
   drawNet theMapList         -- drawNet does all of the drawing
   doHilite currentId, "new"  -- hilite the node that represents the current card
   unlock screen
end makeGlobalMap
```

The DrawNet handler uses graphical techniques similar to those used to construct the block diagramming system in Chapter 7. A handler called **addNode** is used to produce the card field (with style **rectangle**) to represent each card in the target stack. AddDetails is the handler that places the name of each card and the other details about the card (card ID, number of links and destinations of the links) in the corresponding field – the trick used here is to place the name in the first line and locate the other details on lines of the field that are off the bottom of the visible part of the field.

Once all of the cards in the target stack are represented by suitably positioned fields, the links are drawn by a **drawLinks** handler by drawing lines using HyperCard's painting tools. In addition to **addNode**, **addDetails** and **drawLinks**, we also rely on two global variables **penX** and penY, which represent the 'current drawing position' and a collection of graphics primitive handlers called centrePen, moveTo and LineTo which control the notional 'pen' and draw lines, rather like the turtle graphics primitives of Chapter 5.

```
on drawNet theLinks              -- theLinks is the list of cards with their links
   global penX, penY
   sort lines of theLinks descending-- put them in order of number of links
   centrePen                     -- start at the centre of the map area
   planSpace (number of lines of theLinks)-- work out the spacing of 'cells'
   repeat with i = 1 to number of lines of theLinks
      set cursor to busy
      get line i of theLinks
      if it is empty then next repeat
      put word 2 of it into sourceId
      put value(word 3 of it) into details
      put item 2 of it into links
      put item 3 of it into sources
      drawNode sourceId, i       -- make a rectangle field for a card
      addDetails sourceId, details, links, sources
      put penX into curX
      put penY into curY
      repeat with j = 1 to number of words in links
         get word j of links
         drawNode it
         if it is not a number then addDetails it, it
         moveTo curX, curY
      end repeat
   end repeat
   drawLinks
end drawNet
```

Here is how drawNode creates the field to represent each card. It relies on a findFreeCell handler to position the field (findFreeCell is described below; it sets the global variables penX, penY to a suitable position for the next field). DitherNode is a function that randomly offsets each field's position. This is done for two reasons: a map that is organized as a regular array doesn't look attractive, and more importantly, the positions of lines representing the links are less likely to cover each other.

```
on drawNode aCardId, nodeNo
   global penX, penY
   get "node" && aCardId
   if there is no card field it then-- avoid duplicating a node
      if nodeNo ≠ 1 then findFreeCell-- first cell doesn't need placement
      doMenu "New Field"
      get number of card fields   -- new field's number is the number of fields
      set name of card field it to "node" && aCardId
      setOtherProperties it -- sets the height, width, style and textstyle of the field
```

```
        set loc of card field it to ditherNode(penX, penY)-- 'dither' the position to avoid
                                          -- a matrix-like drawing
        choose browse tool
      end if
    end drawNode
```

The problem of laying-out the map is an interesting one; as in most graph-drawing programs, the readability and tidiness of the graph is important – it mustn't look too much like spaghetti! Our program uses an algorithm in which the map area is divided into a number of cells or regions, each somewhat larger than the rectangles used to represent the cards in the target map. When a cell is required for a new field, potential positions are located on the basis of a scan of each of the cells adjacent to the most recently allocated position, extending outwards until a free cell is found. Positions on the map are allocated to target stack cards in order of the number of links leading from them – so the nodes with the most links are located centrally in the map. Here is the findFreeCell handler that finds a cell for a field. It uses the function **segments** to deliver a list of the pairs of coordinates for the eight directions in which it may move from a given cell and a function **isFree** to test that a position is within the map area and isn't already allocated:

```
    on findFreeCell
      global penX, penY
      global hSpacing, vSpacing
      repeat with i = 1 to 7 -- greatest distance between two nodes
        repeat with j = 1 to 8 -- number of different segments
          put line j of segments() into aStep
          put penX + i*(item 1 of aStep)*hSpacing into newX
          put penY + i*(item 2 of aStep)*vSpacing into newY
          if isFree(newX, newY) then
            moveTo newX, newY
            exit findFreeCell
          end if
        end repeat
      end repeat
      beep
      put "insufficent space for map - superimposing some nodes" into msg
    end findFreeCell

    function segments
    return ¬
      ("-1,-1" & return & "0,-1" & return & "1,-1" & return & ¬
      "-1,0" & return & "1,0" & return & ¬
      "-1,1" & return & "0,1" & return & "1,1" & return)
    end segments
```

The **isFree** function uses an interesting technique to determine whether a cell is already occupied – a mouse click operation is simulated at the potential position. This results in a

308   *CHAPTER 14 Hypertext Tools*

mouseDown message that passes to all of the objects lying at that position. We place a mouseDown handler in the card script to receive these messages and to examine their targets. If the target is a card field, then the cell is already occupied, if not then it is free. We have modified this technique to check that the potential position is within the bounds of the mapping area as well – a transparent card button called **Map Area** is used whose extent is the same as the area in which the map is to be drawn. Here is the isFree(X,Y) handler and the associated mouseDown from the card script of the card containing the map:

```
function isFree X,Y
    global targetCell
    put empty into targetCell
    drag from X,Y to 0,0-- synthesizes a mouseDown at X,Y (mouseUp is off the card)
    if targetCell = "Map area" then return true
    else return false
end isFree

on mouseDown
    -- identifies the target of the 'synthetic' mouseDown generated in isFree
    global targetCell
    put short name of the target into targetCell
end mouseDown
```

The construction of the map of an *HT* stack is quite slow, but it is only necessary to re-construct it when the nodes or links are changed, and this is not a problem for *HT* stacks that are changed infrequently or are fixed in their structure. Importantly, it is not a problem for readers of a stack.

14.5 Authoring tools

The *HT Tools* stack is designed to assist with authoring in the *HT* framework. It adds an **HT Tools** menu to the menu bar with three operations: **Show All Popups**, **Show Unlinked Popups** and **Flatten Card**. The first two of these tools provide ways to manage the pop-up fields on any card of an *HT* stack. The problem that they address is the possibility of some pop-up fields that are not linked to any text. This may occur, for example when a piece of hot text is deleted from a card, leaving the pop-up dangling with nothing to activate it. The third tool (**Flatten Card**) extracts all of the text from a hypertext card (including the text from pop-up fields represented as 'footnotes') so that it can be, for instance, copied over to a word processor as a simple piece of text.

To use the *HT Tools* stack, open the target stack, then the *HT Tools* stack. Then go to the card in the target stack that you want to examine and use one of the operations on the **HT Tools** menu. The *HT Tools* stack should be open but the target stack should be the currently active one when you use the **HT Tools** menu.

The implementation is not particularly complex, but it is fairly lengthy, so we refer the reader to the scripts of the stack on the book disk for the full details. Here, we shall illustrate the use of the **start using stack** command to enable the handlers in the *HT Tools* stack script to be invoked when operations on the **HT Tools** menu are invoked. When the stack is first opened, the following **openCard** handler does all that is necessary to create the new menu (via the **addToolsMenu** handler). When a stack is in use, only its stack script is in the current message path. So we can place the **openStack** and **closeStack** handlers in the card script of the first card of the *HT Tools* stack to ensure that they will be invoked only when the tools stack is opened or closed and not when other stacks are opened or closed while it is in use. If we didn't do this, we'd have to use a function like **notMe**; these issues were discussed in Chapter 9.

```
on openStack
  global HTTools
  start using this stack
  put value(last word of long name of this stack) into HTTools
  if there is no menu "HT Tools" then addToolsMenu
  if number of lines in (the stacks) > 1 then
    lock screen
    push card
    go back
    newTarget
  end if
end openStack

on closeStack
  global HTCurrentTarget
  put empty into HTCurrentTarget
  put empty into card field "Target Stack"
  stop using this stack
  if there is a menu "HT Tools" then delete menu "HT Tools"
end closeStack
```

The **newTarget** handler saves the name of the current stack so that it can return to it and makes it the target stack, putting the name in a field in the *HT Tools* stack and then returning to whichever was the current card in the target stack before the *HT Tools* stack was opened:

```
on newTarget
  global HTCurrentTarget, HTTools
  push card
  get short name of this stack
  go stack HTTools
  put it into card field "Target stack"
  put it into HTCurrentTarget
  pop card
end newTarget
```

14.6 Summary

This chapter has shown how to extend the facilities of the *HT* hypertext framework in several directions. Apart from the hypertext index and the history list, each extension is designed as a separate, self-contained stack. This method for extending the facilities of stacks produces a clean, modular structure, minimizing the risk of introducing bugs in working stacks while adding the extensions. Moreover, the extensions can then be used in many stacks.

The *HT* extensions illustrate the range of navigation aids normally found in hypertext systems and exploit many of the more interesting and advanced features of HyperCard and HyperTalk discussed in earlier chapters. The technique for identifying free spaces in the global map used in the **isFree** handler of the *Browser* stack is based on HyperCard's built-in method for targetting messages arising from mouse clicks. It is, we believe, novel, and potentially applicable in many other interactive graphical environments.

CHAPTER 15

Projects

Ideas to keep you going

Now we are nearly at the end of *HyperProgramming*. This chapter gives you some project ideas. These are all stacks and scripts we have written, but we haven't given you the full details here because you'll probably want to develop the ideas in your own ways. You'll have fun working them out: we hope we've given you enough hints to get going and enjoy using your hyperprogramming skills.

15.1 Simple data collection

HyperCard stacks don't have to be complicated to be very useful. A typical school project might be to collect some environmental data, say about air pollution from daily newspapers, over a period of a week and then to draw graphs. HyperCard lends itself to this sort of activity extremely well: depending on the level of the students' expertise with HyperCard, they can start with a stack prepared by their teacher, or could design it themselves with a few suggestions.

Here is one way of starting out. This stack has two fields for nitrogen dioxide and

Air Quality		
Date:	12/5/92	
	Nitrogen dioxide	Sulphur dioxide
London	v good	v good
S England	v good	v good
Wales	v good	poor
C England	v good	poor
N England	v good	v good
Scotland	v good	v good
N Ireland	v good	v good
Average	v good	v good

sulphur dioxide pollution levels in various regions of the United Kingdom. The student makes a new card and fills in the lines in each field. This is really no more than record-keeping, except the student might want to add graphics to the background to personalize the stack. The stack shown is a clear example of using background fields with shared text (for the column of regions, the other column titles and the **Date:** line). The other fields have sharedText false, so that each card can show different text.

Having collected some data, HyperCard can be used to do interesting things with it. The graphics techniques described in Chapter 7 can be used to get some graphs drawn. It is easy to add a new background and to copy the histogram cards from the graphing stack supplied on this book's disk – or you can write your own guided by the chapter. Add a button to copy a week's or month's worth of card data into the fields used by the histogram card to draw a new graph. (If numerical data has been collected, then a line graph or a pie chart may be more appropriate.) You could make the region field handle mouseUp so that it draws a histogram for the data from the other fields taken from the corresponding line: so if you click on Wales, you automatically get a histogram for Welsh air pollution.

The pollution data shown in the illustration here uses terms like 'good' and 'poor'. If you have lots of data to enter, it's a bit tedious typing these words out time and time again. Instead, you could add several buttons for each word, which append the chosen word to the next line in the field (or more precisely, the left-most field that is not yet completed). Another idea is to have a keyDown handler: when the user types g, enter 'good' into the field; when the user types p, put 'poor' into the field, and so on.

The stack above doesn't have any interesting linking between cards. Here are some simple examples of linking that can be used to make useful and interesting stacks.

15.2 Periodic table

H																	He
Li	Be											B	C	N	O	F	Ne
Na	Mg											Al	Si	P	S	Cl	Ar
K	Ca	Sc	Ti	V	Cr	Mn	Fe	Co	Ni	Cu	Zn	Ga	Ge	As	Se	Br	Kr
Rb	Sr	Y	Zr	Nb	Mo	Tc	Ru	Rh	Pd	Ag	Cd	In	Sn	Sb	Te	I	Xe
Cs	Ba	La	Hf	Ta	W	Re	Os	Ir	Pt	Au	Hg	Tl	Pb	Bi	Po	At	Rn
Fr	Ra	Ac	Rf	Ha	—												

The illustration above shows the first card of a stack providing information about the Periodic Table. Click on an element to see details of the chemistry of the element. Cards for elements might be linked to interesting compounds: for example, clicking on `Na` takes you to the card on sodium, and the card on sodium has a button to take you to common salt, and that card is linked to both sodium and chlorine.

The easiest way to draw the periodic table is to start with three fields: top left, a field for `H`, `Li`, `Be`, `Na` and `Mg`; top right, a right-adjusted field for `He` down to `Ar`; then across the bottom a third field for the remaining elements. By using a fixed width font like `Courier`, it is easy to space the letters out evenly, and by choosing a fixed line height you can make the symbols fit neatly into squares. Then use a handler to draw a basic grid which you then touch-up by hand using the eraser tool. You'll probably need to experiment with the numbers and fiddle with the positions of the fields to get good alignment. The example here is based on bold Courier (`like this`) fields with textSize = 14, textHeight = 27. (When the field tool is selected or when **showLines** is true, you can adjust the line size to fit the squares and to align exactly. Then you adjust the handler to draw the squares a bit lower – this is easier and more accurate than moving all three fields the same distance upwards.)

```
on mouseUp
   choose line tool
   doMenu select all
   doMenu clear picture        -- remove old grid
   -- these numbers are for adjusting
   put 16 into l               -- left
   put 525 into r              -- right (approximately)
   put 51 into t               -- top
   put 249 into b              -- bottom (approximately)
   put 27 into s               -- size of squares

   put r-((r-l) mod s) into r  -- make squares have sides exactly s
   put b-((b-t) mod s) into b

   put l into x
   repeat while x <= r         -- draw vertical lines
      drag from x,t to x,b
      add s to x
   end repeat

   put t into y
   repeat while y <= b         -- draw horizontal lines
      drag from l,y to r,y
      add s to y
   end repeat
   choose browse tool
end mouseUp
```

15.3 Tell a story

Young readers like to read stories about themselves. HyperCard makes it very easy to construct personalized stories, to print them out, and (if you have *MacinTalk*) you can also get the Mac to read the story.

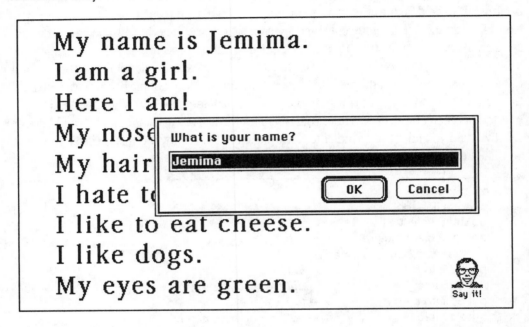

Click on a word to change it. When you click on a word, HyperCard chooses another word of the 'same sort', so clicking on **nose** will get **ear**, then **eye**, then **mouth**. Clicking on **legs** gets **feet**, then **hands** – these are all plural words naming parts of the body. Clicking on a colour gets another colour. The figure shows what happens when you click on the name: here the child has clicked on **Jemima**, and is being asked for a new name. A young child can create interesting sentences, which often say funny things about them, and still make sense. Adding an XCMD to say the words adds to the fun – that's the **Say it!** button in the bottom right. Add some buttons to help draw a face, and a button to print the card and you're finished.

You may want several cards in this stack to share the same background field so that several children can write their own stories before they are all printed at once. A much neater idea is to make the field a shared-text background field. This means that when the stack is used normally, the field is locked and **mouseUp** gets sent to its script when a child clicks on a word. But if you want to edit the text in the field (to add a new sentence or to fix a bug!) you simply change to background mode (***command-B***) and you can edit the field immediately. This method is much easier than setting and unsetting the **lockText** property of the field, which means getting in and out of the field tool mode. The **mouseUp** handler could be based on the following script:

```
on mouseUp                    -- in the field script
  if word 2 of the clickLine = 1 then
    get last word of line 1 of cd field "story"
    delete last char of it
    ask "What is your name?" with it
    if the result ≠ "cancel" then
      if last char of it is not in "!.?" then put "." after it
      put "My name is" && it into line 1 of cd field "story"
    end if
  else
    if number of chars in the clickText ≥ 2 then
      put new_word(the clickText) into the clickChunk
    end if
  end if
end mouseUp
```

15.4 Adventure games

HyperCard is ideal for writing your own adventure games. Each card represents a place, and the user goes on a journey visiting each place – however, to get from some places to others, the user needs to be well-equipped. Each place, which may be a room in a castle, a passage in a maze, an area of a famous city, or even a planet on an extra-terrestial adventure, has its own problems and opportunities. The problem is that the user is not allowed in some places without the right equipment – you can't go into a dark dungeon without the torch; you can't open the door without the key; you can't pacify the dragon without the diamonds – and you have to find where the stuff is hidden.

Typically, each card will have a good picture and some text in a background field describing the place in more detail. Rather than display the descriptive text, it is often just as good to use MacinTalk to speak it; this not only lets the user know where he or she is even though they are admiring the graphics rather than reading, it also lets much younger or non-literate people play the game. The user interface for getting around in an adventure game is easy: the user simply clicks on buttons that take them to other cards representing other places.

Although there need to be four buttons (to permit the user to move north, south, east and west and perhaps up and down and in other directions), it usually won't be sensible for all of the buttons to go places on every card. Rather than have card buttons and write individual scripts for each one on each card, which would be very tedious and difficult to keep track of as you develop the game, it's better to have a hidden field "Go to" with the names of the cards that each button should go to. Then, the buttons can be background buttons (the same throughout the adventure game, the same for each card) and while you develop the game the "Go to" field can remain visible. When you have finished development, simply hide the "Go to" field. The scripts for each button will be something like:

```
on mouseUp
   get line 2 of field "Go to"      -- or line 1, 3 or 4, etc.
   if there is a card it then go card it
   else answer "You can't go East from here!"-- or North, South, West, etc.
end mouseUp
```

Better than the tedious **answer** dialog would be to hide or show the various buttons depending on whether there was a line in the **goto** field. Thus the background's **openCard** could have four lines as follows:

```
set visible of bg button "N" to there is a card line 1 of field "Go to"
set visible of bg button "E" to there is a card line 2 of field "Go to"
set visible of bg button "W" to there is a card line 3 of field "Go to"
set visible of bg button "S" to there is a card line 4 of field "Go to"
```

You may want to have more interesting restrictions on whether you can get places, like you can't get into a room without carrying the right key for its door. One easy way to do this is to have a background field **"locks"**. You cannot get onto a card if you are not carrying all of the items mentioned in the field **"locks"**. The buttons that go to new cards now need modifying with a **lock screen** before the **go card it**. OpenCard then checks whether the user is carrying the right things, and goes back if they aren't. So far as the user is concerned, since the screen is locked, they never managed to get to the card that was 'locked out' – but they did go there, briefly, because that card is the best place to decide whether the user is permitted there. Additionally, a card can have an **OpenCard** script to override or supplement the background **OpenCard** script: this handler can easily impose other restrictions or cause special effects unique to that card.

A background field can be used for keeping track of what gadgets and magic potions are available on each card. It's probably best if the **OpenCard** script reads this background field and re-formats it to fit sensibly in the description field; alternatively you might want to have a few hidden background buttons, and (on **openCard**) set their icons and make them visible to show the things that are in that place. As the user moves around in the adventure, they will be able to pick up and put down items in this field: this is most easily implemented by providing a shared background field, **carrying**, for the things they are carrying (you may want to make the pick-up button restrict the number, weight or combinations of items the user can carry at any one time).

If you implement an adventure game in the way we've described, it has the advantage that you can stop playing at any time and resume later; each thing that has been picked up, carried around, and put down will be wherever it was left. On the other hand, this means that there must be some way of resetting the stack to start a new game! To reset the stack, all that is needed is another background field that contains the initial set up for each card; it will be hidden. You then add two operations to the stack: one, for you while you develop the game, copies the working field into the setup field – you use this when you have put the right things into the field, it's useful because the setup field is hidden; the other operation is for starting a new game (this will probably be a button on the stack's first card) – the script for this button goes through each card in turn and copies the setup field to the working field.

15.5 Testing stacks

Do your stacks work? Chapter 11 gave some ideas for collecting scripts from stacks so that HyperTalk could examine them and check, for example, that all **gos** really went to cards that existed. These sorts of test don't run your stacks, and testing scripts is much harder. Here is one approach.

The following **idle** handler clicks buttons at random, and therefore simulates a random user playing with your stack. If you give it long enough, it should do a quite good test: the approach has several advantages over getting real users to test a stack – it doesn't waste anyone's time, it can test buttons that are hidden, and it's not deceived by perhaps misleading names of buttons. Above all, it won't do what is expected, so it might thereby uncover some bugs.

```
on idle
    put number of card buttons into cb
    get cb + number of background buttons
    if it = 0 then               -- no buttons here
      beep
      answer "No buttons on this card!"
      exit idle
    end if
    get random(it)
    if it ≤ cb then
      click at the loc of button it
    else
      click at the loc of bg button (it-cb)
    end if
    if name of me ≠ name of this stack then
      beep
      answer "That went to another stack" with "Stop", "Go back"
      if it is "Go back" then go back
    end if
    pass idle
end idle
```

The **idle** handler here clicks buttons: you might also want to select menu items. You could modify the handler to **mark** cards; when you have finished a test run, you can find out if any cards failed to be marked by the testing (you obviously have to know that the stack doesn't have buttons that mark cards if you want to do this!). You may want to make the handler more sophisticated, for example not to bother clicking certain buttons (say, one's that merely **go back** or **go recent**); you can do this easily by checking the short name of the button, and only clicking if it doesn't have a dull name like **go back**.

If you only want to check menu items with menu messages (that is, menu items you've defined, rather than standard HyperCard menu items), you can make a list of suitable ones as follows:

```
repeat with i = 1 to number of menus
   repeat with j = 1 to number of menuItems in menu i
      if menuMessage of menuItem j of menu i ≠ empty then
         answer "doMenu" && (menuItem j of menu i) & ", " & name of menu i
      end if
   end repeat
end repeat
```

Using similar methods you can collect commands to test (here, **doMenu**) and use them in a test by picking them out of a global variable at random in an **idle** handler.

Testing stacks randomly is a good approach when being systematic is too complicated. However, there are plenty of features in a stack that can and should be checked systematically. For example, in a stack that you want to distribute with your carefully collected information – how many fields have you accidentally left with **lockText** false? – how many cards have their **cantDelete** false? – have you collected and printed all the scripts in the stack to make sure you haven't forgotten about scripts in hidden buttons or fields?

15.6 Message window history

You use the message window for typing commands to HyperCard. If you are trying to work out how to find the centre of the screen by doing something with the **screenRect**, you're likely to lose track of what commands worked, because the result of each command itself gets written into the message window, so overwriting your commands. You can try using **answer** so that the results of your work is shown in a dialog box and doesn't affect the message window, but there is a better way: modify the stack script (or your Home stack script, or your tools stack script) to keep a history of commands typed into the message window. Here's roughly how to do it.

When the user has typed a command into the message window and hits return, HyperCard sends the message **returnKey**. We handle that to save the message window's text in a global variable **theHistory**. A few details: we don't bother to save an empty message window, and we don't bother to save a repeat of the last line we've already saved (you might prefer not to save anything saved, however long ago).

```
on returnkey
  global theHistory
  if message ≠ empty and message ≠ last line of theHistory then
    put message & return after theHistory
  end if
  pass returnKey
end returnKey
```

The last line of the returnKey handler passes the message returnKey up the current message path, so that HyperCard will get it and know that the user has typed something in the message window that needs working out.

To make use of the history: typing up arrow plus the option key puts the *previous* command into the message window; typing down arrow plus the option key puts the *next* command into the message window. This isn't the only way to get a command history to work, but it behaves intuitively – pressing up arrow several times then down arrow the same number of times gets you back to where you were (unless there was a beep, which indicates you went too far back, further than the history reaches). And when you type new commands, they go at the end of the history, but before the future – you need to try it (or read the script below carefully) if this doesn't seem to make sense. Since the history scheme is so powerful and useful, you might rather have the arrow key work when the option key is up rather than down!

```
on arrowKey key
  global theHistory, theFuture
  if the optionKey = "up" then pass arrowKey
  if key = "down" then              -- go into the theFuture
    get first line of theFuture
    delete first line of theFuture
    if it ≠ empty then put it & return after theHistory
    else beep
  else if key = "up" then           -- go into the past
    if number of lines in theHistory > 1 then
      get last line of theHistory
      delete last line of theHistory
      put it & return before theFuture
    else beep
  end if
  put last line of theHistory
end arrowKey
```

And finally, you'll want to see what the history contains (and what the future contains!), as well as where you are in it. The command history displays the command history in an **answer** dialog box, and takes a bit of care not to make **answer** fall over with a string that is too long for HyperCard to display. The history command also allows the user to 'zap' the history and start again (you might want to script a more refined way of deleting the history – one might only want to zap the future, for instance). A convenient detail is that the command history itself doesn't get put in the history (or, rather, since the message history is sent after returnKey, history will already be in theHistory, having been put there by our returnKey handler, and so it should be deleted).

```
on history
    global theHistory, theFuture
    -- no need to keep this command in the theHistory list!
    if last line of theHistory = "history" and number of lines in theHistory > 1 then
        delete last line of theHistory
    end if
    put max(1, number of lines in theHistory - 3) into start
    if start ≠ 1 then put ":" & return into x
    repeat with i = start to number of lines in theHistory-1
        put "  " & truncate(line i of theHistory) & return after x
    end repeat
    put "•" & truncate(last line of theHistory) & return after x
    put min(3, number of lines in theFuture) into start
    repeat with i = 1 to start
        put "  " & truncate(line i of theFuture) & return after x
    end repeat
    if start ≠ number of lines in theFuture then put ":" after x
    else delete last char of x        -- it's a return
    put last line of theHistory
    answer x with "Zap", "Keep"
    if it = "Zap" then
        put empty into theHistory
        put empty into theFuture
    end if
end history
```

Here's the dialog box history produces, with the present command (which will be in the message window) indicated by the • blob. The two colons indicate that the history and future

extend off the top and bottom of the dialog box.

A utility function **truncate** is used to make sure lines don't get too long for **answer**. We discovered by experimenting that a line of 23 **w** letters (the widest letter in Chicago) and the ... (option plus semicolon) were the most that would fit on one line.

```
function truncate string
   if number of chars in string > 24 then
      return char 1 to 23 of string & "…"
   else return string
end truncate
```

If you have the *Power Tools* stack, you could use the XFCN **ShowList** instead of **answer**.

15.7 Bookmark monitoring

A criticism often levelled at stacks and hypertext more generally is that users have no idea where they are or where they have been. You only have to look at an ordinary book to see that your position in the book is obvious from the thickness of the book before and after your position. At the end of this chapter we'll show how to address this problem and make use of some of the concepts of HyperTalk we've been discussing.

Even in this simple picture of a real book – ▭ – you can see that the reader is nearer the front than the back. The advantage of using a book is that the navigation mechanism (page turning) is the same for all books. The way you tell where you are (from the bookmark or the open page) is utterly familiar. Books, however, aren't programmable.

We'll make a simple stack that performs the same function as a bookmark: it will show the user where in a stack they are and have been and let them go to any card. We could make the bookmark idea far more sophisticated, but the evidence from books is that a *simple* method that works for *all* stacks might be preferable. Some possibilities for major extension are covered in Chapter 14, which provides a more specialized 'book feature' for the hypertext system, *HT*, itself developed in Chapter 13.

The most efficient way to make a bookmark would be to have the feature built inside the stack that needs it. But that would lose out on the benefit of having a general, widely available feature. We will use **start using** to allow us to write a self-contained stack that can monitor the behaviour of any stack we want to have bookmarks for.

The **Bookmark** stack draws a card with little squares, each square representing one card in the monitored stack. When the user goes to a card in the monitored stack, the corresponding square is blacked in.

In the illustration we see the result of monitoring a stack of 17 cards; we have already

visited the first card, the last three, and one near the end. The monitored stack works quite normally, exactly as it did before, except that squares get blacked in the monitoring stack. Furthermore, if the user clicks on a square in the bookmark stack, HyperCard opens the corresponding card in the monitored stack.

How to draw squares

Before we get much further, we'll have to decide how to draw squares. The obvious way to draw squares would be to use rectangular buttons. As trying the following experiment shows, HyperCard is not very good when there are a lot of buttons; if you run the script below that makes lots of buttons, HyperCard gets noticeably slower and slower. A few hundred buttons (the typical number of cards in a stack we might wish to monitor) will have unacceptable performance for our needs.

```
repeat with i = 1 to 100
   doMenu "New Button"
end repeat
```

Instead we shall use graphics and draw the squares ourselves. (We could be more inventive and draw pages or something else more interesting than squares – but our purpose here is simply to show the basic approach.) The following handler draws a square using the line tool:

```
on square h, v               -- draws 10x10 square with top left at h,v
   drag from h,v to h+10,v
   drag from h+10,v to h+10,v+10
   drag from h+10,v+10 to h,v+10
   drag from h,v+10 to h,v
end square
```

We can now draw any number of squares on the card. The handler setup draws as many squares as we need, putting them 24 to the line.

```
on setup n                   -- draw n squares
   choose line tool
   set the height of this card to 40+trunc(n/24)*20
   repeat with l = 1 to n            -- actually, n/24 or so
     repeat with i = 1 to 24
       square i*20, l*20
       subtract 1 from n
       -- stop when we've drawn enough squares
       if n <= 0 then
         choose browse tool
         set the height of this card to l*20+20
         exit setup
       end if
```

```
        end repeat
      end repeat
   end setup
```

We set the card size to make the bookmark look as neat as possible. We have to make sure the card size is big enough before we start, otherwise we would run the risk of drawing squares off the card boundary.

We need to be able to blacken a square, and this is done with the bucket tool:

```
on blacken n                    -- blacken square n
   choose bucket tool
   put trunc((n-1)/24) into y
   put (n-24*y)*20 into x
   put 20*(1+y) into y
   click at x+1,y+1
   choose browse tool
end blacken
```

The following handler helps when we want to erase all the squares we have drawn:

```
on clearCard
   choose select tool
   drag from 0,0 to the bottomRight of this card
   doMenu "clear picture"
end clearCard
```

Using the bookmark stack

We use the bookmark stack to handle openStack and openCard messages generated by other stacks.

Since we've already written blacken to black out squares, the only difficulty is to make the openCard handler call it and be efficient. We do this by locking the screen and messages, and finally pass openCard on for any other stack (or external command) to handle it.

```
on openCard
   global monitoring
   if the short name of this stack = monitoring then
      lock screen
      set lockMessages to true
      go to stack test
      blacken number of target
      go back
      set lockMessages to false
      unlock screen
   end if
```

```
        pass openCard
    end openCard
```

When the user clicks on a square, we want to go to the corresponding card in the monitored stack. The mouseUp handler must be in the card, background or stack so that it can handle mouseUp messages where ever the user has clicked on the card. We have several things to do: what square has the user clicked on, and what stack do we want to go to?

    We use the global variable monitoring to track the name of the stack we are monitoring: thus, if it is empty, we aren't monitoring any stack, and should respond to mouseUp with beep. Otherwise, we have to do some arithmetic to convert the mouse location (where the mouse click was) to a card number, though noting that the user might have clicked *between* squares. Finally, if the user has clicked *on* a square, we go to the corresponding card in the monitored stack.

```
    on mouseUp
        global monitoring, maxcards
        if monitoring is empty then
            beep                        -- no stack open yet
        else                            -- work out where a click was
            get the mouseLoc
            put first item of it - 20 into horiz
            put second item of it - 20 into vert
            -- convert horiz to a number 1 - 24
            -- squares are 10x10 offset by 20
            put trunc(horiz/10) into horiz
            put trunc(vert/10) into vert
            if (horiz mod 2 = 0) and (vert mod 2 = 0) then -- clicked on a square
                get 1 + horiz/2 + 24*(vert/2)
                if it > 0 and it <= maxcards then
                    go to card it of stack monitoring
                else
                    beep                -- missed a square
                end if
            end if
        end if
    end mouseUp
```

Initializing the bookmark

How do we initialize the bookmark stack? OpenStack messages may occur either when we open this stack, or when the stack we want to monitor is opened. If we are opening this stack for the first time, then the global variable monitoring will be empty, and we can then ask the user what stack they want to monitor. Otherwise openStack has been sent by the stack we are monitoring, or perhaps some other stack we are not interested in. If it is the stack we want to monitor, now is the time to find out how many cards it has.

```
on openStack
  global monitoring, maxcards
  get the short name of this stack
  if it ≠ short name of me then
    if monitoring = empty then
      -- initialize from data from other stack
      put it into monitoring
      set lockMessages to true
      put number of cards into maxcards
      go to stack "Bookmark"
      -- clear last time's mess
      clearcard
      -- draw maxcards boxes
      setup maxcards
      choose browse tool
      go back
      set lockMessages to false
    else if it ≠ monitoring then -- tried to monitor two or more stacks - ignore!
      pass openStack
    end if
  else                          -- initialize this stack
    put empty into monitoring
    start using this stack
    go to stack ¬
    "there a stack to play with – Find one with lots of cards!" in a new window
  end if
end openStack
```

The important code in this handler is in the lines:

```
start using this stack
go to stack ¬
"there a stack to play with – Find one with lots of cards!" in a new window
```

The first line tells HyperCard to use this stack (where we are now) to handle messages passed up by the stack we want to monitor (and, in fact, any other stack). Once we've done this we will be getting openCard and openStack messages.

We also get mouseUp messages, so we should make sure we change mouseUp to check that it was sent by the monitor stack, not the monitored stack! We need to add this code to mouseUp:

```
if the short name of this stack ≠ short name of me then
  pass mouseUp
end if
```

The second line (**go to stack** ...) goes to the stack we want to monitor; this will cause the openStack message to be sent (from that stack) and that will initialize the monitoring stack. We've tried to go to a stack with a funny name! HyperCard won't be able to find that stack and it will put up a dialog box to ask the user where it is. This dialog box normally asks **Where is** and then gives the name of the stack you want to open, so by using the pseudo-stack name there a stack to play with – Find one with lots of cards! HyperCard will construct a sensible question!

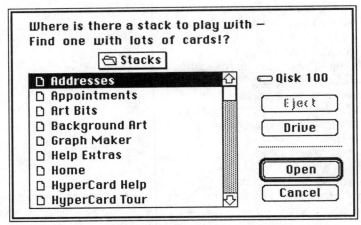

We've used a trick: the spaces between the words Find, one, with were typed as **option–space**, so that they won't break. This enables us to put these words onto a separate line.

There's a problem with the script as we've shown it here. If the stack selected in the dialog box is *already* open, HyperCard won't generate the necessary openStack message. One way to get around this would be to use our own message, rather than openStack, to indicate when we want to keep a bookmark on a stack. Then, after the go to stack "there is a stack to play with…" command, we call that handler directly. This also has the advantage that we are not relying on the monitored stack to pass openStack in its own openStack handler. Another problem you should solve is we used the short name to know which stack is being monitored: It would be much better to use the long name, just in case there are several stacks with the same short name in different folders or on different discs: HyperCard (or your script!) could get confused.

Where's the current card?

By showing a button icon over the current card's square, we can easily simulate a bookmark – we can move a button around the card without having to redraw any graphics ourselves. The following picture shows the bookmark over the last-but-one card.

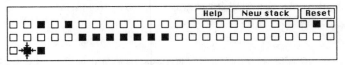

Since the handler blacken already works out where the correct square is, we modify blacken to move the button to the correct place:

```
on blacken n                        -- blacken square n
   choose bucket tool
   put trunc((n-1)/24) into y
   put (n-24*y)*20 into x
   put 20*(1+y) into y
   click at x+1,y+1
   set the loc of card button "current" to x+5,y+5
   show card button "current"
   choose browse tool
end blacken
```

We show the button, assuming that the **Reset** button (see the top right of the card) hides the card button **Current**. It's best to show it after setting its location to the right place, then it isn't made visible in the wrong place, only to be moved. This is the button's icon, by the way:

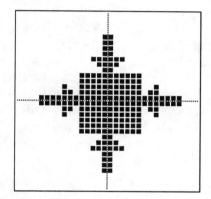

The main thing wrong with the bookmark stack that we haven't already mentioned is that it doesn't bother to save which tool the monitored stack is using: it always goes back to the other stack with the browse tool selected, and this may not be what the other stack expects! Also, we don't check that the right pattern is selected by the bucket tool, and if we did, we should reset the pattern back to whatever it was before coming to this stack. Indeed, it's arguable that a tool like the bookmark stack should be designed for a particular stack (or for particular sorts of simple stacks), since there are so many obscure HyperCard problems to avoid if you want to try and make it a completely general tool. The *HyperCard Objects* stack (on the *HyperProgramming* disk) gives an example of a tailor-made bookmark scheme which does not suffer from any of the drawbacks of this bookmark project.

Regardless of the problems with the bookmark stack, there are many ways to extend it. What about showing backgrounds visited (as well as cards visited) as grey rectangles enclosing several card squares? You may want the bookmark to follow several stacks: if so it will need several cards, one for each stack. But when we start thinking of polishing like this, it's obvious that there are many other things to do too, to make the idea even better – so we leave these developments as an interesting exercise for you.

15.8 MiniCalc – a simple spreadsheet

What is involved in the construction of a spreadsheet?

This section describes how to build a spreadsheet application that has much of the functionality (but few of the frills) of commercial spreadsheet packages.

There are no features built in to HyperCard to support spreadsheet-like applications, so this project provides an interesting insight into techniques for the construction of spreadsheet applications in any language.

In this first spreadsheet – MiniCalc – performance has been sacrificed in favour of simplicity and clarity in the implementation, resulting in a demonstration system whose performance is unsatisfactory with more than 25 cells. At the end of this section we describe a set of enhancements to produce a spreadsheet with a user interface resembling those of commerial spreadsheet packages and that performs adequately for some practical uses but is somewhat more difficult to program (because it uses several simulated data structures).

Both versions can be implemented entirely in HyperTalk. The essential functionality of MiniCalc can be implemented in a background script of 160 lines of HyperTalk. It took us 3 hours to develop a first working version of a MiniCalc stack, and another similar amount of time to develop the version described here.

A problem is that the performance of HyperCard is affected by the number of fields on the current card. Thus although spreadsheets with less than about 50 cells are updated quite quickly, performance is unsatisfactory with 100 or more cells. This was overcome by using fields to model each *column* of cells in the enhanced version.

How spreadsheets work

A spreadsheet is a rectangular array of 'cells' each containing numeric data or text. Cells can be of two types. A 'numeric cell' just contains a numeric value (integer or real) or a text string. A 'formula cell' contains a numeric value and a formula defining the value that should be displayed in the cell in terms of the values in other cells. Whenever the value in any cell changes, all of the formula cells that refer to it must be re-evaluated.

Formulas

Formulas in our model spreadsheet are HyperTalk expressions with embedded references to other cells in the same spreadsheet. Cell references are similar to those used most spreadsheets: they have the form *An* where *A* is an upper- or lower-case letter representing the column number of the cell and *n* is an integer less than 100 representing the row number of the cell. Thus B3 refers to the cell at column 2, row 3 and C5 to the cell at column 3, row 5. The formulas are 'compiled' whenever they have been edited to produce valid HyperTalk expressions. This approach allows the formulas to include any of the arithmetic operations (+, -, *, /, ^), functions (e.g., cos, sin, tan, sqrt, exp, ln) or any of the other operations and functions of HyperTalk. The user can add extra functions using any of the features of HyperTalk, placing them in the card or background script – so the formula notation includes the whole HyperTalk language and is therefore more powerful than the formula notation in most commercial spreadsheets!

How MiniCalc works

	A	B	C	D	E	F
1	*item*	*no in stock*	*price*	*total value*		
2	socks	34	2.95	100.3		
3	shoes	33	32.95	1087.35		
4						
5	2	1		1187.65		

Cells are represented by card fields. The first line of each field contains the current value of the cell – only the first line is visible. The name of each field is its cell reference. (The top left field is called 'A1', the first field in the second row 'A2' etc.) Cells can contain numbers, strings or formulas. The fields representing formula cells are given the shadow style to distinguish them for the user. Buttons are provided to convert formula cells to 'ordinary' cells and vice versa.

Formulas are 'compiled' into HyperTalk expressions when they are entered. The compilation process replaces the *An*-style cell references with references to the corresponding fields. Thus after compilation the formula:

(B3-C3)/[C5]

becomes:

((line 1 of cd fld "B3")-(line 1 of cd fld "C3"))/(line 1 of cd fld "C5")

The compiled formula is stored in the third line of the relevant cell (the uncompiled version is kept in the second line). Hence the need to include 'line 1 of' in the compiled versions of formulas to refer to the values of cells.

Whenever a formula is compiled a list of the cells to which the formula refers is produced. This list is used to update a dependencies table that records, for each cell, references to the other cells that depend on it. The dependencies table is maintained in a hidden background field (called Dependencies). Each line in the dependencies table corresponds to a cell and contains a (possibly empty) list of other cell names that depend upon it. Here is a version of the compile function. Compile depends on a nextToken function to scan the formula from left to right recognizing the elements of it. A token is either a sequence of letters and digits or any other single character. It also uses a function isCellName to examine each token and determine whether it needs to be translated. Only the cell names in formulas are translated, since all of the operations, constants and functions that appear in formulas are expected to be valid in HyperTalk:

```
function compile aFormula     -- Returns a 2-line result:
                              -- line 1: a compiled HyperTalk expression that yields
                              -- the value of the field
                              -- line 2: a list of the fields on which the value
                              -- of this cell depends
    put empty into theExpression
    put empty into dependsOn
```

```
      repeat until aFormula = empty
         get nextToken(aFormula)
         delete char 1 to length of it of aFormula  -- test for a cell reference
         if isCellName(it) then
            put "(line 1 of cd fld"&&quote&it&quote&")" after theExpression
            put it&space after dependsOn
         else
            put it after theExpression
         end if
      end repeat
      return theExpression&return&dependsOn
   end compile
```

Re-calculation

Whenever the value in a cell changes, the corresponding line in the dependencies table must be examined to determine which other cells must be re-calculated. This is a recursive process, since the re-calculated cells can also have their own dependants. The **reCompute** function calls **evaluate** to evaluate each cell. Evaluate evaluates the formula using HyperCard's **value** function and then calls **reCompute** to check for other cells that depend on the one that has just been re-evaluated:

```
   on reCompute aCell --Called from closeField and from evaluate (recursively).
   -- Re-computes the values of all of the "formula" cells that depend on aCell,
   -- or if aCell is empty, all cells.
      get number of cd field aCell -- Offset of relevant line in "Dependencies".
      put line it of bg field "Dependencies" into theDependencies
      repeat with i = 1 to number of words in theDependencies
         evaluate word i of theDependencies
      end repeat
   end reCompute

   on evaluate aFormulaCell --Called from resetFormula and reCompute (recursively).
   -- Re-evaluates the contents of a specific formula cell,
   -- and then makes sure that every cell that depends on it is re-computed.
      put value(line 3 of cd field aFormulaCell) into line 1 of cd field aFormulaCell
      recompute aFormulaCell     -- re-compute the cells that depend on this one
   end evaluate
```

Other aspects

The background script for cards containing spreadsheets holds all of the handlers needed to implement MiniCalc. Each cell in the spreadsheet is a field. Ordinary cells are not locked so users can type new data into a cell. Formula cells are locked, and the **mouseUp** handler shown below is in the background script, so the **resetFormula** function is called when the mouse is clicked on a formula cell. ResetFormula gets a formula from the user and puts it into line 2 of the cell with a compiled version of the formula in line 3. It then calls **upDateDendencies** to note the referenced cells in the dependencies table.

```
on mouseUp                     -- enables the user to edit formulas.
   if name of the target contains "card field" then
      get short name of the target
      if isCellName(it) then resetFormula it
      else pass mouseUp
   else pass mouseUp
end mouseUp

on resetFormula aCell
   ask "Formula for cell "&short name of cd field aCell&":" with line 2 of cd field aCell
   if it ≠ empty then
      put it into theFormula
      get compile(theFormula)
      if it = empty then
         beep
         put "Invalid formula"
      else
         put theFormula into line 2 of card field aCell
         put line 1 of it into line 3 of card field aCell
         upDateDependencies aCell, line 2 of it
         set style of cd field aCell to "Shadow"
         set lockText of cd field aCell to true
         evaluate aCell
      end if
   end if
end resetFormula
```

When a field is closed after entering a new value in it, any cells that depend on its value must be recalculated. The **closeField** takes care of this:

```
on closeField
   if name of the target contains "card field" then
      get short name of the target
      if isCellName(it) then
         reCompute it
      end if
   end if
end closeField
```

UpdateDependencies is called whenever a formula is changed to insert the cell name into the dependency lists of all of the cells that it depends on. The old dependencies must first be removed.

```
on updateDependencies aCell, dependsOn
  --"Dependencies" contains a line for each cell.
  -- Each line contains a word for each dependent cell.
  repeat with i = 1 to number of card fields
    if dependsOn contains short name of card field i then
    -- add a word giving the field name
      if not (line i of bg field "Dependencies" contains aCell&space) then
        put aCell&space after line i of bg field "Dependencies"
      end if
    else                              -- remove any old references
      put offset(aCell&space, line i of bg field "Dependencies") into aChar
      if aChar ≠ 0 then
        put number of words in char 1 to aChar of ¬
        line i of bg field "Dependencies" into theWord
        delete word theWord of line i of bg field "Dependencies"
      end if
    end if
  end repeat
end updateDependencies
```

Enhancements

Here are some suggested enhancements to MiniCalc to make it more like a usable spreadsheet application rather than just a programming exercise:

- Performance enhancement: use a single field for each column (a substantial change, but necessary to provide adequate performance for serious use).

- Check formulas for circular references between cells (cell *a* might be a formula referring to cell *b* and cell *b* might be a formula referring back to cell *a*). Otherwise re-calculation may never stop!

- Insert cell references in formulas by using the mouse to point at cells (you must then use a field for formula construction instead of the **answer** dialog).

- Allow cut and paste contents of whole rows and columns.

- A facility to insert new rows and columns.

- Formulas could include a notation for relative as well as absolute cell references.

You might think that as you add more and more features to MiniCalc you ought to turn to a 'real' programming language, like C. Yet we implemented all but the last three of the above enhancements in only 260 lines of HyperTalk – C programs would run faster, but they'd take longer to write.

15.9 Anti-virus precautions

Since HyperCard is programmable it is susceptible to viruses. There are already some HyperCard viruses written by irresponsible juveniles. There are two things you can do to improve things: first, convince people that virus writing is a puerile form of vandalism – and virus writing is too easy to be a show of skill or virility. Second, you can take a few precautions in writing your stacks.

The problem of trying to avoid viruses is that most techniques you use can often themselves be subverted to work for the virus. Thus, we can't be too specific in giving you recommendations: if we said 'script *exactly* this', then a virus writer would know exactly what he (it usually is a he) was up against.

HyperCard sends messages all the time during its normal operation, from **idle** to **openCard** and **openStack**. It only takes one message to be handled in a virus-infected stack for that stack to start doing malicious things programmed by the virus. Therefore, **lock messages** whenever you don't need them (this also speeds your stack up).

Your Home stack can have a **set** handler to intercept setting the script of objects; a virus would probably want to modify scripts and this is the easiest way of doing it, and hence you can stop it working (or at least ask the user whether he or she wants scripts changing when a **set** is executed).

Your *Home* stack can be locked (**set cantModify to true**), as can stacks you use for tools: any stack open and modifiable when you run a new stack may be modified by a virus. The **cantModify** stack property can be set with a password, and this makes it pretty secure.

Keep the user level as low as possible all the time.

You can use the handlers from Chapter 11 to make a hash code derived from all scripts (for example, a simple hash is the total number of characters in all the scripts). You save this number in a field in the Home script (along with the stack's name). When you open a stack, check that the hash code is unchanged. If it has changed, then you know someone – or something – changed it. Add a button to the Home stack so you can say, 'Don't tell me, I know I've modified this stack!'

You might want to have an **openStack** handler (the more the better, to reduce the chances that a virus has an **openStack** handler that does not **pass openStack** to your handler) that reports which stacks are being opened with an **answer** dialog box to confirm you really want to open them. A virus, of course, might want to open surreptitiously all sorts of stacks to clobber them.

These schemes should give you some ideas of what sort of techniques to use. If you can think of something we haven't mentioned, try and make it simple and reliable – and keep it to yourself. Do use several methods in combination. The fewer people who know how your special method works (so long as it *does* work, at least for some virus attacks), the better.

Don't ever try writing your own virus to test your defences. Many things can go disastrously wrong: the virus may have bugs in it, and your defences may not be up to the virus, bugged or otherwise. Either way you run the very real risk of ruining everything you are doing. It's also illegal.

15.10 Sharing stacks: 'liveware' techniques

HyperCard stacks are for sharing, yet HyperCard itself doesn't provide any direct help with sharing stacks. But you can script some useful sharing facilities relatively easily.

The approach to sharing stacks is called *liveware*, and in this project we'll show how to convert any stack into one that makes sharing cards much easier and practically automatic. You can extend the basic idea to work with stacks used and shared between many different people.

Suppose you have two address list stacks, one on each of your two Macintoshes, and you keep adding new addresses to one or other of the stacks – but you don't keep track of what changes you've been making – then you need liveware to get the stacks sorted out. Or perhaps someone has sent you a floppy disk with their address list on it, and you want to get all their addresses into your own stack. In either case, all you do is select **Share** from a menu, and then leave the scripts to merge the two stacks together and delete any duplicate cards. The result will be a single stack with all the new cards brought in from the other stack.

The standard HyperCard stacks include a suitable address list, *Addresses*, and a diary stack, *Appointments*, both of which can be greatly enhanced with this project. Indeed, the project is a general-purpose tool and will work with (more-or-less) any stack, merely by changing a function and the background name it uses.

Although liveware is a significant idea for extending the power of HyperCard, we've kept it to the project chapter because there is only one picture (below) to illustrate the idea – and it's not a very exciting one!

File Edit Go Tools	**Utilities**
New Stack...	Sort by Name
Open Stack... ⌘O	Sort by Company
Close Stack ⌘W	Sort by Town
! Save a Copy...	Sort by County
	Sort by Post Code
Import Paint...	
Export Paint...	Print Addresses
	Import Text...
Compact Stack	Export Text...
Protect Stack...	
Delete Stack...	✓Addresses
	Stack Overview
Page Setup...	Sort Preferences
Print Field...	Mark Cards
Print Card ⌘P	
Print Stack...	! Share
Print Report...	
Quit HyperCard ⌘Q	

All that has been changed is the addition of a new menu item **Share** at the bottom of the stack's existing **Utilities** menu, with **!** marks put against it and **Save a Copy...** in the **File** menu. (You might prefer to have **Share** in the **File** menu, but we tend to prefer to keep standard menus standard.) Accomplishing this part of the job is easy to script! You simply have to ensure a line livewareMenu "Utilities" is put in the right stack handler – in openStack, for instance – after the menu has been created by the existing handlers.

```
-- HyperProgramming stuff for sharing address stacks -- to go in the stack script --
on livewareMenu itsName
    if there is not a menu itsName then create menu itsName
    put "-,Share" after menu itsname with menuMessage empty,share
end livewareMenu
```

The **!** is put in the menus using the markChar menuItem property. We set the markChar of the two menu items when anybody edits a field. This might help remind you to use **Save a Copy** or **Share**.

```
on closeField -- remind user if stack needs sharing
    if there is a menuItem "Share" of menu "Utilities" then
        set the markChar of menuItem "Share" of menu "Utilities" to "!"
    end if
    if there is a menuItem "Save a Copy..." of menu "File" then
        set the markChar of menuItem "Save a Copy..." of menu "File" to "!"
    end if
end closeField
```

The marks should be remembered for this stack, even when HyperCard has been quit. Thus, whether the **!** mark has been added must be saved in something persistent – a hidden card field on one of the stack's permanent cards (or a sharedText background field on a background with cantDelete set true). Here, we will use the card Stack Overview. Two handlers are required to save and restore the marks; they should be called appropriately in the stack's existing openStack, closeStack, suspendStack and resumeStack handlers.

```
on saveReminders
    put markChar of menuItem "Save a copy..." of menu "File" into a
    put markChar of menuItem "Share" of menu "Utilities" into b
    put a & return & b into card field "Reminders" of card "Stack Overview"
    set markChar of menuItem "Save a copy..." of menu "File" to empty
    set markChar of menuItem "Share" of menu "Utilities" to empty
end saveReminders

on restoreReminders
    get card field "Reminders" of card "Stack Overview"
```

```
    set markChar of menuItem "Save a copy..." of menu "File" to line 1 of it
    set markChar of menuItem "Share" of menu "Utilities" to line 2 of it
end restoreReminders
```

The **!** mark in the **Save a Copy...** menu item is removed when the user saves a copy of this stack. It's simplest to have a **doMenu** handler for this:

```
on doMenu i, m -- remove reminder from the Save menuitem
    if i = "Save a Copy..." then
        set markChar of menuItem i of menu m to empty
    end if
    pass doMenu
end doMenu
```

That's all the easy scripting.

We want to make this a general-purpose liveware facility, so we won't assume that we are dealing with any particular fields. Hence there needs be a function that returns an item list of the fields we're interested in – the fields that contain text that may be changed, and hence which we want to share. It happens that both the *Addresses* and *Appointments* stack define this function for their own purposes, but we give it in full for completeness (it may differ in details in your own stacks).

```
function theFields -- the fields with variable information on
    -- (same as the function in the Address stack's background)
    return "bg fld id 4,bg fld id 97," & ¬
    "bg fld id 6,bg fld id 98,bg fld id 99," & ¬
    "bg fld id 8,bg fld id 100,bg fld id 101," & ¬
    "bg fld id 102,bg fld id 7"
end theFields
```

Incidentally, although a global variable could serve the same purpose as theFields(), and would be faster, it would not be a good idea. If you have several liveware stacks going at once, then the global variable would very easily get corrupted as each stack defines it differently. By using a function, HyperTalk *automatically* ensures that each stack script gets *that* stack's particular definition of the function. In particular, if you choose to write the liveware handlers in a tool stack (one where you will say start using this stack), you will automatically get the right definitions from the stacks that are using it by sending a message to the current card, which then goes up the current message path to find theFields in the relevant stack. So a function is more reliable and more readily extended to tool use; furthermore, handlers that use theFields() can save its value in it or a variable, so in practice its use will be about as fast as a global anyway.

How is this function used? The function theFields() produces at item list of the field IDs, which is no more than a harmless string, but we generally need the fields' values. Thus you can expect to see idioms like: value(item 1 of theFields()) – which will give us the text in the first field in the list; and do "put … into" && item 1 of theFields() – which will put a value into the first field. The most complex part of the entire liveware scripting is the following four lines (we'll meet them properly later), which copies the text in all fields from one card (the first card of background i) to another (the current card):

```
repeat with j = 1 to number of items in theFields
   get item j of theFields
   do "put" && it && "of card 1 of background" && i && "into" && it
end repeat
```

Ideally we should have defined a function theBackground() to give us the background name where we can find these fields. Instead, we will write our handlers assuming that the fields are on a fixed background called Body – however, you are at liberty to use the script editor to replace all Body with theBackground()! The same comments about whether theFields() should be a function or global variable apply also to theBackground().

The **Share** menu item has a menu message share that invokes the stack script handler. This handler opens another stack (in a new window, because this will make things faster when the stacks are shared), and checks carefully that it is a suitable stack. Obviously it would be inappropriate to share with a stack that was not a compatible address list, and we cover this possibility by making the first line of the stack script the comment -- *SharableAddresses*. In a liveware tools stack, a more thorough test would be required, for instance using the value returned by theFields(), which would also be stored on the first line of the script, to check that this stack is meant to be shared with a stack with precisely the same arrangement of fields. Otherwise you would run the risk of sharing an address list with an appointments diary – presumably making a birthday party stack!

Notice that we check that there is enough disk space before getting down to the main work, and we may give the user a hint about compacting his stacks to free up some room. This may seem like fussiness on our part, but there is nothing more frustrating than to embark on a long process (here, sharing) that then aborts half way owing to 'unforeseen circumstances' that should have been foreseen.

```
on share
   set lockMessages to true
   -- if we locked the screen as well, it wouldn't be so interesting to watch!

   put the diskSpace into hereDiskSpace
   put the long name of this stack into here
   put number of this card into cardHere
   put number of cards in background "Body" into numberHere

   go "the other stack to share with" in a new window
   put the long name of this stack into there
   put the diskSpace into thereDiskSpace

   -- check we opened a different stack!
```

```
if here = there then
  beep
  answer "Nothing to share with?"
  go card cardHere of here
  exit share
end if

-- is this a sharable address list?
if word 2 of script of there is not "SharableAddresses" then
  beep
  answer "This stack is not suitable for sharing with."
  doMenu "Close stack"
  go card cardHere of here
  exit share
end if
-- now we KNOW there is a background Body on the stack "there"
put number of cards in background "Body" into numberThere
-- have we enough disk space to proceed?
if hereDiskSpace < the size of there then
  beep
  go card cardHere of here
  if thereDiskSpace > the size of here then
    get "Try from the other stack (it's on a different disk)."
  else get "Try compacting some stacks!"
  answer "There is not enough disk space to do a share." && it
  exit share
end if
```

The sharing itself works by copying all relevant cards from the other stack (called **there**) into the present stack (called **here**). Having done this we will probably have duplicated the background **Body** – resulting in several distinct backgrounds confusingly all with the same name. Since the backgrounds have come from a different stack, even though they have the same name, HyperCard will assume they are different backgrounds: but we don't want this. We therefore use a handler **mergeBackgrounds** to make all the cards on any background *called* **Body** to be on precisely the same background. We then sort the stack (which will make similar cards go next to each other), and then go through card-by-card deleting any cards that are identical. The result will be a stack that has acquired all the new cards from the other stack, and won't repeat any cards we already had.

The following three handler calls are the core of the liveware mechanism.

```
-- now do the sharing
copyCards here, there, numberThere
mergeBackgrounds
deleteDuplicates
```

At this stage, we've completed the sharing process; all that remains to do is to tidy up and tell the user what has been achieved.

```
-- tidy up
put "Compacting stack ..."
doMenu "Compact Stack" -- after all this messing around!
put empty
set the markChar of menuItem "Share" of menu "Utilities" to empty

beep -- wake the user up after all this waiting!

-- then tell the user what's happened
put (number of cards in background "Body") - numberHere into a
if a < 0 then put 0 into a
answer plural(a, "new card") && "acquired from other stack"
put (number of cards in background "Body") - numberThere into b
if b < 0 then put 0 into b
answer plural(b, "new card") && "to give other stack"
if a > 0 or b > 0 then
   answer "You may wish to save a copy of this updated stack to replace" ¬
   && the short name of there
end if
```

Maybe the script should now replace the other stack? In our example, we use **answer** to suggest that the user saves a copy of this stack (that now has everything in it) to replace the other stack. However, there may be problems with insufficient disk space, or maybe the user wants to delete or modify some of the new cards they've just acquired before they replace the other stack. There are so many possibilities that probably the best we can do is to merely make the suggestion without taking any further initiative from the user. It is a good idea to set the markChar of the **Save a Copy...** menu item in the **File** menu (we keep track of its being set by using a hidden field in the stack – and remove the mark when **domenu "Save a Copy..."** is handled). You should add that.

Since we did all the work with no message passing, and we may have come back to a different card in the original stack, we explicitly **send** some messages to get this card and the **Utilities** menu initialized properly.

```
-- we've had lockMessages true; time to reset things (menus, etc)
send openBackground to this background
send openCard to this card
end share
```

We used a simple utility function **plural** to make our English a little better:

```
function plural change, text
   if change = 1 then return 1 && text
   if change = 0 then put "No" into change
   return change && text & "s"
end plural
```

Copying cards from one stack to another is relatively straightforward. We use **repeat** to run through the cards, copying from the **there** stack and pasting into the **here** stack:

```
on copyCards here, there, numberThere -- copy cards from stacks there to here
   repeat with i = 1 to numberThere
      go card i of background "Body" of there
      -- show a count down of progress in the message box
      put "Copying cards from other stack ..." && 1+numberThere-i
      doMenu "Copy Card"
      go here
      doMenu "Paste Card"
   end repeat
   go there -- the repeat left us on stack here
   doMenu "Close stack"
   go here
end copyCards
```

MergeBackgrounds is the most intricate handler of the liveware suite; we described the problem it solves, lots of backgrounds all called **Body**, above. We scan each background, and when we are on a background called **Body** we **add 1 to count**. Thus, when **count** is **1** this can be the 'master' background – the actual one that will remain. When **count** is greater than **1**, we've found a different background also called **Body** and we'll have to copy every field onto a new card in the master background and then delete that card, and do this for each card in that background. Deleting the last card in a background naturally deletes that background.

```
on mergeBackgrounds
   put theFields() into theFields
   put 0 into count
   put 1 into i
   repeat while i ≤ number of backgrounds
      put "Merging backgrounds ..." && 1+number of backgrounds - i
      if short name of background i = "Body" then
         add 1 to count
         if count = 1 then put id of background i into masterID
         else -- there are several backgrounds with the same name!
            repeat for number of cards in background i
               go background id masterID
               doMenu "New Card" -- with the correct background!
               -- now copy the field data over
               repeat with j = 1 to number of items in theFields
                  get item j of theFields
                  do "put" && it && "of card 1 of background" && i && "into" && it
               end repeat
               -- then delete the card on the wrong background
               go card 1 of background i
               if short name of this background = "Body" then -- just being careful!
                  set cantDelete of this background to false -- we may delete its last card
```

```
            end if
            doMenu "Delete Card"
          end repeat
        end if
      end if
      add 1 to i
    end repeat
  end mergeBackgrounds
```

Having got all our cards onto a single background, some of them may be the same. We therefore sort this background, so that similar cards get put close to each other. In particular this will mean that identical cards get put right next to each other, so they are easy to find and fix.

There are several ways to sort, the simplest is to use **sort background "Body" by** sortKey() where the function **sortKey** has the following definition, which makes a single string out of all the relevant fields strung together. The function **canon** will be explained below – we need it in another handler, and it will be easier to understand why its needed when you know about the problem it solves.

```
  function sortKey
    get theFields()
    repeat with i = 1 to number of items in it
      put canon(value(item i of it)) after key
    end repeat
    return key
  end sortKey
```

Sorting means that exactly equal cards end up being adjacent to each other. We then use the last of the three main handlers, **deleteDuplicates**, to run through the cards on the **Body** background looking for cards i and i+1 that make **sameCards(i, i+1)** true, and then delete one of them. **SameCards** is supposed to tell us when two cards are the same – we'll give the HyperTalk for it next after the script for **deleteDuplicates**.

Rather than use card numbers, we refer to all cards by their number in the **Body** background. This ensures the script works correctly even if there are cards from other backgrounds interspersed in the **Body** background (there is no need for all cards in a background to be together).

```
  on deleteDuplicates
    put "Sorting cards ..."
    sort background "Body" by sortKey() -- put cards into a standard order

    -- now go through, and delete cards that are identical
    put 1 into i
    repeat while i < number of cards in background "Body"
      put "Deleting duplicate cards ..." ¬
```

```
      && (number of cards in background "Body") - i
      if sameCards(i, i+1) then
         go card i of background "Body"
         doMenu "Delete Card" -- zaps card i
      else add 1 to i
   end repeat
end deleteDuplicates
```

You may have thought that a **repeat with** would have done just as well as a **repeat while**. However, as cards are deleted, the **number of cards in background "Body"** is reduced. Had we used a simpler **repeat with i = 1 to number of cards in background "Body"**, then this would have used the *original* value of the number of cards. We use **while** to keep working the value out, to allow for its continually changing.

SameCards (below) looks at each of the 'interesting' fields on each of the two cards i and j. If the fields are found to be unequal, we can immediately return **false**. If we've compared all the fields, and they all seem equal, then we return **true**. However, we are not so unsophisticated as to simply check if **field x = field y**! Instead, we check whether **canon(field x) = canon(field y)**. The problem **canon** solves is that many fields will have spaces and returns in them that cannot be seen: **canon** gets rid of them, so that the check that **sameCards** uses is whether cards *look* the same, rather than having identical text.

```
function sameCards i, j
   get theFields()
   repeat with k = 1 to number of items in it
      put value(item k of it && "of card i of background Body") into a
      put value(item k of it && "of card j of background Body") into b
      -- ask a & return & b with it -- an obsolete debugging line!
      if canon(a) ≠ canon(b) then return false
   end repeat
   return true
end sameCards
```

Canon works straightforwardly: it simply deletes everything that you cannot see, and returns what's left of the text. Since many fields are expected to be blank, we make a quick check for this case by counting the number of words.

```
function canon text -- remove everything you can't see
   if number of words in text = 0 then return empty
   repeat while last char of text is in space & return
      delete last char of text
   end repeat
   repeat with i = 1 to number of lines in text
      repeat while last char of line i of text = space
         delete last char of line i of text
      end repeat
```

```
        end repeat
        return text
    end canon
```

That's it. You can now share address lists and appointments – and other stacks – merely by changing theFields function and the name of the Body background.

There are two tiny bugs: using put to copy fields does not copy their text styles (we could use cut-and-paste, but this is *very* slow), and nothing keeps track of card marks. The simplest 'solution' for marking would be to unmark all the cards when the sharing is finished – unmark all cards! More usefully, when a card is deleted, if it is marked the other card concerned might be marked. Some script like the following would work nicely:

```
    put the marked of this card into wasMarked
    doMenu "Delete Card"
    if wasMarked then mark card otherCard
```

This assumes you want to *keep* marks from *both* stacks (had the last line been set mark of otherCard to wasMarked then this would have been incorrect, since it would lose the original mark on the other card). You need to decide whether marks are important enough to be shared like fields, which certainly are worth sharing, and if (for some reason) marks are really that important then cards that differ in their marking must not be deleted. You would then modify mergeBackgrounds to copy marks as well as fields, and you'd modify sameCards to compare marks.

In practice, when you share stacks you'll find many cards are frustratingly similar and you can't decide which ones to keep. The scripting above does not address this problem, except it gets all your cards together into the one stack where they'll be easier to view and manage. How you cope with similar cards depends on what your stack is trying to do: thus, appointments for the same day should be merged, warning about same-time clashes, but of addresses for the same person probably only one can be correct – there isn't a clash, but the person has moved and one address is obsolete.

Here are some concrete suggestions that you may wish to pursue.

- What are similar cards? In an address list, similar cards may be ones whose Name field is the same but which otherwise differ. (This means the liveware scripts have to know which is the crucial Name field.) Another approach is to store a unique number, such as the seconds when the card was created, as the card name. Then, wherever this card goes, it will retain its unique name. With this scheme, similar cards are defined to be ones with the same card name but different fields. The scripts we gave for this project ignore the card names, and there is also a problem that if a user (not being able to see the card name) can delete all the text in the fields of a card and then 'recycle' it as a quite different card – in this case it would have been better to use a distinct Name field, because the user would have changed that as well.

- When two adjacent cards are for the same person (their Name fields are equal) but where their other fields are different, then you should point this out to the user. One way to do this is to unmark all the cards, and then mark these cards. The user can then find the marked cards; add a button to make this facility obvious. Provide a **Flip** button or menu item that quickly flips between any two similar cards – this makes it quite easy to spot the actual differences by eye.

- Add a background field Changed (or use the card name for the same purpose). Normally, this field contains a unique number (**the seconds** will do, put there by a newCard handler), but closeField (which is sent when a field is edited and gets changed) appends a ",changed" string to it. When you scan for similar cards (cards with the same **first item of field "Changed"** but otherwise different), if one has *not* been changed, delete it. Thus, you automatically end up with the most recent changes. If two similar cards *both* have the changed item set, report it as an error and mark both cards so they are easier to find later. At the end of scanning and deleting, you must reset all the Changed fields so they are in their original 'unchanged' state. This scheme automatically deletes obsolete cards which have been modified in the other stack, and it points out if you have accidentally (presumably!) changed the same card two different ways in each of the stacks!

  Warning! If you add a field to a card, some existing scripts may get fouled up. An alternative approach is to store the same information in the card script as comment on its first few lines – so long as nothing already uses the card script for the same purpose!

- The same technique, but instead of putting ",changed" after the Changed field, you put "," & the seconds. When two similar cards are found, you can now automatically delete the older one. When two similar cards have both been changed, if you have the timing information as well, you can recommend to the user that the older one is deleted.

- You may want to share your stack with many people, and the ideas so far suggested are too simplistic to help much. Add a new background field **Livestamp** (which is how liveware really gets interesting). This livestamp field will contain **the seconds** when the card was created (as before) and the user's name who 'owns' the card. (You'll have to have some scheme of passwords and field locking so that users who don't own a card can't alter the text on it.) The livestamp also contains the time of the last change, as in the previous suggestion. Now, when you find two cards created at the same time and owned by the same user, you delete the older one. This scheme means that any number of people can share cards, and you'll always *automatically* get their most recent thoughts – whoever does the sharing and wherever they do it.

Liveware, when it is fully implemented, is such a powerful approach to sharing HyperCard stacks that it is a wonder that the livestamp is not built into cards as a property! The entire process of sharing, user's passwords and the rest could be built into HyperCard, and would be considerably faster and more reliable; it could also work with graphics which any scheme in HyperTalk cannot do very well (because there is no easy way to find out when the card or background picture changes). Nevertheless, even the simple approach to sharing address stacks, that we gave the HyperTalk for in full, is extremely useful and helps you appreciate some of the more interesting things that can be done with HyperTalk working on several stacks.

So, What is Hyperprogramming?

Hyperprogramming is programming in a language like HyperTalk – but just what *is* a language like HyperTalk? What is the 'hyperprogramming paradigm'? What are the powerful, new ideas that HyperTalk and HyperCard represent?

Apart from the features that any decent interactive programming language should anyway have (like arithmetic, conditions, procedures) there are five distinguishing concepts always found in a hyperprogramming language:

Gradual programming – easy to use

Simple aspects of hyperprogramming can be done from dialog boxes, selecting from lists, and by demonstration. A lot can be done without any direct typing. Consider visual effects and linking buttons: HyperCard introduces users to programming gently. They are shortly led into reading scripts and, later, to making serious changes. Of course, HyperTalk is very much a language to be read, and this helps the new user understand how an existing stack is constructed.

Ease of use, particularly in programming languages, is a contentious issue, and a lively research area. The remaining four distinguishing points we have picked out for hyperprogramming systems are not a matter for grades of opinion. Note how the next points separately and collectively enhance the ease of use of any hyperprogramming language.

Objects are the user interface

The central aspect of a hyperprogramming language is that the components of a program (scripts in HyperCard) *are* components of the user interface such as buttons, fields, cards. In other styles of programming language, even object-oriented languages, the user interface is *created* by the program: so things like buttons are drawn by the program (perhaps using library routines) and the connections in the program that determine how they behave are arbitrary. It is helpful to note that HyperCard still lets you create things that are not components of the program: by using painting – whether by hand or by scripting – one creates images that have no directly associated program, just a series of commands and pixel arithmetic. Even though painting in HyperCard can create (what look like) dialog boxes or any other interactive detail, these things are *constructed* and are not objects that *are* dialog boxes. Ideally, a hyperprogramming language would only have object oriented graphics, and every sort of graphical object would be able to have scripts.

Browse binding

Because the program components are part of the user interface, as the user does things, such as selecting a different current card, the associated program components (scripts) become available automatically. So as the user browses in HyperCard, for instance, when changing cards, the objects available, both to programs and to the user, change in concert. Thus, as the user goes from one card to another, HyperCard keeps track of which buttons and fields it should display and which scripts should be available as it runs. In short, the current message path and the user interface are tied intimately together. (The way variables and values are associated in programming languages is called binding, and different languages provide different schemes: static binding, dynamic binding. We call hyperprogramming's scheme *browse binding*, because it combines user browsing with program binding.)

This feature means that the way that hyperprograms are organized corresponds to the way that user interfaces are organized. This is a huge benefit. The correspondence means that simplifying the user interface tends to simplify hyperprograms and, conversely, simplifying hyperprograms tends to simplify the user interface. It means that making a simple change to the user interface (say, we want a button here!) means only making a simple change to the program and making a trivial, almost negligible change, to its structure. In short, it makes programming user interfaces much easier and far more intuitive: if you know how you want the user interface to be organized, you implicitly know how the program structure should be organized. In fact, because in HyperCard programs are created *in* the user interface, rather than in some separate process (which probably involves concepts that are unrelated to the user interface, like compilers and linkers), as you organize a user interface you are *simultaneously* organizing its program. This powerful aspect of hyperprogramming is so natural in HyperCard that one is scarcely conscious of it.

The difficulty of correctly programming menus in HyperCard (particularly when several stacks are involved) is a result of menus *not* being supported by browse binding.

User–programmer equality

A fourth important feature, that follows from the observations above, is that everything a user can do can equally be done in the hyperprogramming language. In HyperCard, users can create new buttons or draw pictures by using the menus and by clicking the mouse and dragging; they can cut and paste; and so on. These user interface activities have, in the most part, corresponding features in the HyperTalk language at a similar level – they are available as simple commands.

Simple user operations (such as moving a window, drawing a polygon, cut and paste) must be simple operations in the hyperprogramming language. Although there are exceptions in HyperCard (such as not being able to edit a brush shape from a script), in an ideal hyperprogramming language every user interface feature is available from the program. Indeed, the ideal HyperCard would itself be programmed in HyperTalk: which would mean that all its dialog boxes, tool menus and so forth, by being (in principle) implemented in HyperTalk would be available *exactly* and uniformly from the hyperprogramming language itself (this feature is technically called *reflection*).

Everything a user did while working in HyperCard could be recorded without loss as a HyperTalk script, and each user action would be a single command in the script. It could then be adapted, rerun, or simplified. (Note that in HyperCard it is very difficult to record what the user is doing unless there are severe restrictions – which suggests an area for improvement.)

Instant persistence

All of the data and program components of a hyperprogram are parts of objects (cards and the fields and buttons on them) and the objects are always permanently stored. This feature greatly simplifies the programming of databases and other applications that need to manipulate permanent data. Whatever the user or the program does to the objects persists from the moment it is created.

Since everything that the user can change is an object – cards, fields, buttons – every change that the user makes persists. In other programming paradigms, the results of computation and changes to the data by users have to be explicitly stored in files; even in so-called persistent programming languages, one has to 'set up' what one wants to persist. In a hyperprogramming language, if you can see something – like a script, graphic, button – it will persist without you doing anything further to it. To emphasize this, we say that in a hyperprogramming language, persistence is *instant* and has no overhead to get it going.

It is interesting that adopting instant persistence has meant that HyperCard avoided the usual Macintosh standard of having a **Save Stack** menu item: HyperCard stacks don't even have to be saved automatically to protect the user from system crashes because they don't need saving – what you see is what you've got on disk (with a few inconsequential provisos).

An important consequence of instant persistence is that you can develop hyperprogramming applications in any order: it is not important to get the program together before entering its data (in HyperCard you can create fields and enter their text well before writing the scripts that make use of the text; or you could do it the other way around – write the scripts, then enter the field texts; or do a bit of one, a bit of another as you develop the stack). Indeed, where most programming languages distinguish between programs and their data, or the files that they use as data, in a hyperprogramming language there is no distinction whatsoever. Objects, such as fields, are as much data as program.

What hyperprogramming buys; what it costs

Hyperprogramming systems are good for developing programs with which users interact directly through a graphical user interface. Hyperprograms are easy to extend; general-purpose tools can be constructed that extend the usefulness of existing programs (such as the Object-property tool of Chapter 9 and the hypertext tools of Chapter 14). Objects can be used to represent the objects in an application (like the use of fields with different styles to represent both the blocks and the labels in the block-diagramming system of Chapter 7).

Hyperprogramming lends itself to the rapid development of interactive programs, capturing the specification of a system in the form of a working prototype which can be continuously refined to the point where it fully meets the user's requirements. It's very easy to extend hyperprograms piecemeal: as you think of new features (such as buttons) they can be added one at a time without having to work out how they relate to the rest of the system.

Hyperprogramming doesn't suit all programming requirements. A price has to be paid for the benefits. There are performance costs in using a high-level, user-oriented programming system. In HyperCard the use of strings to represent all data values, the late binding of handlers to messages and the structuring of information solely as objects all incur significant costs. These costs are not inevitable features of hyperprogramming systems – conventional object-oriented systems that avoid most of them and yet go a long way towards hyperprogramming – they rely on defining the execution environments in terms of classes of objects – this reduces the amount of searching needed to match a message with its handler, whereas in HyperCard the scope for organizing objects is quite limited, and the system has correspondingly more work to do.

There can be complexity costs for the programmer too in using a system that integrates the user interface with the program – not all applications are best designed around their user interface. The advantage of being able to add features incrementally often leads to systems with many features solving small problems; whereas more careful design might have led to something more coherent, more powerful and easier to use.

Summary

HyperCard isn't the ultimate hyperprogramming system; the synergy between HyperTalk and the interfaces built and used in HyperCard is not complete. Yet it is a taste of the new, important class of hyperprogramming systems. We expect to enjoy hyperprogramming in it and its successors in the future, as much as we enjoyed producing the examples and projects that form the subject matter for this book.

Further Reading

Sources for XCMDs and other HyperCard-related software

The best way of writing HyperCard stacks is to find someone else who has done something close enough to what you want, so that you can carry on easily from where they got to. HyperCard, of course, lends itself to working together and sharing stack and scripts, as well as sounds, pictures and ideas. The list of commercial suppliers of stackware is huge, and our best advice to you is to join a HyperCard users' group or at least subscribe to a Macintosh magazine (such as *MacUser*, *MacWorld*, *MacTutor*; some general magazines like *BYTE* have useful articles). If you don't subscribe to a bulletin board or magazine – or know someone who does – you'll get left behind.

Apple's own Developer Group provides support for HyperCard developers, and if you join the Apple developer association, APDA, you will be able to buy various HyperCard products at a discount, as well as the books recommended in the next section such as Apple's own *HyperCard Stack Design Guidelines*.

A sampler of XCMDs and XFCNS

There are thousands of XCMDs and XFCNs available. We give a brief list to give you some idea of the range of facilities available. Look out for stacks that contain many XCMDs and XFCNs – there are shareware and public domain stacks of hundreds of cards, each card describing one or more externals. The following list details some commercially available externals:

3d Graphic Tools (Micro Systems Options) – Colour and monochrome three-dimensional graphics.

AppleTalk Toolkit (Apple) – Contains XCMDs and XFCNs and examples for accessing AppleTalk networks.

Audio Toolkit (Apple) – XCMDs for controlling audio CDs.

CommsTalk Developer Kit (Apple) – Add data communications scripting facilities, including front-ends and general-purpose functions.

CompileIt! (Heizer Software) – Converts HyperTalk into external commands so that it runs much faster.

HyperBASIC (System Technology Corporation) – Supports external commands and functions in BASIC.

HyperExternals Pro (Boojum Computer Systems Inc.) – Collection of lots of general-purpose XCMDs and XFCNs.

OnTrack (Abbate Video Consultants) – Control a video recorder.

Serial Communications Toolkit (Apple) – Contains XCMDs and XFCNs and examples for accessing the Macintosh serial port. Includes an example bulletin board stack.

VideoDisk Toolkit (Apple) – Control video disks from HyperCard.

Voyager CD Audio Stack (The Voyager Company) – Make HyperCard sound resources from off-the shelf audio disks.

Voyager VideoStack (The Voyager Company) – Toolkit for interactive video, allowing HyperCard to control video disk players.

Wild Things (Language Systems Corporation) – Variety of XCMDs for animation, math and statistics.

The following suppliers have most of the available shareware and public domain stacks on disks and CD roms:

BMUG (Berkeley Macintosh Users' Group)   EDUCORP
1442A, Walnut Street #62   7434, Trade Street
Berkeley, CA 94709–1496   San Diego, CA 92121–2410
USA   USA

If you can program in Pascal or C, you can write your own XCMDs; the next section mentions some books that will help you get started.

Selected books and publications

HyperTalk

Apple's *HyperCard 2 Script Language Guide* is the definitive reference on HyperTalk. There are many other reference books on HyperCard and HyperTalk, which we won't attempt to review here.

Gary Bond's *XCMDs for HyperCard* (MIS Press, 1988) gives a detailed discussion of the construction of XCMDs in for HyperCard 1, a selection of utilities you can program in C or Pascal. The *HyperCard 2 Script Language Guide* itself contains sufficient information for experienced Macintosh programmers to get started writing XCMDs in either C or Pascal.

Dan Winkler (creator of HyperTalk) and Scot Kamins have written two useful and informative books: *HyperTalk 2.0: The Book*, published by Bantam Computer Books in 1990 and *Cooking With HyperTalk 2.0* (also Bantam, 1990) which includes a disk. A complete definition of HyperTalk, including its syntax, can be found in *HyperTalk 2.0: The Book*, published by Bantam Computer Books in 1990. Dan Winkler was the creator of HyperTalk, so their book should be definitive – except that HyperTalk does not stand still.

HyperCard

There is an increasing number of books on HyperCard, at all levels, from beginner to expert, from quick reference dictionaries to books of programming tricks. Our best advice is to visit a decent book shop and have a browse around the computer section; failing that, get hold of some book publishers' catalogues. Be warned that there are a lot of impressively thick books of dubious value.

User interface design

Harold Thimbleby's *User Interface Design* (Addison-Wesley/ACM Press, 1990) provides an excellent introduction to the principles of interactive system design, drawing on cognitive psychology, software engineering and mathematics!

Apple Computer are responsible for two of the best books for anyone who is concerned to ensure that their designs are up-to-date and based on the best available guidelines. These are:

HyperCard Stack Design Guidelines, Addison-Wesley, 1989.

Human InterFace Guidelines: The Apple DeskTop Interface, Addison-Wesley, 1987.

We can recommend both of these books to potential designers of HyperCard-based applications. The first focuses on those aspects of stack design that do not require a knowledge of HyperTalk programming and especially on the design of stacks that provide access to information that is organized as hypertext. It includes a set of guidelines that will be of benefit to anyone designing HyperCard stacks for any purpose. The second Apple book gives a more general set of guidelines for interactive system design; these are the guidelines on which the design of most Macintosh applications have been based.

A recommended reference and review of the wider user interface field and other systems is Ben Shneiderman's second edition of *Designing The User Interface*, Addison-Wesley, 1992.

The Apple books on user interface and stack design are excellent sources for ways of designing the appearance of a stack – in contrast to this book, which is an excellent source on how to get stacks to *work*. The Apple books make your programs *look* professional; our book makes your designs – however they look – *work* professionally.

Presentation

Edward Tufte's two books *Envisioning Information*, Graphics Press, 1990, and *The Visual Display of Quantitative Information*, Graphics Press, 1982, are both excellent books and will help you make your stacks more impressive, giving you many ideas for displaying all sorts of information clearly.

You should supplement reading these books with a book on desk top publishing, like the BBC's *Into Print* by Susan Quilliam and Ian Grove-Stephenson (1990) or *Collier's Rules for Desktop Design and Typography* by David Collier, Addison-Wesley, 1990. Both books (and the many others available) will usefully increase your awareness of the importance of good design and well-presented text.

Hypertext

Jakob Nielsen, *HyperText and HyperMedia*, Academic Press, 1990.

Ben Shneiderman and Greg Kiersley, *HyperText Hands On!*, Addison-Wesley, 1989.

Many texts on hypertext are, naturally, available as hypertext documents that you can browse in HyperCard (or in one of its competitors). The classic is a collection of articles (originally published conventionally on paper in 1988 in the Communications of the ACM, volume 31, number 7): *Hypertext on Hypertext*, published by ACM Press.

Graphics

Seymour Papert, *Mindstorms: Children, Computers and Powerful Ideas*, Harvester Press, 1990. An excellent, inspirational book, on the role of LOGO in childrens' education – of course, HyperTalk has now superseded LOGO but the vision remains.

James Foley, Andries van Dam, Steven Feiner and John Hughes, *Fundamentals of Interactive Computer Graphics*, Addison-Wesley, second edition, 1990. This is comprehensive and up-to-date, but you may like to compare it with the other classic, Newman and Sproull:

William Newman and Robert Sproull, *Principles of Interactive Computer Graphics*, McGraw-Hill, second edition, 1979.

Algorithms

Robert Sedgewick, *Algorithms*, Addison-Wesley. Second edition, 1988. Sedgewick's book has 45 chapters covering most algorithms you are likely to need, from graphics, sorting, searching to topics like finding happy marriages. It is available in C and Pascal versions; for HyperTalk programming you'll probably find the Pascal version more useful, since C is very different from HyperTalk.

David Harel, *Algorithmics*, Addison-Wesley, 1987. Subtitled, 'The spirit of computing', this is the best introductory book about algorithms, their speed and correctness.

Object-oriented programming

For an introduction to object-oriented programming, see Tim Corson and John McGregor, 'Understanding Object-Oriented: a Unifying Paradigm', *Communications of the ACM*, volume. 33, number 9, 1990, pp.40–61.

Kurt Schmucker, *Object-Oriented Programming for the Macintosh*, Hayden Book Company, 1986.

Functional programming (see Chapter 11)

Peter Henderson, *Functional Programming: Application and Implementation*, Prentice-Hall, 1980. Henderson's book has the advantage that it also shows you how to implement your own functional system from scratch (in Pascal).

Liveware (see Chapter 15)

I. H. Witten, H. W. Thimbleby, G. F. Coulouris, S. Greenberg, 'Liveware: A New Approach to Sharing Data in Social Networks', *International Journal of Man-Machine Studies*, volume 34, number 3,1991, pp.337–48.

HyperTalk Summary

This appendix contains a handy summary of what HyperTalk 2.0 provides and gives many of the details that a programmer will need to know in order to conceive new stacks and scripts or to day-dream about the scope and possibilities of HyperTalk. There is unfortunately not space to cover *every* corner of the language: you should also rely on the *HyperTalk Reference* stack and your own experiments to test your understanding.

However, since complete references to HyperTalk are so large and bulky, a summary like this appendix can be very useful! We have emphasized details essential to *planning* programming and therefore have not covered the intricacies of HyperTalk's command syntax, which is something that can be sorted out when you know what you want to script. The *Further Reading* chapter suggests some other books that you may wish to refer to for further information.

A.1 Properties

In the *Dictionary of properties* on page 357 we briefly describe every property of HyperCard 2.0 and its objects. Each property description has the following form:

propertyName (types of object it applies to: range of values allowed) = **its default value**
    A brief description of the property.

 If the property is read-only – that is, it can be accessed but not **set** – then the object name is followed by a star: *. The range of values allowed is only mentioned if it needs explaining – it can usually be inferred from the default value. A few properties (such as **cursor**) cannot be read but can only be set; these are mentioned explicitly as being write-only. Some of the default values are determined by HyperCard, others give the value you can expect unless, for example, the User Preferences card in the Home stack overrides them.

Accessing properties

A property is accessed by naming it and specifying the object to which it belongs. Thus:

```
get  rect of button "Next Card"
put rect of me into myRect
get the showPict of this card
```

The word 'the' is always optional before property names. When referring to properties of the HyperCard system you can omit the reference to HyperCard, so the reference to such properties can look very much like a call to a built-in function, as in **the version**, which is short for **the version of HyperCard**.

Some functions, such as **the diskSpace** or **the seconds** really ought to be properties but HyperTalk treats them as functions (for 'reasons' that are irrelevant here)! Note that **number** behaves as *both* a function and property – with different meanings. Finally, there are some things that you might have thought were properties but are actually global variables – we'll summarize those after the dictionary of properties below.

Setting properties

A property is changed using:

set [the] *property* [of *object*] to *value*

You don't always need to mention the object when it is HyperCard itself. The optional word **the** has no significance. **Set** usually knows about the property syntax and expects values of the correct form; thus: **set the bottomRight of button 1 to 4,5** – see the discussion of *rectangle* and *point* properties below.

To add to the confusion – or flexibility? – several properties may be set with special forms: **hide**, **show**, **lock**, and **unlock**. **Hide** *x* and **show** *x* are the same as **set visible of** *x* **to false** (hide) or **true** (show), though you can't do this consistently (**hide groups** works, but **groups** is not an object, so it has no properties; you can hide a button, but you **hide picture of background**; and – in contrast! – **show cards** shows each card one after the other). **Lock** *x* and **unlock** *x*, where *x* is **screen** or **message**, are equivalent to **set** *x* **to true** or **false**. If you want to be consistent (so that **lock recent** and **unlock recent** work) you can always write a handler for **lock** and **unlock**, along these lines:

```
on lock property
   set property to false
end lock
```

Maybe this will be built into a future version of HyperCard?

Modifiers

Some properties (**version**, **name**) can be modified, as in **the short name** or **the long version**.

Point properties

A point is a two-item list of numbers, such as **4,5**. The first number is the horizontal distance, measured in pixels from the left of the reference frame (such as the card window); the second number is the vertical distance down from the top. Both numbers must be positive whole numbers. Given two whole numbers **x** and **y**, the point can be constructed by writing **x & "," & y**. You will normally use the functions **trunc** or **round** if **x** and **y** are not whole numbers, as in **trunc(100*x/pi) & "," & trunc(100*sin(x))**.

Rectangle properties

Many properties are based on the **rectangle** property of the graphical objects. A **rectangle** is an item list of four whole numbers. The first two numbers are the top left point of the object, the last two the bottom right. Thus, a rectangle **1,2,3,4** has top left at **1,2** (that is, horizontal offset 1 pixel right from the far left, vertical offset 2 down from the top) and bottom right at **3,4** (that is, horizontal offset 3 pixels from the far left, 4 pixels down from the top). Windows have their top left fixed at **0,0**.

When you can say the **rectangle of** *object*, you may also say the **topLeft of** *object*, the **center of** *object*, the **height of** *object*, and so forth. However, if **r** is four points representing a rectangle, you cannot use **topLeft**, **height**, **center** or any of the other rectangle properties: instead of **topLeft of r** you have to write **item 1 to 2 of r**. The properties have to be calculated.

When a rectangle property is set, there may be side-effects. Thus setting the **bottom** of a button also moves the top of the button, because the **height** is not changed. The dictionary of properties, below, mentions all such effects.

A.2 Dictionary of properties

autoHilite (button) = false
> Determines whether a button highlights automatically in response to **mouseDown**. With check boxes and radio buttons, **autoHilite** determines whether the button changes from deselected to selected and back.

autoTab (non-scrolling field)
> Determines whether HyperCard inserts a **return** when the insertion point is on the last line of a field (**false**) or moves the insertion point to the next editable field on the card (**true**).

blindTyping (HyperCard)
> Determines whether you can type into the message box when it is not visible. Available only if the **userLevel** is set to **5**.

bottom (card*, button, field, window)
> Equivalent to **item 4** of an object's rectangle. If you set the **bottom** of an object, it moves. The size of the object remains the same.

bottomRight (card*, button, field, window)
>   Equivalent to items 3 and 4 of an object's rectangle. If you set **the bottomRight** of an object, it moves. The size of the object remains the same.

brush (HyperCard: 1-32) = 8
>   The current brush shape number.

cantAbort (HyperCard) = false
>   Determines whether users can type ***command–period*** to stop running handlers.

cantDelete (card, background, stack) = false
>   Determines whether a user can delete an object.

cantModify (stack) = false
>   Determines whether a stack can be changed in any way. If true, a padlock appears in the menu bar.

cantPeek (stack) = false
>   Determines whether ***command–option C, B*** or ***S*** (for card, background or stack) shows scripts, ***command–option*** shows button outlines, ***command–option–shift*** shows field outlines.

centered (HyperCard) = false
>   Determines whether shapes are drawn from the centre rather than a corner.

checkMark (menuItem) = false (for new menus)
>   Determines whether a check mark (a tick) appears in front of a menu item. It uses the character numToChar(18) as the mark character. HyperCard's default menus use check marks as appropriate: for instance to indicate the text style.

commandChar, cmdChar (menuItem: character) = empty (for new menus)
>   The command-key equivalent for a menu item.

cursor (HyperCard: arrow, busy, cross, hand, Ibeam, plus, none, watch)
>   Sets the image that appears as the mouse pointer; you use a number or the name of a CURS resource – you can create new cursors using a resource editor. Property resets on idle to default for current tool. Cursor is write-only.

debugger (HyperCard: debugger name) = ScriptEditor
>   Name of the current HyperTalk debugger.

dontSearch (field, card, background) = false
>   Determines whether find will look for matches in the object.

dontWrap (field)
>   Determines whether a field wraps text that is longer than the width of the field or truncates the text at the edge of the field.

dragSpeed (HyperCard: positive integer) = 0
>   How many pixels per second the pointer will move when manipulated by drag commands. 0 drags as fast as possible. Resets on idle.

editBkgnd (HyperCard) = false
>   Determines where painting or buttons and fields will appear, on the card or the background. Userlevel must be 3 or greater.

enabled (menu, menuItem) = true
>   Determines whether a menu item or a menu is active or inactive (grey).

filled (HyperCard) = false
>   Determines whether shapes are filled with the current pattern.

fixedLineHeight (field)
>   Determines whether a field has uniform line height or each line varies according to largest font size that appears in it.

freeSize (HyperCard*)
>   The amount of free space, in bytes, in the stack.

grid (HyperCard) = false
>   Determines whether most paint tools are constrained to eight-pixel intervals.

hBarLoc (variable watcher window)
>   Determines how many of the variable names and values are visible.

height (window*, button, field, card)
>   An integer equal to the height in pixels of the object. Setting the height of a button or field resizes it, maintaining the centre of the object, expanding or shrinking it on both sides evenly. Setting the height of a card resizes all the cards in a stack.

hideIdle (message watcher window) = true
>   Determines whether to show idle messages in the message watcher.

hideUnused (message watcher window) = true
>   Determines whether to show unused messages in the message watcher.

hilite (button) = false
>   Determines whether a button is highlighted.

icon (button: icon descriptor) = empty
>   The icon displayed by a button. After a set, the result is set to Can't find that icon. if the icon can't be found; otherwise the result is empty.

ID (button*, field*, card*, background*)
>   The ID of the object. All objects apart from menus, menu items and stacks have IDs. The short ID is simply the numeric ID; the ID or the abbreviated ID *may* specify the type of object as well, and the long ID *may* specify the enclosing object (if there is one) and the full name of the stack – depending on the type of object. If the ID of this card is card ID 123, the short ID of this card is 123. (Hint: if you set the name of a background/field/button to empty, the long name of the object gets you what the long ID should have done!)

language (HyperCard: resource name) = English
> The language used for editing scripts.

left (card*, button, field, window)
> Equivalent to item 1 of the object's rectangle. If you set the left of an object, it moves. The size of the object remains the same.

lineSize (HyperCard: 1, 2, 3, 4, 6, or 8) = 1
> Thickness, in pixels, of lines drawn by paint tools.

location, loc (button, field, window, external window: point)
> The centre of a button or field or the top-left of a window.

lockMessages (HyperCard) = false
> Determines whether messages (closeCard, closeBackground, closeStack, openCard, openBackground, openStack, resumeStack, and suspendStack) are sent automatically. Resets to false just before idle.

lockRecent (HyperCard) = false
> Determines whether to update the **Recent** card dialog. HyperCard behaves *as if* lockRecent is true whenever lockScreen is true. LockRecent resets to false just before idle.

lockScreen (HyperCard) = false
> Determines whether the screen is updated when you go to another card: makes HyperCard faster and may have advantages for not confusing the user with irrelevant cards a script needs to visit. LockScreen has a counter: you must set the property to false for every time it has been set to true before it *really* becomes false; however, lockScreen anyway resets to false just before idle, resetting the counter.

lockText (field) = false
> Determines whether the user can edit the text within the field.

longWindowTitles (HyperCard) = false
> Determines whether to display the full pathnames of a stacks in the title bar of all windows.

markChar (menuItem)
> The character used to mark a menu item, or empty if none. Setting this property to other than empty sets the checkMark to true (even if it is not set to a tick mark).

marked (card) = false
> Determines whether a card is marked.

menuMessage, menuMsg (menuItem) = empty
> The message sent to the current card when a menu item is chosen by the user.

messageWatcher (HyperCard: resource name) = MessageWatcher
> The name of the XCMD that displays the message watcher window for tracing scripts.

multiple (HyperCard) = false
>   Determines whether shape tools create multiple images with drag.

multiSpace (HyperCard: 1-100)
>   The minimum space, in pixels, between the edges of multiple shapes drawn when multiple is true.

name (button, field, card, background, stack, menu item, menu)
>   The name of the object, or its ID if it has no explicit name. Can be modified by short or long.

number (button, field, card, background)
>   The number of the object. For buttons and fields, the number determines the front-to-back position relative to other buttons or fields.The menu operation **send farther** increases the number, **bring closer** decreases it; otherwise you cannot change a button or field's number except by deleting other similar objects with lower numbers, or (for cards and backgrounds) by creating objects. For cards, the number determines the position of the card in the stack; this can be changed by cutting-and-pasting. To program the changes described above, use doMenu with the appropriate menu operations.

numberFormat (HyperCard: number format) = 0.######
>   The precision for displaying numbers. Use 0 for each digit, # for optional digits, and a period for the position of the decimal point, if any. Resets just before idle is sent.

pattern (HyperCard: 1 to 40) = 12
>   The current pattern used to fill shapes or to paint with the brush tool.

polySides (HyperCard: 0, 3-50) = 4
>   The number of sides of a polygon drawn by the regular polygon tool. 0 draws a circle.

powerKeys (HyperCard) = true
>   Determines whether painting keyboard shortcuts are available.

printMargins (HyperCard: rectangle) = 0,0,0,0
>   The default margin spacing used by print.

printTextAlign (HyperCard: alignment) = left
>   The default alignment used by print.

printTextFont (HyperCard: font) = Geneva
>   The default text font used by print.

printTextHeight (HyperCard: positive integer) = 13
>   The default text height (or line spacing) used by print.

printTextSize (HyperCard: positive integer) = 10
>   The default text size (or point size) used by print.

printTextStyle (HyperCard: text style list) = plain
>   The default text style used by print.

properties (palette*)
> List of the palette's properties.

rectangle, rect (button, field, card, window, variable watcher*: rectangle)
> The coordinates of the object. Setting the rectangle of a card changes the size of all the cards in a stack; setting the rectangle of the card window resizes the window, not the card. For a window, the point (the first two numbers) is zero. For the variable watcher, the property *must* be spelt rect, and is write-only.

reportTemplates (stack*)
> A return-separated list of the names of the report templates in the stack.

right (card*, button, field, window)
> Equivalent to item 3 of an object's rectangle. If you set the right of an object, it moves. The size of the object remains the same.

script (stack, background, card, field, button: script)
> The script of any object in the current stack or the stack script of another (open) stack.

scriptEditor (debugger: resource name) = ScriptEditor
> The current script editor.

scriptTextFont (debugger: font) = Monaco
> The font used to display scripts in the script editor.

scriptTextSize (debugger: positive integer) = 9
> The size of font used to display scripts in the script editor.

scroll (scrolling field, card window) = 0 (field) or 0,0 (window)
> The number of pixels that have scrolled above the top of a field's rectangle. For windows, the scroll is the top left of the card in its window or of the picture in its window.

sharedHilite (background button) = true
> Determines whether a button shares its hilite property with every card in that background.

sharedText (background field) = false
> Determines whether a field shows the same text on every card of the background.

showLines (field) = false
> Determines whether the text baselines of a field appear.

showName (button) = false
> Determines whether the name of the button is displayed.

showPict (card, background) = true
> Determines whether graphics or paint text for a card or background are visible.

size (stack*)
> The size of the specified stack in bytes. Compacting a stack recovers the space previously occupied by the deleted objects and graphics.

stacksInUse (stack*) = empty

   A **return**-separated list of the full pathnames of stacks in the current message path.

style (button, field) = **roundRect** (button); **rectangle** (field)

   The style of the object. Note that buttons and fields have several incompatible styles – a field cannot be a **roundRect**, for instance, though both can be **rectangle, opaque** and **transparent**.

suspended (HyperCard*)

   Determines whether HyperCard is the currently active application when several applications are open. Typically used to avoid putting up **ask** or **answer** dialogs.

textAlign (HyperCard, field, button) = **left**

   The way paint text, text in a field, or a button name aligns: **left, right,** or **center**.

textArrows (HyperCard)

   Determines whether the arrow keys move the insertion point in a field or change cards. When the **textArrows** property is **false**: right and left arrow keys go to the next and previous cards in the stack; up and down arrow keys go forward and backward through the cards you've already viewed. Holding down the option key when **textArrows** is **true** makes the arrow keys work as if it was **false**.

textFont (HyperCard, field, button: font name) = **Geneva** (fields); **Chicago** (buttons)

   The font of Paint text, text in a field, or a button name.

textHeight (HyperCard, field: positive integer)

   The distance, in pixels, between the baselines of text.

textSize (HyperCard, chunk, field, button) = **12**

   The size, in pixels, of the font.

textStyle (HyperCard, chunk, button, menuItem) = **plain**

   The style in which paint text, field text, button names, or menu items appear. Many styles may occur in fields. These are given as a comma-separated list.

top (card*, button, field, window)

   Equivalent to **item 2** of the object's rectangle. If you set **the top** of an object, it moves. The size of the object remains the same.

topLeft (card*, button, field, window)

   Equivalent to **items 1** and **2** of the object's rectangle. If you set **the topLeft** of an object, it moves. The size of the object remains the same.

traceDelay (debugger: positive integer) = **0**

   The number of ticks in pauses between each statement as the debugger traces a handler.

userLevel (HyperCard: **1-5**)

   The user level: **1** = browsing; **2** = typing; **3** = painting; **4** = authoring; **5** = scripting.

userModify (HyperCard) **= true**
> Determines whether the user can type into fields, use the paint tools, and move or delete objects. If **false**, HyperCard discards any changes when it leaves the current card.

variableWatcher (debugger: resource name) **= VariableWatcher**
> The name of the XCMD that displays the variable watcher window.

version (HyperCard*, stack)
> The version of HyperCard you are running, such as **2.1**. The **long version** gives more information, for example **02108000**. The version number is composed of four pairs of digits: XXYYZZRR, the major revision number, the minor revision number, a release code (**20**: development, **40**: alpha, **60**: beta, **80** final), and a release number. Of a stack, **version** and **long version** both give a five item list: the version of HyperCard that created the stack, the version that last compacted it, the version that last modified it, and the version that first modified it, finally, the time (in seconds) when the stack was last updated before the current sesssion. Example: **02108000, 02108000, 02108000, 02108000, 2790278103**.

visible (button, field, window, external window)
> Determines whether the object is visible. Setting **the visible** of a window to **true** makes it come to the front.

wideMargins (field) **= false**
> Determines whether HyperCard adds extra space between the edges of a field and its text.

width (button, field, card, window)
> Equivalent to the width in pixels of the specified object. Setting **the width** of a button or field resizes it, maintaining the centre of the object, expanding or shrinking it on both sides evenly. Setting **the width** of a card resizes all the cards in a stack.

A.3 Global variables

Unlike properties, global variables *are* variables: they have to be declared **global** and they cannot be assigned by using **set**. (Any variable you use from the message window is taken to be global.) The standard Home stack creates the following globals:

> **UserName**: this is the user name registered in the Home stack.

> **Documents, Applications, Stacks**: HyperCard uses these variables as lines of folders (directories) where HyperCard will look to try and open documents (for reading or writing), applications (for running) and stacks (for going to). If HyperCard cannot find a file it will normally put up a dialog box asking the user to locate the file manually, and then the appropriate global has the new folder added.

> **WhichHomeCard**: the **Home** menu uses this to help go back to the right home card from another stack.

> The script editor normally provides various globals – find out by using the variable

watcher. You should find: ScriptDebugging, ScriptWindowRec, ScriptReplaceString, ScriptWholeWord, ScriptCaseSens, ScriptWrapAround, ScriptFindString.

A.4 Messages and system commands

HyperCard distinguishes between *messages* and *system commands* sent to HyperCard as a result of user actions. Though both are sent automatically, HyperCard only acts on commands, not messages.

Message examples: OpenCard is sent when HyperCard opens a card, but (being a message) has no action unless there is a script with an **opencard** handler in the current message path. HyperCard sends **choose** and **doMenu** as messages when the user chooses a tool or an item from one of HyperCard's menus: since **doMenu** is sent as a message, nothing happens if the user selects an unimplemented menu item (there is not even a dialog box error message). HyperCard sends **close** as a message when the user clicks the close box of a window.

System command examples: In contrast, keyDown, which is sent when the user types, unless it is overridden by a script, will cause the character typed to be inserted into a field or the message window.

To get a better idea of what is going on when you use a stack, type **show window "message watcher"** in the message window. You will get a windoid that shows what messages are currently being generated, but not their parameters if they have any. Here is what you might see if you choose **New Card** from the **Edit** menu. Note that we ran this when we had a check_menus handler defined, as described in Chapter 9, and this causes three sets to be generated; finally, after **openCard** (which is not handled), HyperCard starts sending idle (see the bottom line) again.

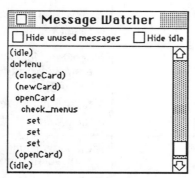

Messages are sent in a fixed order, depending on what event caused them to be sent. The following table summarizes the main events, and the sequence of messages HyperCard will send. Of course, if a message is handled by a handler that does an **exit to HyperCard**, the remaining messages won't get sent.

Event	Message sending order
startup – when HyperCard is initially started	openStack, openBackground, openCard
resume – when the user clicks on HyperCard after running some other application	resume, openStack, openBackground, openCard
new stack – making a new stack, that will appear in the same window (so the current stack must be closed first)	closeCard, closeBackground, closeStack, newStack, newBackground, newCard, openStack, openBackground, openCard
new stack in a new window	suspendStack, newStack, newBackground, newCard, openStack, openBackground, openCard
new background	closeCard, closeBackground, newBackground, newCard, openBackground, openCard
new card	closeCard, newCard, openCard
delete stack	closeCard, closeBackgroud, closeStack, deleteStack
delete background	closeCard, closeBackground, deleteCard, deleteBackground
delete card	closeCard, [closeBackground], deleteCard, [deleteBackground, openBackground], openCard Messages in brackets sent if deleting last card on a background.
cut card	closeCard, [closeBackground], deleteCard, [deleteBackground, openBackground], openCard Messages in brackets sent if cutting last card on a background.
paste card	[newBackground], newCard, [openBackground], openCard Messages in brackets sent if pasting a card into a *potentially* different background.

Event	Message sending order
hiding or revealing the menubar (user types **command–space**)	commandKeyDown space, hide menubar or show menubar
nothing – HyperCard not doing anything else	idle Properties dragSpeed, lockMessages, lockRecent, lockScreen and numberFormat are reset to their default values just before this message is sent (you can't use idle as a command to resent the properties). Visual effects are also cleared.
menu item selected	doMenu *menuItem, menuName* Further messages may be sent, depending on the required menu action. DoMenu is a command and is used to cause the relevant menu action.
resizing or moving a window	sizeWindow, moveWindow (In this order, when both are sent.)
tool selected from tool menu; double-clicking (as on the brush tool) simply gives you two consecutive **choose** messages	choose tool *number*
pattern selected from pattern menu	set pattern to *number*
typing with the control key down (if your keyboard has a control key!)	controlKey *number*
typing with the command key down	commandKeyDown *character*
typing: **return**, an arrow key, tab key, typing any other character	returnKey arrowKey *direction* tabKey keyDown *char*

A.5 Dictionary of messages

Each message in the following dictionary is described by a paragraph in the following form:

Message → where HyperCard sends it
>   a description of when it is sent.

None of the messages in this dictionary has parameters:

closeBackground → current card
>   when a user (or script) quits HyperCard or goes to a card whose background is different than the background of the current card.

closeCard → card
>   when a user (or script) goes to another card or quits HyperCard.

closeField → unlocked field
>   when, after editing, a user (or script) performs an action that closes the field. Sent only when the text changes.

closeStack → current card
>   when a user (or script) opens a different stack in the current window, closes the current window, or quits HyperCard.

deleteBackground → card being deleted
>   when a card is being deleted and if no other cards in the stack share its background. Sent just before the card disappears.

deleteButton → button being deleted
>   when a button is deleted, just before it disappears.

deleteCard → card being deleted
>   when a card that is deleted, just before it disappears.

deleteField → field being deleted
>   when a field that is deleted, just before it disappears.

deleteStack → current card of stack being deleted
>   when a stack is deleted, just before HyperCard erases the stack from the disk.

exitField → unlocked field
>   when, after clicking in a field or tabbing to it, a user (or script) exits the field without changing any text.

idle → current card
>   when no other events are occurring (all handlers have finished running and HyperCard itself isn't sending other messages).

mouseDown → button or locked field, or current card
>   when the user presses the mouse button down and the pointer is inside the rectangle of the button or field.

mouseEnter → button or field
> just after the pointer moves within its rectangle.

mouseLeave → button or field
> just after the pointer moves outside its rectangle.

mouseStillDown → button or locked field, or current card
> while the user holds the mouse button down and the pointer is inside the rectangle of the button or field. Sent after **mouseDown**.

mouseUp → button or locked field, or current card
> when the user releases the mouse button and the pointer is inside the rectangle of same button or field it was in when the user pressed the mouse button (otherwise, HyperCard does not send **mouseUp**).

mouseWithin → button or field
> repeatedly while the pointer is inside its rectangle.

moveWindow → current card
> when the user or a script moves the window. HyperCard usually sends **sizeWindow** before a **moveWindow** message.

newBackground → the first card of the new background
> just after HyperCard creates the background.

newButton → the new button
> just after HyperCard creates it.

newCard → the new card
> just after HyperCard creates it.

newField → the new field
> just after HyperCard creates it.

newStack → the new current card (first card of the new stack)
> just after HyperCard creates the stack.

openBackground → current card
> just after a user (or script) goes to a card whose background differs from the background of the most recent card.

openCard → current card
> just after a user (or handler) goes to the card.

openField → unlocked field
> when a user (or handler) first opens it for text editing. A user opens a field for editing either by clicking in the field or by tabbing from the previous field.

openStack → current card
> when a user (or handler) goes to a card in a different stack than that of the most recent card.

quit → current card
>   when the user chooses **Quit HyperCard** from the **File** menu (or presses command-Q), just before HyperCard quits.

resume → current card
>   when HyperCard resumes running after the user quits an application that he launched from HyperCard.

resumeStack → current card
>   when the stack's window becomes active after being inactive (for example, when the user clicks in a window).

sizeWindow → current card
>   when the user or a script resizes the window. In many cases, HyperCard will send a **moveWindow** message immediately after a **sizeWindow** message.

startUp → first card displayed
>   when HyperCard is first started.

suspend → current card
>   when a user (or handler) launches an application from HyperCard with the **open** command, just before the application is launched.

suspendStack → current card
>   when the stack's window becomes inactive (for example, when the user clicks another card window).

A.6 Named constants

Constant	Meaning	Example
return	ASCII *return* character	put "line 1" & return & "line2" into field 3
space	" "	put date() & space & time() into field 4
empty	"" (the empty string)	if card field 3 is empty then...
quote	" (a single quote)	get quote & "Yes" & quote & "he said"
comma	"," (a comma)	put x & comma & y into z
tab	ASCII *tab* character	
linefeed	ASCII *linefeed* character	
formfeed	ASCII *formfeed* character	
pi	3.14159...(π to 20 decimal places)	2*pi*radius
true	itself: the value true	set the hilite of me to true
false	itself: the value false	set the lockText of me to false
up	itself: "up"	if the mouse is up then ...
down	itself: "down"	if the mouse is down then ...
zero...ten	the integers	put three into x --*x contains 3*

A.7 Operators

Arithmetic operators

+	Add	put thePrice+6.75 into theTotal
-	Subtract	put theTotal-theCredit into amountDue
*	Multiply	put amountDue*1.175 into field "Price"
/	Divide	put amountDue/10 into field "Commission"
^	Power (exponent)	put 4/3*pi*radius^3 into volume
div	Divide with integer result	7 div 3 = 2
mod	Integer remainder	7 mod 3 = 1

The arithmetic operators generate error messages when applied to non-numeric strings.

String concatenation operators

&, &&	concatenate two strings, producing a new string	put "the time is:" & time() into field 3 put time()&&date() into field 3

The double ampersand **&&** interposes a space between the strings: "a" & "b" = "ab", but "a" && "b" = "a b".

Logical operators

and	true when both operands are **true**.	if a > 3 and c < 5 then...
or	true when either operand is true.	if a < 3 or a > 5 then...
not	true if the operand is **false**	set hilite of button 3 to not hilite of button 3

Both operands of **and** and **or** are always evaluated, even if one of them is **true**. The logical operators generate error messages when applied to operands other than **true** and **false**.

Comparison operators

=, is	equal (matching strings)	if x = 0 then put 0 into y if word 3 of field 5 is "foobar" then...
≠, ◇, is not	not equal (the strings do not match)	if x ≠ 0 then... if field 3 is not empty then...
<	less than (alphabetically precedes)	if x < 0 then...
>	greater than (alphabetically follows)	if x > 0 then...
≤, <=	less than or equal (matching or alphabetically precedes)	if x ≤ 0 then...
≥, >=	greater than or equal (matching or alphabetically follows)	if x≥ 0 then...

The comparison operators can be applied to strings of any type. Their meanings for non-numeric operands are described in parentheses.

String-matching operators

contains, is in, is not in	sub-string match	if field 3 contains " Smith " then… if "Jones" is in theList then… if 12 is not in theNumbers then…

The function **offset** may sometimes be more use since it give the position of the matching string; **find** may also be used for some purposes. Various XFCNs are available as well.

Coordinate comparison operators

is within, is not within	test whether a point is within a rectangle	if mouseLoc() is within rect of btn 1 then…

The first operand of **within** must be a point – a string containing two numeric items. The second must be a rectangle, a string containing four numeric items.

String type testing operators

is a is not a	test whether a string is of a given type	if x is not a number then put 0 into x

Permissible type names and their meanings are:

integer	digits optionally preceded by a + or - sign
number	an integer optionally followed by a . and some digits
logical	**true** or **false**
point	two integers separated by a comma
rectangle	four integers separated by commas
date	any of the date formats recognized by HyperCard (such as **12/4/92**)

The following script implements a **whatIs** function:

```
function whatIs x
   if x is a "integer" then return "integer"
   if x is a "number" then return "number"
   if x is a "logical" then return "logical"
   if x is a "point" then return "point"
   if x is a "rectangle" then return "rectangle"
   if x is a "date" then return "date"
   return "string"
end whatIs
```

Object existence operators

there is a
there is not a
	test whether a given object
	exists
		if there is a field "serial number" then
		add 1 to field "serial number"
		end if

The following function returns a new name for a card, guaranteed to be unique:

```
function uniqueName base
    put 1 into n
    repeat while there is a card base & n
        add 1 to n -- or, add random(1000) if you want this function to be faster
    end repeat
    return base & n
end uniqueName
```

A.8 Built-in functions

abs	foundText	round
annuity	heapSpace	screenRect
atan	length	result
average	ln	seconds
charToNum	ln1	selectedChunk
clickChunk	log2	selectedField
clickH	max	selectedLine
clickV	menus	selectedLoc
clickLine	min	selectedText
clickLoc	mouse	shiftKey
clickText	mouseClick	sin
commandKey	mouseH	sound
compound	mouseV	sqrt
cos	mouseLoc	stacks
date	number	tan
diskSpace	numToChar	target
exp	offset	ticks
exp1	optionKey	time
exp2	param	tool
foundChunk	paramCount	trunc
foundField	params	value
foundLine	random	windows

See the *HyperTalk Reference* stack for the full definitions. The definitions of most of these functions can be inferred from their names (and from the way they are used throughout this book). We note some important details:

Compound is used for doing compound interest calculations. Compound(rate, periods) calculates $(1+rate)^{periods}$ more accurately than you can easily do directly. Annuity is similar, but works out $(1-(1+rate)^{periods})/rate$. If your credit card interest is 25% compounded monthly and you currently owe the credit company £1200, you'll owe them something like compound(0.25/12, 12)*1200 after twelve months – but you need to be very careful what the definitions your credit company use for interest rates and how *they* work them out as they usually express things to make the loan look more attractive than it really is.

All the trigonometric functions work in radians. If you prefer degrees, you need to convert degrees to radians using 360 degrees equals 2π radians: as in sin(degrees*pi/180) or atan(ratio)*180/pi.

The naming of ln, ln1, log2, exp, exp1 and exp2 is misleading. Quite conventionally, ln gives the natural logarithm (to base e = 2.7183), and exp gives e raised to a power. Log2 gives the logarithm base 2 (which is the number of binary bits that a number requires), and exp2 returns 2 raised to a power, so exp2(x) is the same as 2^x. However, ln1(x) gives the value of ln(1+x), which is preferable when x is small, and exp1(x) gives the same value as exp(x)-1 – which isn't as useful a function except that exp1(ln1(x))=x, as does exp(ln(x)).

The date can provide the current date in a variety of formats; date() is equivalent to the date but can be overridden by your own definitions. We also have:

the abbr date the abbrev date the abbreviated date	Thu, Jun 18, 1992
the date	18/6/92
the long date	Thursday, June 18, 1992
the short date	18/6/92

The exact formats depend on how the Macintosh is set up at the time the function is called. Thus, if you want stored dates (ones displayed in a field) in a stack to be valid anywhere, you should use seconds (which are the same everywhere!) as follows:

```
get the secs
convert it to long date -- or you can convert to any other date format
```

when you need to show the date in whatever the local format is.

A.9 Commands

add	dial	import paint from file	reset
answer	disable	lock screen	returnInField
answer file	divide	mark	returnKey
arrowKey	doMenu	multiply	save
ask	drag from	open	select
ask file	edit script	open file	set
beep	enable	open printing	show
choose	enterInField	open report printing	sort
click at	enterKey	palette	start using
close file	export paint to file	picture	stop using
close printing	find	play	subtract
convert	flash	play stop	tabKey
create menu	functionKey	pop card	type
create stack	get	print	unlock screen
debug	go	push	unmark
delete	help	put	visual
delete menu	hide	read from file	wait
			write

See the *HyperTalk Reference* stack for the full definitions.

Commands can be intercepted by your own handlers, and in the first instance you should write a handler like:

```
on open
    answer the params
end open
```

so that you can see what the complicated parameters of **open** end up as. For example even if you wrote **choose lasso tool**, your handler would be called with two parameters **tool 5** – in the opposite order.

Some keywords (**send, return, pass**) look like commands, but do not generate messages that you can intercept; however, **set** *is* a command and it is very often useful to have your own handler for it (use **pass set** to get HyperCard to do the work after you have intercepted it).

A.10 Synonyms and abbreviations

Here is a list of synonyms and abbreviations that you can use in scripts and in the message box. Upper- and lower-case letters are always equivalent. The table does not give syntactical abbreviations, such as the freedom to omit to in go [to] commands.

Full terms	Synonyms
abbreviated	abbr, abbrev
background	bg, bkgnd
backgrounds	bgs, bkgnds
bottomRight	botRight
button	btn
buttons	btns
card	cd
cards	cds
center	centre
character	char
characters	chars
commandChar	cmdChar
commandKey	cmdKey
dissolve	fade
field	fld
fields	flds
gray	grey
hilite	highlite, hilight, highlight
in	of
location	loc
menuMessages	menuMessage, menuMsg, menuMsgs
message box	message, msg box, msg
message watcher	msg watcher
middle	mid
of	in
picture	pict
polygon	poly
previous	prev
rectangle	rect
regular polygon	reg poly
round rectangle	round rect
second	sec, secs, seconds
spray can	spray
tick	ticks

Sec, seconds and secs are synonyms for second only as a unit of time. You cannot use them as a synonym for the ordinal second, hence the second card cannot be abbreviated the sec card.

Pascal to HyperTalk

Hypertalk for Pascal programmers

If you know Pascal this appendix shows how to translate Pascal concepts into HyperTalk: any Pascal programmer should find the information here interesting and well worth reading. Programmers familiar with other block-structured languages (C or Modula-2, for example) should find it useful too. It is in alphabetical order to make it easier to reference.

HyperTalk has many features that are not found in Pascal (such as objects), but if you still 'think in Pascal' this appendix will be a useful entré into HyperTalk's approach. Take special note of HyperTalk's **go to** command which is *not* the same as Pascal's or BASIC's **goto**. After reading this appendix a Pascal programmer should be able to read HyperTalk programs, though HyperCard's new concepts must still be learnt from the book, particularly Chapter 3 (mainly about objects) and Chapter 4 (mainly about message passing).

Abbreviations

Pascal provides no abbreviations: every name has to be spelt out in full, and different spellings are always different things. HyperTalk is more flexible and permits many of its common keywords to be abbreviated to save you typing. You can write **bg** as a short form for **background**, **cd** as a short form for **card**. There is a complete list of HyperTalk's abbreviations in *Synonyms and abbreviations* on page 377. Convenient as abbreviation is, HyperTalk does not have any standard rules for abbreviations, and some words cannot be abbreviated at all. You can only abbreviate HyperTalk keywords, not your own variable names.

Arrays: `a[i]`

Where Pascal uses `a[i]`, in HyperTalk one writes **char i of a**, or **line i of a**. In Pascal, the way the array is used ('subscripted') does not depend on what each element of the array is. In HyperTalk, all the containers (variables, fields, etc.) hold sequences of characters. The contents of containers can be accessed as sequences of characters, sequences of words (words are terminated by a **space** or a **return** character), sequences of lines (lines are terminated by a **return** character) or sequences of items (items are terminated by commas). You first have to decide how to store the information and then to write *each* use of the array accordingly, using char, word, line or item.

If the information you want to access is organized in sub-sequences of characters that are words, lines or comma-separated, then HyperTalk can subscript them. Otherwise you have to think of some other way to access the data (perhaps by using the offset function, or the contains operator to locate the line of text that contains the data you want, then choosing the portion of the line you want with character counts).

If you declare a Pascal variable a as var a: array [1..10] of char; you can subscript it with a[i], getting characters. In HyperTalk, you'd write char i of a. HyperTalk does not require the declaration; in particular it does not restrict you to a particular size (like 10). You can simulate two-dimensional arrays by using a combination of two sorts of chunk, for example, a Pascal array: a: array [1..10, 1..20] of integer could be simulated by a container holding 20 lines, each of 10 words, where the words are integers. Pascal's a[i,j] would be written word j of line i of a. You could then generate such an array in any container (any variable or field) by setting the contents of the container to be the appropriate number of words containing 0s:

```
repeat with i = 1 to 20
  repeat with j = 1 to 10
    put 0 into word j of line i of b
  end repeat
end repeat
```

Unlike Pascal, you can insert and delete entries. For example:

```
put "123" & return after line 3 of a
```

inserts an extra line between lines 3 and 4 of a. The new line becomes line 4, and what was previously line 4 becomes line 5. Similarly, you can delete parts of sequences:

```
delete line 4 of a
```

removes line 4 of a and what was previously line 5 becomes line 4.

You can use HyperCard's stacks of cards as an array, by referring to cards by number. Hence multi-dimensional arrays (a[i,j,k]) may be simulated by line i of field j of card k.

Assignment: a := b

HyperTalk writes assignments the other way around from Pascal. HyperTalk's put x into y achieves the same as Pascal's y := x.

Some common forms of assignment, such as x := x+1 and x := x*2 can be written more conveniently in HyperTalk (add 1 to x and multiply x by 2) rather than using put.

Blocks: begin … end

Commands can be grouped together in Pascal by using begin and end. There is no equivalent in HyperTalk. Where grouping is necessary, for instance in loops, each HyperTalk command has its own special end. This is rather like Pascal's repeat … until, which does not need a **begin** and **end** to group the commands between **repeat** and **until**. Thus,

Pascal	HyperTalk

```if e then```
```begin```
   ```blah; blah```
```end```
	if e then
	  blah
	  blah
	end if

Case

HyperTalk provides no ```case``` command or equivalent. You can either write the ```case``` statement out as a series of **if** ... **else if** ... commands, or (if each **case** constant is an enumerated type value) you could convert it to message sending by defining handlers (Pascal: procedures) with the names of the enumerated type and use **send x** (which then effectively calls the procedure of the right name) instead of ```case x```.

Comments: { }, (* *)

HyperTalk's comments start with the symbol -- and extend to the end of the line. Unlike Pascal you cannot comment out several lines without repeating the comment symbol on each line; however the script editor provides a menu command to do this easily.

Conditions: if ... then ... else

HyperTalk's conditional commands are very similar to Pascal's. **If** commands in HyperTalk must end with **end if** (in contrast, Pascal uses ```begin``` and ```end```) unless the command can be fitted onto one line.

Constants: const

Like Pascal, HyperTalk provides a few standard constants (**true**, **false**, **pi**) but it provides no straightforward way for the programmer to define their own constants (like Pascal's ```const age = 36```); the work-around is to use functions:

```
function age
    return 36
end age
```

Files

As in Pascal, there are commands in HyperTalk for opening, closing, reading and writing files of characters, but since HyperCard stacks already provide persistent storage, the only normal use for files is to import data from, or export data to other programs:

```
open file "Fred" for reading
read from file "Fred" until return
read from file "Fred" at 100 for 12
read from file "Fred" until end
write myVar to file "Fred" at 200
```

For loop: for i := 1 to 20 do

HyperTalk provides loops that are practically the same as Pascal's. In HyperTalk, a loop must be ended by end repeat.

Pascal	HyperTalk
`for i := 1 to 20 do write(i);`	repeat with i = 1 to 20 answer i end repeat

for i := 20 downto 1 do
begin
  s := s+i
end;
	repeat with i = 20 down to 1
	   add i to s
	end repeat

for i := 1 to 10 by 2 do
  think(i);
	repeat with ii = 1 to 5
	   put 2*ii into i
	   think(i)
	end repeat

Functions

Pascal's functions return to the caller when they execute to their end; in HyperTalk, the keyword return can be used at any point to make the function return a value.

Pascal	HyperTalk

`function f(x: integer):`
`Boolean;`
`begin`
`    f := true`
`end;`
	function f x
	   return true
	end f

`function found(key: Char):`
`Boolean;`
`var i: integer;`
`begin`
`    found := false;`
`    for i := 1 to 10 do`
`        if a[i] = key then`
`found := true`
`end;`
	function found key
	   repeat with i = 1 to 10
	     if line i of field "a" = key then
	       return true
	     end if
	   end repeat
	   return false
	end found

The second example in the table shows how the function name in Pascal can be used to save a default value for the function. In the Pascal example, found is set to false, in case the for loop never sets it to true. In HyperTalk you cannot do this, since saying **return** makes a function return immediately; this happens to make the example more efficient in HyperTalk since once **found** is **true** there is no point continuing the **repeat** loop anyway – in Pascal, the loop continues right to the end regardless.

Jumps: Goto

Although HyperTalk has a goto (written **go to**, either as two words *with* a space, or with the word **to** omitted) its action is completely different from Pascal's. In HyperCard, **go to** changes the current card, and subsequent references to fields, buttons and so on, are taken from the card you have gone to. **Go to** does *not* change what commands HyperTalk is executing.

Goto is sometimes used in Pascal to exit while, repeat and for loops. HyperTalk provides the **exit repeat** command for this restricted purpose.

HyperTalk can perform gos that exit control structures (**exit repeat**), exit handlers (**exit opencard**), and stop all scripts running (**exit to HyperCard**).

Input: read

You can read and write to files in HyperTalk in much the same way that you do in Pascal. However, for reading and writing interactively, HyperCard's style is completely different.

Instead of Pascal's write('Type a number'); read(x); you could use

```
ask "Type a number"
put it into x
```

but there are usually better ways of doing it, for example using a field that the user can type into directly.

See also *Files* on page 381.

Labels

Labels are used in Pascal as the destination of goto commands. Their use is generally frowned on, except for special purposes such as getting to the end of a procedure. HyperTalk has no labels (its **go to** command does something completely different – see *Jumps* : Goto) but provides a command, **exit**, that can be used to get to the end of a **repeat**, **function** or **procedure** (handler).

Loops: repeat **and** while

Pascal provides while and repeat ... until so that tests can be placed before or after loops. HyperTalk provides a **repeat while** and a **repeat until**. The test is always at the start of the loop:

Pascal	HyperTalk
`while a < b do a := a*2;`	repeat while a < b 　put 2*a into a end repeat

`while n > 0 do`
`begin`
`   n := n/2;`
`   x := x+1`
`end;`
	repeat while n > 0
	　divide n by 2
	　add 1 to x
	end repeat

`repeat`
`    finished := true;`
`    something`
`until finished;`
	put false into finished
	repeat until finished
	　put true into finished
	　something
	end repeat

HyperTalk's **repeat** must be ended by **end repeat**, though this means that `begin` and `end` need never be used even when several lines of commands are being repeated.

Pascal's `while true` can be written in HyperTalk as **repeat forever**, or just as **repeat**, more briefly.

Names

Pascal's names are fixed. If you declare something to be **teamwork**, say, then it will *always* be called **teamwork**.

HyperTalk differs in two respects.

Objects, like fields and buttons, can have their names *changed* as a program runs. Suppose **People** is the name of a field, then writing **set name of field "people" to "famous people"** will change the name of the field to **famous people**. Now you have to refer to its value as **field "famous people"**. You can generally refer to objects in other ways, such as using their number, so that changing their names does not confuse programs.

Secondly, you can use programs to construct names, or indeed any part of a program. The standard function **value** returns the value of its parameter. Thus **value("x")** is the value of the variable **x**. Since **"team" & "work"** is a string whose value is **"teamwork"**, you could use **value("team" & "work")** to get its value. This function comes into its own when you want to calculate names, for example, **value("team" & i)** could be used to find the values of **team1**, **team2**, and so on.

More generally the command **do** x takes the expression x and evaluates it as a command. Thus:

```
put "beep" into x
do x
```

is equivalent to **beep**.

Operators

Like Pascal, HyperTalk provides a range of operators. Some of Pascal's operators are simply not available in HyperTalk since the corresponding types are not provided (for example, set operators).

Pascal's and HyperTalk's string operators are *different*. In particular, when Pascal says that two strings are equal they are exactly equal, but HyperTalk ignores differences in case. Thus, in HyperTalk a and A are equal, but they are different in Pascal; similarly, the operators < and > would treat a > B in Pascal but a < B in HyperTalk.

Output: write

You can read and write to files in HyperTalk in much the same way that you do in Pascal. However, for reading and writing interactively, HyperCard's style is completely different.

HyperTalk's **answer** is a bit like `write` (or `writeln`), except that it only shows one thing at a time. A simple Pascal program could be converted by changing `writes` to **answers**, but you would never see all the output at once. Instead, you would normally write text to a field that can get bigger and bigger, or to a scrolling field.

If there is a field called **output**, `write(x)` could be translated as **put x after field "output"**; and **writeln(x)** can be done by **put x & return after field "output"**.

Pointers

HyperTalk provides no pointers, and no `new`. Objects can be referred to by their identification numbers (IDs), and in some cases these can be used like pointers. You could, for example, simulate an array of pointers to cards by using a variable or field storing one card ID per line.

Objects (such as cards, buttons, fields, even stacks) can be dynamically created – created while a program is running – using **doMenu "New Button"** (or **New Card**). Likewise, they can be deleted by using **doMenu "Clear Card"** (**button, field** ...), or by using **doMenu "Cut Card"** if you want to repaste them somewhere else.

Procedures

HyperTalk *handlers*, declared using the **on** keyword, correspond to Pascal's `procedure` declarations. Pascal's procedures return to the caller when they execute right to their end; in HyperTalk, **exit** can be used at any point to make the procedure return immediately.

Pascal	HyperTalk

`procedure p(x: integer);`
`begin`
`    { ... }`
`end;`
	on p x
	  -- ...
	end p

You cannot really define local procedures in HyperTalk. In Pascal if you nest a procedure within another one, then (like other variables) its name is local to the containing procedure –

another procedure cannot use it. HyperTalk's handlers do not nest. However, there is a nesting where stacks contain backgrounds, backgrounds contain cards, and cards contain buttons and fields. Handlers defined at one level in this hierarchy cannot normally use handlers defined further in. Thus, if a card calls the handler **whatsit**, either it must define it itself, or HyperTalk will find a definition of it in the background, or failing that in the stack – or further up the hierarchy (see Chapter 4).

Programs

Pascal programs start with the keyword `program` and finish at the last `end`. A Pascal program need not contain any procedures. Pascal can only run one program at a time.

HyperCard's programs are called *scripts* and are always parts of stacks and other objects. Stacks consist of many scripts, which in turn contain *handlers*, HyperTalk's equivalent of procedures. A HyperCard script can be empty or can contain handlers, though a simple HyperCard stack can still be constructed with no scripts whatsoever. HyperCard can run many stacks at once.

Records

Instead of records, HyperCard can use *fields*. Instead of a Pascal record `var a: record x,y: integer end`, you would create two fields with names **x** and **y**. Rather than `write a.x`, you write **field "x"**, or possibly **field "x" of card a**. If a Pascal program only has one large record (or an array of records), consider making each element a card rather than a field.

You may like to think of HyperCard's objects (cards, buttons and so forth) rather as Pascal records. Then, what HyperTalk calls *properties* are what Pascal would call record fields. Objects have properties such as their *script* (a string, being the HyperTalk program associated with the object), and various numbers (their *rectangle* property) giving where they are displayed on the screen. If **x** is an object, you get properties by writing **script of x**, rather than Pascal's style `x.script`. Sadly, HyperTalk does not let you add more properties to an object: you have to live with the ones they're made with.

Semicolon: ;

Commands in Pascal are separated by a semicolon. In HyperTalk, commands are written one per line, separated by return characters. It is not possible to write several commands on one line in HyperTalk. Commands that are too long for a single line are split with a special marker: '¬' which is typed by *option–return*.

Sets

HyperTalk has no sets, so there is no operator in, and the operators + and - don't work on sets – on the other hand, most sets can be represented as strings of words, and then HyperTalk's string operator **is in** can be used to much the same effect. Note that if you add an element to a

Pascal set that already contains the element, the set will only contain one element: with strings, you must first check that an element is not already in the set before adding another. (You would probably choose to use the operator **&&** for adding elements to a HyperTalk string.)

Types

HyperCard has no types, and no need for type declarations. All values are considered strings of characters: you can write things like **character 1 of pi**, which will be a 3; **character 2** is a dot, and so on. However, **character 1 of "pi"** will be **p**, since "pi" is a string of two characters, **p** and **i**.

Although everything is a string in HyperTalk, naturally many of its operations – such as addition – only make sense when they are applied to values of the right type, like numbers. HyperTalk provides a convenient operator **is a** (with variants: **is an**, **is not a**, **is not an**) that you can use to determine the type of a string:

> *expression* **is a** *type*
> *expression* **is not a** *type*

where type is: **number, integer, point, rectangle, date, logical**. A number is anything that you can do arithmetic on, such as **10** or **2.3**; whereas an integer has to be a whole number. A point is two whole numbers separated by a comma, and to be a sensible point both numbers must be non-negative (such as **234,234**). A rectangle is two points separated by a comma, four whole numbers in all. A date is any string that HyperCard can flexibly interpret as a valid date. A logical value is either **true** or **false**.

Variable declarations: `var x: integer`

Local variables are not declared in HyperTalk. Global variables (which would be declared first in a Pascal program) can be declared anywhere, by using **global**. In Pascal, if a variable is defined outside of a procedure it is known inside it, but in HyperTalk *all* variables used inside handlers (procedures) are local unless declared as global.

The following Pascal and HyperTalk programs do the same thing. Each declares a procedure (handler) **p**, which uses a global variable **x** and a local variable **y**. In Pascal, the global variable **x** is defined outside of **p**, whereas in HyperTalk it is defined inside. The local variable **y** has to be defined in Pascal, but is not defined in HyperTalk – it is assumed to be local.

Pascal	HyperTalk
| ```
var x: integer;
procedure p;
var y: integer;
begin
   y := x;
   x := 2*y
end;
``` | ```
on p
  global x
  put x into y
  put 2*y into x
end p
``` |

Var parameters: `procedure p(var c: char)`

All procedure (handler) and function parameters in HyperTalk are passed by value: there is no equivalent to Pascal's `var`. (However, it is possible to pass the quoted name of the argument and then use **value** inside the handler if the variable is global and suitably declared in both handlers.)

With

HyperTalk provides no equivalent of `with`, except that **go to** changes which card is being used for resolving names. In a sense, Pascal's `with x write(y)`, which takes `y`'s value from record `x`, is a bit like:

> go to card "x"
> put field "y"

since the value in field **"y"** is taken from that field in card **x**. (Without the **with**, you'd have to write `x.y` in Pascal; and without the **go**, you'd have to write field **"y"** of card **"x"** in HyperTalk.) HyperTalk's **go to**, however, is vastly more flexible than Pascal's `with`.

Index of Handlers

A

addIndexMenus 293
addLink 279
addStyle 286
aMenu 188
AnObjectAt 201
area 68
arrowKey 319

B

bk 100
bkg 226
black 173
blacken 323, 327
busy cursor 125

C

canon 342
cardLinkScript 282
cardPlace 160
changeStyle 286
check_menus 189
clear 101
clearCard 323
clickText 258
closeAllPopUps 286
closeCard 106, 293

closeField 29, 153, 256, 260, 301,
    331, 335
closeStack 16, 27, 93, 193, 194, 202,
    309
connect 139
containsExample 224
copyCards 340
count 245, 247
courier 186
createMakeLinkMenu 283
createMenu 195

D

deleteDuplicates 341
deleteIndexMenus 293
deleteLink 280
deleteLinkBack 296
deleteMenu 195
deletePendingLink 283
demo 106
doCardLink 281, 284
doMenu 86, 185, 336
dot 248
doTopic 292
draw 100
drawBar 135
drawBarAxes 134
drawGround 161

Index

Symbols

A

B